# THE OFFICIAL®

# 1996 BLACKBOOK PRICE GUIDE OF UNITED STATES POSTAGE STAMPS

## EIGHTEENTH EDITION

## BY MARC HUDGEONS, N.L.G.

HOUSE OF COLLECTIBLES • NEW YORK

*Important Notice.* All of the information, including valuations, in this book has been compiled from the most reliable sources, and every effort has been made to eliminate errors and questionable data. Nevertheless, the possibility of error, in a work of such immense scope, always exists. The publisher will not be held responsible for losses which may occur in the purchase, sale, or other transaction of items because of information contained herein. Readers who feel they have discovered errors are invited to *write* and inform us, so they may be corrected in subsequent editions. Those seeking further information on the topics covered in this book are advised to refer to the complete line of *Official Price Guides* published by the House of Collectibles.

© 1995 by Random House, Inc.

𝓗𝒞 This is a registered trademark of Random House, Inc.

All rights reserved under International and Pan-American Copyright Conventions.

Published by: House of Collectibles
            201 East 50th Street
            New York, New York 10022

Distributed by Ballantine Books, a division of Random House, Inc., New York, and simultaneously in Canada by Random House of Canada Limited, Toronto.

Manufactured in the United States of America

ISSN: 0195-3559

ISBN: 0-876-37931-5

Cover design by Kristine Mills
Cover photo by George Kerrigan

Eighteenth Edition: July 1995

10  9  8  7  6  5  4  3  2  1

# TABLE OF CONTENTS

# OFFICIAL BOARD OF CONTRIBUTORS

The publisher also wishes to express special thanks to Mr. Armin R. Crowe at the Collectors Institute, Ltd., Omaha, Nebraska 68144, and for the special help provided by *Linn's Stamp Journal*. The designs for the stamps issued from 1978 to date are copyrighted by the U.S. Postal Service and are used by permission from the U.S. Postal Service.

# NOTE TO READERS

# THE OFFICIAL®

# 1996
# BLACKBOOK PRICE GUIDE OF UNITED STATES POSTAGE STAMPS

# MARKET REVIEW

The USPS issued over 140 major varieties of stamps and postal stationary in 1994. There were ninety-four commemorative, nine definitive, ten special, one stamped envelope,

and twenty-four postcards (the most ever produced in one year). The most innovative series issued were the "Classic Collection," which was a series of twenty different stamps based on a central topic. The stamps were framed with a four-color printed salvage, and there was a detailed description printed on the back of each stamp. The first set in the series, "Legends of the Old West," included the most controversial stamp design error in history. Bill Pickett, one of the series' subjects, was pictured incorrectly. The "Bill Pickett" stamp design error was compounded by a series of events that began with the premature release of over 150 paines containing the error stamp. Distribution was halted and a recall was issued January 14, 1994. The Postal Service board was inundated with requests to release more of the error stamps. On June 10, 1994, 150,000 paines were offered on a limited lottery type sale and distribution began December 1994. The remaining stamps from the print run of 5.2 million were destroyed. The error was corrected and the redesigned series was reprinted and re-released October 1994. The redesigned series not only had visible differences in the picture of Bill Pickett, but it seems that the other stamps in the series also had subtitle variations, which meant that there would be an additional sixteen variations possible in the series.

There was another USPS print error that stimulated collector interest. The $1.19 World Cup souvenir sheet incorrectly showed New York as one of the sites where the soccer matches would be played. Since the stamps were already printed, the USPS made amends to the correct state, New Jersey, by moving the opening day ceremonies to New Jersey and by creating a free commemorative panel that depicted the "Giants" stadium.

Various control features were also incorporated into the printing of stamps. Micro printing of dates and security words were used, in addition to salvage markings that included pricing information for the postal clerks. All of these changes represented new challenges for the collector.

Increased 1995 postal rates resulted in over 150 new stamp issues alone scheduled for 1995. Changes in design, content, markings, perforations, adhesives, and presentation formats have created many new avenues for the collector. The USPS seems to be concentrating their focus on a new market by appealing to the potential collector with new products and stimulating interest in the hobby by bombarding the public with advertising programs in all types of media. In addition to the new issue releases, USPS offering of philatelic collectibles includes: uncut press sheets, uncut press sheets that are autographed by the designing artist, stamps that were flown in space, gold-plated sterling silver replicas of stamps, mint singles, and block folders. This aggressive campaign is working.

Attendance records at most major shows are at a level not seen since the 1970s. The activity at the Annual American Stamp Dealers Association's Postage Stamp Mega-Event at New York City's Madison Square Garden was unprecedented. Dealers in modestly priced stamps were particularly busy, indicating increased activity and attendance by the intermediate collector. Many dealers reported sales that were twice what they had experienced at last year's show.

An additional incentive provided by the USPS now enables you to order stamps, toll-free, from the USPS. See page 17 for details.

Stamp collecting as a hobby and as an industry is on a definite upswing, driven by USPS innovations, products, and advertising. Many dealers, publishers, and collectors within the hobby are increasingly taking steps to promote the hobby with a more positive look to building future collectors.

# THE STORY OF U.S. STAMPS

The world's first postage stamps were issued by Great Britain in 1840 and pictured its new queen, Victoria, then 21 years old. It was not until 1847 that the U.S. released postage stamps, but prior to that time some city postmasters issued stamps of their own. These very valuable stamps, known as "postmaster provisionals," were used in St. Louis, New York, Annapolis and a number of other cities.

The first federally released postage stamps comprised a 5¢ denomination picturing Benjamin Franklin and a 10¢ showing George Washington. Their size was very similar to that of modern non-commemoratives and they had gummed backs, just like our stamps. The chief difference was that they carried no little holes or perforations between each specimen on a sheet, to aid in separation. Instead they had to be cut apart with scissors or creased and torn by hand. These stamps are called "imperforates," or "without perforations." All stamps in those days, including Europe's, were made in this way. The U.S. did not start perforating its stamps until 1857, ten years later.

Imperforates rank today as the hobby's aristocrats, its elder statesmen and foremost classics. They have long been dear to the hearts of collectors, and not merely on grounds of their antiquity. Some specialists maintain that these issues, every one of them bearing a statesman's portrait, are more elegantly engraved than any of their descendants. In addition, they can be found (with luck and the necessary cash) in super specimens that put ordinary perforated stamps to shame. When a stamp is perforated, every one on the sheet is of identical size. Some sheets may be better centered than others, depending on how the paper is fed, but no specimens will be physically larger than any others. With imperforates, it's quite another matter. The cutting was never done very evenly. Some specimens were cropped or cut into by scissor wielders and left with margins so immense that portions of all the surrounding stamps are visible. These are called jumbo margin copies and the prices collectors will give for them are often astronomic, provided the condition is otherwise good. It is not at all unusual for one of these oversized beauties to command three or four times the normal sum. Collectors must take care though, because in philately, as in most other things, all that sparkles is not necessarily diamonds. Larcenous persons have been known to take very ordinary average stamps and add fake margins.

Not all imperforates are equally easy (or hard) to get with four full margins. This is all a matter of how closely together they were printed on the sheet. The cutter is less apt to make a mistake if the stamps are further apart on the sheet. Scott's #11, the 3¢ 1851, is by far the most difficult to find with full margins. It also happens to be the least expensive imperforate, thanks to the enormous quantities printed. While the usual specimen will fetch only $8–$10 used, a jumbo margin #11 has no trouble selling for $20, $30 or more.

The second series of imperforates, issued from 1851 to 1856, comprised values from 1¢ to 12¢. There were five stamps, with Washington appearing on three of them; the other two used portraits of Franklin and Jefferson. In 1857 the same group of stamps was released again, this time with perforations and three high values: a 24¢ and 90¢ pictured Washington, and a 30¢ portrayed Franklin. The 90¢ stamp was not exceeded in face value until the Columbian Exposition series in 1893. Because very little mail required the paying of so much postage, most specimens of the 90¢, 1857–1861 that went to private hands never got on letters. Consequently, this stamp is much more difficult to find used than unused, a rare circumstance for a U.S. issue. Needless to say, counterfeit cancels exist.

There was no question that by this time postage stamps had scored a big success. Any doubts or complaints that some users may have had about them at the beginning had long since vanished. Certain persons became so fond of stamps that they began saving them, used as well as unused, and thus the hobby of philately was born. For the government, stamps brought greater economy to the postal service than anticipated. They also allowed mail to travel faster. There was just one problem: some people were abusing the system. During the Civil War, and shortly thereafter, it became apparent that many stamps were going through the mails twice or more. People were cleaning off the cancels and using them again. This may have been done by individuals but, more likely, it was a large-scale operation in which used stamps were cleaned in wholesale quantities and sold to business houses and other volume mailers at a discount. The government was being bilked out of thousands of dollars, but there seemed no solution until a plan was devised to use "grills" on the faces of stamps in 1867. These were networks of tiny embossed dots which weakened the paper and would, presumably, cause it to break apart if any attempt was made at erasing the cancel. After just two years the grill was dropped, but it had appeared on enough stamps in that short time to provide philatelists with an intriguing subspecialty. Not all the grills were alike. They differed in size and style and collecting them is quite a sport.

The year 1869 marked the first year of U.S. pictorial stamps that portrayed things or events rather than portraits. They cannot really be termed commemoratives in the modern sense, but they were extremely pictorial. Subjects included a pony express rider, a rail locomotive, panoramas of the landing of Columbus, the signing of the Declaration of Independence, and others. This series also presented the first stamps to be printed in more than one color. Multicolor printing was no small operation in those days. It required two separate plates; one consisting of frames to be printed in one color, and the other central designs to be printed in a different color. The sheets were fed through one press, allowed to dry, then fed into the next to receive the final printing. As the feeding was done by hand, human error occasionally occurred. A few sheets were fed upside down the second time around, resulting in the first, but not the most famous, U.S. inverts, or stamps with upside down centers. These are very valuable and seldom offered on the market. The king of all United States inverts is a twentieth-century stamp, the 24¢ airmail of 1918. This small stamp has a central design of a Curtiss

Jenny single engine plane. It was printed 100 to a sheet. On the day it was issued, a Washington, D.C. collector, William T. Robey, took a few minutes from his lunch hour to go into the local post office and buy a sheet. He had no intention of using the stamps but merely wanted them for his collection. After putting down his $24 he received what appeared to be a normal sheet, but after looking closer, Mr. Robey found that on every stamp the airplane was upside down. This incident stirred a furor of considerable proportion. The government was embarrassed since it had claimed that the old 1869 inverts could not happen again with its new machinery and rigid controls. It tried, without success, to buy the sheet back from Robey. Meanwhile it notified postmasters around the country to check their stocks for further error sheets. No more were found, and when it became evident that Robey's sheet was the only one in existence he began receiving substantial offers from collectors and dealers. The offers seemed tempting and he finally sold his treasure for $15,000 to Eugene Klein of Philadelphia, a prominent dealer. Klein immediately resold the sheet to Col. Edward H. R. Green of New York, the legendary collector who also owned the only five known specimens of the 1913 Liberty nickel. It is believed Green paid at least $17,500 for this philatelic morsel, a huge sum in those days but only about one third as much as each of the 100 stamps are now individually worth. Green broke up the sheet into blocks, selling most of them and recovering his entire cost. Several single specimens were subsequently lost; one was supposed to have disappeared into a vacuum cleaner while Green's housekeeper was tidying up.

# FACTORS BEHIND
# STAMP PRICES

The collector value (or "market value") of any stamp rests with a variety of factors. Philately becomes a bit less mysterious when one understands the forces at work in the stamp marketplace.

A beginner will normally presume that expensive stamps are expensive because of rarity. Certainly there is a great deal of talk about stamp rarities within the hobby, and so it is natural enough to ascribe high prices to the phenomenon of rarity. In fact, rarity is only one of several factors that influence stamp prices, and the influence it carries is not particularly clear-cut.

In this book you will note some stamps (mostly among the early regular issues) with values of $1,000, $2,000, and even higher. Obviously these stamps are rarer than those selling for $10 or $15. But once having said that, we have virtually summed up our useful knowledge of rarity and its effect on prices. A comparison of prices, between stamps in roughly similar ranges of value, does not indicate which is the rarer. A stamp selling for $1,000 is not necessarily rarer than one selling for $500. A $10,000 stamp may actually be more abundant than one which commands $5,000. This hard-to-comprehend fact of philatelic life prevails because of the other factors involved in determining a stamp's price. If rarity were the only factor, one could, of course, easily see which stamps are the rarest by the prices they fetch.

The word "rare" is an elixir to many collectors, not only of stamps but other collectors' items. Sellers are well aware of this, and seldom fail to sprinkle the word liberally in their sales literature. There is no law against calling a stamp rare, as this represents a personal opinion more than anything else and opinions are allowable in advertising. Unfortunately, there is no standard definition for rarity. Does "rare" mean just a handful of specimens in existence, with one reaching the sales portals once in five years? Does it mean 100 in existence, or 1,000, or some other number? Since stamps are—today, at any rate—printed in the multimillions, a thousand surviving specimens might seem a very tiny total to some people. Further complicating this situation is the fact that the specific rarity of most stamps cannot be determined, or even estimated, with any hope of accuracy. The quantities printed are recorded for most of our stamps, going back even into the nineteenth century, but the quantity *surviving* of any particular stamp is anyone's guess. It is obvious that a stamp that goes through the auction rooms once a year is fairly rare, but this provides no sound basis for guessing the number of specimens in existence. That could only be accomplished if some sort of grand census could be taken, and all specimens tallied. This, of course, is nothing but a pipe dream. Some collectors would not participate in such a census; some might be unaware that it was being conducted. Then, too, there are many scarce or rare stamps in hands other than those of collectors, such as dealers and museums. Additionally, there could be (and probably are) existing specimens of rare stamps yet to be discovered, as fresh discoveries are made periodically in the hobby through attic cleaning and the like.

In terms of influence on price, rarity is outdistanced somewhat by *popularity*. Some stamps, for one reason or other, are simply more popular than others. They have a sort of innate appeal for hobbyists, either through reputation, exquisite designing, circumstances of issue, oddity, or various other potential reasons. These stamps sell out rapidly from the stocks of dealers, while some stamps that are supposedly scarcer will linger in stock albums for ages and ages waiting to tempt a customer. It is no wonder, then, that the prices of popular stamps rise more quickly than those that are scarce but not in brisk demand. The Columbian series typifies the effect of popularity on stamp values. If stamp prices were fixed by scarcity alone, none of the Columbians would be selling for nearly as much. Much of their value derives from their overwhelming popularity with collectors of U.S. stamps. It would be safe to say, in fact, that *all* of the Columbians from the lowest face value to the $5, are more plentiful than other U.S. stamps selling for precisely the same sums. Every dealer has Columbians in stock, and quite a few dealers have the high value of the set, too. They are not "hard to get." But they *are* very costly.

Popularity, of course, does not remain constant forever. There are shifts in philatelic popularity, usually slight but occasionally extreme. The popularity of commemoratives as a whole versus regular issues as a whole can change from time to time. Then, too, there are swings of popularity for airmails, first day covers, blocks, coil pairs, mint sheets, and all other philatelic material. A climb or decline in the price of any philatelic item is often an indication of the forces of popularity at work. Then there are activities of investors to consider, whose buying habits seldom reflect those of the pure collector. A great deal of buying by investors in any short period of time (such as occurred during 1979 and 1980, and to less extent in 1981) can make prices seem well out of balance.

Also on the subject of prices, it is important for the beginner to realize that arithmetic is usually futile when dealing with stamp values. You cannot determine the price of one philatelic item by knowing the value of a similar one. This can best be shown by the relative values of singles and blocks of four. A block of four is, as one would expect, worth *more* than four times as much as single specimens of that stamp. It is not just four specimens of the stamp, but four of them *attached*, which lends added scarcity and appeal. The difficulty lies in trying to use mathematics to determine a block's value. Some blocks are worth five times as much as the single stamp; some six times; some ten times as much or even more. Almost all blocks—except very common ones—will vary somewhat in value, in relation to the value of the individual stamp. There is no satisfactory explanation for this, other than the presumption that some blocks are scarcer than others or just in greater demand than others.

In the case of common philatelic items, the value hinges greatly on the method of sale. If you want to buy one specimen of a common cover, you may have to pay $1.50. But if you were willing to buy a hundred common first day covers *of the dealer's choice*, you could very likely get them for $75 or 75¢ each. Buying in quantity, and allowing the dealer to make the selections, can save a great deal of money. Of course one may then ask: What is the real value of those covers? Is it $1.50 or 75¢? The only answer is that it depends on how you buy!

If this article seems to raise a great many questions without supplying many answers, it will, hopefully, serve to show that stamp collecting is not bound to rigid formulas. What happens in the stamp market is largely beyond prediction, or precise explanation. This, indeed, is one of the exciting aspects of the hobby.

# STAMP COLLECTORS' TERMINOLOGY

**Adhesives**—A term given to stamps that have gummed backs and are intended to be pasted on articles and items that are to be mailed.

**Aerophilately**—The collecting of airmail or any form of stamps related to mail carried by air.

**Airmail**—Any mail carried by air.

**Albino**—An uncolored embossed impression of a stamp generally found on envelopes.

**Approvals**—Stamps sent to collectors. They are examined by the collector, who selects stamps to purchase and returns balance with payment for the stamps he retained.

**Arrow Block**—An arrow-like mark found on blocks of stamps in the selvage. This mark is used as a guide for cutting or perforating stamps.

**As-is**—A term used when selling a stamp. It means no representation is given as to its condition or authenticity. Buyers should beware.

**Backprint**—Any printing that may appear on reverse of stamp.

**Backstamp**—The postmark on the back of a letter indicating what time or date the letter arrived at the post office.

**Bantams**—A miniature stamp given to a war economy issue of stamps from South Africa.

**Batonne**—Watermarked paper used in printing stamps.

**Bicolored**—A two-color printed stamp.

**Bisect**—A stamp that could be used by cutting in half and at half the face value.

**Block**—A term used for a series of four or more stamps attached at least two high and two across.

**Bourse**—A meeting or convention of stamp collectors and dealers where stamps are bought, sold, and traded.

**Cachet**—A design printed on the face of an envelope, generally celebrating the commemoration of a new postage stamp issue. Generally called a first day cover.

**Cancellation**—A marking placed on the face of a stamp to show that it has been used.

**Cancelled to Order**—A stamp cancelled by the government without being used. Generally remainder stamps or special issues. Common practice of Russian nations.

**Centering**—The manner in which the design of a stamp is printed and centered upon the stamp blank. A perfectly centered stamp would have equal margins on all sides.

**Classic**—A popular, unique, highly desired or very artistic stamp. Not necessarily a rare stamp, but one sought after by the collector. Generally used only for nineteenth-century issues.

**Coils**—Stamps sold in rolls for use in vending machines.

**Commemorative**—A stamp issued to commemorate or celebrate a special event.

**Crease**—A fold or wrinkle in a stamp.

**Cut Square**—An embossed staple removed from the envelope by cutting.

**Dead Country**—A country no longer issuing stamps.

**Demonetized**—A stamp no longer valid for use.

**Error**—A stamp printed or produced with a major design or color defect.

**Essay**—Preliminary design for a postage stamp.

**Face Value**—The value of a stamp indicated on the face or surface of the stamp.

**Frank**—A marking on the face of an envelope indicating the free and legal use of postage. Generally for government use.

**Fugitive Inks**—A special ink used to print stamps, which can be rubbed or washed off easily, to eliminate erasures and forgeries.

**General Collector**—One who collects all kinds of issues and all types of stamps from different countries.

**Granite Paper**—A type of paper containing colored fibers to prevent forgery.

**Gum**—The adhesive coating on the back of a stamp.

**Handstamped**—A stamp that has been handcancelled.

**Hinge**—A specially gummed piece of glassine paper used to attach a stamp to the album page.

**Imperforate**—A stamp without perforations.

**Inverted**—Where one portion of a stamp's design is inverted or upside down from the remainder of the design.

**Local Stamps**—Stamps that are only valid in a limited area.

**Margin**—The unprinted area around a stamp.

**Miniature Sheet**—A smaller than usual sheet of stamps.

**Mint Condition**—A stamp in original condition as it left the postal printing office.

**Mirror Print**—A stamp error printed in reverse as though looking at a regular stamp reflected in a mirror.

**Multicolored**—A stamp printed in three or more colors.

**Never Hinged**—A stamp in original mint condition never hinged in an album.

**Off Paper**—A used stamp that has been removed from the envelope to which it was attached.

**On Paper**—A used stamp still attached to the envelope.

**Original Gum**—A stamp with the same or original adhesive that was applied in the manufacturing process.

**Pair**—Two stamps unseparated.

**Pen Cancellation**—A stamp cancelled by pen or pencil.

**Perforation Gauge**—A printed chart containing various sizes of perforation holes used in determining the type or size of perforation of a stamp.

**Perforations**—Holes punched along stamp designs allowing stamps to be easily separated.

**Philatelist**—One who collects stamps.

**Pictorial Stamps**—Stamps that bear large pictures of animals, birds, flowers, etc.

**Plate Block Number**—The printing plate number used to identify a block of four or more stamps taken from a sheet of stamps.

**Postally Used**—A stamp that has been properly used and cancelled.

**Precancels**—A stamp that has been cancelled in advance. Generally used on bulk mail.

**Reissue**—A new printing of an old stamp that has been out of circulation.

**Revenue Stamp**—A label or stamp affixed to an item as evidence of tax payment.

**Seals**—An adhesive label that looks like a stamp, used for various fund raising campaigns.

**Se-tenant**—Two or more stamps joined together, each having a different design or value.

*Sheet*—A page of stamps as they are printed, usually separated before distribution to post offices.

*Soaking*—Removing used stamps from paper to which they are attached by soaking in water. *(NOTE: Colored cancels may cause staining to other stamps.)*

*Souvenir Sheet*—One or more specially designed stamps printed by the government in celebration of a special stamp.

*Splice*—The splice made between rolls of paper in the printing operation. Stamps printed on this splice are generally discarded.

*Tete-Bechs*—A pair of stamps printed together so that the images point in opposite vertical directions.

*Transit Mark*—A mark made by an intermediate post office between the originating and final destination post office.

*Typeset Stamp*—A stamp printed with regular printer's type, as opposed to engraved, lithographed, etc.

*Ungummed*—Stamps printed without an adhesive back.

*Unhinged*—A stamp that has never been mounted with the use of a hinge.

*Unperforated*—A stamp produced without perforations.

*Vignette*—The central design portion of a stamp.

*Want List*—A list of stamps a collector needs to fill gaps in his collection.

*Watermark*—A mark put into paper by the manufacturer, not readily seen by the naked eye.

*Wrapper*—A strip of paper with adhesive on one end, used for wrapping bundles of mail. Especially in Britain, it refers to any bit of paper to which a used stamp is still attached.

# HOW TO GRADE STAMPS

A person need not be an expert to judge the quality or grade of a stamp. All he needs is a discerning eye, possibly a small linear measuring device, and the grading instructions listed below.

The major catalogs traditionally list stamps simply as "Unused" or "Used." Auction houses, however, will describe the stamps for sale in a more informative manner. The greater the value of the stamp, the more thoroughly it is described.

There is no officially accepted system of grading stamps. What we have done in this book is essentially to set up a system of grading stamps using the suggestions and practices of stamp dealers from all over the country. Total agreement was made to the following categories and grades of stamps that are most frequently traded.

## CATEGORIES

*Mint*—The perfect stamp with superb centering, no faults and usually with original gum (if issued with gum).

*Unused*—Although unused this stamp may have a hinge mark or may have suffered some change in its gum since it was issued.

*Used*—Bascially this will be the normal stamp that passed through the government postal system and will bear an appropriate cancellation.

*Cancelled to Order*—These are stamps that have not passed through the postal system but have been carefully cancelled by the government usually for a commemo-

Average
Centering

Fine
Centering

Very Fine
Centering

Extra Fine
Centering

Superb
Centering

ration. These are generally considered undesirable by collectors.

## GRADE—STAMP CENTERING

*Average*—The perforations cut slightly into the design.

*Fine*—The perforations do not touch the design at all, but the design will be off center by 50% or more of a superb centered stamp.

*Very Fine*—The design will be off center by less than 50% of a superb stamp. The off centered design will be visibly noticeable.

*Extra Fine*—The design will be almost perfectly centered. The margin will be off by less than 25% of a superb stamp.

*Superb*—This design will be perfectly centered with all four margins exactly the same. On early imperforate issues, superb specimens will have four clear margins that do not touch the design at any point.

## GRADE—STAMP GUM

*Original Gum*—This stamp will have the same gum on it that it had the day it was issued.

*Regummed*—This stamp will have new gum applied to it as compared to an original gummed stamp. Regummed stamps are worth no more than those with gum missing.

*No Gum*—This stamp will have had its gum removed or it may have not been issued with gum.

*Never Hinged*—This stamp has never been hinged so the gum should not have been disturbed in any way.

*Lightly Hinged*—This stamp has had a hinge applied. A lightly wetted or peelable hinge would do very little damage to the gum when removed.

*Heavily Hinged*—This stamp has had a hinge applied in such a manner as to secure it to the stamp extremely well. Removal of this hinge usually proves to be disastrous, in most cases, since either part of the hinge remains on the stamp or part of the stamp comes off on the hinge, causing thin spots on the stamp.

## GRADE—STAMP FAULTS

Any fault in a stamp such as thin paper, bad perforations, creases, tears, stains, ink marks, pin holes, etc., and depending upon the seriousness of the fault, usually results in grading the stamp to a lower condition.

## OTHER STAMP CONSIDERATIONS

### CANCELLATIONS

*Light Cancel*—This stamp has been postally cancelled but the wording and lines are very light and almost unreadable.

*Normal Cancel*—This stamp has been postally cancelled with just the right amount of pressure. Usually the wording and lines are not distorted and can be made out.

*Heavy Cancel*—This stamp has been postally cancelled. In the process excessive pressure was used, and the wording and lines are extremely dark and sometimes smeared and in most cases unreadable.

### PERFORATIONS

Not to be overlooked in the appearance of a stamp are its

perforations. The philatelist might examine these "tear apart" holes with a magnifying glass or microscope to determine the cleanliness of the separations. One must also consider that the different types of paper, upon which the stamp was printed, will sometimes make a difference in the cleanliness of the separations. The term "pulled perf" is used to denote a badly separated stamp in which the perforations are torn or ragged.

## COLOR

Other important factors such as color affect the appearance and value of stamps. An expert will have a chart of stamp colors. Chemical changes often occur in inks. Modern printing sometimes uses metallic inks. These "printings" will oxidize upon contact with the natural secretions from animal skin.

The color of certain stamps has been deliberately altered by chemicals to produce a rare shade. Overprints can be eliminated. Postmarks may be eradicated. Replacing gum is a simple process. Some stamps have been found to bear forged watermarks. The back of the paper was cut away and then the stamps rebacked with appropriately watermarked paper.

There are stamp experts who earn a living in the business of stamp repairing. They are craftsmen of the first order. A thin spot on a stamp can be repaired by gluing it on a new layer of paper. Missing perforations can be added. Torn stamps can be put back together. Pieces of stamps may be joined.

In some countries it is accepted practice for an expert, upon examination of a stamp, to certify the authenticity by affixing his signature to the back of the stamp. If the stamp is not genuine, it is his right and duty to so designate on the stamp; but these signatures can also be faked.

# REPAIRS, FAKES, AND OTHER UNDESIRABLES

Philately, like most hobbies, is not without its pitfalls. The collector who buys from reputable dealers runs very little risk, as today's stamp pros have high principles and are hard to fool. Buying from auction sales and small dealers, who may not have expert knowledge, is another matter. Here the collector must call into play his own expertise and learn to distinguish the bad from the good.

In the early years of philately, stamps provided a playground for fakers and swindlers. They took advantage of the public's gullibility and the general lack of published information about stamps. Copies were printed of rare stamps, as well as of stamps that never existed in the first place. Cancels were bleached from used specimens to make them appear unused. Fake margins were added to imperforates, to allow ordinary copies to be sold as "superb with jumbo margins." Perforated stamps were reperforated to make them better centered. Thin spots in the paper were filled in, tears closed, missing portions of paper replaced. Stamps were doctored and manipulated in more ways than could be imagined, all in the hope of fooling collectors and making anywhere from a few extra cents to thousands of dollars on them. One of the favorite tricks of fakers was to apply bogus overprints or surcharges. By merely using a rubber handstamp and a pad of ink, they could stamp out a hundred or more "rarities" in a few minutes, turning ordinary British or other issues into varieties not found in any catalog. It was all a great game and proved very profitable, until collectors and the philatelic public at large became wary of such practices. Even though most of these fakes from the hobby's pioneer years have disappeared out of circulation, a few still turn up and must be guarded against.

United States stamps have not been faked nearly so extensively as those of many other nations, notably South America and Japan. Still, the collector should learn to watch for fakes and also repaired specimens.

***Total Fake.*** The counterfeit stamp always varies somewhat from a genuine specimen, though the difference may be very slight. Detection can usually be made if the suspect stamp is examined alongside one known to be genuine. By using a magnifier, the lines of engraving and paper quality can be compared. The ink on a fake is likely to have a fresher appearance and will lie on the surface as a result of being printed at a later date and on less sophisticated equipment; however, this is not always the case. Experts say that when a stamp appears to be a fake, or a reprint, the odds are very good that it is. Some experience is necessary before anyone can get a first glance reaction to a stamp. The presence or absence of a cancel has no bearing on the likelihood of a stamp being a fake, as cancels can be faked too.

***Faked Cancel.*** Faked cancels are very rare on U.S. stamps, as nearly all are worth more unused than used. One notable exception is the 90¢, 1857–1861. These are applied either with a fake handstamp or simply drawn with pen and ink. Skillfully drawn faked cancels can be very deceptive. Faked cancels are *much more numerous* on covers than loose stamps.

***Removed Cancels.*** So-called cleaned copies of used stamps, sold as unused, were once very plentiful and are still encountered from time to time. The faker, of course, chooses lightly cancelled specimens from which the obliteration can be removed without leaving telltale evidence. In the case of imperforates he may trim down the margins to remove part of the cancel. Rarely will he attempt to clean a stamp whose cancel falls across the face or any important portion of the stamp. Holding the stamp to a strong light may reveal the cancel lines. X-ray examination provides positive proof.

***Added Margin(s).*** When margins have been added to an imperforate stamp, the paper fibers are woven together (after moistening) along the back and at the front where the margin extends beyond the stamp's design. They can usually be detected by looking closely for a seam or joint at the point where the design ends and the margin begins. A magnifying glass will be necessary for this. When held against a light, the reverse side will probably show evidence of the weaving operation. Sometimes the added margins are of a slightly different grade of paper.

**Reperforated.** A stamp that has been reperforated to improve its centering will usually be slightly smaller than a normal specimen, and this can be revealed by placing it atop an untampered copy.

**Filled in Thin Spots.** If held to a light and examined with a good magnifier, filled in thin spots will normally appear darker than the remainder of the stamp. Such spots are often mistaken for discoloration by beginners. Thin spots are filled in by making a paste of paper pulp and glue and applying it gradually to the injured area. After drying, the stamp is placed in a vise so that no telltale hills or valleys are left. This is not really considered forgery but honest repair work; it becomes forgery only if done with the intent of selling the stamp as undamaged.

**Closed Tears.** These are almost always visible against a light with a magnifier, even if small. A routine examination of any rare stamp should include a check of its margins for possible closed or open tears.

# HOW TO USE THIS BOOK

The main section of this book lists all U.S. stamps with the exception of special issues such as airmail, revenues, etc. Special issues are grouped separately in sections of their own. Please refer to the Table of Contents.

Before pricing your stamps, be sure they are correctly identified. Use the photo section as an aid. In some cases, two or more stamp issues are very similar in appearance and can be distinguished only by minor details. These are always noted in the text. Sometimes the evidence is obvious. If a stamp has perforations, it cannot be earlier than 1857.

Prices are given in columns for used and unused specimens, usually in two grades of condition. You need only refer to the column that applies to your stamp and its condition grade.

Prices shown in this book are actual selling prices, so one should not necessarily expect to receive a discount when buying from dealers.

When a dash (—) appears in place of a price, this indicates that the item is either unavailable in that condition grade or is so seldom available that its price is open to question. It should not be assumed, however, that such items are invariably more valuable than those for which prices are shown.

Prices are given for hinged stamps that have been in collections. In today's stamp market a premium value is placed on stamps that have never been hinged. To determine the premium on any stamp, refer to the premium percentages shown on every page.

The stated values are general guides only and cannot

reflect the price of occasional superb specimens, such as imperforates with four wide margins, which may sell considerably higher.

A small box has been provided to the left of each listing for keeping a record of the stamps in your collection.

## IMPORTANT

Because of the space limitation on each page we have not been able to include very fine, extra fine, never hinged, or lightly hinged pricing on each stamp. To determine these prices please use the following procedure.

*Very Fine Pricing*—Prior to 1941: *Double the average price quoted.*

*Very Fine Pricing*—After 1941; *Add 25% to the fine price.*

*Extra Fine Pricing*—Prior to 1941: *Triple the average price quoted.*

*Never Hinged Pricing*—Prior to 1941: *Add the percentage indicated at the right of the issue to any price listed. Example (N-H add 5%).*

*Never Hinged Pricing*—After 1941: *Add 15% to any price listed.*

*Lightly Hinged Pricing*—*Add one half of the N-H percentage indicated for each issue to any price listed.*

## DEALER BUYING PRICES

Buying prices will vary greatly depending upon condition, rarity, and existing dealers' stock of a particular stamp. With these facts in mind, a dealer can be expected to buy stamps between 40 percent and 50 percent of their quoted prices; but this will depend upon supply and demand.

# EQUIPMENT

To collect stamps properly a collector will need some "tools of the trade." These need not be expensive and need not all be bought at the very outset. That might, in fact, be the worst thing to do. Many a beginning collector has spent his budget on equipment, only to have little or nothing left for stamps and then loses interest in the hobby.

It may be economical in the long run to buy the finest quality accessories, but few collectors, just starting out, have a clear idea of what they will and will not be needing. It is just as easy to make impulse purchases of accessories as of stamps and just as unwise. Equipment must be purchased on the basis of what sort of collection is being built *now*, rather than on what the collection may be in the future. There is no shame in working up from an elementary album.

***Starter Kits.*** Starter or beginner outfits are sold in just about every variety shop, drugstore, etc. These come in attractive boxes and contain a juvenile or beginner's album; some stamps, which may be on paper and in need of removal; a packet of gummed hinges; tongs; a pocket stockbook or file; and often other items such as a perforation gauge, booklet on stamp collecting, magnifier, and watermark detector. These kits are specially suited to young collectors and can provide a good philatelic education.

***Albums.*** When the hobby began, more than a century ago, collectors mounted their stamps in whatever albums were at hand. Scrapbooks, school exercise tablets and diaries all were used, as well as homemade albums. Today a number of firms specialize in printing albums of all kinds for philatelists, ranging from softbounds for the cautious type to huge multi-volume sets that cost hundreds of dollars. There are general worldwide albums, country albums, U.N. albums, and albums for mint sheets, covers, and every other conceivable variety of philatelic material. Choose your album according to the specialty you intend to pursue. It is not necessary, however, to buy a printed album at all. Many collectors feel there is not enough room for creativity in a printed album and prefer to use a binder with unprinted sheets. This allows items to be arranged at will on the page, rather than following the publisher's format, and for a personal write-up to be added. Rod-type binders will prove more durable and satisfactory than ring binders for heavy collections. The pages of an album should not be too thin, unless only one side is used. The presence of tiny crisscrossing lines (quadrilled sheets) is intended as an aid to correct alignment. Once items have been mounted and written up, these lines are scarcely visible and do not interfere with the attractiveness of the page.

*Hinges.* These are small rectangular pieces of lightweight paper, usually clear or semiopaque, gummed and folded. One side is moistened and affixed to the back of the stamp and the other to the album page. Hinges are sold in packets of 1,000 and are very inexpensive. Though by far the most popular device for mounting stamps, the hobbyist has his choice of a number of other products if hinges are not satisfactory to him. These include cello mounts, which encase the stamp in clear sheeting and have a black background to provide a kind of frame. These are self-sticking. Their cost is much higher than hinges. The chief advantage of cello mounts is that they prevent injuries to the stamp and eliminate the moistening necessary in using hinges; however, they add considerably to the weight of each page, making flipping through an album less convenient, and become detached from the page more readily than hinges.

*Glassine Interleaving.* These are sheets made of thin semitransparent glassine paper, the same used to make envelopes in which stamps are stored. They come punched to fit albums of standard size and are designed to be placed between each set of sheets, to prevent stamps on one page from becoming entangled with those on the facing page. Glassine interleaving is not necessary if cello mounts are used, but any collection mounted with conventional hinges should be interleaved. The cost is small. Glassine interleaving is sold in packets of 100 sheets.

*Magnifier.* A magnifier is a necessary tool for *most* stamp collectors, excepting those who specialize in first day covers or other items that would not likely require study by magnification. There are numerous types and grades on the market, ranging in price from about $1 to more than $20. The quality of magnifier to buy should be governed by the extent to which it is likely to be used, and the collector's dependence upon it for identification and study. A collector of plate varieties ought to have the best magnifier he can afford and carry it whenever visiting dealers, shows or anywhere that he may wish to examine specimens. A good magnifier is also necessary for a specialist in grilled stamps and for collectors of Civil War and other nineteenth-century covers. Those with built-in illumination are best in these circumstances.

*Tongs.* Beginners have a habit of picking up stamps with their fingers, which can cause injuries, smudges and grease stains. Efficient handling of tongs is not difficult to learn, and the sooner the better. Do not resort to ordinary tweezers, but get a pair of philatelic tongs which are specially shaped and of sufficiently large size to be easily manipulated.

*Perforation Gauge.* A very necessary inexpensive article, as the identification of many stamps depends upon a correct measuring of their perforations.

# TIPS ON STAMP BUYING

There are many ways to buy stamps: packets, poundage mixtures, approvals, new issue services, auctions and a number of others. To buy wisely, a collector must get to know the language of philately and the techniques used by dealers and auctioneers in selling stamps.

Packets of all different worldwide stamps are sold in graduated sizes from 1,000 up to 50,000. True to their word, they contain no duplicates. The stamps come from all parts of the world and date from the 1800s to the present. Both mint and used are included. When you buy larger quantities of most things, a discount is offered; with stamp packets, it works in reverse. The larger the packet, the higher its price per stamp. This is because the smaller packets are filled almost exclusively with low-grade material.

Packets are suitable only as a collection base. A collector should never count on them to build his entire collection. The contents of one worldwide packet are much like that of another. Country jackets are sold in smaller sizes, but there are certain drawbacks with packets.

**1.** Most packets contain some cancelled-to-order stamps, which are not very desirable for a collection. These are stamps released with postmarks already on them, and are classified as used but have never gone through the mail. Eastern Europe and Russia are responsible for many C.T.O.'s.

**2.** The advertised value of packets bears little relation to the actual value. Packet makers call attention to the catalog values of their stamps, based on prices listed in standard reference works. The lowest sum at which a stamp can be listed in these books is 2¢, therefore, a packet of 1,000 automatically has a minimum catalog value of $20. If the retail price is $3 this seems like a terrific buy when, in fact, most of those thousand stamps are so common they are almost worthless.

Poundage mixtures are very different than packets. Here the stamps are all postally used (no C.T.O.'s) and still attached to small fragments of envelopes or parcel wrappings. Rather than sold by count, poundage mixtures are priced by the pound or ounce and quite often by kilos. Price varies depending on the grade, and the grade depends on where the mixture was assembled. Bank mixtures are considered the best, as banks receive a steady flow of foreign registered mail. Mission mixtures are also highly rated. Of course, the mixture should be sealed and unpicked. Unless a mixture is advertised as unpicked, the high values have been removed. The best poundage mixtures are sold only by mail. Those available in shops are of medium or low quality. Whatever the grade, poundage mixtures can be counted on to contain duplicates.

If you want to collect the stamps of a certain country, you can leave a standing order for its new releases with a new issue service. Whenever that government puts out stamps, they will be sent to the collector along with a bill. Usually the service will supply only mint copies. The price charged is not the face value, but the face value with a surcharge added to meet the costs of importing, handling and the like. New issue services are satisfactory only if the collector is positive he wants all the country's stamps, no matter what. Remember that its issues could include semipostals, long and maybe expensive sets, and extra high values.

By far the most popular way to buy stamps is via approvals. There is nothing new about approvals, as they go back to the Victorian era. Not all services are alike, though. Some offer sets, while others sell penny approvals. Then there are remainder approvals, advanced approvals, and seconds on approval. Penny approvals are really a thing of the past, though the term is still used. Before inflation, dealers would send a stockbook containing several thousand stamps, all priced at a penny each. If all the stamps were kept, the collector got a discount plus the book! Today the same sort of service can be found, but instead of 1¢ per stamp, the price is anywhere from 3¢ to 10¢. Remainder approvals are made up from collection remainders. Rather than dismount and sort stamps from incoming collections, the approval merchant saves himself time by sending them out right on the album pages. The collector receives leaves from someone else's collection with stamps mounted just as he arranged them. Seconds on approval are slightly defective specimens of scarce stamps, which would cost more if perfect. Advanced approvals are designed for specialized collectors who know exactly what they want and have a fairly substantial stamp budget.

In choosing an approval service you should know the ground rules of approval buying and not be unduly influenced by promotional offers. Most approval merchants allow the selections to be kept for ten days to two weeks. The unbought stamps are then returned along with payment for those kept. As soon as the selection is received back, another is mailed. This will go on, regardless of how much or how little is bought, until the company is notified to refrain from sending further selections. The reputable services will always stop when told.

Approval ads range from splashy full pagers in the stamp publications to small three-line classified announcements in magazines and newspapers. Most firms catering to beginners offer loss leaders, or stamps on which they take a loss for the sake of getting new customers. If an approval dealer offers 100 pictorials for a dime, it is obvious he is losing money on that transaction, as 10¢ will not even pay the postage. It is very tempting to order these premiums. Remember that when ordering approvals. What sort of service is it? Will it offer the kind of stamps desired? Will prices be high to pay for the loss leaders? Be careful of confusing advertisements. Sometimes the premium offers seem to promise more than they actually do. A rare, early stamp may be pictured. Of course you do not receive the stamp, but merely a modern commemorative picturing it.

*Auction Sales.* Stamp auctions are held all over the country and account for millions of dollars in sales annually. Buying at auction is exciting and can be economical. Many sleepers turn up—stamps that can be bought at less than their actual value. To be a good auction buyer, the philatelist must know stamps and their prices pretty well, and know the ropes of auctions. An obvious drawback of auctions is that purchases are not returnable. A dealer will take back a stamp that proves not to a collector's liking, but an auctioneer will not. Also, auctioneers require immediate payment while a dealer may extend credit.

Stamps sold at auction come from private collections and the stocks of dealers; not necessarily defunct dealers, but those who want to get shelf space. Because they were brought together from a variety of sources, the nature and condition will vary. In catalog descriptions the full book value will be given for each stamp, but of course defective stamps will sell for much less than these figures. A bidder must calculate how much less. Other lots which can be difficult for the bidder to evaluate are those containing more than one stamp. Sometimes a superb specimen will be lotted along with a defective one. Then there are bulk lots which contain odds and ends from collections and such. It is usual in auctioning a collection for the better stamps to be removed and sold separately. The remainder is then offered in a single lot, which may consist of thousands or even tens of thousands of stamps. By all means examine lots before bidding. A period of inspection is always allowed before each sale, usually for several days. There may or may not be an inspection on sale day. If the bidder is not able to make a personal examination but must bid on strength of the catalog description, he should scale his bids for bulk lots much lower than for single stamp lots. He might bid $50 on a single stamp lot with a catalog value of $100, if the condition is listed as top notch, but to bid one-half catalog value on a bulk lot would not be very wise. These lots are not scrutinized very carefully by the auctioneers and some stamps are bound to be disappointing. There may be some heavily canceled, creased, torn, etc. Also, there will very likely be duplication. A bid of one-fifth the catalog value on a bulk lot is considered high. Often a one-tenth bid is successful.

The mechanics of stamp auctions may strike the beginner as complicated. They are run no differently than other auctions. All material to be sold is lotted by the auctioneer; that is, broken down into lots or units and bidding is by lot. Everything in the lot must be bid on, even if just one of the stamps is desired. The motive of bulk lotting is to save time and give each lot a fair sales value.

Before the sale a catalog is published listing all the lots, describing the contents and sometimes picturing the better items. Catalogs are in the mail about 30 days before the sale date. If a bid is to be mailed, it must be sent early. Bids that arrive after the sale are disqualified, even if they would have been successful.

When the bid is received it is entered into a bidbook, along with the bidder's name and address. On sale day each lot opens on the floor at one level above the second highest mail bid. Say the two highest mail bids are $30 and $20. The floor bidding would begin at $25. If the two highest bids are $100 and $500, the opening bid would probably be $150. The larger the amounts involved, the bigger will be the advances. The auctioneer will not accept an advance of $5 on a $500 lot; but on low value lots even dollar advances are sometimes made. Then it becomes a contest of floor versus book. The auctioneer acts as an agent, bidding for the absentee until his limit is reached. If the floor tops him, he has lost. If the floor does not get as high as his bid, he wins the lot at one advance over the highest floor bid.

When a collector buys stamps by mail from a dealer, he should choose one who belongs to the American Stamp Dealers' Association or A.S.D.A. The emblem is carried in their ads.

## HOW TO ORDER STAMPS "TOLL-FREE" FROM THE USPS

You can now order stamps, toll-free, from the USPS by calling the Philatelic Fulfillment Service Center located in Kansas City, Missouri, 1-800-782-6724. Listening to a computerized voice, you can choose from six options using a touchtone phone; 1) ordering stamps, 2) personalized envelopes, post offices and official mail agencies, 3) catalog requests, subscription programs information, 4) customer assistance, 5) direct extension dialing, and 6) first-day cancellation service. This is a very useful service. It is recommended that you first order one of the catalogs, "Stamps, Etc." or "Not Just Stamps" in order to correctly place your order for stamps.

# SELLING YOUR STAMPS

Almost every collector becomes a stamp seller sooner or later. Duplicates are inevitably accumulated, no matter how careful one may be in avoiding them. Then there are the G and VG stamps that have been replaced with F and VF specimens, and have become duplicates by intent. In addition to duplicates, a more advanced collector is likely to have stamps that are not duplicates but for which he has no further use. These will be odds and ends, sometimes quite valuable ones, that once suited the nature of his collection but are now out of place. Collectors' tastes change. The result is a stockpile of stamps that can be converted back to cash.

The alternative to selling the stamps you no longer need or want is trading them with a collector who does want them, and taking his unwanted stamps in return. All stamp clubs hold trading sessions. Larger national stamp societies operate trade-by-mail services for their members. The APS (American Philatelic Society) keeps $8,000,000 worth of stamps constantly circulating in its trading books or "circuit" books. Trading can be an excellent way of disposing of surplus stamps. In most cases it takes a bit longer than selling. Another potential drawback, especially if you are not a club member, is finding the right person with the right stamps.

The nature and value of the material involved may help in deciding whether to sell outright or trade. Also, there are your own personal considerations. If you're not going to continue in the stamp hobby, or need cash for some purpose other than stamp buying, trading is hardly suitable. Likewise, if you have developed an interest in some very exotic group of stamps or other philatelic items it may be impossible to find someone to trade with.

Once you have decided to sell, if indeed you do make that decision, the matter revolves upon how. To a stamp shop? To another collector? Through an auction house? Possibly by running your own advertisements and issuing price lists, if you have enough stamps and spare time to make this worthwhile?

While some individuals have an absolute horror at the prospect of selling anything, stamp collectors tend to enjoy selling. It is difficult to say why. Some enjoy it so much they keep right on selling stamps, as a business, long after their original objective is achieved. Nearly all professional stamp dealers were collectors before entering the trade.

Selling your stamps outright to a dealer, especially a local dealer whom you can personally visit, is not necessarily the most financially rewarding but it is quick and very problem-free. Of course it helps if the dealer knows you and it's even better if he knows some of your stamps. Dealers have no objection to repurchasing stamps they've sold to you. You will find that the dealers encourage their customers to sell to them just as much as they encourage them to buy. The dealers are really anxious to get your stamps if you have good salable material from popular countries. In fact most dealers would prefer buying from the public rather than any other source.

The collector selling stamps to a dealer has to be reasonable in his expectations. A dealer may not be able to use all the stamps you have. It is simply not smart business for a dealer to invest money in something he may not be able to sell. So, if you have esoteric or highly specialized items for sale, it might be necessary to find a specialist who deals in those particular areas rather than selling to a neighborhood stamp shop.

The local stamp shop will almost certainly want to buy anything you can offer in the way of medium to better grade United States stamps of all kinds, including the so-called "back of the book" items. He may not want plate blocks or full sheets of commemoratives issued within the past 20 years. Most dealers are well supplied with material of this nature and have opportunities to buy more of it every day. The same is true of first day covers, with a few exceptions, issued from the 1960s to the present. The dealers either have these items abundantly or can get them from a whole-saler at rock-bottom prices. They would rather buy stamps that are a bit harder to get from the wholesalers, or for which the wholesalers charge higher prices. On the whole you will meet with a favorable reception when offering U.S. stamps to a local dealer. With foreign stamps it becomes another matter: what do you have and how flexible are you in price? Nearly all the stamp shops in this country do stock foreign stamps to one extent or another. They do not, as a rule, attempt to carry comprehensive or specialized stocks of them. In the average shop you will discover that the selection of general foreign consists of a combination of modern mint sets, topicals, souvenir sheets, packets, which come from the wholesaler, and a small sprinkling of older material, usually pre-1900. The price range of this older material will be $5 to $50. Non-specialist collectors of foreign stamps buy this type of item and that is essentially who the local shop caters to. When a local dealer buys rare foreign stamps or a large foreign collection, it is not for himself. He buys with the intent of passing them along to another dealer who has the right customers lined up. He acts only as a middleman or go-between. Therefore the price you receive for better grade foreign stamps tends to be lower than for better grade U.S., which the dealer buys for his own use.

What is a fair price to get for your stamps? This is always difficult to say, as many variable factors are involved. Consider their condition. Think in terms of what the dealer could reasonably hope to charge for them at retail and stand a good chance of selling them. Some of your stamps may have to be discounted because of no gum, poor centering, bent perfs, hinge remnants, repairs, or other problems. But even if your stamps are primarily F or VF, a dealer cannot pay book values for them. If you check his selling prices on his specimens of those same stamps, you can usually count on receiving from 40 to 50 percent of those prices. Considering the discount made from book values by the dealer in pricing his stock, your payment may work out to about 25 percent of book values. For rare United States stamps in top condition you can do better than 25 percent, but on most stamps sold to a dealer this is considered a fair offer. Keep in mind that the difference between a dealer's buying and selling prices is not just "profit margin." Most of the markup goes toward operating costs, for without this markup, there would be no stamp dealers.

# THE AMERICAN PHILATELIC SOCIETY

The American Philatelic Society is an internationally recognized association of stamp experts and enthusiasts that offers a number of services and educational opportunities for stamp collectors. The APS is the national representative to the Federation Internationale de Philatelie and is affiliated with more than 700 local stamp clubs (APS Chapters) and almost 200 "specialty groups" (APS Affiliates).

The services that are available with an APS membership include a subscription to *The American Philatelist*, one of the premier stamp magazines in the world, as well as numerous other brochures and publications that are available at a discount to members. The APS Sales Division provides an opportunity for collectors to buy or sell stamps through the mail. Members may request "circuits" of stamps or covers in more than 150 categories of countries and topics. Selections of circuit books are mailed at intervals, and members can choose any items they wish to purchase, and then mail the books on to the next APS member on the circuit. The items are priced by the submitting members, and most range from under $1.00 to $5.00.

The APS also provides an insurance program for members living in the United States and Canada. The insurance policy does not require a detailed inventory, only a general description of a collection and a value estimate, and may be applied for along with a membership application.

The Society also runs the American Philatelic Research Library, with a wide range of resource material including thousands of books, journals, auction catalogs, and other material that are loaned or photocopied and available to members by mail for a nominal fee. The APRL also publishes the *Philatelic Literature Review*, a quarterly journal covering literature of interest to collectors. The magazine is available by separate subscription.

The APS offers, in association with Pennsylvania State University, correspondence courses ranging from "Beginning Collecting" to "Printing Techniques" and week-long summer seminars on philately that feature hands-on instruction by prominent experts. In addition, the APS Education Department produces many brochures and other materials and answers inquiries from beginner and intermediate collectors on various "how-to" aspects of the hobby.

Other APS services include identification of members' stamps by the APS Expert Committee, estate advice, a translation service for international trading, and an annual convention-exhibition stamp show.

## THE AMERICAN PHILATELIST

The Society's monthly magazine, which is included in the membership fee, features a monthly column for beginning stamp collectors; regular columns on stamp clubs, exhibitions, topical collecting, and more; articles by experienced philatelists; how-to columns on using the Society's Sales Division; commentary on important issues to collectors from the state of the stamp market to insights on stamp condition and auctions; and detailed listings of all new stamps and postal stationery issued by the U.S. Postal Service.

## MEMBERSHIP INFORMATION

The APS offers a variety of memberships including special rates for spouses and children, foreign members, and lifetime memberships. The Society operates on a calendar year, and membership fees are pro-rated on a quarterly basis and include a $3.00 admission fee. The 1991 schedule of membership fees is listed below.

| Application received by<br>APS National Headquarters | Admission<br>Fee | Membership<br>Fee | U.S. | Canada | Foreign |
|---|---|---|---|---|---|
| October, November, December | $3.00 | $22.00 | $25.00 | $28.00 | $31.00 |
| January, February, March | 3.00 | 16.50 | 19.50 | 21.75 | 24.00 |
| April, May, June | 3.00 | 11.00 | 14.00 | 15.50 | 17.00 |
| July, August, September | 3.00 | 5.50 | 8.50 | 9.25 | 10.00 |

For more information, call or write the American Philatelic
Society at:

> APS
> P.O. Box 8000, Dept. HC
> State College, PA 16803
> (814) 237-3803

**IMPORTANT NOTICE:** On stamps issued before 1890, prices of unused specimens are for ones without original gum. Specimens with original gum can be expected to command a premium of as much as 50 percent. Beware of regummed specimens.

| Scott No. | | Fine Unused Each | Ave. Unused Each | Fine Used Each | Ave. Used Each |
|---|---|---|---|---|---|
| **GENERAL ISSUES** | | | | | |
| **1847. FIRST ISSUE** | | | | | |
| ☐1 | 5¢ Red Brown | — | 2800.00 | 510.00 | 360.00 |
| ☐2 | 10¢ Black | — | 10,000.00 | 1500.00 | 800.00 |
| **1875. REPRODUCTIONS OF 1847 ISSUE** | | | | | |
| ☐3 | 5¢ Red Brown | 1000.00 | 700.00 | — | — |
| ☐4 | 10¢ Black | 1200.00 | 850.00 | — | — |
| **1851–1856. REGULAR ISSUE—IMPERFORATE** | | | | | |
| ☐5A | 1¢ Blue (1b) | — | — | 3650.00 | 2100.00 |
| ☐6 | 1¢ Blue (1a) | — | — | 5600.00 | 3200.00 |
| ☐7 | 1¢ Blue (II) | 475.00 | 300.00 | 90.00 | 60.00 |
| ☐8 | 1¢ Blue (III) | — | — | 1300.00 | 810.00 |
| ☐8A | 1¢ Blue (IIIa) | — | 1250.00 | 550.00 | 325.00 |
| ☐9 | 1¢ Blue (IV) | 400.00 | 200.00 | 80.00 | 50.00 |
| ☐10 | 3¢ Orange Brown (I) | — | 650.00 | 42.¢ | 30.00 |
| ☐11 | 3¢ Dull Red (I) | 110.00 | 65.00 | 7.00 | 5.00 |
| ☐12 | 5¢ Red Brown (I) | — | — | 1000.00 | 625.00 |
| ☐13 | 10¢ Green (I) | — | — | 625.00 | 365.00 |
| ☐14 | 10¢ Green (II) | — | 1000.00 | 250.00 | 160.00 |
| ☐15 | 10¢ Green (III) | — | 1100.00 | 250.00 | 170.00 |
| ☐16 | 10¢ Green (IV) | — | — | 1200.00 | 725.00 |
| ☐17 | 12¢ Black | — | 1300.00 | 250.00 | 145.00 |
| **1857–1861. SAME DESIGNS AS 1851–1856 ISSUE—PERF. 15** | | | | | |
| ☐18 | 1¢ Blue (I) | 700.00 | 400.00 | 350.00 | 210.00 |
| ☐19 | 1¢ Blue (Ia) | — | — | 2200.00 | 1500.00 |
| ☐20 | 1¢ Blue (II) | 400.00 | 240.00 | 130.00 | 80.00 |
| ☐21 | 1¢ Blue (III) | — | 2100.00 | 1150.00 | 670.00 |
| ☐22 | 1¢ Blue (IIIa) | 700.00 | 380.00 | 230.00 | 140.00 |
| ☐23 | 1¢ Blue (IV) | — | 1500.00 | 300.00 | 175.00 |

| Scott No. | | | Fine Unused Each | Ave. Unused Each | Fine Used Each | Ave. Used Each |
|---|---|---|---|---|---|---|
| ☐24 | 1¢ | Blue (V) | 125.00 | 65.00 | 27.00 | 15.00 |
| ☐25 | 3¢ | Rose (I) | — | 415.00 | 30.00 | 17.00 |
| ☐26 | 3¢ | Dull Red (II) | 45.00 | 28.00 | 4.00 | 2.10 |
| ☐26A | 3¢ | Dull Red (IIa) | 105.00 | 75.00 | 24.00 | 14.00 |
| ☐27 | 5¢ | Brick Red (I) | — | 4300.00 | 750.00 | 475.00 |
| ☐28 | 5¢ | Red Brown (I) | — | 800.00 | 260.00 | 150.00 |
| ☐28A | 5¢ | Indian Red (I) | — | — | 1750.00 | 1100.00 |
| ☐29 | 5¢ | Brown (I) | 740.00 | 400.00 | 200.00 | 100.00 |
| ☐30 | 5¢ | Orange Brown (II) | 715.00 | 400.00 | 875.00 | 460.00 |
| ☐30A | 5¢ | Brown (II) | 400.00 | 220.00 | 190.00 | 110.00 |
| ☐31 | 10¢ | Green (I) | — | 3000.00 | 500.00 | 275.00 |
| ☐32 | 10¢ | Green (II) | 2000.00 | 1200.00 | 170.00 | 105.00 |
| ☐33 | 10¢ | Green (III) | 2000.00 | 1200.00 | 170.00 | 100.00 |
| ☐34 | 10¢ | Green (IV) | — | — | 1500.00 | 810.00 |
| ☐35 | 10¢ | Green (IV) | 180.00 | 90.00 | 52.00 | 34.00 |
| ☐36 | 12¢ | Black (I) | 310.00 | 180.00 | 80.00 | 50.00 |
| ☐36b | 12¢ | Black (II) | 300.00 | 160.00 | 100.00 | 62.00 |
| ☐37 | 24¢ | Gray Lilac | 600.00 | 300.00 | 200.00 | 120.00 |
| ☐38 | 30¢ | Orange | 675.00 | 410.00 | 260.00 | 150.00 |
| ☐39 | 90¢ | Blue | 1100.00 | 700.00 | — | — |

## 1875. REPRINTS OF 1857–1861 ISSUE

| ☐40 | 1¢ | Bright Blue | 600.00 | 400.00 | — | — |
|---|---|---|---|---|---|---|
| ☐41 | 3¢ | Scarlet | 3000.00 | 1900.00 | — | — |
| ☐42 | 5¢ | Orange Brown | 1000.00 | 700.00 | — | — |
| ☐43 | 10¢ | Blue Green | 2300.00 | 1500.00 | — | — |
| ☐44 | 12¢ | Greenish Black | 2800.00 | 1800.00 | — | — |
| ☐45 | 24¢ | Blackish Violet | 3000.00 | 1850.00 | — | — |
| ☐46 | 30¢ | Yellow Orange | 3000.00 | 1900.00 | — | — |
| ☐47 | 90¢ | Deep Blue | 4000.00 | 2900.00 | — | — |

## 1861. FIRST DESIGNS—PERF. 12

| ☐56 | 3¢ | Brown Red | 700.00 | 450.00 | — | — |
|---|---|---|---|---|---|---|
| ☐62B | 10¢ | Dark Green | — | — | 500.00 | 300.00 |

## 1861–1862. SECOND DESIGNS

| ☐63 | 1¢ | Blue | 120.00 | 75.00 | 18.00 | 11.00 |
|---|---|---|---|---|---|---|
| ☐63b | 1¢ | Dark Blue | 150.00 | 88.00 | 27.00 | 21.00 |
| ☐64 | 3¢ | Pink | — | 1900.00 | 300.00 | 180.00 |

| Scott No. | | | Fine Unused Each | Ave. Unused Each | Fine Used Each | Ave. Used Each |
|---|---|---|---|---|---|---|
| ☐64b | 3¢ | Rose Pink | 260.00 | 150.00 | 43.00 | 25.00 |
| ☐65 | 3¢ | Rose | 62.00 | 32.00 | 1.80 | .90 |
| ☐66 | 3¢ | Lake | — | 1000.00 | — | — |
| ☐67 | 5¢ | Buff | — | 2600.00 | 360.00 | 200.00 |
| ☐68 | 10¢ | Yellow Green | 230.00 | 130.00 | 28.00 | 17.00 |
| ☐69 | 12¢ | Black | 475.00 | 285.00 | 49.00 | 28.00 |
| ☐70 | 24¢ | Red Lilac | 600.00 | 350.00 | 75.00 | 41.00 |
| ☐70b | 24¢ | Steel Blue | — | — | 260.00 | 140.00 |
| ☐70c | 24¢ | Violet | — | 2100.00 | 500.00 | 275.00 |
| ☐71 | 30¢ | Orange | 465.00 | 280.00 | 62.00 | 38.00 |
| ☐72 | 90¢ | Blue | 1200.00 | 650.00 | 230.00 | 130.00 |

## 1861–1866. NEW VALUES OR NEW COLORS

| | | | | | | |
|---|---|---|---|---|---|---|
| ☐73 | 2¢ | Black | 150.00 | 70.00 | 23.50 | 12.00 |
| ☐74 | 3¢ | Scarlet | 3900.00 | 2700.00 | 1800.00 | 1100.00 |
| ☐75 | 5¢ | Red Brown | 1250.00 | 750.00 | 215.00 | 125.00 |
| ☐76 | 5¢ | Brown | 340.00 | 190.00 | 55.00 | 32.00 |
| ☐77 | 15¢ | Black | 500.00 | 280.00 | 60.00 | 35.00 |
| ☐78 | 24¢ | Lilac | 265.00 | 150.00 | 46.00 | 30.00 |

## 1867. SAME DESIGNS AS 1861–1866 ISSUE
## GRILL WITH POINTS UP
### A. GRILL COVERING ENTIRE STAMP

| | | | | | | |
|---|---|---|---|---|---|---|
| ☐79 | 3¢ | Rose | 1700.00 | 950.00 | 410.00 | 215.00 |

### C. GRILL ABOUT 13 x 16 MM.

| | | | | | | |
|---|---|---|---|---|---|---|
| ☐83 | 3¢ | Rose | 1800.00 | 1150.00 | 370.00 | 210.00 |

## GRILL WITH POINTS DOWN
### D. GRILL ABOUT 12 x 14 MM.

| | | | | | | |
|---|---|---|---|---|---|---|
| ☐84 | 2¢ | Black | 2900.00 | 2000.00 | 1000.00 | 610.00 |
| ☐85 | 3¢ | Rose | 1600.00 | 1100.00 | 400.00 | 230.00 |

### Z. GRILL ABOUT 11 x 14 MM.

| | | | | | | |
|---|---|---|---|---|---|---|
| ☐85B | 2¢ | Black | 1500.00 | 900.00 | 350.00 | 185.00 |
| ☐85C | 3¢ | Rose | 2500.00 | 2000.00 | 900.00 | 500.00 |
| ☐85E | 12¢ | Black | 2000.00 | 1200.00 | 500.00 | 285.00 |

### E. GRILL ABOUT 11 x 13 MM.

| | | | | | | |
|---|---|---|---|---|---|---|
| ☐86 | 1¢ | Blue | 850.00 | 475.00 | 230.00 | 145.00 |

| Scott No. | | | Fine Unused Each | Ave. Unused Each | Fine Used Each | Ave. Used Each |
|---|---|---|---|---|---|---|
| ☐87 | 2¢ | Black | 370.00 | 200.00 | 65.00 | 36.00 |
| ☐88 | 3¢ | Rose | 280.00 | 160.00 | 10.00 | 6.00 |
| ☐89 | 10¢ | Green | 1400.00 | 875.00 | 160.00 | 96.00 |
| ☐90 | 12¢ | Black | 1700.00 | 1000.00 | 180.00 | 110.00 |
| ☐91 | 15¢ | Black | 3600.00 | 2000.00 | 400.00 | 240.00 |

## F. GRILL ABOUT 9 x 13 MM.

| | | | | | | |
|---|---|---|---|---|---|---|
| ☐92 | 1¢ | Blue | 390.00 | 230.00 | 95.00 | 55.00 |
| ☐93 | 2¢ | Black | 140.00 | 75.00 | 26.00 | 15.00 |
| ☐94 | 3¢ | Red | 110.00 | 58.00 | 4.00 | 2.00 |
| ☐95 | 5¢ | Brown | 1100.00 | 700.00 | 215.00 | 125.00 |
| ☐96 | 10¢ | Yellow Green | 700.00 | 410.00 | 100.00 | 58.00 |
| ☐97 | 12¢ | Black | 750.00 | 400.00 | 110.00 | 65.00 |
| ☐98 | 15¢ | Black | 700.00 | 415.00 | 120.00 | 69.00 |
| ☐99 | 24¢ | Gray Lilac | 1500.00 | 780.00 | 425.00 | 250.00 |
| ☐100 | 30¢ | Orange | 2000.00 | 1100.00 | 350.00 | 190.00 |
| ☐101 | 90¢ | Blue | 4100.00 | 2300.00 | 850.00 | 500.00 |

## 1875. RE-ISSUE OF 1861–1866 ISSUES

| | | | | | | |
|---|---|---|---|---|---|---|
| ☐102 | 1¢ | Blue | — | 370.00 | — | 550.00 |
| ☐103 | 2¢ | Black | — | 1800.00 | — | 2600.00 |
| ☐104 | 3¢ | Brown Red | — | 2300.00 | — | 3100.00 |
| ☐105 | 5¢ | Light Brown | — | 1400.00 | — | 1800.00 |
| ☐106 | 10¢ | Green | — | 1400.00 | — | 2400.00 |
| ☐107 | 12¢ | Black | — | 2000.00 | — | 2800.00 |
| ☐108 | 15¢ | Black | — | 2100.00 | — | 3150.00 |
| ☐109 | 24¢ | Deep Violet | — | 2600.00 | — | 3800.00 |
| ☐110 | 30¢ | Brownish Orange | — | 3000.00 | — | 4400.00 |
| ☐111 | 90¢ | Blue | — | 4000.00 | — | 11,000.00 |

## 1869. PICTORIAL ISSUES
## GRILL ABOUT 9¹/₂ x 9¹/₂ MM.

| | | | | | | |
|---|---|---|---|---|---|---|
| ☐112 | 1¢ | Buff | 210.00 | 130.00 | 60.00 | 35.00 |
| ☐113 | 2¢ | Brown | 170.00 | 100.00 | 28.00 | 16.50 |
| ☐114 | 3¢ | Ultramarine | 150.00 | 85.00 | 7.00 | 4.00 |
| ☐115 | 6¢ | Ultramarine | 700.00 | 390.00 | 86.00 | 55.00 |
| ☐116 | 10¢ | Yellow | 750.00 | 420.00 | 89.00 | 52.00 |
| ☐117 | 12¢ | Green | 780.00 | 410.00 | 90.00 | 52.00 |
| ☐118 | 15¢ | Brown & Blue (I) | 1600.00 | 1000.00 | 280.00 | 165.00 |

| Scott No. | | Fine Unused Each | Ave. Unused Each | Fine Used Each | Ave. Used Each |
|---|---|---|---|---|---|
| ☐119 15¢ | Brown & Blue (II) | 825.00 | 490.00 | 140.00 | 82.00 |
| ☐120 24¢ | Green & Violet | 2100.00 | 1200.00 | 450.00 | 260.00 |
| ☐121 30¢ | Blue & Carmine | 2000.00 | 1100.00 | 215.00 | 125.00 |
| ☐122 90¢ | Carmine & Black | 5000.00 | 2700.00 | 1100.00 | 700.00 |

## 1875. RE-ISSUE OF 1869 ISSUE, HARD WHITE PAPER—WITHOUT GRILL

| Scott No. | | Fine Unused Each | Ave. Unused Each | Fine Used Each | Ave. Used Each |
|---|---|---|---|---|---|
| ☐123 1¢ | Buff | 310.00 | 180.00 | 210.00 | 120.00 |
| ☐124 2¢ | Brown | 360.00 | 200.00 | 300.00 | 180.00 |
| ☐125 3¢ | Blue | 2800.00 | 2000.00 | 1100.00 | 900.00 |
| ☐126 6¢ | Blue | — | 500.00 | — | 370.00 |
| ☐127 10¢ | Yellow | — | 840.00 | — | 800.00 |
| ☐128 12¢ | Green | — | 900.00 | — | 800.00 |
| ☐129 15¢ | Brown & Blue (III) | — | 900.00 | — | 425.00 |
| ☐130 24¢ | Green & Violet | — | 700.00 | — | 360.00 |
| ☐131 30¢ | Blue & Carmine | — | 1000.00 | — | 725.00 |
| ☐132 90¢ | Carmine & Black | — | 3400.00 | — | 4300.00 |

## 1880. SAME AS ABOVE—SOFT POROUS PAPER

| Scott No. | | Fine Unused Each | Ave. Unused Each | Fine Used Each | Ave. Used Each |
|---|---|---|---|---|---|
| ☐133 1¢ | Buff | 180.00 | 115.00 | 135.00 | 80.00 |

## 1870–1871. PRINTED BY NATIONAL BANK NOTE CO.—GRILLED

| Scott No. | | Fine Unused Each | Ave. Unused Each | Fine Used Each | Ave. Used Each |
|---|---|---|---|---|---|
| ☐134 1¢ | Ultramarine | 650.00 | 400.00 | 52.00 | 30.00 |
| ☐135 2¢ | Red Brown | 400.00 | 210.00 | 32.00 | 21.00 |
| ☐136 3¢ | Green | 290.00 | 170.00 | 10.00 | 6.50 |
| ☐137 6¢ | Carmine | 1500.00 | 850.00 | 250.00 | 155.00 |
| ☐138 7¢ | Vermilion | 1100.00 | 600.00 | 230.00 | 140.00 |
| ☐139 10¢ | Brown | 1400.00 | 800.00 | 380.00 | 230.00 |
| ☐140 12¢ | Light Violet | — | — | 1600.00 | 850.00 |
| ☐141 15¢ | Orange | 1800.00 | 1300.00 | 660.00 | 380.00 |
| ☐142 24¢ | Purple | — | — | — | 6200.00 |
| ☐143 30¢ | Black | — | 2600.00 | 800.00 | 450.00 |
| ☐144 90¢ | Carmine | — | 3200.00 | 700.00 | 375.00 |

## 1870–1871. SAME AS ABOVE—WITHOUT GRILL

| Scott No. | | Fine Unused Each | Ave. Unused Each | Fine Used Each | Ave. Used Each |
|---|---|---|---|---|---|
| ☐145 1¢ | Ultramarine | 160.00 | 95.00 | 7.00 | 4.50 |
| ☐146 2¢ | Red Brown | 78.00 | 42.00 | 4.50 | 3.00 |
| ☐147 3¢ | Green | 120.00 | 70.00 | .70 | .40 |

| Scott No. | | Fine Unused Each | Ave. Unused Each | Fine Used Each | Ave. Used Each |
|---|---|---|---|---|---|
| ☐148 6¢ | Carmine | 240.00 | 135.00 | 11.00 | 6.00 |
| ☐149 7¢ | Vermilion | 315.00 | 170.00 | 46.00 | 27.00 |
| ☐150 10¢ | Brown | 240.00 | 130.00 | 11.00 | 7.00 |
| ☐151 12¢ | Dull Violet | 500.00 | 280.00 | 56.00 | 34.00 |
| ☐152 15¢ | Bright Orange | 490.00 | 270.00 | 55.00 | 32.00 |
| ☐153 24¢ | Purple | 580.00 | 330.00 | 73.00 | 45.00 |
| ☐154 30¢ | Black | 980.00 | 540.00 | 90.00 | 51.00 |
| ☐155 90¢ | Carmine | 1300.00 | 700.00 | 160.00 | 95.00 |

## 1873. SAME DESIGNS AS 1870–1871 ISSUE— WITH SECRET MARKS PRINTED BY THE CONTINENTAL BANK NOTE CO. THIN HARD GRAYISH WHITE PAPER

| | | | | | |
|---|---|---|---|---|---|
| ☐156 1¢ | Ultramarine | 62.00 | 40.00 | 1.95 | 1.35 |
| ☐157 2¢ | Brown | 180.00 | 100.00 | 9.00 | 5.00 |
| ☐158 3¢ | Green | 55.00 | 28.00 | .22 | .20 |
| ☐159 6¢ | Dull Pink | 200.00 | 110.00 | 9.00 | 6.00 |
| ☐160 7¢ | Orange Vermilion | 420.00 | 230.00 | 52.00 | 28.00 |
| ☐161 10¢ | Brown | 230.00 | 130.00 | 9.10 | 6.00 |
| ☐162 12¢ | Black Violet | 650.00 | 360.00 | 62.00 | 34.00 |
| ☐163 15¢ | Yellow Orange | 600.00 | 350.00 | 55.00 | 33.00 |
| ☐165 30¢ | Gray Black | 690.00 | 360.00 | 58.00 | 35.00 |
| ☐166 90¢ | Rose Carmine | 1300.00 | 750.00 | 175.00 | 100.00 |

## 1875. REGULAR ISSUE

| | | | | | |
|---|---|---|---|---|---|
| ☐178 2¢ | Vermilion | 175.00 | 90.00 | 4.50 | 3.00 |
| ☐179 5¢ | Blue | 200.00 | 115.00 | 9.00 | 5.00 |

## 1879. SAME DESIGNS AS 1870–1875 ISSUES PRINTED BY THE AMERICAN BANK NOTE CO. SOFT POROUS YELLOWISH WHITE PAPER

| | | | | | |
|---|---|---|---|---|---|
| ☐182 1¢ | Dark Ultramarine | 130.00 | 70.00 | 1.40 | .85 |
| ☐183 2¢ | Vermilion | 60.00 | 32.00 | 1.40 | .85 |
| ☐184 3¢ | Green | 48.00 | 28.00 | .26 | .20 |
| ☐185 5¢ | Blue | 285.00 | 135.00 | 8.00 | 4.50 |
| ☐186 6¢ | Pink | 450.00 | 250.00 | 11.00 | 7.00 |
| ☐187 10¢ | Brown (no secret mark) | 750.00 | 390.00 | 13.00 | 8.00 |

| Scott No. | | Fine Unused Each | Ave. Unused Each | Fine Used Each | Ave. Used Each |
|---|---|---|---|---|---|
| ☐188 | 10¢ Brown (secret mark) | 500.00 | 280.00 | 15.00 | 9.00 |
| ☐188b | 10¢ Black Brown | 675.00 | 360.00 | 70.00 | 28.00 |
| ☐189 | 15¢ Red Orange | 165.00 | 90.00 | 16.00 | 8.50 |
| ☐190 | 30¢ Full Black | 475.00 | 250.00 | 30.00 | 17.50 |
| ☐191 | 90¢ Carmine | 1000.00 | 600.00 | 140.00 | 80.00 |

## 1882. REGULAR ISSUE

| | | | | | |
|---|---|---|---|---|---|
| ☐205 | 5¢ Yellow Brown | 110.00 | 60.00 | 4.50 | 3.00 |

## 1881–1882. DESIGNS OF 1873 ISSUE RE-ENGRAVED (N-H ADD 95%)

| | | | | | |
|---|---|---|---|---|---|
| ☐206 | 1¢ Gray Blue | 32.00 | 18.00 | .85 | .40 |
| ☐207 | 3¢ Blue Green | 38.00 | 21.00 | .28 | .19 |
| ☐208 | 6¢ Rose | 215.00 | 115.00 | 46.00 | 27.00 |
| ☐208a | 6¢ Brown Red | 195.00 | 110.00 | 52.00 | 31.00 |
| ☐209 | 10¢ Brown | 70.00 | 41.00 | 2.50 | 1.50 |
| ☐209b | 10¢ Black Brown | 100.00 | 58.00 | 9.00 | 6.00 |

## 1883. REGULAR ISSUE

| | | | | | |
|---|---|---|---|---|---|
| ☐210 | 2¢ Red Brown | 28.00 | 17.00 | .22 | .18 |
| ☐211 | 4¢ Blue Green | 135.00 | 75.00 | 7.25 | 4.00 |

## 1887. REGULAR ISSUE

| | | | | | |
|---|---|---|---|---|---|
| ☐212 | 1¢ Ultramarine | 55.00 | 30.00 | .80 | .46 |
| ☐213 | 2¢ Green | 21.00 | 11.00 | .26 | .20 |
| ☐214 | 3¢ Vermilion | 40.00 | 25.00 | 32.00 | 20.00 |

## 1888. SAME DESIGNS AS 1870–1883 ISSUES

| | | | | | |
|---|---|---|---|---|---|
| ☐215 | 4¢ Carmine | 140.00 | 70.00 | 11.00 | 6.00 |
| ☐216 | 5¢ Indigo | 135.00 | 75.00 | 7.00 | 4.00 |
| ☐217 | 30¢ Orange Brown | 290.00 | 185.00 | 75.00 | 42.00 |
| ☐218 | 90¢ Purple | 600.00 | 375.00 | 125.00 | 73.00 |

**IMPORTANT NOTICE:** From this point onward, values of unused stamps and blocks are for specimens with original gum. Prices given for **blocks** are for blocks of 4, **without** plate number.

| Scott No. | Fine Unused Block | Ave. Unused Block | Fine Unused Each | Ave. Unused Each | Fine Used Each | Ave. Used Each |
|---|---|---|---|---|---|---|
| **1890–1893. SMALL DESIGN (N-H ADD 95%)** | | | | | | |
| ☐219 1¢ Dull Blue | | | | | | |
| | 100.00 | 80.00 | 15.00 | 11.00 | .21 | .18 |
| ☐219D 2¢ Lake | | | | | | |
| | 800.00 | 625.00 | 130.00 | 80.00 | .48 | .28 |
| ☐220 2¢ Carmine | | | | | | |
| | 90.00 | 70.00 | 16.00 | 9.00 | .16 | .14 |
| ☐220a 2¢ Carmine (Cap on left 2) | | | | | | |
| | 150.00 | 125.00 | 40.00 | 30.00 | 1.10 | .85 |
| ☐220c 2¢ Carmine (Cap both 2's) | | | | | | |
| | 165.00 | 135.00 | 110.00 | 66.00 | 7.00 | 5.00 |
| ☐221 3¢ Purple | | | | | | |
| | 250.00 | 200.00 | 50.00 | 30.00 | 4.50 | 3.00 |
| ☐222 4¢ Dark Brown | | | | | | |
| | 300.00 | 230.00 | 48.00 | 28.00 | 1.80 | 1.10 |
| ☐223 5¢ Chocolate | | | | | | |
| | 280.00 | 225.00 | 48.00 | 29.00 | 1.80 | 1.10 |
| ☐224 6¢ Brown Red | | | | | | |
| | 290.00 | 240.00 | 50.00 | 35.00 | 14.00 | 9.00 |
| ☐225 8¢ Lilac | | | | | | |
| | 275.00 | 240.00 | 38.00 | 25.00 | 8.00 | 6.00 |
| ☐226 10¢ Green | | | | | | |
| | 460.00 | 390.00 | 87.00 | 60.00 | 2.00 | 1.10 |
| ☐227 15¢ Indigo | | | | | | |
| | 700.00 | 600.00 | 125.00 | 85.00 | 15.00 | 9.00 |
| ☐228 30¢ Black | | | | | | |
| | 1000.00 | 875.00 | 190.00 | 100.00 | 18.00 | 12.00 |
| ☐229 90¢ Orange | | | | | | |
| | 1800.00 | 1600.00 | 300.00 | 200.00 | 88.00 | 52.00 |
| **1893. COLUMBIAN ISSUE (N-H ADD 95%)** | | | | | | |
| ☐230 1¢ Blue | | | | | | |
| | 100.00 | 82.00 | 20.00 | 14.00 | .40 | .30 |
| ☐231 2¢ Violet | | | | | | |
| | 100.00 | 85.00 | 21.00 | 13.00 | .19 | .14 |
| ☐231c 2¢ "Broken Hat" | | | | | | |
| | 260.00 | 215.00 | 56.00 | 40.00 | .48 | .30 |
| ☐232 3¢ Green | | | | | | |
| | 275.00 | 230.00 | 41.00 | 28.00 | 14.00 | 10.00 |

| Scott No. | Fine Unused Block | Ave. Unused Block | Fine Unused Each | Ave. Unused Each | Fine Used Each | Ave. Used Each |
|---|---|---|---|---|---|---|
| ☐233 4¢ Ultramarine | | | | | | |
| | 430.00 | 340.00 | 58.00 | 40.00 | 6.50 | 4.00 |
| ☐234 5¢ Chocolate | | | | | | |
| | 480.00 | 340.00 | 66.00 | 45.00 | 7.00 | 5.00 |
| ☐235 6¢ Purple | | | | | | |
| | 480.00 | 340.00 | 59.00 | 40.00 | 18.00 | 13.00 |
| ☐236 8¢ Magenta | | | | | | |
| | 380.00 | 300.00 | 55.00 | 36.00 | 8.50 | 5.00 |
| ☐237 10¢ Black Brown | | | | | | |
| | 600.00 | 430.00 | 100.00 | 75.00 | 7.00 | 5.00 |
| ☐238 15¢ Dark Green | | | | | | |
| | 1650.00 | 900.00 | 185.00 | 135.00 | 62.00 | 45.00 |
| ☐239 30¢ Orange Brown | | | | | | |
| | 2900.00 | 2000.00 | 290.00 | 180.00 | 82.00 | 60.00 |
| ☐240 50¢ Slate Blue | | | | | | |
| | 2900.00 | 2000.00 | 375.00 | 210.00 | 128.00 | 85.00 |
| ☐241 $1 Salmon | | | | | | |
| | — | — | 1100.00 | 700.00 | 540.00 | 350.00 |
| ☐242 $2 Brown Red | | | | | | |
| | — | — | 1200.00 | 800.00 | 450.00 | 300.00 |
| ☐243 $3 Yellow Green | | | | | | |
| | — | — | 2200.00 | 1600.00 | 900.00 | 650.00 |
| ☐244 $4 Crimson Lake | | | | | | |
| | — | — | 2800.00 | 2000.00 | 1250.00 | 850.00 |
| ☐245 $5 Black | | | | | | |
| | — | — | 4200.00 | 2600.00 | 1500.00 | 1050.00 |

## 1894. UNWATERMARKED (N-H ADD 95%)

| Scott No. | Fine Unused Block | Ave. Unused Block | Fine Unused Each | Ave. Unused Each | Fine Used Each | Ave. Used Each |
|---|---|---|---|---|---|---|
| ☐246 1¢ Ultramarine | | | | | | |
| | 90.00 | 82.00 | 20.00 | 14.00 | 2.90 | 2.00 |
| ☐247 1¢ Blue | | | | | | |
| | 200.00 | 175.00 | 46.00 | 32.00 | 1.80 | 1.10 |
| ☐248 2¢ Pink, Type I | | | | | | |
| | 100.00 | 70.00 | 16.00 | 10.00 | 1.90 | 1.15 |
| ☐249 2¢ Carmine Lake, Type I | | | | | | |
| | 550.00 | 425.00 | 95.00 | 70.00 | 1.35 | .85 |
| ☐250 2¢ Carmine, Type I | | | | | | |
| | 190.00 | 170.00 | 18.00 | 11.00 | .26 | .16 |

| Scott No. | Fine Unused Block | Ave. Unused Block | Fine Unused Each | Ave. Unused Each | Fine Used Each | Ave. Used Each |
|---|---|---|---|---|---|---|
| ☐251 2¢ Carmine, Type II | | | | | | |
| | 1400.00 | 1100.00 | 150.00 | 92.00 | 2.50 | 1.25 |
| ☐252 2¢ Carmine, Type III | | | | | | |
| | 400.00 | 300.00 | 82.00 | 55.00 | 3.00 | 1.75 |
| ☐253 3¢ Purple | | | | | | |
| | 400.00 | 300.00 | 64.00 | 46.00 | 6.50 | 4.00 |
| ☐254 4¢ Dark Brown | | | | | | |
| | 500.00 | 375.00 | 76.00 | 42.00 | 3.00 | 1.80 |
| ☐255 5¢ Chocolate | | | | | | |
| | 450.00 | 380.00 | 65.00 | 40.00 | 4.00 | 2.50 |
| ☐256 6¢ Dull Brown | | | | | | |
| | 850.00 | 600.00 | 120.00 | 80.00 | 16.00 | 10.00 |
| ☐257 8¢ Violet Brown | | | | | | |
| | 875.00 | 600.00 | 90.00 | 62.00 | 11.00 | 7.00 |
| ☐258 10¢ Dark Green | | | | | | |
| | 1400.00 | 900.00 | 160.00 | 100.00 | 5.00 | 4.00 |
| ☐259 15¢ Dark Blue | | | | | | |
| | 1800.00 | 1000.00 | 210.00 | 150.00 | 37.00 | 26.00 |
| ☐260 50¢ Orange | | | | | | |
| | 2000.00 | 1200.00 | 260.00 | 170.00 | 70.00 | 48.00 |
| ☐261 $1 Black (I) | | | | | | |
| | 5200.00 | 4000.00 | 600.00 | 400.00 | 230.00 | 150.00 |
| ☐261A $1 Black (II) | | | | | | |
| | — | — | 1400.00 | 850.00 | 415.00 | 275.00 |
| ☐262 $2 Blue | | | | | | |
| | — | — | 1800.00 | 1200.00 | 575.00 | 425.00 |
| ☐263 $5 Dark Green | | | | | | |
| | — | — | 2500.00 | 1600.00 | 1050.00 | 600.00 |

## 1895. DOUBLE LINE WATERMARKED "U.S.P.S." PERF. 12 (N-H ADD 95%)

| Scott No. | Fine Unused Block | Ave. Unused Block | Fine Unused Each | Ave. Unused Each | Fine Used Each | Ave. Used Each |
|---|---|---|---|---|---|---|
| ☐264 1¢ Blue | | | | | | |
| | 46.00 | 37.00 | 5.00 | 3.00 | .18 | .16 |
| ☐265 2¢ Carmine, Type I | | | | | | |
| | 220.00 | 155.00 | 18.00 | 13.00 | .74 | .50 |
| ☐266 2¢ Carmine, Type II | | | | | | |
| | 275.00 | 190.00 | 17.00 | 13.00 | 2.75 | 1.65 |
| ☐267 2¢ Carmine, Type III | | | | | | |
| | 50.00 | 38.00 | 4.00 | 3.00 | .16 | .15 |

| Scott No. | Fine Unused Block | Ave. Unused Block | Fine Unused Each | Ave. Unused Each | Fine Used Each | Ave. Used Each |
|---|---|---|---|---|---|---|
| ☐268 3¢ Purple | | | | | | |
| | 290.00 | 170.00 | 29.00 | 20.00 | 1.20 | .75 |
| ☐269 4¢ Dark Brown | | | | | | |
| | 300.00 | 240.00 | 29.00 | 20.00 | 1.35 | .80 |
| ☐270 5¢ Chocolate | | | | | | |
| | 300.00 | 250.00 | 30.00 | 19.00 | 1.90 | 1.20 |
| ☐271 6¢ Dull Brown | | | | | | |
| | 380.00 | 290.00 | 50.00 | 40.00 | 3.90 | 2.25 |
| ☐272 8¢ Violet Brown | | | | | | |
| | 215.00 | 150.00 | 40.00 | 23.00 | 1.15 | .65 |
| ☐273 10¢ Dark Green | | | | | | |
| | 370.00 | 240.00 | 50.00 | 38.00 | 1.20 | .80 |
| ☐274 15¢ Dark Blue | | | | | | |
| | 800.00 | 600.00 | 130.00 | 80.00 | 9.00 | 6.00 |
| ☐275 50¢ Dull Orange | | | | | | |
| | 1200.00 | 950.00 | 200.00 | 140.00 | 19.00 | 12.00 |
| ☐276 $1 Black (I) | | | | | | |
| | 2400.00 | 1800.00 | 500.00 | 300.00 | 62.00 | 40.00 |
| ☐276A $1 Black (II) | | | | | | |
| | — | — | 1100.00 | 750.00 | 115.00 | 75.00 |
| ☐277 $2 Blue | | | | | | |
| | — | — | 800.00 | 500.00 | 260.00 | 160.00 |
| ☐278 $5 Dark Green | | | | | | |
| | — | — | 1600.00 | 1200.00 | 400.00 | 250.00 |

## 1898. REGULAR ISSUE PERF. (N-H ADD 95%)

| Scott No. | Fine Unused Block | Ave. Unused Block | Fine Unused Each | Ave. Unused Each | Fine Used Each | Ave. Used Each |
|---|---|---|---|---|---|---|
| ☐279 1¢ Deep Green | | | | | | |
| | 85.00 | 48.00 | 8.50 | 5.00 | .18 | .14 |
| ☐279B 2¢ Red | | | | | | |
| | 85.00 | 48.00 | 8.00 | 5.00 | .18 | .14 |
| ☐279C 2¢ Rose Carmine | | | | | | |
| | 690.00 | 600.00 | 140.00 | 82.00 | 35.00 | 21.00 |
| ☐279D 2¢ Orange Red | | | | | | |
| | 80.00 | 50.00 | 10.50 | 8.00 | .21 | .16 |
| ☐280 4¢ Rose Brown | | | | | | |
| | 210.00 | 130.00 | 26.00 | 19.00 | .90 | .60 |
| ☐281 5¢ Dark Blue | | | | | | |
| | 210.00 | 140.00 | 28.00 | 19.00 | .90 | .62 |

| Scott No. | Fine Unused Block | Ave. Unused Block | Fine Unused Each | Ave. Unused Each | Fine Used Each | Ave. Used Each |
|---|---|---|---|---|---|---|
| ☐282 6¢ Lake | | | | | | |
| | 375.00 | 250.00 | 39.00 | 28.00 | 2.50 | 1.40 |
| ☐282a 6¢ Purplish Lake | | | | | | |
| | 500.00 | 375.00 | 52.00 | 30.00 | 3.00 | 1.50 |
| ☐282C 10¢ Brown (I) | | | | | | |
| | 900.00 | 675.00 | 120.00 | 79.00 | 2.30 | 1.50 |
| ☐283 10¢ Orange Brown (III) | | | | | | |
| | 750.00 | 475.00 | 82.00 | 48.00 | 2.15 | 1.25 |
| ☐284 15¢ Olive Green | | | | | | |
| | 875.00 | 575.00 | 115.00 | 70.00 | 7.00 | 4.00 |

## 1898. TRANS-MISSISSIPPI EXPOSITION ISSUE (N-H ADD 90%)

| Scott No. | Fine Unused Block | Ave. Unused Block | Fine Unused Each | Ave. Unused Each | Fine Used Each | Ave. Used Each |
|---|---|---|---|---|---|---|
| ☐285 1¢ Yellow Green | | | | | | |
| | 250.00 | 125.00 | 24.00 | 20.00 | 6.00 | 4.00 |
| ☐286 2¢ Copper Red | | | | | | |
| | 250.00 | 125.00 | 21.00 | 18.00 | 1.75 | 1.00 |
| ☐287 4¢ Orange | | | | | | |
| | 910.00 | 650.00 | 120.00 | 90.00 | 24.00 | 15.00 |
| ☐288 5¢ Dull Blue | | | | | | |
| | 910.00 | 650.00 | 110.00 | 80.00 | 21.00 | 14.00 |
| ☐289 8¢ Violet Brown | | | | | | |
| | 1050.00 | 750.00 | 150.00 | 98.00 | 37.00 | 24.00 |
| ☐290 10¢ Gray Violet | | | | | | |
| | 1200.00 | 1000.00 | 165.00 | 115.00 | 20.00 | 14.00 |
| ☐291 50¢ Sage Green | | | | | | |
| | — | — | 575.00 | 440.00 | 160.00 | 95.00 |
| ☐292 $1 Black | | | | | | |
| | — | — | 1300.00 | 1000.00 | 480.00 | 325.00 |
| ☐293 $2 Orange Brown | | | | | | |
| | — | — | 2100.00 | 1600.00 | 760.00 | 500.00 |

## 1901. PAN-AMERICAN ISSUE (N-H ADD 75%)

| Scott No. | Fine Unused Block | Ave. Unused Block | Fine Unused Each | Ave. Unused Each | Fine Used Each | Ave. Used Each |
|---|---|---|---|---|---|---|
| ☐294 1¢ Green & Black | | | | | | |
| | 220.00 | 200.00 | 17.00 | 9.00 | 4.00 | 3.00 |
| ☐295 2¢ Carmine & Black | | | | | | |
| | 220.00 | 200.00 | 15.00 | 9.00 | 1.40 | .80 |
| ☐296 4¢ Chocolate & Black | | | | | | |
| | 2100.00 | 1600.00 | 82.00 | 55.00 | 16.50 | 11.00 |

| Scott No. | | Fine Unused Block | Ave. Unused Block | Fine Unused Each | Ave. Unused Each | Fine Used Each | Ave. Used Each |
|---|---|---|---|---|---|---|---|
| □297 | 5¢ Ultramarine & Black | | | | | | |
| | | 2300.00 | 1800.00 | 90.00 | 60.00 | 16.50 | 11.00 |
| □298 | 8¢ Brown Violet Black | | | | | | |
| | | 3000.00 | 2200.00 | 118.00 | 78.00 | 60.00 | 48.00 |
| □299 | 10¢ Yellow Brown Black | | | | | | |
| | | 4800.00 | 3800.00 | 175.00 | 110.00 | 29.00 | 19.00 |

## 1902–1903. PERF. 12 (N-H ADD 80%)

| Scott No. | | Fine Unused Block | Ave. Unused Block | Fine Unused Each | Ave. Unused Each | Fine Used Each | Ave. Used Each |
|---|---|---|---|---|---|---|---|
| □300 | 1¢ Blue Green | | | | | | |
| | | 140.00 | 90.00 | 8.00 | 6.00 | .16 | .14 |
| □301 | 2¢ Carmine | | | | | | |
| | | 140.00 | 90.00 | 10.00 | 7.00 | .16 | .14 |
| □302 | 3¢ Violet | | | | | | |
| | | 480.00 | 310.00 | 40.00 | 30.00 | 3.60 | 2.00 |
| □303 | 4¢ Brown | | | | | | |
| | | 480.00 | 310.00 | 40.00 | 30.00 | 1.30 | .75 |
| □304 | 5¢ Blue | | | | | | |
| | | 610.00 | 500.00 | 45.00 | 40.00 | 1.10 | .70 |
| □305 | 6¢ Claret | | | | | | |
| | | 610.00 | 475.00 | 45.00 | 41.00 | 2.80 | 1.50 |
| □306 | 8¢ Violet Black | | | | | | |
| | | 450.00 | 325.00 | 32.00 | 21.00 | 2.00 | 1.40 |
| □307 | 10¢ Red Brown | | | | | | |
| | | 750.00 | 650.00 | 52.00 | 45.00 | 1.70 | 1.00 |
| □308 | 13¢ Purple Black | | | | | | |
| | | 400.00 | 300.00 | 32.00 | 28.00 | 9.00 | 6.00 |
| □309 | 15¢ Olive Green | | | | | | |
| | | 1200.00 | 750.00 | 100.00 | 70.00 | 7.00 | 5.00 |
| □310 | 50¢ Orange | | | | | | |
| | | 3800.00 | 2800.00 | 350.00 | 300.00 | 25.00 | 14.00 |
| □311 | $1 Black | | | | | | |
| | | 5200.00 | 4200.00 | 575.00 | 400.00 | 50.00 | 34.00 |
| □312 | $2 Dark Blue | | | | | | |
| | | — | — | 750.00 | 500.00 | 170.00 | 115.00 |
| □313 | $5 Dark Green | | | | | | |
| | | — | — | 1700.00 | 1100.00 | 550.00 | 380.00 |

## 1906–1908. IMPERFORATED (N-H ADD 70%)

| Scott No. | | Fine Unused Block | Ave. Unused Block | Fine Unused Each | Ave. Unused Each | Fine Used Each | Ave. Used Each |
|---|---|---|---|---|---|---|---|
| □314 | 1¢ Blue Green | | | | | | |
| | | 180.00 | 150.00 | 24.00 | 18.00 | 17.00 | 11.00 |

| Scott No. | Fine Unused Block | Ave. Unused Block | Fine Unused Each | Ave. Unused Each | Fine Used Each | Ave. Used Each |
|---|---|---|---|---|---|---|
| ☐315  5¢ Blue | | | | | | |
| | 4200.00 | 3600.00 | 400.00 | 290.00 | 200.00 | 125.00 |

## 1903. PERF. 12 (N-H ADD 50%)

| | | | | | | |
|---|---|---|---|---|---|---|
| ☐319  2¢ Carmine | | | | | | |
| | 80.00 | 68.00 | 6.25 | 4.85 | .18 | .14 |
| ☐319a 2¢ Lake | | | | | | |
| | 115.00 | 90.00 | 7.25 | 5.00 | .27 | .22 |

## 1906. IMPERFORATED (N-H ADD 70%)

| | | | | | | |
|---|---|---|---|---|---|---|
| ☐320  2¢ Carmine | | | | | | |
| | 225.00 | 190.00 | 21.00 | 12.50 | 16.50 | 9.50 |
| ☐320a 2¢ Lake | | | | | | |
| | 350.00 | 300.00 | 64.00 | 42.00 | 39.00 | 26.00 |

## 1904. LOUISIANA PURCHASE ISSUE
## PERF. 12 (N-H ADD 75%)

| | | | | | | |
|---|---|---|---|---|---|---|
| ☐323  1¢ Green | | | | | | |
| | 185.00 | 140.00 | 23.00 | 15.00 | 5.00 | 2.80 |
| ☐324  2¢ Carmine | | | | | | |
| | 185.00 | 140.00 | 21.00 | 13.00 | 1.90 | .90 |
| ☐325  3¢ Violet | | | | | | |
| | 800.00 | 550.00 | 72.00 | 45.00 | 31.00 | 21.00 |
| ☐326  5¢ Dark Blue | | | | | | |
| | 900.00 | 700.00 | 78.00 | 55.00 | 20.00 | 15.00 |
| ☐327 10¢ Red Brown | | | | | | |
| | 1600.00 | 1200.00 | 140.00 | 95.00 | 31.00 | 21.00 |

## 1907. JAMESTOWN EXPOSITION ISSUE
## (N-H ADD 75%)

| | | | | | | |
|---|---|---|---|---|---|---|
| ☐328  1¢ Green | | | | | | |
| | 240.00 | 200.00 | 19.00 | 11.00 | 4.00 | 3.00 |
| ☐329  2¢ Carmine | | | | | | |
| | 340.00 | 300.00 | 22.00 | 12.00 | 5.50 | 3.50 |
| ☐330  5¢ Blue | | | | | | |
| | 1900.00 | 1600.00 | 96.00 | 62.00 | 26.50 | 15.00 |

| Scott No. | Fine Unused Block | Ave. Unused Block | Fine Unused Each | Ave. Unused Each | Fine Used Each | Ave. Used Each |
|---|---|---|---|---|---|---|

## 1908–1909. DOUBLE LINE WATERMARKED "U.S.P.S." PERF. 12 (N-H ADD 50%)

| Scott No. | | Fine Unused Block | Ave. Unused Block | Fine Unused Each | Ave. Unused Each | Fine Used Each | Ave. Used Each |
|---|---|---|---|---|---|---|---|
| ☐331 | 1¢ Green | 66.00 | 45.00 | 6.00 | 4.00 | .21 | .14 |
| ☐332 | 2¢ Carmine | 62.00 | 47.00 | 6.00 | 4.25 | .21 | .14 |
| ☐333 | 3¢ Violet | 300.00 | 260.00 | 28.00 | 18.00 | 3.15 | 1.90 |
| ☐334 | 4¢ Orange Brown | 310.00 | 260.00 | 30.00 | 20.00 | 1.10 | .70 |
| ☐335 | 5¢ Blue | 510.00 | 410.00 | 39.00 | 26.00 | 2.30 | 1.50 |
| ☐336 | 6¢ Red Orange | 425.00 | 320.00 | 48.00 | 30.00 | 4.75 | 3.00 |
| ☐337 | 8¢ Olive Green | 360.00 | 230.00 | 34.00 | 24.00 | 3.00 | 1.90 |
| ☐338 | 10¢ Yellow | 600.00 | 450.00 | 48.00 | 35.00 | 1.50 | .90 |
| ☐339 | 13¢ Blue Green | 425.00 | 300.00 | 32.00 | 23.00 | 23.00 | 11.00 |
| ☐340 | 15¢ Pale Ultramarine | 425.00 | 310.00 | 42.00 | 31.00 | 6.00 | 3.50 |
| ☐341 | 50¢ Violet | 1700.00 | 1100.00 | 250.00 | 145.00 | 17.00 | 10.00 |
| ☐342 | $1 Violet Black | 2600.00 | 1800.00 | 380.00 | 240.00 | 74.00 | 46.00 |

## IMPERFORATE (N-H ADD 65%)

| Scott No. | | Fine Unused Block | Ave. Unused Block | Fine Unused Each | Ave. Unused Each | Fine Used Each | Ave. Used Each |
|---|---|---|---|---|---|---|---|
| ☐343 | 1¢ Green | 60.00 | 42.00 | 6.00 | 4.75 | 4.00 | 2.90 |
| ☐344 | 2¢ Carmine | 100.00 | 80.00 | 8.00 | 6.00 | 4.15 | 2.90 |
| ☐345 | 3¢ Deep Violet | 200.00 | 160.00 | 18.00 | 11.00 | 14.00 | 10.00 |
| ☐346 | 4¢ Orange Brown | 310.00 | 260.00 | 26.00 | 17.00 | 18.00 | 12.00 |
| ☐347 | 5¢ Blue | 450.00 | 310.00 | 42.00 | 29.00 | 29.00 | 20.00 |

| Scott No. | Fine Unused Line Pair | Ave. Unused Line Pair | Fine Unused Each | Ave. Unused Each | Fine Used Each | Ave. Used Each |
|---|---|---|---|---|---|---|

## 1908–1910. COIL STAMPS
## PERF. 12 HORIZONTALLY (N-H ADD 70%)

| Scott No. | Fine Unused Line Pair | Ave. Unused Line Pair | Fine Unused Each | Ave. Unused Each | Fine Used Each | Ave. Used Each |
|---|---|---|---|---|---|---|
| ☐348 1¢ Green | 150.00 | 100.00 | 22.00 | 16.00 | 12.00 | 7.50 |
| ☐349 2¢ Carmine | 240.00 | 140.00 | 36.00 | 21.00 | 8.00 | 4.50 |
| ☐350 4¢ Orange Brown | 700.00 | 425.00 | 85.00 | 50.00 | 68.00 | 40.00 |
| ☐351 5¢ Blue | 710.00 | 425.00 | 100.00 | 62.00 | 84.00 | 50.00 |

## PERF. 12 VERTICALLY (N-H ADD 70%)

| Scott No. | Fine Unused Line Pair | Ave. Unused Line Pair | Fine Unused Each | Ave. Unused Each | Fine Used Each | Ave. Used Each |
|---|---|---|---|---|---|---|
| ☐352 1¢ Green | 275.00 | 200.00 | 45.00 | 30.00 | 26.00 | 18.00 |
| ☐353 ¢ Carmine | 265.00 | 180.00 | 42.00 | 25.00 | 7.50 | 4.00 |
| ☐354 4¢ Orange Brown | 700.00 | 500.00 | 95.00 | 66.00 | 49.00 | 31.00 |
| ☐355 5¢ Blue | 775.00 | 600.00 | 100.00 | 75.00 | 70.00 | 42.00 |
| ☐356 10¢ Yellow | — | — | 1300.00 | 700.00 | 600.00 | 390.00 |

| Scott No. | Fine Unused Block | Ave. Unused Block | Fine Unused Each | Ave. Unused Each | Fine Used Each | Ave. Used Each |
|---|---|---|---|---|---|---|

## 1909. BLUISH GRAY PAPER
## PERF. 12 (N-H ADD 70%)

| Scott No. | Fine Unused Block | Ave. Unused Block | Fine Unused Each | Ave. Unused Each | Fine Used Each | Ave. Used Each |
|---|---|---|---|---|---|---|
| ☐357 1¢ Green | 700.00 | 525.00 | 90.00 | 60.00 | 80.00 | 56.00 |
| ☐358 2¢ Carmine | 700.00 | 500.00 | 82.00 | 55.00 | 60.00 | 40.00 |
| ☐359 3¢ Violet | — | — | 1400.00 | 1000.00 | — | — |
| ☐360 4¢ Orange Brown | — | — | 15,000.00 | 10,000.00 | — | — |
| ☐361 5¢ Blue | — | — | 3000.00 | 2000.00 | — | — |

| Scott No. | Fine Unused Block | Ave. Unused Block | Fine Unused Each | Ave. Unused Each | Fine Used Each | Ave. Used Each |
|---|---|---|---|---|---|---|
| □362  6¢ Orange | | | | | | |
| | — | — | 1100.00 | 650.00 | — | — |
| □363  8¢ Olive Green | | | | | | |
| | — | — | 15,000.00 | 10,000.00 | — | — |
| □364 10¢ Yellow | | | | | | |
| | — | — | 1100.00 | 700.00 | — | — |
| □365 13¢ Blue Green | | | | | | |
| | — | — | 1900.00 | 1250.00 | — | — |
| □366 15¢ Pale Ultramarine | | | | | | |
| | — | — | 900.00 | 650.00 | — | — |

## 1909. LINCOLN MEMORIAL ISSUE (N-H ADD 75%)

| Scott No. | Fine Unused Block | Ave. Unused Block | Fine Unused Each | Ave. Unused Each | Fine Used Each | Ave. Used Each |
|---|---|---|---|---|---|---|
| □367  2¢ Carmine | | | | | | |
| | 120.00 | 85.00 | 7.00 | 4.00 | 2.10 | 1.50 |
| □368  2¢ Carmine, Impf. | | | | | | |
| | 200.00 | 140.00 | 21.00 | 16.00 | 17.00 | 11.00 |
| □369  2¢ Carmine (On B.G. Paper) | | | | | | |
| | 1100.00 | 1000.00 | 190.00 | 120.00 | 185.00 | 125.00 |

## 1909. ALASKA-YUKON ISSUE (N-H ADD 70%)

| Scott No. | Fine Unused Block | Ave. Unused Block | Fine Unused Each | Ave. Unused Each | Fine Used Each | Ave. Used Each |
|---|---|---|---|---|---|---|
| □370  2¢ Carmine | | | | | | |
| | 200.00 | 150.00 | 9.00 | 6.00 | 2.00 | — |
| □371  2¢ Carmine, Impf. | | | | | | |
| | 225.00 | 165.00 | 29.00 | 20.00 | 19.00 | 13.00 |

## 1909. HUDSON-FULTON ISSUE (N-H ADD 70%)

| Scott No. | Fine Unused Block | Ave. Unused Block | Fine Unused Each | Ave. Unused Each | Fine Used Each | Ave. Used Each |
|---|---|---|---|---|---|---|
| □372  2¢ Carmine | | | | | | |
| | 240.00 | 180.00 | 12.00 | 9.00 | 3.75 | 2.25 |
| □373  2¢ Carmine, Impf. | | | | | | |
| | 250.00 | 190.00 | 31.00 | 24.00 | 22.00 | 18.50 |

## 1910–1911. SINGLE LINE WATERMARKED "U.S.P.S." PERF. 12 (N-H ADD 75%)

| Scott No. | Fine Unused Block | Ave. Unused Block | Fine Unused Each | Ave. Unused Each | Fine Used Each | Ave. Used Each |
|---|---|---|---|---|---|---|
| □374  1¢ Green | | | | | | |
| | 69.00 | 51.00 | 6.00 | 4.00 | .18 | .14 |
| □375  2¢ Carmine | | | | | | |
| | 72.00 | 53.00 | 7.00 | 5.00 | .18 | .14 |
| □376  3¢ Deep Violet | | | | | | |
| | 130.00 | 100.00 | 16.00 | 11.50 | 1.75 | 1.10 |

| Scott No. | Fine Unused Block | Ave. Unused Block | Fine Unused Each | Ave. Unused Each | Fine Used Each | Ave. Used Each |
|---|---|---|---|---|---|---|
| ☐377 4¢ Brown | | | | | | |
| | 166.00 | 115.00 | 23.00 | 16.00 | .50 | .30 |
| ☐378 5¢ Blue | | | | | | |
| | 200.00 | 150.00 | 25.00 | 17.00 | .50 | .28 |
| ☐379 6¢ Red Orange | | | | | | |
| | 300.00 | 170.00 | 29.00 | 20.00 | .85 | .56 |
| ☐380 8¢ Olive Green | | | | | | |
| | 550.00 | 400.00 | 92.00 | 65.00 | 13.00 | 8.00 |
| ☐381 10¢ Yellow | | | | | | |
| | 425.00 | 365.00 | 86.00 | 64.00 | 4.20 | 2.50 |
| ☐382 15¢ Ultramarine | | | | | | |
| | 1200.00 | 900.00 | 210.00 | 145.00 | 13.50 | 8.75 |

## IMPERFORATE (N-H ADD 70%)

| Scott No. | Fine Unused Block | Ave. Unused Block | Fine Unused Each | Ave. Unused Each | Fine Used Each | Ave. Used Each |
|---|---|---|---|---|---|---|
| ☐383 1¢ Green | | | | | | |
| | 50.00 | 40.00 | 2.80 | 1.90 | 2.25 | 1.50 |
| ☐384 2¢ Carmine | | | | | | |
| | 130.00 | 93.00 | 5.00 | 2.80 | 1.60 | .85 |

| Scott No. | Fine Unused Line Pair | Ave. Unused Line Pair | Fine Unused Each | Ave. Unused Each | Fine Used Each | Ave. Used Each |
|---|---|---|---|---|---|---|
| | | | | | | |

## 1910–1913. COIL STAMPS
## PERF. 12 HORIZONTALLY (N-H ADD 70%)

| Scott No. | Fine Unused Line Pair | Ave. Unused Line Pair | Fine Unused Each | Ave. Unused Each | Fine Used Each | Ave. Used Each |
|---|---|---|---|---|---|---|
| ☐385 1¢ Green | | | | | | |
| | 210.00 | 125.00 | 21.00 | 15.00 | 12.00 | 5.50 |
| ☐386 2¢ Carmine | | | | | | |
| | 410.00 | 270.00 | 35.00 | 22.00 | 13.00 | 8.00 |

## PERF. 12 VERTICALLY (N-H ADD 70%)

| Scott No. | Fine Unused Line Pair | Ave. Unused Line Pair | Fine Unused Each | Ave. Unused Each | Fine Used Each | Ave. Used Each |
|---|---|---|---|---|---|---|
| ☐387 1¢ Green | | | | | | |
| | 285.00 | 200.00 | 60.00 | 40.00 | 28.50 | 16.00 |
| ☐388 2¢ Carmine | | | | | | |
| | 2600.00 | 2100.00 | 425.00 | 340.00 | 130.00 | 85.00 |

## PERF. 8½ HORIZONTALLY (N-H ADD 70%)

| Scott No. | Fine Unused Line Pair | Ave. Unused Line Pair | Fine Unused Each | Ave. Unused Each | Fine Used Each | Ave. Used Each |
|---|---|---|---|---|---|---|
| ☐390 1¢ Green | | | | | | |
| | 23.00 | 16.00 | 4.00 | 2.50 | 3.50 | 3.00 |

| Scott No. | | Fine Unused Line Pair | Ave. Unused Line Pair | Fine Unused Each | Ave. Unused Each | Fine Used Each | Ave. Used Each |
|---|---|---|---|---|---|---|---|
| ☐391 | 2¢ Carmine | | | | | | |
| | | 160.00 | 120.00 | 24.00 | 16.50 | 8.50 | 5.00 |

## PERF. 8½ VERTICALLY (N-H ADD 70%)

| | | | | | | | |
|---|---|---|---|---|---|---|---|
| ☐392 | 1¢ Green | | | | | | |
| | | 100.00 | 70.00 | 16.00 | 10.00 | 15.00 | 12.00 |
| ☐393 | 2¢ Carmine | | | | | | |
| | | 160.00 | 110.00 | 32.00 | 21.00 | 6.50 | 4.50 |
| ☐394 | 3¢ Violet | | | | | | |
| | | 235.00 | 155.00 | 36.00 | 26.00 | 37.00 | 28.00 |
| ☐395 | 4¢ Brown | | | | | | |
| | | 235.00 | 155.00 | 38.00 | 26.00 | 32.00 | 28.00 |
| ☐396 | 5¢ Blue | | | | | | |
| | | 235.00 | 155.00 | 38.00 | 26.00 | 32.00 | 28.00 |

| Scott No. | | Fine Unused Block | Ave. Unused Block | Fine Unused Each | Ave. Unused Each | Fine Used Each | Ave. Used Each |
|---|---|---|---|---|---|---|---|

## 1913–1915. PANAMA-PACIFIC ISSUE
## PERF. 12 (N-H ADD 80%)

| | | | | | | | |
|---|---|---|---|---|---|---|---|
| ☐397 | 1¢ Green | | | | | | |
| | | 130.00 | 90.00 | 13.00 | 8.00 | 1.90 | 1.10 |
| ☐398 | 2¢ Carmine | | | | | | |
| | | 215.00 | 145.00 | 15.00 | 9.00 | .80 | .50 |
| ☐399 | 5¢ Blue | | | | | | |
| | | 525.00 | 400.00 | 60.00 | 45.00 | 10.00 | 5.50 |
| ☐400 | 10¢ Orange Yellow | | | | | | |
| | | 810.00 | 575.00 | 95.00 | 65.00 | 17.00 | 12.00 |
| ☐400A | 10¢ Orange | | | | | | |
| | | 1400.00 | 1200.00 | 175.00 | 125.00 | 20.00 | 11.00 |

## PERF. 10 (N-H ADD 80%)

| | | | | | | | |
|---|---|---|---|---|---|---|---|
| ☐401 | 1¢ Green | | | | | | |
| | | 260.00 | 190.00 | 19.00 | 15.00 | 7.00 | 4.50 |
| ☐402 | 2¢ Carmine | | | | | | |
| | | 450.00 | 300.00 | 70.00 | 52.00 | 2.00 | 1.50 |
| ☐403 | 5¢ Blue | | | | | | |
| | | 1500.00 | 1000.00 | 150.00 | 100.00 | 17.00 | 12.00 |

| Scott No. | Fine Unused Block | Ave. Unused Block | Fine Unused Each | Ave. Unused Each | Fine Used Each | Ave. Used Each |
|---|---|---|---|---|---|---|
| ☐404 10¢ Orange | | | | | | |
| | 6000.00 | 4000.00 | 810.00 | 550.00 | 65.00 | 42.00 |

## 1912–1914. REGULAR ISSUE
## PERF. 12 (N-H ADD 70%)

| Scott No. | Fine Unused Block | Ave. Unused Block | Fine Unused Each | Ave. Unused Each | Fine Used Each | Ave. Used Each |
|---|---|---|---|---|---|---|
| ☐405 1¢ Green | | | | | | |
| | 90.00 | 62.00 | 5.00 | 2.25 | .18 | .15 |
| ☐406 2¢ Carmine | | | | | | |
| | 95.00 | 75.00 | 4.50 | 3.00 | .18 | .15 |
| ☐407 7¢ Black | | | | | | |
| | 500.00 | 400.00 | 72.00 | 48.00 | 7.50 | 4.50 |

## IMPERFORATE (N-H ADD 70%)

| Scott No. | Fine Unused Block | Ave. Unused Block | Fine Unused Each | Ave. Unused Each | Fine Used Each | Ave. Used Each |
|---|---|---|---|---|---|---|
| ☐408 1¢ Green | | | | | | |
| | 19.00 | 15.00 | 1.10 | .70 | .60 | .35 |
| ☐409 2¢ Carmine | | | | | | |
| | 34.00 | 26.00 | 1.25 | .82 | .60 | .36 |

| Scott No. | Fine Unused Line Pair | Ave. Unused Line Pair | Fine Unused Each | Ave. Unused Each | Fine Used Each | Ave. Used Each |
|---|---|---|---|---|---|---|

## 1912. COIL STAMPS
## PERF. 8½ HORIZONTALLY (N-H ADD 70%)

| Scott No. | Fine Unused Line Pair | Ave. Unused Line Pair | Fine Unused Each | Ave. Unused Each | Fine Used Each | Ave. Used Each |
|---|---|---|---|---|---|---|
| ☐410 1¢ Green | | | | | | |
| | 30.00 | 20.00 | 5.00 | 3.75 | 3.40 | 2.00 |
| ☐411 2¢ Carmine | | | | | | |
| | 36.00 | 26.00 | 7.00 | 4.25 | 3.15 | 1.90 |

## PERF. 8½ VERTICALLY (N-H ADD 80%)

| Scott No. | Fine Unused Line Pair | Ave. Unused Line Pair | Fine Unused Each | Ave. Unused Each | Fine Used Each | Ave. Used Each |
|---|---|---|---|---|---|---|
| ☐412 1¢ Green | | | | | | |
| | 78.00 | 50.00 | 17.50 | 10.00 | 5.50 | 3.40 |
| ☐413 2¢ Carmine | | | | | | |
| | 160.00 | 98.00 | 27.00 | 19.00 | .72 | .50 |

| Scott No. | Fine Unused Block | Ave. Unused Block | Fine Unused Each | Ave. Unused Each | Fine Used Each | Ave. Used Each |
|---|---|---|---|---|---|---|

**1912–1914. SINGLE LINE WATERMARKED "U.S.P.S." PERF. 12 (N-H ADD 75%)**

| Scott No. | Fine Unused Block | Ave. Unused Block | Fine Unused Each | Ave. Unused Each | Fine Used Each | Ave. Used Each |
|---|---|---|---|---|---|---|
| ☐414 8¢ Olive Green | 320.00 | 210.00 | 34.00 | 22.00 | 1.35 | 1.00 |
| ☐415 9¢ Salmon Red | 500.00 | 360.00 | 43.00 | 28.00 | 13.00 | 8.50 |
| ☐416 10¢ Orange Yellow | 380.00 | 260.00 | 30.00 | 20.00 | .45 | .26 |
| ☐417 12¢ Claret Brown | 360.00 | 240.00 | 34.00 | 24.00 | 4.00 | 2.75 |
| ☐418 15¢ Gray | 500.00 | 360.00 | 55.00 | 38.00 | 3.40 | 2.25 |
| ☐419 20¢ Ultramarine | 1000.00 | 725.00 | 138.00 | 88.00 | 14.00 | 9.50 |
| ☐420 30¢ Orange Red | 700.00 | 500.00 | 100.00 | 70.00 | 14.00 | 9.50 |
| ☐421 50¢ Violet | 2400.00 | 1750.00 | 375.00 | 265.00 | 16.00 | 10.00 |

**1912. DOUBLE LINE WATERMARKED "U.S.P.S." (N-H ADD 75%)**

| Scott No. | Fine Unused Block | Ave. Unused Block | Fine Unused Each | Ave. Unused Each | Fine Used Each | Ave. Used Each |
|---|---|---|---|---|---|---|
| ☐422 50¢ Violet | 1275.00 | 1000.00 | 190.00 | 120.00 | 18.00 | 9.00 |
| ☐423 $1 Violet Black | 3000.00 | 2100.00 | 425.00 | 275.00 | 60.00 | 40.00 |

**1914–1915. SINGLE LINE WATERMARKED "U.S.P.S." PERF. 10 (N-H ADD 55%)**

| Scott No. | Fine Unused Block | Ave. Unused Block | Fine Unused Each | Ave. Unused Each | Fine Used Each | Ave. Used Each |
|---|---|---|---|---|---|---|
| ☐424 1¢ Green | 32.00 | 22.00 | 2.30 | 1.40 | .18 | .14 |
| ☐425 2¢ Carmine | 22.00 | 16.00 | 2.00 | 1.35 | .18 | .14 |
| ☐426 3¢ Deep Violet | 110.00 | 75.00 | 11.00 | 7.60 | 1.60 | .90 |
| ☐427 4¢ Brown | 230.00 | 80.00 | 27.00 | 20.00 | .58 | .40 |
| ☐428 5¢ Blue | 260.00 | 150.00 | 23.00 | 15.75 | .58 | .40 |

| Scott No. | Fine Unused Block | Ave. Unused Block | Fine Unused Each | Ave. Unused Each | Fine Used Each | Ave. Used Each |
|---|---|---|---|---|---|---|
| ☐429 6¢ Orange | | | | | | |
| | 280.00 | 185.00 | 29.00 | 21.00 | 1.30 | .95 |
| ☐430 7¢ Black | | | | | | |
| | 700.00 | 600.00 | 70.00 | 55.00 | 5.00 | 3.50 |
| ☐431 8¢ Olive Green | | | | | | |
| | 310.00 | 300.00 | 30.00 | 20.00 | 1.70 | .90 |
| ☐432 9¢ Salmon Red | | | | | | |
| | 500.00 | 400.00 | 39.00 | 30.00 | 10.00 | 5.00 |
| ☐433 12¢ Orange Yellow | | | | | | |
| | 500.00 | 400.00 | 35.00 | 26.00 | .35 | .19 |
| ☐434 11¢ Dark Green | | | | | | |
| | 190.00 | 120.00 | 17.00 | 12.00 | 7.25 | 5.00 |
| ☐435 12¢ Claret Brown | | | | | | |
| | 220.00 | 150.00 | 21.00 | 15.00 | 5.00 | 3.25 |
| ☐435a 12¢ Copper Red | | | | | | |
| | 250.00 | 160.00 | 23.00 | 14.00 | 6.00 | 4.00 |
| ☐437 15¢ Gray | | | | | | |
| | 700.00 | 575.00 | 88.00 | 65.00 | 6.00 | 4.00 |
| ☐438 20¢ Ultramarine | | | | | | |
| | 1900.00 | 1500.00 | 170.00 | 118.00 | 3.50 | 2.60 |
| ☐439 30¢ Orange Red | | | | | | |
| | 2800.00 | 1900.00 | 215.00 | 160.00 | 16.00 | 11.00 |
| ☐440 50¢ Violet | | | | | | |
| | 9000.00 | 6500.00 | 540.00 | 425.00 | 17.00 | 12.00 |

| Scott No. | Fine Unused Line Pair | Ave. Unused Line Pair | Fine Unused Each | Ave. Unused Each | Fine Used Each | Ave. Used Each |
|---|---|---|---|---|---|---|

## 1914. COIL STAMPS
## PERF. 10 HORIZONTALLY (N-H ADD 75%)

| | | | | | | |
|---|---|---|---|---|---|---|
| ☐441 1¢ Green | | | | | | |
| | 7.50 | 5.00 | .90 | .80 | .90 | .68 |
| ☐442 2¢ Carmine | | | | | | |
| | 55.00 | 38.00 | 7.50 | 5.00 | 7.00 | 4.10 |

## PERF. 10 VERTICALLY (N-H ADD 70%)

| | | | | | | |
|---|---|---|---|---|---|---|
| ☐443 1¢ Green | | | | | | |
| | 90.00 | 63.00 | 18.00 | 12.00 | 6.00 | 5.00 |

| Scott No. | Fine Unused Line Pair | Ave. Unused Line Pair | Fine Unused Each | Ave. Unused Each | Fine Used Each | Ave. Used Each |
|---|---|---|---|---|---|---|
| ☐444 | 2¢ Carmine | | | | | |
| | 150.00 | 98.00 | 24.00 | 16.00 | 1.30 | 1.25 |
| ☐445 | 3¢ Violet | | | | | |
| | 825.00 | 650.00 | 185.00 | 125.00 | 100.00 | 80.00 |
| ☐446 | 4¢ Brown | | | | | |
| | 500.00 | 375.00 | 100.00 | 75.00 | 33.00 | 25.00 |
| ☐447 | 5¢ Blue | | | | | |
| | 180.00 | 130.00 | 36.00 | 25.00 | 22.00 | 15.00 |

## 1914–1916. ROTARY PRESS COIL STAMPS PERF. 10 HORIZONTALLY (N-H ADD 70%)

| | | | | | | |
|---|---|---|---|---|---|---|
| ☐448 | 1¢ Green | | | | | |
| | 36.00 | 24.00 | 7.00 | 4.00 | 2.75 | 1.90 |
| ☐449 | 2¢ Red (I) | | | | | |
| | — | — | 1700.00 | 850.00 | 200.00 | 150.00 |
| ☐450 | 2¢ Carmine (III) | | | | | |
| | 48.00 | 36.00 | 11.00 | 8.10 | 3.25 | 1.90 |

## PERF. 10 VERTICALLY (N-H ADD 70%)

| | | | | | | |
|---|---|---|---|---|---|---|
| ☐452 | 1¢ Green | | | | | |
| | 62.00 | 40.00 | 9.00 | 6.00 | 1.50 | 1.10 |
| ☐453 | 2¢ Red (I) | | | | | |
| | 440.00 | 340.00 | 90.00 | 75.00 | 4.00 | 2.75 |
| ☐454 | 2¢ Carmine (II) | | | | | |
| | 400.00 | 300.00 | 82.00 | 64.00 | 10.00 | 7.00 |
| ☐455 | 2¢ Carmine (III) | | | | | |
| | 50.00 | 42.00 | 7.50 | 5.00 | .90 | .45 |
| ☐456 | 3¢ Violet | | | | | |
| | 500.00 | 400.00 | 210.00 | 160.00 | 90.00 | 64.00 |
| ☐457 | 4¢ Brown | | | | | |
| | 124.00 | 88.00 | 21.00 | 16.00 | 16.00 | 10.00 |
| ☐458 | 5¢ Blue | | | | | |
| | 130.00 | 88.00 | 30.00 | 20.00 | 16.00 | 11.00 |

## IMPERFORATE (N-H ADD 60%)

| | | | | | | |
|---|---|---|---|---|---|---|
| ☐459 | 2¢ Carmine | | | | | |
| | 1300.00 | 850.00 | 400.00 | 275.00 | — | — |

| Scott No. | Fine Unused Block | Ave. Unused Block | Fine Unused Each | Ave. Unused Each | Fine Used Each | Ave. Used Each |
|---|---|---|---|---|---|---|

## 1915. DOUBLE LINE WATERMARKED "U.S.P.S." PERF. 10 (N-H ADD 60%)

☐460 $1 Violet Black

| | 4000.00 | 3400.00 | 700.00 | 500.00 | 88.00 | 62.00 |

## 1915. SINGLE LINE WATERMARKED "U.S.P.S." PERF. 11 (N-H ADD 60%)

☐461 2¢ Pale Carmine Rose

| | 300.00 | 190.00 | 100.00 | 65.00 | 140.00 | 65.00 |

## 1916–1917. UNWATERMARKED PERF. 10 (N-H ADD 70%)

☐462 1¢ Green

| | 110.00 | 75.00 | 7.00 | 5.00 | .38 | .22 |

☐463 2¢ Carmine

| | 98.00 | 62.00 | 4.25 | 2.75 | .18 | .15 |

☐464 3¢ Violet

| | 1000.00 | 700.00 | 68.00 | 50.00 | 13.50 | 8.50 |

☐465 4¢ Orange Brown

| | 500.00 | 400.00 | 41.00 | 25.00 | 2.10 | 1.25 |

☐466 5¢ Blue

| | 850.00 | 650.00 | 65.00 | 40.00 | 2.10 | 1.50 |

☐467 5¢ Carmine (error)

| | — | 1100.00 | 600.00 | 480.00 | — | — |

☐468 6¢ Red Orange

| | 600.00 | 470.00 | 72.00 | 46.00 | 7.10 | 4.10 |

☐469 7¢ Black

| | 500.00 | 400.00 | 98.00 | 65.00 | 13.00 | 7.00 |

☐470 58¢ Olive Green

| | 460.00 | 310.00 | 46.00 | 31.00 | 6.00 | 3.50 |

☐471 9¢ Salmon Red

| | 420.00 | 310.00 | 48.00 | 34.00 | 14.00 | 9.00 |

☐472 12¢ Orange Yellow

| | 900.00 | 700.00 | 85.00 | 70.00 | 1.00 | .65 |

☐473 11¢ Dark Green

| | 236.00 | 165.00 | 27.00 | 20.00 | 16.00 | 11.00 |

☐474 12¢ Claret Brown

| | 450.00 | 300.00 | 43.00 | 31.00 | 5.75 | 4.50 |

☐475 15¢ Gray

| | 900.00 | 710.00 | 140.00 | 90.00 | 12.00 | 7.00 |

| Scott No. | | Fine Unused Block | Ave. Unused Block | Fine Unused Each | Ave. Unused Each | Fine Used Each | Ave. Used Each |
|---|---|---|---|---|---|---|---|
| ☐476 | 20¢ | Ultramarine | | | | | |
| | | 2100.00 | 1800.00 | 210.00 | 160.00 | 12.00 | 8.00 |
| ☐477 | 50¢ | Light Violet | | | | | |
| | | 6000.00 | 4800.00 | 1000.00 | 710.00 | 68.00 | 42.00 |
| ☐478 | $1 | Violet Black | | | | | |
| | | 4000.00 | 2600.00 | 650.00 | 500.00 | 20.00 | 12.00 |

## 1916–1917. DESIGN OF 1902–1903 PERF. 10 (N-H ADD 70%)

| Scott No. | | Fine Unused Block | Ave. Unused Block | Fine Unused Each | Ave. Unused Each | Fine Used Each | Ave. Used Each |
|---|---|---|---|---|---|---|---|
| ☐479 | $2 | Dark Blue | | | | | |
| | | 2100.00 | 1500.00 | 400.00 | 280.00 | 41.00 | 30.00 |
| ☐480 | $5 | Light Green | | | | | |
| | | 2100.00 | 1500.00 | 300.00 | 210.00 | 46.00 | 30.00 |

## IMPERFORATE (N-H ADD 70%)

| Scott No. | | Fine Unused Block | Ave. Unused Block | Fine Unused Each | Ave. Unused Each | Fine Used Each | Ave. Used Each |
|---|---|---|---|---|---|---|---|
| ☐481 | 1¢ | Green | | | | | |
| | | 10.00 | 8.00 | .90 | .55 | .75 | .45 |
| ☐482 | 2¢ | Carmine | | | | | |
| | | 20.00 | 15.00 | 1.25 | .70 | 1.30 | .90 |
| ☐483 | 3¢ | Violet (I) | | | | | |
| | | 110.00 | 82.00 | 12.00 | 8.50 | 8.00 | 5.00 |
| ☐484 | 3¢ | Violet (II) | | | | | |
| | | 90.00 | 64.00 | 9.00 | 7.00 | 4.10 | 3.00 |

| Scott No. | | Fine Unused Line Pair | Ave. Unused Line Pair | Fine Unused Each | Ave. Unused Each | Fine Used Each | Ave. Used Each |
|---|---|---|---|---|---|---|---|

## 1916–1922. ROTARY PRESS COIL STAMPS PERF. 10 HORIZONTALLY (N-H ADD 60%)

| Scott No. | | Fine Unused Line Pair | Ave. Unused Line Pair | Fine Unused Each | Ave. Unused Each | Fine Used Each | Ave. Used Each |
|---|---|---|---|---|---|---|---|
| ☐486 | 1¢ | Green | | | | | |
| | | 4.00 | 3.00 | .75 | .60 | .28 | .16 |
| ☐487 | 2¢ | Carmine (II) | | | | | |
| | | 100.00 | 75.00 | 13.00 | 9.00 | 2.75 | 1.80 |
| ☐488 | 2¢ | Carmine (III) | | | | | |
| | | 16.00 | 11.00 | 3.00 | 1.65 | 1.80 | 1.00 |
| ☐489 | 3¢ | Violet | | | | | |
| | | 31.00 | 21.00 | 4.25 | 3.00 | 1.30 | .75 |

| Scott No. | Fine Unused Line Pair | Ave. Unused Line Pair | Fine Unused Each | Ave. Unused Each | Fine Used Each | Ave. Used Each |
|---|---|---|---|---|---|---|

## PERF. 10 VERTICALLY (N-H ADD 60%)

| Scott No. | | Fine Unused Line Pair | Ave. Unused Line Pair | Fine Unused Each | Ave. Unused Each | Fine Used Each | Ave. Used Each |
|---|---|---|---|---|---|---|---|
| ☐490 | 1¢ Green | | | | | | |
| | | 4.50 | 4.00 | .65 | .42 | .24 | .16 |
| ☐491 | 2¢ Carmine (II) | | | | | | |
| | | — | — | 1200.00 | 800.00 | 420.00 | 300.00 |
| ☐492 | 2¢ Carmine (III) | | | | | | |
| | | 51.00 | 40.00 | 9.00 | 6.00 | .18 | .14 |
| ☐493 | 3¢ Violet (I) | | | | | | |
| | | 95.00 | 70.00 | 15.00 | 11.00 | 3.00 | 1.90 |
| ☐494 | 3¢ Violet (II) | | | | | | |
| | | 56.00 | 48.00 | 8.50 | 6.75 | .75 | .60 |
| ☐495 | 4¢ Orange Brown | | | | | | |
| | | 65.00 | 50.00 | 10.00 | 6.50 | 5.00 | 3.00 |
| ☐496 | 5¢ Blue | | | | | | |
| | | 26.00 | 18.00 | 5.00 | 3.00 | 1.00 | .70 |
| ☐497 | 10¢ Orange Yellow | | | | | | |
| | | 98.00 | 75.00 | 21.00 | 16.00 | 8.00 | 5.00 |

| Scott No. | Fine Unused Block | Ave. Unused Block | Fine Unused Each | Ave. Unused Each | Fine Used Each | Ave. Used Each |
|---|---|---|---|---|---|---|

## 1917–1919. FLAT PLATE PRINTING
## PERF. 11 (N-H ADD 60%)

| Scott No. | | Fine Unused Block | Ave. Unused Block | Fine Unused Each | Ave. Unused Each | Fine Used Each | Ave. Used Each |
|---|---|---|---|---|---|---|---|
| ☐498 | 1¢ Green | | | | | | |
| | | 13.00 | 11.00 | .50 | .36 | .18 | .15 |
| ☐499 | 2¢ Rose (I) | | | | | | |
| | | 16.00 | 12.00 | .42 | .30 | .18 | .15 |
| ☐500 | 2¢ Deep Rose (Ia) | | | | | | |
| | | 1300.00 | 1000.00 | 210.00 | 155.00 | 116.00 | 70.00 |
| ☐501 | 3¢ Violet (I) | | | | | | |
| | | 140.00 | 90.00 | 11.00 | 8.00 | .24 | .20 |
| ☐502 | 3¢ Violet (II) | | | | | | |
| | | 160.00 | 120.00 | 15.00 | 9.00 | .34 | .23 |
| ☐503 | 4¢ Brown | | | | | | |
| | | 160.00 | 100.00 | 10.00 | 5.50 | .24 | .15 |
| ☐504 | 5¢ Blue | | | | | | |
| | | 125.00 | 85.00 | 8.50 | 5.50 | .21 | .15 |
| ☐505 | 5¢ Rose (error) | | | | | | |
| | | — | — | 400.00 | 280.00 | — | — |

| Scott No. | | Fine Unused Block | Ave. Unused Block | Fine Unused Each | Ave. Unused Each | Fine Used Each | Ave. Used Each |
|---|---|---|---|---|---|---|---|
| ☐506 | 6¢ Red Orange | | | | | | |
| | | 190.00 | 125.00 | 12.00 | 7.50 | .40 | .22 |
| ☐507 | 7¢ Black | | | | | | |
| | | 340.00 | 200.00 | 26.00 | 16.00 | 1.50 | .78 |
| ☐508 | 8¢ Olive Bistre | | | | | | |
| | | 180.00 | 110.00 | 9.50 | 6.50 | 1.10 | .90 |
| ☐509 | 9¢ Salmon Red | | | | | | |
| | | 175.00 | 100.00 | 14.00 | 10.00 | 2.20 | 1.60 |
| ☐510 | 10¢ Orange Yellow | | | | | | |
| | | 200.00 | 150.00 | 15.00 | 9.00 | .20 | .15 |
| ☐511 | 11¢ Light Green | | | | | | |
| | | 135.00 | 90.00 | 8.50 | 3.20 | 3.10 | 2.30 |
| ☐512 | 12¢ Claret Brown | | | | | | |
| | | 120.00 | 80.00 | 8.00 | 4.50 | .60 | .55 |
| ☐513 | 13¢ Apple Green | | | | | | |
| | | 125.00 | 85.00 | 10.00 | 6.50 | 7.00 | 6.00 |
| ☐514 | 15¢ Gray | | | | | | |
| | | 550.00 | 350.00 | 37.00 | 25.00 | .90 | .70 |
| ☐515 | 20¢ Ultramarine | | | | | | |
| | | 600.00 | 410.00 | 44.00 | 31.00 | .35 | .24 |
| ☐516 | 30¢ Orange Red | | | | | | |
| | | 500.00 | 350.00 | 40.00 | 28.00 | 1.00 | .80 |
| ☐517 | 50¢ Red Violet | | | | | | |
| | | 1200.00 | 700.00 | 71.00 | 50.00 | .75 | .65 |
| ☐518 | $1 Violet Brown | | | | | | |
| | | 900.00 | 600.00 | 65.00 | 42.00 | 1.90 | 1.20 |
| ☐518b | $1 Deep Brown | | | | | | |
| | | 2100.00 | 1700.00 | 800.00 | 480.00 | 450.00 | 275.00 |

## 1917. DOUBLE LINE WATERMARKED "U.S.P.S." DESIGN OF 1908–1909 PERF. 11 (N-H ADD 60%)

| | | | | | | | |
|---|---|---|---|---|---|---|---|
| ☐519 | 2¢ Carmine | | | | | | |
| | | 1800.00 | 1600.00 | 225.00 | 125.00 | 250.00 | 150.00 |

## 1918. UNWATERMARKED PERF. 11 (N-H ADD 55%)

| | | | | | | | |
|---|---|---|---|---|---|---|---|
| ☐523 | $2 Orange Red & Black | | | | | | |
| | | 7000.00 | 5600.00 | 725.00 | 475.00 | 210.00 | 115.00 |
| ☐524 | $5 Deep Green & Black | | | | | | |
| | | 3100.00 | 2200.00 | 350.00 | 200.00 | 25.00 | 17.00 |

| Scott No. | Unused Block | FineAve. Unused Block | Fine Unused Each | Ave. Unused Each | Fine Used Each | Ave. Used Each |
|---|---|---|---|---|---|---|

## 1918–1920. OFFSET PRINTING PERF. 11 (N-H ADD 60%)

| | | | | | | |
|---|---|---|---|---|---|---|
| ☐525 1¢ Gray Green | | | | | | |
| | 16.00 | 13.00 | 1.75 | .90 | .80 | .56 |
| ☐526 2¢ Carmine (IV) | | | | | | |
| | 165.00 | 130.00 | 26.00 | 13.00 | 4.00 | 2.50 |
| ☐527 2¢ Carmine (V) | | | | | | |
| | 90.00 | 70.00 | 12.00 | 7.00 | 1.15 | .65 |
| ☐528 2¢ Carmine (Va) | | | | | | |
| | 49.00 | 30.00 | 7.50 | 4.00 | .22 | .15 |
| ☐528A 2¢ Carmine (VI) | | | | | | |
| | 250.00 | 200.00 | 41.00 | 27.00 | 1.00 | .75 |
| ☐528B 2¢ Carmine (VII) | | | | | | |
| | 110.00 | 78.00 | 15.00 | 11.00 | .18 | .15 |
| ☐529 3¢ Violet (III) | | | | | | |
| | 48.00 | 32.00 | 2.80 | 2.25 | .18 | .15 |
| ☐530 3¢ Purple (IV) | | | | | | |
| | 9.00 | 5.50 | 1.00 | .60 | .18 | .15 |

## IMPERFORATE (N-H ADD 60%)

| | | | | | | |
|---|---|---|---|---|---|---|
| ☐531 1¢ Gray Green | | | | | | |
| | 70.00 | 55.00 | 8.00 | 6.50 | 7.00 | 6.00 |
| ☐532 2¢ Carmine (IV) | | | | | | |
| | 220.00 | 185.00 | 34.00 | 24.00 | 29.00 | 22.00 |
| ☐533 2¢ Carmine (V) | | | | | | |
| | 1100.00 | 800.00 | 180.00 | 140.00 | 59.00 | 45.00 |
| ☐534 2¢ Carmine (Va) | | | | | | |
| | 90.00 | 65.00 | 10.00 | 7.50 | 8.00 | 6.00 |
| ☐534A 2¢ Carmine (VI) | | | | | | |
| | 250.00 | 210.00 | 30.00 | 25.00 | 28.00 | 20.00 |
| ☐534B 2¢ Carmine (VII) | | | | | | |
| | — | — | 1400.00 | 900.00 | 500.00 | 280.00 |
| ☐535 3¢ Violet | | | | | | |
| | 60.00 | 40.00 | 8.00 | 6.00 | 6.50 | 4.50 |

## PERF. 12 ½ (N-H ADD 65%)

| | | | | | | |
|---|---|---|---|---|---|---|
| ☐536 1¢ Gray Green | | | | | | |
| | 125.00 | 88.00 | 11.00 | 8.00 | 11.00 | 7.00 |

**IMPORTANT NOTICE:** Beginning here, prices of **blocks** are for blocks of 4 with **plate number attached**. Ordinary blocks of 4 bring lower prices. Plate blocks consisting of more than 4 stamps would sell higher than these sums. Always check the **headings** of price columns to accurately value your stamps.

| Scott No. | Fine Unused Plate Blk | Ave. Unused Plate Blk | Fine Unused Each | Ave. Unused Each | Fine Used Each | Ave. Used Each |
|---|---|---|---|---|---|---|
| **1919. VICTORY ISSUE (N-H ADD 45%)** | | | | | | |
| ☐537  3¢ Violet | | | | | | |
| | 90.00 | 78.00 | 8.00 | 6.00 | 4.10 | 2.50 |
| **1919–1921. REGULAR ISSUE ROTARY PRESS PRINTING PERF. 11 x 10 (N-H ADD 70%)** | | | | | | |
| ☐538  1¢ Green | | | | | | |
| | 75.00 | 49.00 | 9.00 | 6.00 | 9.00 | 5.00 |
| ☐538a  Same Impf. Horiz. Pair | | | | | | |
| | — | — | 50.00 | 34.00 | — | — |
| ☐539  2¢ Carmine Rose (II) | | | | | | |
| | — | — | 2600.00 | 1300.00 | 1000.00 | 600.00 |
| ☐540  2¢ Carmine Rose (III) | | | | | | |
| | 78.00 | 50.00 | 9.00 | 6.00 | 8.50 | 6.00 |
| ☐530a  Same Impf. Horiz. Pair | | | | | | |
| | — | — | 42.00 | 32.00 | — | — |
| ☐541  3¢ Violet | | | | | | |
| | 300.00 | 210.00 | 29.00 | 21.00 | 28.50 | 21.00 |
| **PERF. 10 x 11 (N-H ADD 70%)** | | | | | | |
| ☐542  1¢ Green | | | | | | |
| | 125.00 | 90.00 | 9.00 | 6.00 | 1.10 | .75 |
| **PERF. 10 x 10 (N-H ADD 70%)** | | | | | | |
| ☐543  1¢ Green | | | | | | |
| | 15.00 | 9.00 | .50 | .45 | .20 | .16 |
| **PERF. 11 x 11 (N-H ADD 70%)** | | | | | | |
| ☐544  1¢ Green | | | | | | |
| | — | — | — | 2100.00 | 1500.00 | |
| ☐545  1¢ Green | | | | | | |
| | 700.00 | 560.00 | 120.00 | 73.00 | 110.00 | 75.00 |

| Scott No. | Fine Unused Plate Blk | Ave. Unused Plate Blk | Fine Unused Each | Ave. Unused Each | Fine Used Each | Ave. Used Each |
|---|---|---|---|---|---|---|
| □546 2¢ Carmine Rose | | | | | | |
| | 490.00 | 400.00 | 80.00 | 41.00 | 78.00 | 52.00 |

## FLAT PLATE PRINTING PERF. 11 (N-H ADD 60%)
| | | | | | | |
|---|---|---|---|---|---|---|
| □547 $2 Carmine & Black | | | | | | |
| | — | — | 200.00 | 175.00 | 36.00 | 27.00 |

## 1920. PILGRIM ISSUE (N-H ADD 55%)
| | | | | | | |
|---|---|---|---|---|---|---|
| □548 1¢ Green | | | | | | |
| | 40.00 | 34.00 | 4.10 | 2.75 | 2.60 | 1.75 |
| □549 2¢ Carmine Rose | | | | | | |
| | 58.00 | 45.00 | 7.00 | 3.50 | 2.00 | 1.50 |
| □550 5¢ Deep Blue | | | | | | |
| | 400.00 | 300.00 | 48.00 | 30.00 | 14.00 | 13.00 |

## 1922–1925. PERF. FLAT PLATE PRINTING PERF. 11 (N-H ADD 55%)
| | | | | | | |
|---|---|---|---|---|---|---|
| □551 ½¢ Olive Brown | | | | | | |
| | 7.50 | 6.00 | .26 | .16 | .19 | .14 |
| □552 1¢ Deep Green | | | | | | |
| | 25.00 | 18.00 | 1.75 | 1.20 | .19 | .14 |
| □553 1½¢ Yellow Brown | | | | | | |
| | 30.00 | 24.00 | 2.50 | 1.90 | .35 | .23 |
| □554 2¢ Carmine | | | | | | |
| | 21.00 | 17.00 | 1.75 | 1.15 | .20 | .14 |
| □555 3¢ Violet | | | | | | |
| | 165.00 | 135.00 | 16.00 | 12.00 | 1.00 | .70 |
| □556 4¢ Yellow Brown | | | | | | |
| | 170.00 | 150.00 | 17.00 | 12.00 | .35 | .20 |
| □557 5¢ Dark Blue | | | | | | |
| | 185.00 | 160.00 | 17.00 | 13.00 | .19 | .14 |
| □558 6¢ Red Orange | | | | | | |
| | 340.00 | 300.00 | 30.00 | 20.00 | .82 | .60 |
| □559 7¢ Black | | | | | | |
| | 68.00 | 55.00 | 9.00 | 6.00 | .80 | .55 |
| □560 8¢ Olive Green | | | | | | |
| | 490.00 | 400.00 | 41.00 | 28.00 | .85 | .55 |
| □561 9¢ Rose | | | | | | |
| | 150.00 | 110.00 | 14.00 | 7.50 | 1.20 | .90 |

| Scott No. | Fine Unused Plate Blk | Ave. Unused Plate Blk | Fine Unused Each | Ave. Unused Each | Fine Used Each | Ave. Used Each |
|---|---|---|---|---|---|---|
| □562 10¢ Orange | | | | | | |
| | 220.00 | 190.00 | 17.00 | 13.00 | .20 | .15 |
| □563 11¢ Blue/Green | | | | | | |
| | 30.00 | 24.00 | 2.00 | 1.15 | .40 | .30 |
| □564 12¢ Brown Violet | | | | | | |
| | 75.00 | 68.00 | 7.00 | 4.50 | .19 | .14 |
| □565 14¢ Dark Blue | | | | | | |
| | 52.00 | 40.00 | 6.00 | 3.00 | 1.00 | .62 |
| □566 15¢ Gray | | | | | | |
| | 260.00 | 200.00 | 24.00 | 16.00 | .19 | .14 |
| □567 20¢ Carmine Rose | | | | | | |
| | 215.00 | 180.00 | 21.00 | 15.00 | .19 | .14 |
| □568 25¢ Green | | | | | | |
| | 210.00 | 150.00 | 20.00 | 13.00 | .60 | .34 |
| □569 30¢ Olive Brown | | | | | | |
| | 300.00 | 250.00 | 45.00 | 38.00 | .45 | .34 |
| □570 50¢ Lilac | | | | | | |
| | 1000.00 | 700.00 | 58.00 | 43.00 | .20 | .16 |
| □571 $1 Violet Black | | | | | | |
| | 450.00 | 300.00 | 42.00 | 34.00 | .48 | .28 |
| □572 $2 Deep Blue | | | | | | |
| | 1400.00 | 1100.00 | 100.00 | 58.00 | 10.00 | 6.25 |
| □573 $5 Carmine & Blue | | | | | | |
| | 8000.00 | 5000.00 | 210.00 | 170.00 | 13.00 | 9.50 |

## IMPERFORATE (N-H ADD 45%)

| Scott No. | Fine Unused Plate Blk | Ave. Unused Plate Blk | Fine Unused Each | Ave. Unused Each | Fine Used Each | Ave. Used Each |
|---|---|---|---|---|---|---|
| □575 1¢ Green | | | | | | |
| | 72.00 | 60.00 | 8.00 | 6.50 | 3.50 | 2.20 |
| □576 1½¢ Yellow Brown | | | | | | |
| | 21.00 | 18.00 | 2.00 | .95 | 1.70 | .80 |
| □577 2¢ Carmine | | | | | | |
| | 24.00 | 17.00 | 2.15 | 1.10 | 1.80 | .85 |

## 1923–1926. ROTARY PRESS PRINTING PERF. 11 x 10 (N-H ADD 55%)

| Scott No. | Fine Unused Plate Blk | Ave. Unused Plate Blk | Fine Unused Each | Ave. Unused Each | Fine Used Each | Ave. Used Each |
|---|---|---|---|---|---|---|
| □578 1¢ Green | | | | | | |
| | 585.00 | 425.00 | 58.00 | 41.00 | 51.00 | 34.00 |
| □579 2¢ Carmine | | | | | | |
| | 375.00 | 240.00 | 51.00 | 32.00 | 45.00 | 28.50 |

| Scott No. | Fine Unused Plate Blk | Ave. Unused Plate Blk | Fine Unused Each | Ave. Unused Each | Fine Used Each | Ave. Used Each |
|---|---|---|---|---|---|---|

## PERF. 10 (N-H ADD 55%)

| Scott No. | Fine Unused Plate Blk | Ave. Unused Plate Blk | Fine Unused Each | Ave. Unused Each | Fine Used Each | Ave. Used Each |
|---|---|---|---|---|---|---|
| □581 1¢ Green | | | | | | |
| | 95.00 | 75.00 | 8.00 | 4.50 | .80 | .65 |
| □582 1½¢ Brown | | | | | | |
| | 42.00 | 28.00 | 4.00 | 3.00 | .80 | .55 |
| □583 2¢ Carmine | | | | | | |
| | 28.00 | 24.00 | 2.10 | 1.25 | .20 | .16 |
| □584 3¢ Violet | | | | | | |
| | 240.00 | 180.00 | 25.00 | 16.00 | 2.00 | 1.15 |
| □585 4¢ Yellow Brown | | | | | | |
| | 165.00 | 125.00 | 14.00 | 8.50 | .65 | .34 |
| □586 5¢ Blue | | | | | | |
| | 140.00 | 125.00 | 14.00 | 9.00 | .32 | .19 |
| □587 6¢ Red Orange | | | | | | |
| | 70.00 | 50.00 | 6.50 | 5.00 | .62 | .38 |
| □588 7¢ Black | | | | | | |
| | 100.00 | 70.00 | 9.00 | 6.00 | 5.00 | 3.00 |
| □589 8¢ Olive Green | | | | | | |
| | 210.00 | 175.00 | 20.00 | 13.00 | 3.15 | 2.00 |
| □590 9¢ Rose | | | | | | |
| | 46.00 | 28.00 | 4.00 | 2.75 | 2.15 | 1.40 |
| □591 10¢ Orange | | | | | | |
| | 600.00 | 500.00 | 52.00 | 40.00 | .20 | .15 |

## PERF. 11

| Scott No. | Fine Unused Plate Blk | Ave. Unused Plate Blk | Fine Unused Each | Ave. Unused Each | Fine Used Each | Ave. Used Each |
|---|---|---|---|---|---|---|
| □595 2¢ Carmine | | | | | | |
| | 1400.00 | 1000.00 | 185.00 | 105.00 | 180.00 | 110.00 |

| Scott No. | Fine Unused Line Pair | Ave. Unused Line Pair | Fine Unused Each | Ave. Unused Each | Fine Used Each | Ave. Used Each |
|---|---|---|---|---|---|---|

## 1923–1929. ROTARY PRESS COIL STAMPS PERF. 10 VERTICALLY (N-H ADD 55%)

| Scott No. | Fine Unused Line Pair | Ave. Unused Line Pair | Fine Unused Each | Ave. Unused Each | Fine Used Each | Ave. Used Each |
|---|---|---|---|---|---|---|
| □597 1¢ Green | | | | | | |
| | 2.00 | 1.60 | .40 | .22 | .20 | .16 |
| □598 1½¢ Deep Brown | | | | | | |
| | 5.00 | 4.00 | .65 | .47 | .20 | .16 |
| □599 2¢ Carmine (I) | | | | | | |
| | 2.00 | 1.25 | .40 | .28 | .20 | .16 |

| Scott No. | Fine Unused Line Pair | Ave. Unused Line Pair | Fine Unused Each | Ave. Unused Each | Fine Used Each | Ave. Used Each |
|---|---|---|---|---|---|---|
| ☐599A 2¢ Carmine (II) | | | | | | |
| | 550.00 | 360.00 | 120.00 | 65.00 | 13.50 | 7.50 |
| ☐600 3¢ Deep Violet | | | | | | |
| | 27.00 | 20.00 | 6.50 | 4.00 | .18 | .15 |
| ☐601 4¢ Yellow Brown | | | | | | |
| | 28.00 | 20.00 | 4.00 | 2.60 | .50 | .29 |
| ☐602 5¢ Dark Blue | | | | | | |
| | 10.00 | 6.00 | 1.75 | .95 | .26 | .16 |
| ☐603 10¢ Orange | | | | | | |
| | 21.00 | 15.00 | 4.00 | 2.70 | .18 | .16 |

## PERF. 10 HORIZONTALLY (N-H ADD 55%)

| | | | | | | |
|---|---|---|---|---|---|---|
| ☐604 1¢ Green | | | | | | |
| | 3.00 | 1.50 | .30 | .20 | .19 | .16 |
| ☐605 1½¢ Yellow Brown | | | | | | |
| | 2.75 | 1.50 | .30 | .20 | .25 | .16 |
| ☐606 2¢ Carmine | | | | | | |
| | 2.00 | 1.10 | .30 | .20 | .19 | .16 |

| Scott No. | Fine Unused Plate Blk | Ave. Unused Plate Blk | Fine Unused Each | Ave. Unused Each | Fine Used Each | Ave. Used Each |
|---|---|---|---|---|---|---|
| **1923. HARDING MEMORIAL ISSUE (N-H ADD 45%)** | | | | | | |
| ☐610 2¢ Black, pf. 11 | | | | | | |
| | 22.00 | 16.00 | .75 | .50 | .21 | .16 |
| ☐611 2¢ Black, imperf. | | | | | | |
| | 100.00 | 80.00 | 7.50 | 6.00 | 5.00 | 4.00 |
| ☐612 2¢ Black, pf. 10 rotary | | | | | | |
| | 260.00 | 200.00 | 14.00 | 11.00 | 2.30 | 1.80 |
| **1924. HUGUENOT-WALLOON ISSUE (N-H ADD 45%)** | | | | | | |
| ☐614 1¢ Green | | | | | | |
| | 40.00 | 26.00 | 4.00 | 2.70 | 3.10 | 2.40 |
| ☐615 2¢ Carmine Rose | | | | | | |
| | 72.00 | 58.00 | 7.00 | 4.10 | 3.10 | 2.10 |
| ☐616 5¢ Dark Blue | | | | | | |
| | 340.00 | 260.00 | 30.00 | 25.00 | 18.00 | 12.00 |

| Scott No. | Fine Unused Plate Blk | Ave. Unused Plate Blk | Fine Unused Each | Ave. Unused Each | Fine Used Each | Ave. Used Each |
|---|---|---|---|---|---|---|

## 1925. LEXINGTON-CONCORD SESQUICENTENNIAL (N-H ADD 45%)

□617  1¢  Green

| | 40.00 | 31.00 | 4.10 | 3.00 | 3.00 | 1.65 |

□618  2¢  Carmine Rose

| | 70.00 | 52.00 | 7.00 | 4.00 | 3.20 | 2.80 |

□619  5¢  Dark Blue

| | 300.00 | 200.00 | 30.00 | 21.00 | 15.00 | 9.00 |

## 1925. NORSE-AMERICAN ISSUE (N-H ADD 40%)

□620  2¢  Carmine & Black

| | 170.00 | 115.00 | 6.00 | 3.50 | 5.00 | 2.25 |

□621  5¢  Dark Blue & Black

| | 575.00 | 400.00 | 20.00 | 16.00 | 14.00 | 11.00 |

## 1925–1926.

□622 13¢  Green

| | 140.00 | 100.00 | 14.00 | 10.00 | .70 | .62 |

□623 17¢  Black

| | 180.00 | 125.00 | 16.00 | 13.00 | .37 | .30 |

## 1926–1927. COMMEMORATIVES
## 1926. SESQUICENTENNIAL EXPOSITION (N-H ADD 50%)

□627  2¢  Carmine Rose

| | 45.00 | 32.00 | 3.50 | 2.10 | .60 | .42 |

## 1926. ERICSSON MEMORIAL ISSUE (N-H ADD 50%)

□628  5¢  Gray Lilac

| | 90.00 | 68.00 | 6.00 | 4.00 | 3.50 | 2.60 |

## 1926. BATTLE OF WHITE PLAINS (N-H ADD 45%)

□629  2¢  Carmine Rose

| | — | 40.00 | 2.50 | 1.50 | 2.00 | 1.15 |

□630  2¢  Souv. Sheet of 25

| | — | — | 440.00 | 330.00 | — | — |

| Scott No. | Fine Unused Plate Blk | Ave. Unused Plate Blk | Fine Unused Each | Ave. Unused Each | Fine Used Each | Ave. Used Each |
|---|---|---|---|---|---|---|
| **1926–1928. DESIGNS OF 1922–1925 ROTARY PRESS PRINTING IMPERFORATE (N-H ADD 40%)** | | | | | | |
| ☐631 1½¢ Brown | 58.00 | 45.00 | 2.00 | 1.40 | 1.70 | 1.10 |
| **PERF. 11 x 10½ (N-H ADD 50%)** | | | | | | |
| ☐632 1¢ Green | 2.50 | 1.60 | .23 | .21 | .18 | .14 |
| ☐633 1½¢ Yellow Brown | 76.00 | 62.00 | 2.00 | 1.50 | .19 | .14 |
| ☐634 2¢ Carmine (I) | 1.50 | 1.00 | .24 | .21 | .18 | .14 |
| ☐634A 2¢ Carmine (II) | — | — | 200.00 | 150.00 | 16.00 | 10.00 |
| ☐635 3¢ Violet | 8.00 | 6.00 | .42 | .30 | .19 | .15 |
| ☐636 4¢ Yellow Brown | 78.00 | 64.00 | 2.60 | 2.00 | .18 | .14 |
| ☐637 5¢ Dark Blue | 20.00 | 16.00 | 2.20 | 1.60 | .18 | .14 |
| ☐638 6¢ Red Orange | 20.00 | 16.00 | 2.20 | 1.60 | .19 | .15 |
| ☐639 7¢ Black | 20.00 | 16.00 | 2.20 | 1.60 | .18 | .14 |
| ☐640 8¢ Olive Green | 20.00 | 16.00 | 2.20 | 1.60 | .18 | .14 |
| ☐641 9¢ Orange Red | 20.00 | 16.00 | 2.20 | 1.60 | .18 | .14 |
| ☐642 10¢ Orange | 30.00 | 21.00 | 4.50 | 3.20 | .18 | 14 |
| **1927. VERMONT SESQUICENTENNIAL (N-H ADD 45%)** | | | | | | |
| ☐643 2¢ Carmine Rose | 43.00 | 36.00 | 1.30 | .75 | 1.00 | .85 |
| **1927. BURGOYNE CAMPAIGN ISSUE (N-H ADD 45%)** | | | | | | |
| ☐644 2¢ Carmine | 46.00 | 40.00 | 3.50 | 2.50 | 2.75 | 1.75 |

| Scott No. | Fine Unused Plate Blk | Ave. Unused Plate Blk | Fine Unused Each | Ave. Unused Each | Fine Used Each | Ave. Used Each |
|---|---|---|---|---|---|---|
| **1928. VALLEY FORGE ISSUE (N-H ADD 45%)** | | | | | | |
| ☐645  2¢ Carmine | | | | | | |
| | 34.00 | 26.00 | 1.00 | .75 | .60 | .42 |
| **1928. BATTLE OF MONMOUTH (N-H ADD 45%)** | | | | | | |
| ☐646  2¢ Carmine | | | | | | |
| | 39.00 | 31.00 | 1.50 | .80 | 1.00 | .75 |
| **1928. DISCOVERY OF HAWAII (N-H ADD 40%)** | | | | | | |
| ☐647  2¢ Carmine Rose | | | | | | |
| | 125.00 | 73.00 | 5.00 | 3.00 | 4.50 | 2.25 |
| ☐648  5¢ Blue | | | | | | |
| | 250.00 | 175.00 | 13.00 | 9.00 | 12.00 | 7.50 |
| **1928. AERONAUTICS CONFERENCE (N-H ADD 40%)** | | | | | | |
| ☐649  2¢ Carmine | | | | | | |
| | 14.00 | 10.00 | 1.25 | 1.00 | .92 | .62 |
| ☐650  5¢ Blue | | | | | | |
| | 68.00 | 44.00 | 6.50 | 4.00 | 3.90 | 2.85 |
| **1929. GEORGE ROGERS CLARK (N-H ADD 40%)** | | | | | | |
| ☐651  2¢ Carmine & Black | | | | | | |
| | 12.00 | 7.50 | .75 | .50 | .68 | .42 |
| **1929. DESIGNS OF 1922–1925 ROTARY PRESS PRINTING—PERF. 11 x 10½ (N-H ADD 40%)** | | | | | | |
| ☐653  ½¢ Olive Brown | | | | | | |
| | 1.10 | .75 | .25 | .19 | .20 | .15 |
| **1929. EDISON COMMEMORATIVE FLAT PLATE PRINTING—PERF. 11 (N-H ADD 40%)** | | | | | | |
| ☐654  2¢ Carmine Rose | | | | | | |
| | 30.00 | 20.00 | 1.00 | .70 | .75 | .55 |
| **ROTARY PRESS PRINTING—PERF. 11 x 10½ (N-H ADD 40%)** | | | | | | |
| ☐655  2¢ Carmine Rose | | | | | | |
| | 46.00 | 30.00 | .75 | .55 | .40 | .30 |

| Scott No. | Fine Unused Line Pair | Ave. Unused Line Pair | Fine Unused Each | Ave. Unused Each | Fine Used Each | Ave. Used Each |
|---|---|---|---|---|---|---|

## ROTARY PRESS COIL STAMPS—PERF. 10 VERTICALLY (N-H ADD 40%)

| | Fine Unused Line Pair | Ave. Unused Line Pair | Fine Unused Each | Ave. Unused Each | Fine Used Each | Ave. Used Each |
|---|---|---|---|---|---|---|
| ☐656 2¢ Carmine Rose | 61.00 | 41.00 | 13.00 | 8.50 | 2.00 | 1.15 |

| Scott No. | Fine Unused Plate Blk | Ave. Unused Plate Blk | Fine Unused Each | Ave. Unused Each | Fine Used Each | Ave. Used Each |
|---|---|---|---|---|---|---|

## 1929. SULLIVAN EXPEDITION (N-H ADD 40%)

| | Fine Unused Plate Blk | Ave. Unused Plate Blk | Fine Unused Each | Ave. Unused Each | Fine Used Each | Ave. Used Each |
|---|---|---|---|---|---|---|
| ☐657 2¢ Carmine Rose | 32.00 | 19.00 | .85 | .68 | .60 | .50 |

## 1929. 632–42 OVERPRINTED (KANS.) (N-H ADD 45%)

| | Fine Unused Plate Blk | Ave. Unused Plate Blk | Fine Unused Each | Ave. Unused Each | Fine Used Each | Ave. Used Each |
|---|---|---|---|---|---|---|
| ☐658 1¢ Green | 30.00 | 21.00 | 2.00 | 1.50 | 1.85 | 1.15 |
| ☐659 ½¢ Brown | 42.00 | 30.00 | 2.50 | 1.90 | 2.00 | 2.10 |
| ☐660 2¢ Carmine | 35.00 | 29.00 | 3.00 | 2.10 | .85 | .65 |
| ☐661 3¢ Violet | 150.00 | 110.00 | 14.00 | 11.00 | 10.00 | 5.00 |
| ☐662 4¢ Yellow Brown | 150.00 | 115.00 | 15.00 | 11.00 | 8.50 | 6.00 |
| ☐663 5¢ Deep Blue | 130.00 | 90.00 | 11.00 | 8.50 | 8.50 | 7.25 |
| ☐664 6¢ Red Orange | 320.00 | 215.00 | 24.00 | 19.00 | 15.00 | 11.00 |
| ☐665 7¢ Black | 310.00 | 225.00 | 22.00 | 17.00 | 18.00 | 13.00 |
| ☐666 8¢ Olive Green | 550.00 | 415.00 | 62.00 | 46.00 | 62.00 | 46.00 |
| ☐667 9¢ Light Rose | 200.00 | 115.00 | 12.00 | 9.00 | 8.00 | 7.50 |
| ☐668 10¢ Orange Yellow | 310.00 | 220.00 | 16.00 | 13.00 | 9.00 | 7.50 |

| Scott No. | Fine Unused Plate Blk | Ave. Unused Plate Blk | Fine Unused Each | Ave. Unused Each | Fine Used Each | Ave. Used Each |
|---|---|---|---|---|---|---|

## 1929. 632–42 OVERPRINTED (NEBR.) (N-H ADD 45%)

| | Fine Unused Plate Blk | Ave. Unused Plate Blk | Fine Unused Each | Ave. Unused Each | Fine Used Each | Ave. Used Each |
|---|---|---|---|---|---|---|
| ☐669 1¢ Green | 30.00 | 22.00 | 2.00 | 1.40 | 1.80 | 1.10 |
| ☐670 1½¢ Brown | 40.00 | 30.00 | 2.50 | 1.75 | 2.00 | 1.10 |
| ☐671 2¢ Carmine | 29.00 | 20.00 | 2.20 | 1.00 | .75 | .45 |
| ☐672 3¢ Violet | 140.00 | 100.00 | 10.00 | 7.50 | 7.50 | 5.00 |
| ☐673 4¢ Brown | 160.00 | 100.00 | 15.00 | 9.00 | 9.50 | 6.00 |
| ☐674 5¢ Blue | 165.00 | 115.00 | 13.00 | 9.00 | 11.00 | 7.50 |
| ☐675 6¢ Orange | 425.00 | 300.00 | 34.00 | 22.00 | 17.00 | 12.00 |
| ☐676 7¢ Black | 210.00 | 160.00 | 20.00 | 14.00 | 13.00 | 7.50 |
| ☐677 8¢ Olive Green | 300.00 | 220.00 | 24.00 | 17.00 | 19.00 | 12.00 |
| ☐678 9¢ Rose | 360.00 | 250.00 | 30.00 | 20.00 | 21.00 | 14.00 |
| ☐679 10¢ Orange Yellow | 700.00 | 450.00 | 88.00 | 60.00 | 16.00 | 10.00 |

## 1929. BATTLE OF FALLEN TIMBERS (N-H ADD 35%)

| | Fine Unused Plate Blk | Ave. Unused Plate Blk | Fine Unused Each | Ave. Unused Each | Fine Used Each | Ave. Used Each |
|---|---|---|---|---|---|---|
| ☐680 2¢ Carmine Rose | 30.00 | 21.00 | .90 | .65 | .85 | .63 |

## 1929. OHIO RIVER CANALIZATION (N-H ADD 30%)

| | Fine Unused Plate Blk | Ave. Unused Plate Blk | Fine Unused Each | Ave. Unused Each | Fine Used Each | Ave. Used Each |
|---|---|---|---|---|---|---|
| ☐681 2¢ Carmine Rose | 21.00 | 15.00 | 1.00 | .55 | .75 | .54 |

## 1930–1931. COMMEMORATIVES
## 1930. MASSACHUSETTS BAY COLONY (N-H ADD 35%)

| | Fine Unused Plate Blk | Ave. Unused Plate Blk | Fine Unused Each | Ave. Unused Each | Fine Used Each | Ave. Used Each |
|---|---|---|---|---|---|---|
| ☐682 2¢ Carmine Rose | 30.00 | 21.00 | .88 | .80 | .50 | .38 |

| Scott No. | Fine Unused Plate Blk | Ave. Unused Plate Blk | Fine Unused Each | Ave. Unused Each | Fine Used Each | Ave. Used Each |
|---|---|---|---|---|---|---|

## 1930. CAROLINA-CHARLESTON ISSUE (N-H ADD 35%)

| Scott No. | Fine Unused Plate Blk | Ave. Unused Plate Blk | Fine Unused Each | Ave. Unused Each | Fine Used Each | Ave. Used Each |
|---|---|---|---|---|---|---|
| ☐683 2¢ Carmine Rose | 50.00 | 42.00 | 1.30 | 1.00 | 1.25 | 1.15 |

## 1930. REGULAR ISSUE ROTARY PRESS PRINTING—PERF. 11 x 10½ (N-H ADD 35%)

| Scott No. | Fine Unused Plate Blk | Ave. Unused Plate Blk | Fine Unused Each | Ave. Unused Each | Fine Used Each | Ave. Used Each |
|---|---|---|---|---|---|---|
| ☐684 1½¢ Brown | 3.00 | 2.10 | .38 | .30 | .19 | .15 |
| ☐685 4¢ Brown | 11.00 | 7.20 | .85 | .62 | .19 | .15 |

| Scott No. | Fine Unused Line Pair | Ave. Unused Line Pair | Fine Unused Each | Ave. Unused Each | Fine Used Each | Ave. Used Each |
|---|---|---|---|---|---|---|

## ROTARY PRESS COIL STAMPS PERF. 10 VERTICALLY (N-H ADD 40%)

| Scott No. | Fine Unused Line Pair | Ave. Unused Line Pair | Fine Unused Each | Ave. Unused Each | Fine Used Each | Ave. Used Each |
|---|---|---|---|---|---|---|
| ☐686 1½¢ Brown | 8.00 | 6.00 | 1.70 | 1.15 | .19 | .14 |
| ☐687 4¢ Brown | 14.00 | 10.00 | 3.50 | 2.10 | .55 | .32 |

| Scott No. | Fine Unused Plate Blk | Ave. Unused Plate Blk | Fine Unused Each | Ave. Unused Each | Fine Used Each | Ave. Used Each |
|---|---|---|---|---|---|---|

## 1930. BATTLE OF BRADDOCK'S FIELD (N-H ADD 40%)

| Scott No. | Fine Unused Plate Blk | Ave. Unused Plate Blk | Fine Unused Each | Ave. Unused Each | Fine Used Each | Ave. Used Each |
|---|---|---|---|---|---|---|
| ☐688 2¢ Carmine Rose | 42.00 | 32.00 | .90 | .80 | .85 | .66 |

## 1930. VON STEUBEN ISSUE (N-H ADD 40%)

| Scott No. | Fine Unused Plate Blk | Ave. Unused Plate Blk | Fine Unused Each | Ave. Unused Each | Fine Used Each | Ave. Used Each |
|---|---|---|---|---|---|---|
| ☐689 2¢ Carmine Rose | 24.00 | 18.00 | .60 | .50 | .45 | .40 |

## 1931. PULASKI ISSUE (N-H ADD 40%)

| Scott No. | Fine Unused Plate Blk | Ave. Unused Plate Blk | Fine Unused Each | Ave. Unused Each | Fine Used Each | Ave. Used Each |
|---|---|---|---|---|---|---|
| ☐690 2¢ Carmine Rose | 16.00 | 12.00 | .28 | .22 | .20 | .16 |

| Scott No. | Fine Unused Plate Blk | Ave. Unused Plate Blk | Fine Unused Each | Ave. Unused Each | Fine Used Each | Ave. Used Each |
|---|---|---|---|---|---|---|

## 1931. DESIGNS OF 1922–1926 ROTARY PRESS PRINTING—PERF. 11 x 10½ (N-H ADD 40%)

| | Fine Unused Plate Blk | Ave. Unused Plate Blk | Fine Unused Each | Ave. Unused Each | Fine Used Each | Ave. Used Each |
|---|---|---|---|---|---|---|
| ☐692 11¢ Light Blue | 15.00 | 11.00 | 3.10 | 1.60 | .20 | .15 |
| ☐693 12¢ Brown Violet | 25.00 | 20.00 | 4.60 | 3.50 | .19 | .14 |
| ☐694 13¢ Yellow Green | 15.00 | 11.00 | 2.15 | 1.65 | .25 | .17 |
| ☐695 14¢ Dark Blue | 18.00 | 12.00 | 3.00 | 2.10 | .60 | .30 |
| ☐696 15¢ Gray | 40.00 | 32.00 | 8.00 | 6.00 | .19 | .14 |

## PERF. 10½ x 11 (N-H ADD 40%)

| | | | | | | |
|---|---|---|---|---|---|---|
| ☐697 17¢ Black | 25.00 | 19.00 | 4.75 | 2.90 | .42 | .24 |
| ☐698 20¢ Carmine Rose | 41.00 | 26.00 | 9.50 | 7.00 | .19 | .14 |
| ☐699 25¢ Blue Green | 42.00 | 26.00 | 9.25 | 6.00 | .18 | .15 |
| ☐700 30¢ Brown | 72.00 | 42.00 | 15.00 | 10.00 | .19 | .15 |
| ☐701 50¢ Lilac | 200.00 | 110.00 | 43.00 | 35.00 | .19 | .15 |

## 1931. RED CROSS ISSUE (N-H ADD 40%)

| | | | | | | |
|---|---|---|---|---|---|---|
| ☐702 2¢ Black & Red | 3.00 | 1.90 | .28 | .20 | .19 | .17 |

## 1931. SURRENDER OF YORKTOWN (N-H ADD 40%)

| | | | | | | |
|---|---|---|---|---|---|---|
| ☐703 2¢ Carmine Rose & Black | 4.00 | 3.20 | .50 | .42 | .48 | .36 |

## 1932. WASHINGTON BICENTENNIAL (N-H ADD 40%)

| | | | | | | |
|---|---|---|---|---|---|---|
| ☐704 ½¢ Olive Brown | 4.25 | 3.60 | .25 | .21 | .19 | .14 |
| ☐705 1¢ Green | 5.00 | 4.00 | .23 | .21 | .19 | .14 |

| Scott No. | Fine Unused Plate Blk | Ave. Unused Plate Blk | Fine Unused Each | Ave. Unused Each | Fine Used Each | Ave. Used Each |
|---|---|---|---|---|---|---|
| ☐706 1½¢ Brown | | | | | | |
| | 17.00 | 12.50 | .36 | .21 | .19 | .14 |
| ☐707 2¢ Carmine | | | | | | |
| | 2.00 | 1.25 | .23 | .21 | .19 | .14 |
| ☐708 3¢ Purple | | | | | | |
| | 13.00 | 10.00 | .70 | .47 | .19 | .14 |
| ☐709 4¢ Light Brown | | | | | | |
| | 6.00 | 5.00 | .34 | .22 | .19 | .14 |
| ☐710 5¢ Blue | | | | | | |
| | 18.00 | 15.00 | 1.60 | 1.10 | .19 | .14 |
| ☐711 6¢ Orange | | | | | | |
| | 62.00 | 50.00 | 4.00 | 2.80 | .19 | .14 |
| ☐712 7¢ Black | | | | | | |
| | 7.50 | 5.75 | .38 | .30 | .23 | .18 |
| ☐713 8¢ Olive Bistre | | | | | | |
| | 65.00 | 46.00 | 3.50 | 3.00 | .90 | .55 |
| ☐714 9¢ Pale Red | | | | | | |
| | 42.00 | 31.00 | 3.10 | 2.10 | .32 | .19 |
| ☐715 10¢ Orange Yellow | | | | | | |
| | 115.00 | 90.00 | 12.00 | 8.50 | .17 | .15 |

## 1932. COMMEMORATIVES
## 1932. OLYMPIC WINTER GAMES (N-H ADD 30%)

| | | | | | | |
|---|---|---|---|---|---|---|
| ☐716 2¢ Carmine Rose | | | | | | |
| | 14.00 | 10.00 | .60 | .35 | .28 | .22 |

## 1932. ARBOR DAY ISSUE (N-H ADD 30%)

| | | | | | | |
|---|---|---|---|---|---|---|
| ☐717 2¢ Carmine Rose | | | | | | |
| | 9.00 | 8.00 | .25 | .20 | .17 | .15 |

## 1932. OLYMPIC SUMMER GAMES (N-H ADD 30%)

| | | | | | | |
|---|---|---|---|---|---|---|
| ☐718 3¢ Purple | | | | | | |
| | 16.00 | 12.00 | 1.95 | 1.50 | .19 | .15 |
| ☐719 5¢ Blue | | | | | | |
| | 24.00 | 19.00 | 3.10 | 2.15 | .30 | .22 |

| Scott No. | Fine Unused Line Pair | Ave. Unused Line Pair | Fine Unused Each | Ave. Unused Each | Fine Used Each | Ave. Used Each |
|---|---|---|---|---|---|---|
| **1932. ROTARY PRESS** | | | | | | |
| □720 3¢ Deep Violet | | | | | | |
| | — | — | .25 | .20 | .19 | .15 |
| **COIL PERF. 10 VERTICALLY (N-H ADD 30%)** | | | | | | |
| □721 3¢ Deep Violet | | | | | | |
| | 7.00 | 4.25 | 3.00 | 2.10 | .19 | .15 |
| **COIL PERF. 10 HORIZONTALLY (N-H ADD 30%)** | | | | | | |
| □722 3¢ Deep Violet | | | | | | |
| | 5.00 | 4.25 | 1.80 | 1.00 | .75 | .60 |
| **COIL DESIGN OF 1922–1925—PERF. 10 VERTICALLY (N-H ADD 30%)** | | | | | | |
| □723 6¢ Deep Orange | | | | | | |
| | 50.00 | 35.00 | 11.00 | 7.25 | .26 | .19 |

| Scott No. | Fine Unused Plate Blk | Ave. Unused Plate Blk | Fine Unused Each | Ave. Unused Each | Fine Used Each | Ave. Used Each |
|---|---|---|---|---|---|---|
| **1932. WILLIAM PENN ISSUE (N-H ADD 30%)** | | | | | | |
| □724 3¢ Violet | | | | | | |
| | 13.00 | 10.50 | .35 | .29 | .26 | .18 |
| **1932. DANIEL WEBSTER ISSUE (N-H ADD 30%)** | | | | | | |
| □725 3¢ Violet | | | | | | |
| | 25.00 | 20.00 | .48 | .38 | .35 | .29 |
| **1933. COMMEMORATIVES** | | | | | | |
| **1933. GEORGIA BICENTENNIAL (N-H ADD 30%)** | | | | | | |
| □726 3¢ Violet | | | | | | |
| | 16.00 | 12.00 | .30 | .28 | .24 | .17 |
| **1933. PEACE SESQUICENTENNIAL (N-H ADD 30%)** | | | | | | |
| □727 3¢ Violet | | | | | | |
| | 7.00 | 5.00 | .25 | .20 | .18 | .15 |

| Scott No. | Fine Unused Plate Blk | Ave. Unused Plate Blk | Fine Unused Each | Ave. Unused Each | Fine Used Each | Ave. Used Each |
|---|---|---|---|---|---|---|

## 1933. CENTURY OF PROGRESS EXPOSITION (N-H ADD 30%)

☐728  1¢  Yellow Green

| | 3.25 | 2.50 | .24 | .20 | .18 | .15 |

☐729  3¢  Purple

| | 4.00 | 3.10 | .24 | .20 | .18 | .15 |

## 1933. A.P.S. CONVENTION AND EXHIBITION AT CHICAGO IMPERFORATE—UNGUMMED (N-H ADD 30%)

☐730  1¢  Yellow Green, sheet of 25

| | — | — | 36.00 | 31.00 | — | — |

☐730a 1¢  Yellow Green, sgl.

| | — | — | .80 | .62 | .55 | .37 |

☐731  3¢  Violet, sheet of 25

| | — | — | 32.00 | — | 30.00 | — |

☐731a 3¢  Violet, single

| | — | — | .65 | .52 | .46 | .36 |

## 1933. N.R.A. ISSUE (N-H ADD 25%)

☐732  3¢  Violet

| | 2.75 | 1.85 | .23 | .20 | .19 | .15 |

## 1933. BYRD ANTARCTIC EXPEDITION (N-H ADD 30%)

☐733  3¢  Dark Blue

| | 17.00 | 14.00 | .65 | .50 | .60 | .52 |

## 1933. KOSCIUSZKO ISSUE (N-H ADD 30%)

☐734  5¢  Blue

| | 38.00 | 29.00 | .72 | .50 | .45 | .24 |

## 1934. NATIONAL PHILATELIC EXHIBITION IMPERFORATE—UNGUMMED (N-H ADD 30%)

☐735  3¢  Dark Blue, sheet of 6

| | — | — | 20.00 | — | 16.00 | 11.00 |

☐735a 3¢  Dark Blue, sgl.

| | — | — | 2.50 | 2.10 | 2.00 | 1.70 |

| Scott No. | Fine Unused Plate Blk | Ave. Unused Plate Blk | Fine Unused Each | Ave. Unused Each | Fine Used Each | Ave. Used Each |
|---|---|---|---|---|---|---|

## 1934. COMMEMORATIVES
## 1934. MARYLAND TERCENTENARY (N-H ADD 30%)

| ☐736 3¢ Rose | | | | | | |
|---|---|---|---|---|---|---|
| | 12.00 | 8.50 | .22 | .20 | .18 | .15 |

## 1934. MOTHER'S DAY ISSUE ROTARY PRESS PRINTING—PERF. 11 x 10½ (N-H ADD 30%)

| ☐737 3¢ Deep Violet | | | | | | |
|---|---|---|---|---|---|---|
| | 2.00 | 1.40 | .25 | .19 | .16 | .15 |

## FLAT PRESS PRINTING—PERF. 11 (N-H ADD 30%)

| ☐738 3¢ Deep Violet | | | | | | |
|---|---|---|---|---|---|---|
| | 5.00 | 4.00 | .28 | .20 | .21 | .16 |

## 1934. WISCONSIN TERCENTENARY (N-H ADD 30%)

| ☐739 3¢ Deep Violet | | | | | | |
|---|---|---|---|---|---|---|
| | 4.75 | 3.60 | .26 | .20 | .19 | .15 |

## 1934. NATIONAL PARKS ISSUE (N-H ADD 25%)

| | Fine Unused Plate Blk | Ave. Unused Plate Blk | Fine Unused Each | Ave. Unused Each | Fine Used Each | Ave. Used Each |
|---|---|---|---|---|---|---|
| ☐740 1¢ Green | | | | | | |
| | 1.85 | 1.25 | .25 | .19 | .18 | .15 |
| ☐741 2¢ Red | | | | | | |
| | 1.80 | 1.40 | .25 | .19 | .18 | .15 |
| ☐742 3¢ Purple | | | | | | |
| | 2.50 | 1.65 | .25 | .19 | .18 | .15 |
| ☐743 4¢ Brown | | | | | | |
| | 9.75 | 7.00 | .47 | .30 | .42 | .30 |
| ☐744 5¢ Blue | | | | | | |
| | 12.00 | 9.50 | .95 | .70 | .65 | .42 |
| ☐745 6¢ Indigo | | | | | | |
| | 21.00 | 15.00 | 1.20 | .90 | .80 | .65 |
| ☐746 7¢ Black | | | | | | |
| | 15.00 | 9.50 | .76 | .60 | .55 | .55 |
| ☐747 8¢ Green | | | | | | |
| | 21.00 | 15.00 | 2.00 | 1.50 | 1.25 | 1.00 |
| ☐748 9¢ Salmon | | | | | | |
| | 20.00 | 16.00 | 2.10 | 1.60 | .72 | .55 |
| ☐749 10¢ Gray Black | | | | | | |
| | 31.00 | 22.00 | 4.00 | 3.00 | 1.10 | .70 |

| Scott No. | Fine Unused Plate Blk | Ave. Unused Plate Blk | Fine Unused Each | Ave. Unused Each | Fine Used Each | Ave. Used Each |
|---|---|---|---|---|---|---|

## 1934. A.P.S. CONVENTION AND EXHIBITION AT ATLANTIC CITY IMPERFORATE SOUVENIR SHEET (N-H ADD 25%)

| | | | | | | |
|---|---|---|---|---|---|---|
| ☐750  3¢  Purple, sheet of 6 | | | | | | |
| | — | — | 36.00 | — | 30.00 | 20.00 |
| ☐750a 3¢ Purple, single | | | | | | |
| | — | — | 5.00 | 4.00 | 3.00 | 2.60 |

## 1934. TRANS-MISSISSIPPI PHILATELIC EXPOSITION ANDCONVENTION AT OMAHA IMPERFORATE SOUVENIR SHEET (N-H ADD 25%)

| | | | | | | |
|---|---|---|---|---|---|---|
| ☐751  1¢  Green, sheet of 6 | | | | | | |
| | — | — | 16.00 | — | 12.00 | 8.50 |
| ☐751a 1¢ Green, single | | | | | | |
| | — | — | 2.00 | 1.70 | 1.60 | 1.25 |

| Scott No. | Plate Block | Block Plain | Mint Each | Used Each |
|---|---|---|---|---|

## 1935. "FARLEY SPECIAL PRINTINGS" DESIGNS OF 1933–1934 PERF. 10½ x 11— UNGUMMED (N-H ADD 25%)

| | | | | |
|---|---|---|---|---|
| ☐752  3¢  Violet | 15.00 | 4.50 | .17 | .15 |

## PERF. 11—GUMMED (N-H ADD 25%)

| | | | | |
|---|---|---|---|---|
| ☐753  3¢  Dark Blue | 20.00 | 4.15 | .58 | .50 |

## IMPERFORATE—UNGUMMED (N-H ADD 25%)

| | | | | |
|---|---|---|---|---|
| ☐754  3¢  Deep Violet | 20.00 | 3.60 | .62 | .50 |
| ☐755  3¢  Deep Violet | 20.00 | 4.75 | .65 | .60 |

## NATIONAL PARKS
## IMPERFORATE—UNGUMMED (N-H ADD 25%)

| | | | | |
|---|---|---|---|---|
| ☐756  1¢  Green | 6.50 | 1.65 | .21 | .15 |
| ☐757  2¢  Red | 7.00 | 1.60 | .28 | .19 |

| Scott No. | Plate Block | Block Plain | Mint Each | Used Each |
|---|---|---|---|---|

| | | | | |
|---|---|---|---|---|
| ☐758  3¢  Deep Violet | 18.00 | 11.00 | .65 | .55 |

| Scott No. | | Plate Block | Block Plain | Mint Each | Used Each |
|---|---|---|---|---|---|
| ☐759 | 4¢ Brown | 23.00 | 12.00 | 1.15 | 1.00 |
| ☐760 | 5¢ Blue | 26.00 | 18.00 | 2.25 | 2.00 |
| ☐761 | 6¢ Dark Blue | 50.00 | 25.00 | 2.90 | 2.50 |
| ☐762 | 7¢ Black | 40.00 | 21.00 | 2.00 | 1.90 |
| ☐763 | 8¢ Sage Green | 45.00 | 22.00 | 2.30 | 2.00 |
| ☐764 | 9¢ Red Orange | 50.00 | 32.00 | 2.30 | 2.00 |
| ☐765 | 10¢ Gray Black | 62.00 | 40.00 | 4.00 | 3.75 |

## IMPERFORATE—UNGUMMED (N-H ADD 25%)

| Scott No. | | Plate Block | Block Plain | Mint Each | Used Each |
|---|---|---|---|---|---|
| ☐766a | 1¢ Yellow Green | — | 15.00 | .80 | .56 |
| ☐767a | 3¢ Violet | — | 15.00 | .80 | .56 |
| ☐768a | 3¢ Dark Blue | — | 19.00 | 3.00 | 2.80 |
| ☐769a | 1¢ Green | — | 12.00 | 1.90 | 1.25 |
| ☐770a | 3¢ Deep Violet | — | 28.00 | 3.50 | 2.75 |

## DESIGN OF CE 1 (N-H ADD 30%)

| Scott No. | | Plate Block | Block Plain | Mint Each | Used Each |
|---|---|---|---|---|---|
| ☐771 | 16¢ Dark Blue | 90.00 | 41.00 | 3.00 | 2.75 |

## 1935-1936. COMMEMORATIVES

| Scott No. | | Fine Unused Plate Blk | Ave. Unused Plate Blk | Mint Each | Used Each |
|---|---|---|---|---|---|

## 1935. CONNECTICUT TERCENTENARY (N-H ADD 25%)

| ☐772 | 3¢ Red Violet | 2.50 | 1.65 | .21 | .16 |
|---|---|---|---|---|---|

## 1935. CALIFORNIA PACIFIC EXPOSITION (N-H ADD 25%)

| ☐773 | 3¢ Purple | 2.10 | 1.70 | .21 | .16 |
|---|---|---|---|---|---|

## 1935. BOULDER DAM ISSUE (N-H ADD 25%)

| ☐774 | 3¢ Purple | 2.50 | 2.25 | .21 | .16 |
|---|---|---|---|---|---|

## 1935. MICHIGAN CENTENARY (N-H ADD 25%)

| ☐775 | 3¢ Purple | 2.00 | 1.50 | .21 | .16 |
|---|---|---|---|---|---|

## 1936. TEXAS CENTENNIAL (N-H ADD 25%)

| ☐776 | 3¢ Purple | 2.00 | 1.65 | .21 | .16 |
|---|---|---|---|---|---|

| Scott No. | Plate Block | Block Plain | Mint Each | Used Each |
|---|---|---|---|---|

## 1936. RHODE ISLAND TERCENTENARY (N-H ADD 25%)

| | | | | |
|---|---|---|---|---|
| ☐777  3¢ Purple | 2.50 | 1.90 | .21 | .16 |

## 1936. THIRD INTL. PHILATELIC EXHIBITION "TIPEX" IMPERFORATE SOUVENIR SHEET DESIGNS OF 772, 773, 775, 776 (N-H ADD 25%)

| | | | | |
|---|---|---|---|---|
| ☐778  3¢ Red Violet, sheet of 4 | | | | |
| | — | — | 3.10 | 2.80 |
| ☐778a 3¢ Red Violet, single | — | — | .75 | .65 |
| ☐778b 3¢ Red Violet, single | — | — | .75 | .65 |
| ☐778c 3¢ Red Violet, single | — | — | .75 | .65 |
| ☐778d 3¢ Red Violet, single | — | — | .75 | .65 |

## 1936. ARKANSAS CENTENNIAL (N-H ADD 25%)

| | | | | |
|---|---|---|---|---|
| ☐782  3¢ Purple | 2.10 | 1.65 | .21 | .16 |

| Scott No. | Fine Unused Plate Blk | Ave. Unused Plate Blk | Fine Unused Each | Ave. Unused Each | Fine Used Each | Ave. Used Each |
|---|---|---|---|---|---|---|

## 1936. OREGON TERRITORY CENTENNIAL (N-H ADD 25%)

| | | | | | | |
|---|---|---|---|---|---|---|
| ☐783  3¢ Purple | | | | | | |
| | 2.00 | 1.50 | .21 | .17 | .16 | .14 |

## 1936. SUFFRAGE FOR WOMEN ISSUE (N-H ADD 25%)

| | | | | | | |
|---|---|---|---|---|---|---|
| ☐784  3¢ Dark Violet | | | | | | |
| | 1.50 | 1.00 | .21 | .17 | .16 | .14 |

## 1936–1937. ARMY AND NAVY ISSUE ARMY COMMEMORATIVES (N-H ADD 20%)

| | | | | | | |
|---|---|---|---|---|---|---|
| ☐785  1¢ Green | | | | | | |
| | 1.50 | 1.10 | .21 | .18 | .16 | .14 |
| ☐786  2¢ Carmine | | | | | | |
| | 1.50 | 1.10 | .21 | .18 | .16 | .14 |
| ☐787  3¢ Purple | | | | | | |
| | 1.90 | 1.50 | .26 | .21 | .16 | .14 |

| Scott No. | Fine Unused Plate Blk | Ave. Unused Plate Blk | Fine Unused Each | Ave. Unused Each | Fine Used Each | Ave. Used Each |
|---|---|---|---|---|---|---|
| ☐788 4¢ Gray | | | | | | |
| | 16.00 | 11.00 | .50 | .40 | .38 | .19 |
| ☐789 5¢ Ultramarine | | | | | | |
| | 18.00 | 10.50 | .85 | .55 | .40 | .19 |

## NAVY COMMEMORATIVES (N-H ADD 25%)

| | | | | | | |
|---|---|---|---|---|---|---|
| ☐790 1¢ Green | | | | | | |
| | — | 1.20 | .23 | .18 | .16 | .14 |
| ☐791 2¢ Carmaine | | | | | | |
| | 1.60 | 1.25 | .23 | .20 | .16 | .14 |
| ☐792 3¢ Purple | | | | | | |
| | 1.90 | 1.65 | .23 | .22 | .16 | .15 |
| ☐793 4¢ Gray | | | | | | |
| | 14.00 | 12.00 | .50 | .40 | .34 | .18 |
| ☐794 5¢ Ultramarine | | | | | | |
| | 18.00 | 13.00 | .85 | .60 | .38 | .22 |

## 1937. COMMEMORATIVES
## 1937. NORTHWEST ORDINANCE ISSUE (N-H ADD 25%)

| | | | | | | |
|---|---|---|---|---|---|---|
| ☐795 3¢ Violet | | | | | | |
| | 1.90 | 1.35 | .26 | .17 | .20 | .16 |

## 1937. VIRGINIA DARE ISSUE (N-H ADD 20%)

| | | | | | | |
|---|---|---|---|---|---|---|
| ☐796 5¢ Gray Blue | | | | | | |
| | 10.00 | 8.50 | .31 | .25 | .22 | .16 |

## 1937. S.P.A. CONVENTION ISSUE (N-H ADD 25%)
## DESIGN OF 749 IMPERFORATE SOUVENIR SHEET

| | | | | | | |
|---|---|---|---|---|---|---|
| ☐797 10¢ Blue Green | | | | | | |
| | — | — | 1.50 | — | .80 | .60 |

## 1937. CONSTITUTIONAL SESQUICENTENNIAL (N-H ADD 25%)

| | | | | | | |
|---|---|---|---|---|---|---|
| ☐798 3¢ Red Violet | | | | | | |
| | 2.10 | 1.80 | .22 | .20 | .18 | .14 |

| Scott No. | Fine Unused Plate Blk | Ave. Unused Plate Blk | Fine Unused Each | Ave. Unused Each | Fine Used Each | Ave. Used Each |
|---|---|---|---|---|---|---|

## 1937. TERRITORIAL PUBLICITY ISSUE (N-H ADD 25%)

| Scott No. | | Fine Unused Plate Blk | Ave. Unused Plate Blk | Fine Unused Each | Ave. Unused Each | Fine Used Each | Ave. Used Each |
|---|---|---|---|---|---|---|---|
| ☐799 | 3¢ Violet | | | | | | |
| | | 2.00 | 1.60 | .22 | .17 | .18 | .14 |
| ☐800 | 3¢ Violet | | | | | | |
| | | 2.00 | 1.60 | .22 | .17 | .18 | .14 |
| ☐801 | 3¢ Bright Violet | | | | | | |
| | | 2.00 | 1.60 | .22 | .17 | .18 | .14 |
| ☐802 | 3¢ Light Violet | | | | | | |
| | | 2.00 | 1.60 | .22 | .17 | .18 | .14 |

## 1938. PRESIDENTIAL SERIES ROTARY PRESS PRINTING—PERF. 11 x 10$^1$/$_2$ (N-H ADD 25%)

| Scott No. | | Fine Unused Plate Blk | Ave. Unused Plate Blk | Fine Unused Each | Ave. Unused Each | Fine Used Each | Ave. Used Each |
|---|---|---|---|---|---|---|---|
| ☐803 | ½¢ Red Orange | | | | | | |
| | | .60 | .50 | .22 | .19 | .16 | .14 |
| ☐804 | 1¢ Green | | | | | | |
| | | .50 | .40 | .22 | .19 | .16 | .14 |
| ☐805 | 1½¢ Bistre Brown | | | | | | |
| | | .55 | .40 | .22 | .19 | .16 | .14 |
| ☐806 | 2¢ Rose Carmine | | | | | | |
| | | .60 | .50 | .22 | .19 | .16 | .14 |
| ☐807 | 3¢ Deep Violet | | | | | | |
| | | .55 | .45 | .22 | .19 | .16 | .14 |
| ☐808 | 4¢ Red Violet | | | | | | |
| | | 3.00 | 2.60 | .85 | .19 | .16 | .14 |
| ☐809 | 4½¢ Dark Gray | | | | | | |
| | | 2.00 | 1.50 | .22 | .19 | .16 | .14 |
| ☐810 | 5¢ Bright Blue | | | | | | |
| | | 1.50 | 1.30 | .25 | .21 | .18 | .16 |
| ☐811 | 6¢ Red Orange | | | | | | |
| | | 2.00 | 1.60 | .28 | .21 | .18 | .16 |
| ☐812 | 7¢ Sepia | | | | | | |
| | | 2.10 | 1.80 | .36 | .24 | .18 | .16 |
| ☐813 | 8¢ Olive Green | | | | | | |
| | | 2.50 | 2.10 | .38 | .26 | .18 | .16 |
| ☐814 | 9¢ Rose Pink | | | | | | |
| | | 2.60 | 2.40 | .38 | .26 | .18 | .16 |
| ☐815 | 10¢ Brown Red | | | | | | |
| | | 2.00 | 1.80 | .35 | .24 | .18 | .16 |

| Scott No. | Fine Unused Plate Blk | Ave. Unused Plate Blk | Fine Unused Each | Ave. Unused Each | Fine Used Each | Ave. Used Each |
|---|---|---|---|---|---|---|
| ☐816 11¢ Ultramarine | | | | | | |
| | 5.00 | 4.00 | .70 | .35 | .18 | .16 |
| ☐817 12¢ Bright Violet | | | | | | |
| | 8.00 | 7.00 | 1.20 | .40 | .18 | .16 |
| ☐818 13¢ Blue Green | | | | | | |
| | 10.00 | 8.00 | 1.80 | .50 | .18 | .16 |
| ☐819 14¢ Blue | | | | | | |
| | 6.00 | 5.00 | 1.10 | .45 | .18 | .16 |
| ☐820 15¢ Blue Gray | | | | | | |
| | 3.00 | 3.00 | .60 | .35 | .18 | .16 |
| ☐821 16¢ Black | | | | | | |
| | 8.00 | 6.00 | 1.15 | .60 | .50 | .45 |
| ☐822 17¢ Rose Red | | | | | | |
| | 7.00 | 5.50 | 1.00 | .45 | .18 | .16 |
| ☐823 18¢ Brown Carmine | | | | | | |
| | 13.00 | 10.00 | 2.00 | 1.40 | .18 | .16 |
| ☐824 19¢ Bright Violet | | | | | | |
| | 10.00 | 9.00 | 1.80 | .90 | .55 | .50 |
| ☐825 20¢ Bright Blue Green | | | | | | |
| | 6.00 | 4.75 | 1.00 | .75 | .18 | .16 |
| ☐826 21¢ Dull Blue | | | | | | |
| | 12.00 | 9.00 | 2.20 | 1.35 | .18 | .16 |
| ☐827 22¢ Vermilion | | | | | | |
| | 16.00 | 12.00 | 1.35 | .72 | .60 | .50 |
| ☐828 24¢ Gray Black | | | | | | |
| | 24.00 | 18.00 | 4.00 | 2.50 | .35 | .21 |
| ☐829 25¢ Deep Red Lilac | | | | | | |
| | 6.00 | 4.00 | 1.00 | .50 | .18 | .16 |
| ☐830 30¢ Deep Ultramarine | | | | | | |
| | 27.00 | 21.00 | 4.50 | 3.40 | .18 | .16 |
| ☐831 50¢ Light Red Violet | | | | | | |
| | 42.00 | 34.00 | 8.00 | 5.00 | .18 | .16 |

## FLAT PLATE PRINTING—PERF. 11 (N-H ADD 20%)

| Scott No. | Fine Unused Plate Blk | Ave. Unused Plate Blk | Fine Unused Each | Ave. Unused Each | Fine Used Each | Ave. Used Each |
|---|---|---|---|---|---|---|
| ☐832 $1 Purple & Black | | | | | | |
| | 50.00 | 38.00 | 9.00 | 6.00 | .28 | .16 |
| ☐832b $1 Watermarked | | | | | | |
| | — | — | 310.00 | 240.00 | 70.00 | 55.00 |

| Scott No. | Fine Unused Plate Blk | Ave. Unused Plate Blk | Fine Unused Each | Ave. Unused Each | Fine Used Each | Ave. Used Each |
|---|---|---|---|---|---|---|
| □832c $1 Dry Printing, Thick Paper (1954) | | | | | | |
| | 40.00 | 34.00 | 8.00 | 6.50 | .26 | .15 |
| □833 $2 Green & Black | | | | | | |
| | 160.00 | 140.00 | 30.00 | 21.00 | 8.00 | 6.00 |
| □834 $5 Carmine & Black | | | | | | |
| | 600.00 | 400.00 | 115.00 | 100.00 | 6.00 | 4.00 |

## 1938–1939. COMMEMORATIVES
## 1938. CONSTITUTION RATIFICATION (N-H ADD 25%)
□835 3¢ Deep Violet

| | 6.00 | 4.50 | .42 | .24 | .20 | .16 |
|---|---|---|---|---|---|---|

## 1938. SWEDISH-FINNISH TERCENTENARY (N-H ADD 25%)
□836 3¢ Red Violet

| | 5.00 | 3.00 | .28 | .24 | .20 | .16 |
|---|---|---|---|---|---|---|

## 1938. NORTHWEST COLONIZATION (N-H ADD 25%)
□837 3¢ Bright Violet

| | 12.00 | 9.50 | .25 | .24 | .20 | .16 |
|---|---|---|---|---|---|---|

## 1938. IOWA TERRITORY CENTENNIAL (N-H ADD 25%)
□838 3¢ Violet

| | 9.00 | 7.00 | .25 | .24 | .20 | .16 |
|---|---|---|---|---|---|---|

| Scott No. | Fine Unused Line Pair | Ave. Unused Line Pair | Fine Unused Each | Ave. Unused Each | Fine Used Each | Ave. Used Each |
|---|---|---|---|---|---|---|

## 1939. ROTARY PRESS COIL STAMPS
## PERF. 10 VERTICALLY (N-H ADD 25%)
□839 1¢ Green

| | 1.35 | 1.00 | .40 | .26 | .18 | .15 |
|---|---|---|---|---|---|---|
| □840 1½¢ Bistre Brown | | | | | | |
| | 1.60 | 1.25 | .45 | .26 | .18 | .15 |
| □841 2¢ Rose Carmine | | | | | | |
| | 2.00 | 1.50 | .40 | .30 | .20 | .15 |
| □842 3¢ Deep Violet | | | | | | |
| | 1.60 | 1.40 | .62 | .40 | .22 | .15 |

| Scott No. | Fine Unused Line Pair | Ave. Unused Line Pair | Fine Unused Each | Ave. Unused Each | Fine Used Each | Ave. Used Each |
|---|---|---|---|---|---|---|
| ☐843 4¢ Red Violet | | | | | | |
| | 26.00 | 20.00 | 9.00 | 7.00 | .55 | .40 |
| ☐844 4¹/₂¢ Dark Gray | | | | | | |
| | 5.50 | 4.00 | .90 | .70 | .60 | .40 |
| ☐845 5¢ Bright Blue | | | | | | |
| | 26.00 | 20.00 | 7.00 | 5.00 | .50 | .35 |
| ☐846 6¢ Red Orange | | | | | | |
| | 7.00 | 5.50 | 2.00 | 1.10 | .20 | .15 |
| ☐847 10¢ Brown Red | | | | | | |
| | 44.00 | 37.00 | 15.00 | 9.00 | .70 | .50 |

## PERF. 10 HORIZONTALLY (N-H ADD 25%)

| Scott No. | Fine Unused Line Pair | Ave. Unused Line Pair | Fine Unused Each | Ave. Unused Each | Fine Used Each | Ave. Used Each |
|---|---|---|---|---|---|---|
| ☐848 1¢ Green | | | | | | |
| | 2.75 | 2.25 | .90 | .70 | .21 | .15 |
| ☐849 1¹/₂¢ Bistre Brown | | | | | | |
| | 3.50 | 3.00 | 1.50 | 1.25 | .55 | .45 |
| ☐850 2¢ Rose Carmine | | | | | | |
| | 6.50 | 4.50 | 3.40 | 2.50 | .65 | .50 |
| ☐851 3¢ Deep Violet | | | | | | |
| | 6.50 | 6.00 | 3.00 | 2.30 | .55 | .48 |

| Scott No. | Fine Unused Plate Blk | Ave. Unused Plate Blk | Fine Unused Each | Ave. Unused Each | Fine Used Each | Ave. Used Each |
|---|---|---|---|---|---|---|
| **1939. GOLDEN GATE INTERNATIONAL EXPOSITION (N-H ADD 25%)** | | | | | | |
| ☐852 3¢ Bright Purple | | | | | | |
| | 2.00 | 1.50 | .25 | .20 | .18 | .15 |
| **1939. NEW YORK WORLD'S FAIR (N-H ADD 20%)** | | | | | | |
| ☐853 3¢ Deep Purple | | | | | | |
| | 2.40 | 1.75 | .25 | .20 | .18 | .15 |
| **1939. WASHINGTON INAUGURATION SESQUICENTENNIAL (N-H ADD 20%)** | | | | | | |
| ☐854 3¢ Bright Red Violet | | | | | | |
| | 5.50 | 3.75 | .58 | .35 | .20 | .15 |

| Scott No. | Fine Unused Plate Blk | Ave. Unused Plate Blk | Fine Unused Each | Ave. Unused Each | Fine Used Each | Ave. Used Each |
|---|---|---|---|---|---|---|

## 1939. BASEBALL CENTENNIAL (N-H ADD 20%)

☐855  3¢  Violet

| | 9.00 | 7.00 | 1.75 | .60 | .21 | .16 |

## 1939. 25TH ANNIVERSARY PANAMA CANAL (N-H ADD 20%)

☐856  3¢  Deep Red Violet

| | 4.00 | 3.50 | .25 | .21 | .17 | .15 |

## 1939. COLONIAL PRINTING TERCENTENARY (N-H ADD 20%)

☐857  3¢  Rose Violet

| | 1.80 | 1.60 | .23 | .16 | .16 | .15 |

## 1939. 50TH ANNIVERSARY OF STATEHOOD (N-H ADD 20%)

☐858  3¢  Rose Violet

| | 2.00 | 1.65 | .22 | .18 | .16 | .15 |

## 1940. FAMOUS AMERICANS SERIES
## AMERICAN AUTHORS (N-H ADD 20%)

☐859  1¢  Bright Blue Green

| | 1.70 | 1.50 | .26 | .18 | .16 | .15 |

☐860  2¢  Rose Carmine

| | 1.70 | 1.35 | .26 | .18 | .16 | .15 |

☐861  3¢  Bright Red Violet

| | 1.80 | 1.50 | .26 | .18 | .16 | .15 |

☐862  5¢  Ultramarine

| | 18.00 | 13.00 | .45 | .40 | .36 | .40 |

☐863 10¢  Dark Brown

| | 58.00 | 42.00 | 2.60 | 2.10 | 1.90 | 1.50 |

## AMERICAN POETS (N-H ADD 20%)

☐864  1¢  Bright Blue Green

| | 2.65 | 2.15 | .26 | .24 | .19 | .14 |

| Scott No. | Fine Unused Plate Blk | Ave. Unused Plate Blk | Fine Unused Each | Ave. Unused Each | Fine Used Each | Ave. Used Each |
|---|---|---|---|---|---|---|
| ☐865  2¢ Rose Carmine | | | | | | |
| | 2.65 | 2.40 | .26 | .24 | .19 | .14 |
| ☐866  3¢ Bright Red Violet | | | | | | |
| | 3.25 | 2.75 | .26 | .24 | .19 | .14 |
| ☐867  5¢ Ultramarine | | | | | | |
| | 16.00 | 11.00 | .50 | .45 | .38 | .30 |
| ☐868 10¢ Dark Brown | | | | | | |
| | 52.00 | 40.00 | 2.60 | 2.30 | 2.25 | 2.00 |

## AMERICAN EDUCATORS (N-H ADD 20%)

| Scott No. | Fine Unused Plate Blk | Ave. Unused Plate Blk | Fine Unused Each | Ave. Unused Each | Fine Used Each | Ave. Used Each |
|---|---|---|---|---|---|---|
| ☐869  1¢ Bright Blue Green | | | | | | |
| | 3.10 | 2.75 | .24 | .22 | .19 | .14 |
| ☐870  2¢ Rose Carmine | | | | | | |
| | 2.00 | 1.75 | .24 | .22 | .19 | .14 |
| ☐871  3¢ Bright Red Violet | | | | | | |
| | 4.00 | 3.00 | .28 | .25 | .19 | .14 |
| ☐872  5¢ Ultramarine | | | | | | |
| | 16.00 | 12.00 | .55 | .45 | .40 | .30 |
| ☐873 10¢ Dark Brown | | | | | | |
| | 41.00 | 32.00 | 2.40 | 2.00 | 1.90 | 1.70 |

## AMERICAN SCIENTISTS (N-H ADD 20%)

| Scott No. | Fine Unused Plate Blk | Ave. Unused Plate Blk | Fine Unused Each | Ave. Unused Each | Fine Used Each | Ave. Used Each |
|---|---|---|---|---|---|---|
| ☐874  1¢ Bright Blue Green | | | | | | |
| | 1.60 | 1.50 | .24 | .20 | .19 | .14 |
| ☐875  2¢ Rose Carmine | | | | | | |
| | 1.40 | 1.25 | .24 | .20 | .19 | .14 |
| ☐876  3¢ Bright Red Violet | | | | | | |
| | 1.75 | 1.40 | .24 | .20 | .19 | .14 |
| ☐877  5¢ Ultramarine | | | | | | |
| | 10.00 | 7.50 | .40 | .38 | .35 | .29 |
| ☐878 10¢ Dark Brown | | | | | | |
| | 33.00 | 29.00 | 1.80 | 1.65 | 1.60 | 1.30 |

## AMERICAN COMPOSERS (N-H ADD 20%)

| Scott No. | Fine Unused Plate Blk | Ave. Unused Plate Blk | Fine Unused Each | Ave. Unused Each | Fine Used Each | Ave. Used Each |
|---|---|---|---|---|---|---|
| ☐879  1¢ Bright Blue Green | | | | | | |
| | 1.75 | 1.50 | .24 | .20 | .18 | .14 |
| ☐880  2¢ Rose Carmine | | | | | | |
| | 1.80 | 1.50 | .24 | .20 | .18 | .14 |
| ☐881  3¢ Bright Red Violet | | | | | | |
| | 1.85 | 1.60 | .24 | .20 | .18 | .15 |

| Scott No. | Fine Unused Plate Blk | Ave. Unused Plate Blk | Fine Unused Each | Ave. Unused Each | Fine Used Each | Ave. Used Each |
|---|---|---|---|---|---|---|
| ☐882 5¢ Ultramarine | | | | | | |
| | 15.00 | 11.00 | .65 | .48 | .34 | .30 |
| ☐883 10¢ Dark Brown | | | | | | |
| | 50.00 | 39.00 | 5.00 | 3.75 | 1.85 | 1.75 |

## AMERICAN ARTISTS (N-H ADD 20%)

| | | | | | | |
|---|---|---|---|---|---|---|
| ☐884 1¢ Bright Blue Green | | | | | | |
| | 1.50 | 1.25 | .24 | .20 | .18 | .14 |
| ☐885 2¢ Rose Carmine | | | | | | |
| | 1.50 | 1.25 | .24 | .20 | .18 | .14 |
| ☐886 3¢ Bright Red Violet | | | | | | |
| | 1.50 | 1.25 | .24 | .20 | .18 | .14 |
| ☐887 5¢ Ultramarine | | | | | | |
| | 14.00 | 10.00 | .75 | .60 | .34 | .30 |
| ☐888 10¢ Dark Brown | | | | | | |
| | 41.00 | 34.00 | 2.40 | 1.90 | 1.65 | 1.45 |

## AMERICAN INVENTORS (N-H ADD 20%)

| | | | | | | |
|---|---|---|---|---|---|---|
| ☐889 1¢ Bright Blue Green | | | | | | |
| | 3.00 | 2.50 | .24 | .20 | .18 | .14 |
| ☐890 2¢ Rose Carmine | | | | | | |
| | 1.80 | 1.40 | .24 | .20 | .18 | .14 |
| ☐891 3¢ Bright Red Violet | | | | | | |
| | 2.75 | 2.30 | .40 | .21 | .18 | .15 |
| ☐892 5¢ Ultramarine | | | | | | |
| | 21.00 | 18.00 | 1.30 | .90 | .50 | .45 |
| ☐893 10¢ Dark Brown | | | | | | |
| | 120.00 | 90.00 | 13.00 | 11.00 | 3.20 | 2.60 |

## 1940. COMMEMORATIVES
## 1940. 80TH ANNIVERSARY OF PONY EXPRESS (N-H ADD 20%)

| | | | | | | |
|---|---|---|---|---|---|---|
| ☐894 3¢ Henna Brown | | | | | | |
| | 5.00 | 3.50 | .30 | .25 | .21 | .16 |

## 1940. 50TH ANNIVERSARY OF PAN-AMERICAN UNION (N-H ADD 20%)

| | | | | | | |
|---|---|---|---|---|---|---|
| ☐895 3¢ Light Violet | | | | | | |
| | 5.00 | 4.00 | .28 | .20 | .19 | .14 |

| Scott No. | Fine Unused Plate Blk | Ave. Unused Plate Blk | Fine Unused Each | Ave. Unused Each | Fine Used Each | Ave. Used Each |
|---|---|---|---|---|---|---|
| **1940. 50TH ANNIVERSARY OF IDAHO (N-H ADD 20%)** | | | | | | |
| ☐896 3¢ Bright Violet | | | | | | |
| | 3.25 | 2.50 | .24 | .19 | .16 | .14 |
| **1940. 50TH ANNIVERSARY OF WYOMING (N-H ADD 20%)** | | | | | | |
| ☐897 3¢ Brown Violet | | | | | | |
| | 2.50 | 2.00 | .24 | .19 | .16 | .14 |
| **1940. 400TH ANNIVERSARY OF COLORADO EXPEDITION (N-H ADD 20%)** | | | | | | |
| ☐898 3¢ Violet | | | | | | |
| | 2.50 | 2.00 | .24 | .19 | .16 | .14 |
| **1940. NATIONAL DEFENSE ISSUE (N-H ADD 20%)** | | | | | | |
| ☐899 1¢ Bright Blue Green | | | | | | |
| | .70 | .50 | .24 | .19 | .16 | .14 |
| ☐900 2¢ Rose Carmine | | | | | | |
| | .70 | .50 | .24 | .19 | .16 | .14 |
| ☐901 3¢ Bright Violet | | | | | | |
| | .90 | .80 | .24 | .19 | .16 | .14 |
| **1940. 75TH ANNIVERSARY EMANCIPATION AMENDMENT (N-H ADD 20%)** | | | | | | |
| ☐902 3¢ Deep Violet | | | | | | |
| | 5.00 | 3.75 | .26 | .23 | .21 | .16 |

**IMPORTANT NOTICE:** Values for mint sheets are provided for the following listings. To command the stated prices, sheets must be complete as issued with the plate number (or numbers) intact.

| Scott No. | Mint Sheet | Plate Block | Fine Unused Each | Fine Used Each |
|---|---|---|---|---|
| **1941–1943. COMMEMORATIVES** | | | | |
| **1941. VERMONT STATEHOOD** | | | | |
| ☐903 3¢ Light Violet | 10.50 | 2.30 | .24 | .16 |

| Scott No. | Mint Sheet | Plate Block | Fine Unused Each | Fine Used Each |
|---|---|---|---|---|

## 1942. KENTUCKY SESQUICENTENNIAL ISSUE

| | | | | |
|---|---|---|---|---|
| ☐904  3¢  Violet | 8.00 | 1.65 | .24 | .16 |

## 1942. WIN THE WAR ISSUE

| | | | | |
|---|---|---|---|---|
| ☐905  3¢  Violet | 11.00 | .75 | .24 | .16 |

## 1942. CHINA ISSUE

| | | | | |
|---|---|---|---|---|
| ☐906  5¢  Bright Blue | 20.00 | 12.00 | .30 | .27 |

## 1943. ALLIED NATIONS ISSUE

| | | | | |
|---|---|---|---|---|
| ☐907  2¢  Rose Carmine | 6.50 | .55 | .24 | .16 |

## 1943. FOUR FREEDOMS ISSUE

| | | | | |
|---|---|---|---|---|
| ☐908  1¢  Green | 6.50 | .75 | .24 | .16 |

## 1943–1944. OVERRUN COUNTRIES SERIES

| | | | | |
|---|---|---|---|---|
| ☐909  5¢  (Poland) | 15.00 | 8.00 | .24 | .19 |
| ☐910  5¢  (Czechoslovakia) | 12.00 | 4.50 | .24 | .16 |
| ☐911  5¢  (Norway) | 8.50 | 2.00 | .24 | .16 |
| ☐912  5¢  (Luxembourg) | 8.00 | 1.75 | .24 | .16 |
| ☐913  5¢  (Netherlands) | 8.00 | 1.35 | .24 | .16 |
| ☐914  5¢  (Belgium) | 8.00 | 1.35 | .24 | .16 |
| ☐915  5¢  (France) | 8.00 | 1.35 | .24 | .16 |
| ☐916  5¢  (Greece) | 34.00 | 15.00 | .53 | .45 |
| ☐917  5¢  (Yugoslavia) | 22.00 | 8.00 | .38 | .29 |
| ☐918  5¢  (Albania) | 17.00 | 8.00 | .27 | .22 |
| ☐919  5¢  (Austria) | 15.00 | 6.00 | .27 | .23 |
| ☐920  5¢  (Denmark) | 19.00 | 6.50 | .30 | .27 |
| ☐921  5¢  (Korea) | 12.00 | 6.00 | .26 | .24 |

## 1944. COMMEMORATIVES
## 1944. RAILROAD ISSUE

| | | | | |
|---|---|---|---|---|
| ☐922  3¢  Violet | 14.00 | 1.75 | .26 | .21 |

## 1944. STEAMSHIP ISSUE

| | | | | |
|---|---|---|---|---|
| ☐923  3¢  Violet | 7.00 | 1.75 | .26 | .16 |

*No hinge pricing from 1941 to date is figured at (N-H ADD 15%)

| Scott No. | Mint Sheet | Plate Block | Fine Unused Each | Fine Used Each |
|---|---|---|---|---|

**1944. TELEGRAPH ISSUE**

| ☐924 3¢ Bright Red Violet | 6.50 | 1.25 | .26 | .16 |

**1944. CORREGIDOR ISSUE**

| ☐925 3¢ Deep Violet | 6.50 | 1.35 | .26 | .16 |

**1944. MOTION PICTURE ISSUE**

| ☐926 3¢ Deep Violet | 7.50 | 1.35 | .26 | .16 |

**1945. COMMEMORATIVES**
**1945. FLORIDA ISSUE**

| ☐927 3¢ Bright Red Violet | 5.50 | .90 | .26 | .16 |

**1945. PEACE CONFERENCE ISSUE**

| ☐928 5¢ Ultramarine | 5.50 | .80 | .26 | .16 |

**1945. IWO JIMA ISSUE**

| ☐929 3¢ Yellow Green | 5.50 | .80 | .26 | .16 |

**1945–1946. ROOSEVELT MEMORIAL ISSUE**

| ☐930 1¢ Blue Green | 2.50 | .50 | .26 | .16 |
| ☐931 2¢ Carmine Rose | 3.00 | .52 | .26 | .16 |
| ☐932 3¢ Purple | 6.00 | .72 | .26 | .16 |
| ☐933 5¢ Bright Blue | 6.50 | .70 | .26 | .16 |

**1945. ARMY ISSUE**

| ☐934 3¢ Olive Gray | 6.00 | .65 | .23 | .14 |

**1945. NAVY ISSUE**

| ☐935 3¢ Blue | 6.00 | .65 | .23 | .14 |

**1945. COAST GUARD ISSUE**

| ☐936 3¢ Bright Blue Green | 6.00 | .65 | .23 | .14 |

**1945. ALFRED SMITH ISSUE**

| ☐937 3¢ Purple | 11.00 | .65 | .23 | .14 |

**1945. TEXAS CENTENNIAL ISSUE**

| ☐938 3¢ Blue | 6.00 | .65 | .23 | .14 |

*No hinge pricing from 1941 to date is figured at (N-H ADD 15%)

| Scott No. | Mint Sheet | Plate Block | Fine Unused Each | Fine Used Each |
|---|---|---|---|---|

## 1946-1947. COMMEMORATIVES
## 1946. MERCHANT MARINE ISSUE

| ☐939 3¢ Blue Green | 5.50 | .70 | .22 | .14 |
|---|---|---|---|---|

## 1946. HONORABLE DISCHARGE EMBLEM ISSUE

| ☐940 3¢ Dark Violet | 12.00 | .70 | .22 | .14 |
|---|---|---|---|---|

## 1946. TENNESSEE ISSUE

| ☐941 3¢ Dark Violet | 6.00 | .70 | .22 | .14 |
|---|---|---|---|---|

## 1946. IOWA STATEHOOD ISSUE

| ☐942 3¢ Deep Blue | 6.00 | .70 | .22 | .14 |
|---|---|---|---|---|

## 1946. SMITHSONIAN INSTITUTION ISSUE

| ☐943 3¢ Violet Brown | 6.00 | .70 | .22 | .14 |
|---|---|---|---|---|

## 1946. NEW MEXICO ISSUE

| ☐944 3¢ Brown Violet | 6.00 | .70 | .22 | .14 |
|---|---|---|---|---|

## 1947. EDISON ISSUE

| ☐945 3¢ Bright Red Violet | 8.00 | .70 | .22 | .14 |
|---|---|---|---|---|

## 1947. PULITZER PRIZE

| ☐946 3¢ Purple | 6.00 | .70 | .22 | .14 |
|---|---|---|---|---|

## 1947. U.S. POSTAGE STAMP CENTENARY

| ☐947 3¢ Deep Blue | 6.00 | .70 | .22 | .14 |
|---|---|---|---|---|

## 1947. "CIPEX" SOUVENIR SHEET

| ☐948 5¢ & 10¢ Sheet of 2 | — | — | .90 | .75 |
|---|---|---|---|---|
| ☐948a 5¢ Blue, sgl. stp. | — | — | .34 | .25 |
| ☐948b 10¢ Brown Orange, sgl. stp. | | | | |
|  | — | — | .52 | .34 |

## 1947. DOCTORS ISSUE

| ☐949 3¢ Brown Violet | 6.00 | .70 | .22 | .14 |
|---|---|---|---|---|

## 1947. UTAH ISSUE

| ☐950 3¢ Dark Violet | 6.00 | .70 | .22 | .14 |
|---|---|---|---|---|

| Scott No. | Mint Sheet | Plate Block | Fine Unused Each | Fine Used Each |
|---|---|---|---|---|
| **1947. U.S.F. CONSTITUTION ISSUE** | | | | |
| ☐951  3¢  Blue Green | 6.00 | .70 | .22 | .14 |
| **1947. EVERGLADES ISSUE** | | | | |
| ☐952  3¢  Bright Green | 6.00 | .70 | .22 | .14 |
| **1948. COMMEMORATIVES** | | | | |
| **1948. CARVER ISSUE** | | | | |
| ☐953  3¢  Red Violet | 7.00 | .70 | .22 | .14 |
| **1948. GOLD RUSH ISSUE** | | | | |
| ☐954  3¢  Dark Violet | 6.00 | .70 | .22 | .14 |
| **1948. MISSISSIPPI TERRITORY ISSUE** | | | | |
| ☐955  3¢  Brown Violet | 6.00 | .70 | .22 | .14 |
| **1948. FOUR CHAPLAINS ISSUE** | | | | |
| ☐956  3¢  Gray Black | 6.00 | .70 | .22 | .16 |
| **1948. WISCONSIN CENTENNIAL ISSUE** | | | | |
| ☐957  3¢  Dark Violet | 6.00 | .70 | .22 | .16 |
| **1948. SWEDISH PIONEER ISSUE** | | | | |
| ☐958  5¢  Deep Blue | 7.00 | .70 | .22 | .16 |
| **1948. 100 YEARS PROGRESS OF WOMEN** | | | | |
| ☐959  3¢  Dark Violet | 6.00 | .70 | .22 | .16 |
| **1948. WILLIAM ALLEN WHITE ISSUE** | | | | |
| ☐960  3¢  Red Violet | 7.50 | .80 | .22 | .16 |
| **1948. U.S.-CANADA FRIENDSHIP** | | | | |
| ☐961  3¢  Blue | 6.00 | .70 | .22 | .16 |
| **1948. FRANCIS SCOTT KEY ISSUE** | | | | |
| ☐962  3¢  Rose Pink | 6.00 | .70 | .22 | .16 |

*No hinge pricing from 1941 to date is figured at (N-H ADD 15%)

| Scott No. | Mint Sheet | Plate Block | Fine Unused Each | Fine Used Each |
|---|---|---|---|---|

**1948. SALUTE TO YOUTH ISSUE**

| ☐963 3¢ Deep Blue | 6.00 | .70 | .22 | .16 |

**1948. OREGON TERRITORY ISSUE**

| ☐964 3¢ Brown Red | 6.00 | .70 | .22 | .16 |

**1948. HARLAN FISKE STONE**

| ☐965 3¢ Bright Red Violet | 7.00 | .70 | .22 | .16 |

**1948. MT. PALOMAR OBSERVATORY**

| ☐966 3¢ Blue | 7.50 | .70 | .22 | .16 |

**1948. CLARA BARTON ISSUE**

| ☐967 3¢ Rose Pink | 6.00 | .70 | .22 | .16 |

**1948. POULTRY ISSUE**

| ☐968 3¢ Sepia | 6.00 | .70 | .22 | .16 |

**1948. GOLD STAR MOTHERS**

| ☐969 3¢ Orange Yellow | 6.00 | .70 | .22 | .16 |

**1948. FORT KEARNY ISSUE**

| ☐970 3¢ Violet | 6.00 | .70 | .22 | .16 |

**1948. VOLUNTEER FIREMEN**

| ☐971 3¢ Bright Rose Carmine | 6.00 | .70 | .22 | .16 |

**1948. INDIAN CENTENNIAL**

| ☐972 3¢ Dark Brown | 6.00 | .70 | .22 | .16 |

**1948. ROUGH RIDERS**

| ☐973 3¢ Violet Brown | 6.00 | .70 | .22 | .16 |

**1948. JULIETTE LOW**

| ☐974 3¢ Blue Green | 6.00 | .70 | .22 | .16 |

*No hinge pricing from 1941 to date is figured at (N-H ADD 15%)

| Scott No. | Mint Sheet | Plate Block | Fine Unused Each | Fine Used Each |
|---|---|---|---|---|
| **1948. WILL ROGERS** | | | | |
| ☐975 3¢ Bright Red Violet | 9.00 | .70 | .22 | .16 |
| **1948. FORT BLISS** | | | | |
| ☐976 3¢ Henna Brown | 9.00 | .70 | .22 | .16 |
| **1948. MOINA MICHAEL** | | | | |
| ☐977 3¢ Rose Pink | 7.00 | .70 | .22 | .16 |
| **1948. GETTYSBURG ADDRESS** | | | | |
| ☐978 3¢ Bright Blue | 6.00 | .70 | .22 | .16 |
| **1948. AMERICAN TURNERS** | | | | |
| ☐979 3¢ Carmine | 6.00 | .70 | .22 | .16 |
| **1948. JOEL CHANDLER HARRIS** | | | | |
| ☐980 3¢ Bright Red Violet | 8.00 | .80 | .22 | .16 |
| **1949-1950. COMMEMORATIVES** | | | | |
| **1949. MINNESOTA CENTENNIAL** | | | | |
| ☐981 3¢ Blue Green | 6.00 | .70 | .22 | .16 |
| **1949. WASHINGTON & LEE UNIVERSITY** | | | | |
| ☐982 3¢ Ultramarine | 6.00 | .70 | .22 | .16 |
| **1949. PUERTO RICO ISSUE** | | | | |
| ☐983 3¢ Green | 6.00 | .70 | .22 | .16 |
| **1949. ANNAPOLIS TERCENTENARY** | | | | |
| ☐984 3¢ Aquamarine | 6.00 | .70 | .22 | .16 |
| **1949. G.A.R. ISSUE** | | | | |
| ☐985 3¢ Bright Rose Carmine | 6.00 | .70 | .22 | .16 |
| **1950. EDGAR ALLAN POE** | | | | |
| ☐986 3¢ Bright Red Violet | 8.00 | .70 | .22 | .16 |
| **1950. BANKERS ASSOCIATION** | | | | |
| ☐987 3¢ Yellow Green | 6.00 | .70 | .22 | .16 |

| Scott No. | | Mint Sheet | Plate Block | Fine Unused Each | Fine Used Each |
|---|---|---|---|---|---|

## 1950. SAMUEL GOMPERS

| ☐988 3¢ Bright Red Violet | 8.00 | .70 | .22 | .16 |
|---|---|---|---|---|

## 1950. WASHINGTON SESQUICENTENNIAL

| ☐989 3¢ Bright Blue | 6.00 | .70 | .22 | .16 |
|---|---|---|---|---|
| ☐990 3¢ Deep Green | 6.00 | .70 | .22 | .16 |
| ☐991 3¢ Light Violet | 6.00 | .70 | .22 | .16 |
| ☐992 3¢ Rose Violet | 6.00 | .70 | .22 | .16 |

## 1950. RAILROAD ENGINEERS

| ☐993 3¢ Violet Brown | 6.00 | .70 | .22 | .16 |
|---|---|---|---|---|

## 1950. KANSAS CITY CENTENARY

| ☐994 3¢ Violet | 6.00 | .70 | .22 | .16 |
|---|---|---|---|---|

## 1950. BOY SCOUTS ISSUE

| ☐995 3¢ Sepia | 6.00 | .70 | .22 | .16 |
|---|---|---|---|---|

## 1950. INDIANA SESQUICENTENNIAL

| ☐996 3¢ Bright Blue | 6.00 | .70 | .22 | .16 |
|---|---|---|---|---|

## 1950. CALIFORNIA STATEHOOD

| ☐997 3¢ Yellow Orange | 6.00 | .70 | .22 | .16 |
|---|---|---|---|---|

## 1951-1952. COMMEMORATIVES
## 1951. UNITED CONFEDERATE VETERANS

| ☐998 3¢ Gray | 6.00 | .70 | .22 | .16 |
|---|---|---|---|---|

## 1951. NEVADA SETTLEMENT

| ☐999 3¢ Light Olive Green | 6.00 | .70 | .22 | .16 |
|---|---|---|---|---|

## 1951. LANDING OF CADILLAC

| ☐1000 3¢ Bright Blue | 6.00 | .70 | .22 | .16 |
|---|---|---|---|---|

## 1951. COLORADO STATEHOOD

| ☐1001 3¢ Violet Blue | 6.00 | .70 | .22 | .16 |
|---|---|---|---|---|

*No hinge pricing from 1941 to date is figured at (N-H ADD 15%)

| Scott No. | Mint Sheet | Plate Block | Fine Unused Each | Fine Used Each |
|---|---|---|---|---|
| **1951. AMERICAN CHEMICAL SOCIETY** | | | | |
| ☐ 1002 3¢ Violet Brown | 6.00 | .70 | .22 | .16 |
| **1951. BATTLE OF BROOKLYN ISSUE** | | | | |
| ☐ 1003 3¢ Violet | 7.00 | .70 | .22 | .16 |
| **1952. BETSY ROSS ISSUE** | | | | |
| ☐ 1004 3¢ Carmine Rose | 6.00 | .70 | .22 | .16 |
| **1952. 4-H CLUB ISSUE** | | | | |
| ☐ 1005 3¢ Blue Green | 6.00 | .70 | .22 | .16 |
| **1952. BALTIMORE & OHIO RAILROAD** | | | | |
| ☐ 1006 3¢ Bright Blue | 6.25 | .70 | .22 | .16 |
| **1952. AMERICAN AUTOMOBILE ASSOCIATION (AAA)** | | | | |
| ☐ 1007 3¢ Deep Blue | 6.00 | .70 | .22 | .16 |
| **1952. NORTH ATLANTIC TREATY ORGANIZATION** | | | | |
| ☐ 1008 3¢ Deep Violet | 11.00 | .70 | .22 | .16 |
| **1952. GRAND COULEE DAM ISSUE** | | | | |
| ☐ 1009 3¢ Blue Green | 6.00 | .70 | .22 | .16 |
| **1952. ARRIVAL OF LAFAYETTE** | | | | |
| ☐ 1010 3¢ Ultramarine | 6.00 | .70 | .22 | .16 |
| **1952. MOUNT RUSHMORE** | | | | |
| ☐ 1011 3¢ Blue Green | 6.00 | .70 | .22 | .16 |
| **1952. SOCIETY OF CIVIL ENGINEERS** | | | | |
| ☐ 1012 3¢ Violet Blue | 6.00 | .70 | .22 | .16 |
| **1952. WOMEN IN ARMED FORCES** | | | | |
| ☐ 1013 3¢ Deep Blue | 6.00 | .70 | .22 | .16 |

*No hinge pricing from 1941 to date is figured at (N-H ADD 15%)

| Scott No. | Mint Sheet | Plate Block | Fine Unused Each | Fine Used Each |
|---|---|---|---|---|

## 1952. GUTENBERG PRINTING
☐1014 3¢ Violet 6.00 .70 .22 .16

## 1952. NEWSPAPERBOYS
☐1015 3¢ Violet 6.00 .70 .22 .16

## 1952. INTERNATIONAL RED CROSS
☐1016 3¢ Deep Blue & Carmine
6.00 .70 .22 .16

## 1953-1954. COMMEMORATIVES
## 1953. NATIONAL GUARD
☐1017 3¢ Bright Blue 7.00 .70 .22 .16

## 1953. OHIO STATEHOOD
☐1018 3¢ Chocolate 8.00 .70 .22 .16

## 1953. WASHINGTON TERRITORY
☐1019 3¢ Green 6.00 .70 .22 .16

## 1953. LOUISIANA PURCHASE
☐1020 3¢ Violet Brown 6.00 .70 .22 .16

## 1953. OPENING OF JAPAN
☐1021 3¢ Green 7.25 .90 .22 .16

## 1953. AMERICAN BAR ASSOCIATION
☐1022 3¢ Rose Violet 5.75 .70 .22 .16

## 1953. SAGAMORE HILL
☐1023 3¢ Yellow Green 5.75 .70 .22 .16

## 1953. FUTURE FARMERS
☐1024 3¢ Deep Blue 5.75 .70 .22 .16

## 1953. TRUCKING INDUSTRY
☐1025 3¢ Violet 5.75 .70 .22 .16

## 1953. GENERAL PATTON
☐1026 3¢ Blue Violet 7.50 .70 .22 .16

*No hinge pricing from 1941 to date is figured at (N-H ADD 15%)

| Scott No. | Mint Sheet | Plate Block | Fine Unused Each | Fine Used Each |
|---|---|---|---|---|
| **1953. NEW YORK CITY** | | | | |
| ☐1027 3¢ Bright Red Violet | 5.75 | .70 | .22 | .16 |
| **1953. GADSDEN PURCHASE** | | | | |
| ☐1028 3¢ Copper Brown | 5.75 | .70 | .22 | .16 |
| **1954. COLUMBIA UNIVERSITY** | | | | |
| ☐1029 3¢ Blue | 5.75 | .70 | .22 | .16 |
| **1954-1961. LIBERTY SERIES** | | | | |
| ☐1030 ½¢ Red Orange | 6.50 | .70 | .22 | .16 |
| ☐1031 1¢ Dark Green | 6.50 | .70 | .22 | .16 |
| ☐1031A 1¼¢ Turquoise | 6.50 | .70 | .22 | .16 |
| ☐1032 1½¢ Brown | 10.00 | 2.50 | .22 | .16 |
| ☐1033 2¢ Rose Carmine | 9.00 | .70 | .22 | .16 |
| ☐1034 2½¢ Dark Blue | 12.00 | .70 | .22 | .16 |
| ☐1035 3¢ Deep Violet | 12.00 | .70 | .22 | .16 |
| ☐1036 4¢ Red Violet | 10.00 | .80 | .22 | .16 |
| ☐1037 4½¢ Green | 12.00 | .80 | .22 | .16 |
| ☐1038 5¢ Deep Blue | 14.00 | .70 | .22 | .16 |
| ☐1039 6¢ Orange Red | 35.00 | 1.60 | .38 | .16 |
| ☐1040 7¢ Deep Carmine | 38.00 | 3.10 | .36 | .16 |
| ☐1041 8¢ Dark Violet Blue, Carmine | 30.00 | 3.00 | .24 | .16 |
| ☐1042 8¢ Violet Blue, Carmine (Re-engraved) | 34.00 | 1.40 | .26 | .14 |
| ☐1042A 8¢ Brown | 30.00 | 1.40 | .30 | .16 |
| ☐1043 9¢ Rose Lilac | 48.00 | 2.00 | .45 | .16 |
| ☐1044 10¢ Rose Lake | 34.00 | 1.40 | .32 | .16 |
| ☐1044A 11¢ Carmine, Violet Blue | 36.00 | 1.60 | .45 | .16 |
| ☐1045 12¢ Red | 45.00 | 2.00 | .45 | .16 |
| ☐1046 15¢ Maroon | 100.00 | 4.50 | 1.10 | .16 |
| ☐1047 20¢ Ultramarine | 80.00 | 3.00 | .60 | .16 |
| ☐1048 25¢ Green | 130.00 | 7.00 | 1.50 | .16 |
| ☐1049 30¢ Black | 130.00 | 5.50 | 1.35 | .16 |
| ☐1050 40¢ Brown Carmine | 300.00 | 13.00 | 2.40 | .16 |

*No hinge pricing from 1941 to date is figured at (N-H ADD 15%)

| Scott No. | Mint Sheet | Plate Block | Fine Unused Each | Fine Used Each |
|---|---|---|---|---|
| ☐1051 50¢ Bright Violet | 200.00 | 8.50 | 1.85 | .16 |
| ☐1052 $1 Deep Violet | 900.00 | 30.00 | 6.50 | .22 |
| ☐1053 $5 Black | 10,000.00 | 425.00 | 90.00 | 8.50 |

## 1954-1965. ROTARY PRESS COIL STAMPS PERF. 10 VERTICALLY OR HORIZONTALLY

| Scott No. | Fine Unused Line Pair | Ave. Unused Line Pair | Fine Unused Each | Ave. Unused Each | Fine Used Each | Ave. Used Each |
|---|---|---|---|---|---|---|
| ☐1054 1¢ Deep Green | | | | | | |
| | 1.10 | 1.00 | .28 | .24 | .21 | .16 |
| ☐1055 2¢ Rose Carmine | | | | | | |
| | .70 | .60 | .25 | .24 | .21 | .16 |
| ☐1056 2½¢ Gray Blue | | | | | | |
| | 4.00 | 3.00 | .32 | .24 | .21 | .18 |
| ☐1057 3¢ Deep Violet | | | | | | |
| | .70 | .65 | .25 | .24 | .21 | .16 |
| ☐1058 4¢ Red Violet | | | | | | |
| | .70 | .65 | .28 | .24 | .21 | .16 |
| ☐1059 4½¢ Green | | | | | | |
| | 16.00 | 12.00 | 1.60 | 1.45 | 1.25 | 1.00 |
| ☐1059A 25¢ Green | | | | | | |
| | 2.00 | 1.75 | .80 | .50 | .90 | .24 |

| Scott No. | Mint Sheet | Plate Block | Fine Unused Each | Fine Used Each |
|---|---|---|---|---|

## 1954. NEBRASKA TERRITORY

| | | | | |
|---|---|---|---|---|
| ☐1060 3¢ Violet | 5.75 | .70 | .21 | .16 |

## 1954. KANSAS TERRITORY

| | | | | |
|---|---|---|---|---|
| ☐1061 3¢ Brown Orange | 5.75 | .70 | .21 | .16 |

## 1954. GEORGE EASTMAN ISSUE

| | | | | |
|---|---|---|---|---|
| ☐1062 3¢ Violet Brown | 8.0 | .70 | .21 | .16 |

*No hinge pricing from 1941 to date is figured at (N-H ADD 15%)

| Scott No. | Mint Sheet | Plate Block | Fine Unused Each | Fine Used Each |
|---|---|---|---|---|
| **1954. LEWIS & CLARK EXPEDITION** | | | | |
| ☐1063 3¢ Dark Brown | 5.75 | .70 | .22 | .16 |
| **1955. COMMEMORATIVES** | | | | |
| **1955. PENNSYLVANIA ACADEMY OF FINE ARTS** | | | | |
| ☐1064 3¢ Rose Brown | 5.75 | .70 | .22 | .16 |
| **1955. LAND GRANT COLLEGES** | | | | |
| ☐1065 3¢ Green | 5.75 | .70 | .22 | .16 |
| **1955. ROTARY INTERNATIONAL ISSUE** | | | | |
| ☐1066 8¢ Deep Blue | 11.00 | 1.50 | .23 | .16 |
| **1955. ARMED FORCES RESERVE** | | | | |
| ☐1067 3¢ Red Violet | 5.75 | .70 | .22 | .16 |
| **1955. OLD MAN OF THE MOUNTAINS** | | | | |
| ☐1068 3¢ Blue Green | 7.00 | .70 | .22 | .16 |
| **1955. SOO LOCKS CENTENNIAL** | | | | |
| ☐1069 3¢ Blue | 5.75 | .70 | .22 | .16 |
| **1955. ATOMS FOR PEACE** | | | | |
| ☐1070 3¢ Blue | 5.75 | .70 | .22 | .16 |
| **1955. FORT TICONDEROGA BICENTENNIAL** | | | | |
| ☐1071 3¢ Sepia | 5.75 | .70 | .22 | .16 |
| **1955. ANDREW MELLON ISSUE** | | | | |
| ☐1072 3¢ Deep Carmine | 8.00 | .70 | .22 | .16 |
| **1956. COMMEMORATIVES** | | | | |
| **1956. 250TH ANNIVERSARY FRANKLIN'S BIRTH** | | | | |
| ☐1073 3¢ Rose Carmine | 6.00 | .70 | .22 | .16 |
| **1956. BOOKER T. WASHINGTON ISSUE** | | | | |
| ☐1074 3¢ Deep Blue | 5.75 | .70 | .22 | .16 |

*No hinge pricing from 1941 to date is figured at (N-H ADD 15%)

| Scott No. | Mint Sheet | Plate Block | Fine Unused Each | Fine Used Each |
|---|---|---|---|---|

### 1956. FIFTH INTL. PHILATELIC EXHIBITION DESIGNS OF 1035 & 1041 IN IMPERF. SOUVENIR SHEET

| | | | | |
|---|---|---|---|---|
| ☐1075 3¢ & 8¢ Sheet of 2 | — | — | 3.00 | 2.00 |

### 1956. FIFTH INTL. PHILATELIC EXHIBITION

| | | | | |
|---|---|---|---|---|
| ☐1076 3¢ Deep Violet | 5.75 | .70 | .22 | — |

### 1956. WILDLIFE CONSERVATION ISSUE

| | | | | |
|---|---|---|---|---|
| ☐1077 3¢ Rose Lake | 5.75 | .70 | .22 | .16 |
| ☐1078 3¢ Brown | 5.75 | .70 | .22 | .16 |
| ☐1079 3¢ Green | 5.75 | .70 | .22 | .16 |

### 1956. PURE FOOD & DRUG ACT

| | | | | |
|---|---|---|---|---|
| ☐1080 3¢ Dark Blue Green | 5.75 | .70 | .22 | .16 |

### 1956. HOME OF PRESIDENT BUCHANAN

| | | | | |
|---|---|---|---|---|
| ☐1081 3¢ Black Brown | 5.75 | .70 | .22 | .16 |

### 1956. LABOR DAY ISSUE

| | | | | |
|---|---|---|---|---|
| ☐1082 3¢ Deep Blue | 5.75 | .70 | .22 | .16 |

### 1956. NASSAU HALL—PRINCETON

| | | | | |
|---|---|---|---|---|
| ☐1083 3¢ Black on Orange | 5.75 | .70 | .22 | .16 |

### 1956. DEVIL'S TOWER

| | | | | |
|---|---|---|---|---|
| ☐1084 3¢ Purple | 5.75 | .70 | .22 | .16 |

### 1956. CHILDREN'S ISSUE

| | | | | |
|---|---|---|---|---|
| ☐1085 3¢ Dark Blue | 5.75 | .70 | .22 | .16 |

### 1957. COMMEMORATIVES
### 1957. ALEXANDER HAMILTON ISSUE

| | | | | |
|---|---|---|---|---|
| ☐1086 3¢ Rose Red | 5.75 | .70 | .22 | .16 |

### 1957. POLIO ISSUE

| | | | | |
|---|---|---|---|---|
| ☐1087 3¢ Light Purple | 5.75 | .70 | .22 | .16 |

*No hinge pricing from 1941 to date is figured at (N-H ADD 15%)

| Scott No. | Mint Sheet | Plate Block | Fine Unused Each | Fine Used Each |
|---|---|---|---|---|

### 1957. COAST & GEODETIC SURVEY
☐ 1088 3¢ Dark Blue     5.75     .70     .22     .16

### 1957. ARCHITECTS ISSUE
☐ 1089 3¢ Red Lilac     5.75     .70     .22     .16

### 1957. STEEL INDUSTRY CENTENNIAL
☐ 1090 3¢ Bright Ultra     5.75     .70     .22     .16

### 1957. INTERNATIONAL NAVAL REVIEW
☐ 1091 3¢ Blue Green     6.00     .70     .22     .16

### 1957. OKLAHOMA STATEHOOD
☐ 1092 3¢ Dark Blue     5.75     .70     .22     .16

### 1957. SCHOOL TEACHERS
☐ 1093 3¢ Rose Lake     5.75     .70     .22     .16

### 1957. U.S. FLAG ISSUE
☐ 1094 4¢ Blue & Red     6.50     .70     .22     .16

### 1957. 350TH SHIPBUILDING ANNIVERSARY
☐ 1095 3¢ Purple     8.00     .70     .22     .16

### 1957. PHILIPPINES—CHAMPION OF LIBERTY
☐ 1096 8¢ Red, Blue & Gold     10.00     1.10     .26     .16

### 1957. BIRTH OF LAFAYETTE
☐ 1097 3¢ Maroon     6.50     .70     .22     .16

### 1957. WILDLIFE CONSERVATION ISSUE
☐ 1098 3¢ Blue, Green & Yellow
    5.75     .70     .22     .16

### 1957. RELIGIOUS FREEDOM
☐ 1099 3¢ Black     5.75     .70     .22     .16

*No hinge pricing from 1941 to date is figured at (N-H ADD 15%)

| Scott No. | Mint Sheet | Plate Block | Fine Unused Each | Fine Used Each |
|---|---|---|---|---|

## 1958. COMMEMORATIVES

## 1958. GARDENING & HORTICULTURE

| ☐ 1100 3¢ Deep Green | 5.50 | .70 | .22 | .16 |
|---|---|---|---|---|

## 1958. BRUSSELS EXHIBITION

| ☐ 1104 3¢ Deep Claret | 5.50 | .70 | .22 | .16 |
|---|---|---|---|---|

## 1958. JAMES MONROE BICENTENNIAL

| ☐ 1105 3¢ Purple | 8.00 | .70 | .22 | .16 |
|---|---|---|---|---|

## 1958. MINNESOTA STATEHOOD

| ☐ 1106 3¢ Green | 5.75 | .70 | .22 | .16 |
|---|---|---|---|---|

## 1958. INTERNATIONAL GEOPHYSICAL YEAR

| ☐ 1107 3¢ Black & Orange | 5.75 | .70 | .22 | .16 |
|---|---|---|---|---|

## 1958. GUNSTON HALL BICENTENARY

| ☐ 1108 3¢ Light Green | 5.75 | .70 | .22 | .16 |
|---|---|---|---|---|

## 1958. MACKINAC BRIDGE ISSUE

| ☐ 1109 3¢ Bluish Green | 5.75 | .70 | .22 | .16 |
|---|---|---|---|---|

## 1958. SOUTH AMERICA—CHAMPION OF LIBERTY

| ☐ 1110 4¢ Olive Bistre | 8.00 | .70 | .22 | .16 |
|---|---|---|---|---|
| ☐ 1111 8¢ Red, Blue & Gold | 16.00 | 2.00 | .26 | .16 |

## 1958. ATLANTIC CABLE CENTENNIAL

| ☐ 1112 4¢ Reddish Purple | 6.50 | .60 | .22 | .16 |
|---|---|---|---|---|

## 1958-1959. LINCOLN COMMEMORATIVE ISSUE

| ☐ 1113 1¢ Green | 3.00 | .60 | .22 | .16 |
|---|---|---|---|---|
| ☐ 1114 3¢ Rust Brown | 6.00 | .70 | .22 | .16 |
| ☐ 1115 4¢ Sepia | 8.00 | .70 | .22 | .16 |
| ☐ 1116 4¢ Blue | 9.00 | .70 | .22 | .16 |

## 1958. HUNGARY—CHAMPION OF LIBERTY

| ☐ 1117 4¢ Bluish Green | 8.75 | .70 | .22 | .16 |
|---|---|---|---|---|
| ☐ 1118 8¢ Red, Blue & Gold | 18.00 | 1.75 | .26 | .16 |

*No hinge pricing from 1941 to date is figured at (N-H ADD 15%)

| Scott No. | Mint Sheet | Plate Block | Fine Unused Each | Fine Used Each |
|---|---|---|---|---|
| **1958. FREEDOM OF THE PRESS** | | | | |
| ☐1119 4¢ Black | 6.00 | .70 | .22 | .16 |
| **1958. OVERLAND MAIL CENTENNIAL** | | | | |
| ☐1120 4¢ Crimson Rose | 6.00 | .70 | .22 | .16 |
| **1958. NOAH WEBSTER** | | | | |
| ☐1121 4¢ Dark Carmine Rose | | | | |
| | 8.50 | .70 | .22 | .16 |
| **1958. FOREST CONSERVATION** | | | | |
| ☐1122 4¢ Yellow, Brown & Green | | | | |
| | 6.50 | .70 | .22 | .16 |
| **1958. FORT DUQUESNE BICENTENNIAL** | | | | |
| ☐1123 4¢ Blue | 6.50 | .70 | .22 | .16 |
| **1959. COMMEMORATIVES** | | | | |
| **1959. OREGON STATEHOOD** | | | | |
| ☐1124 4¢ Blue Green | 6.50 | .70 | .22 | .16 |
| **1959. ARGENTINA & CHILE—CHAMPION OF LIBERTY** | | | | |
| ☐1125 4¢ Blue | 8.50 | .70 | .22 | .16 |
| ☐1126 8¢ Red, Blue & Gold | 16.00 | 1.30 | .22 | .16 |
| **1959. 10TH ANNIVERSARY N.A.T.O.** | | | | |
| ☐1127 4¢ Blue | 8.50 | .70 | .22 | .16 |
| **1959. ARCTIC EXPLORATIONS** | | | | |
| ☐1128 4¢ Blue | 6.50 | .70 | .22 | .16 |
| **1959. WORLD PEACE & TRUST** | | | | |
| ☐1129 8¢ Maroon | 11.00 | 1.10 | .26 | .16 |
| **1959. SILVER DISCOVERY CENTENNIAL** | | | | |
| ☐1130 4¢ Black | 6.50 | .70 | .22 | .16 |

*No hinge pricing from 1941 to date is figured at (N-H ADD 15%)

| Scott No. | Mint Sheet | Plate Block | Fine Unused Each | Fine Used Each |
|---|---|---|---|---|

## 1959. ST. LAWRENCE SEAWAY ISSUE

| | | | | |
|---|---|---|---|---|
| ☐ 1131 4¢ Red & Blue | 6.50 | .70 | .22 | .16 |

## 1959. 49-STAR FLAG ISSUE

| | | | | |
|---|---|---|---|---|
| ☐ 1132 4¢ Blue, Red & Yellow | | | | |
| | 6.50 | .70 | .22 | .16 |

## 1959. SOIL CONSERVATION

| | | | | |
|---|---|---|---|---|
| ☐ 1133 4¢ Yellow, Green & Blue | | | | |
| | 6.50 | .70 | .22 | .16 |

## 1959. PETROLEUM INDUSTRY CENTENNIAL

| | | | | |
|---|---|---|---|---|
| ☐ 1134 4¢ Brown | 6.50 | .70 | .22 | .16 |

## 1959. DENTAL HEALTH ISSUE

| | | | | |
|---|---|---|---|---|
| ☐ 1135 4¢ Green | 10.50 | 1.00 | .22 | .16 |

## 1959. GERMANY—CHAMPION OF LIBERTY

| | | | | |
|---|---|---|---|---|
| ☐ 1136 4¢ Gray | 9.00 | .70 | .22 | .16 |
| ☐ 1137 8¢ Red, Blue & Gold | 16.00 | 1.25 | .26 | .16 |

## 1959. DR. EPHRAIM McDOWELL

| | | | | |
|---|---|---|---|---|
| ☐ 1138 4¢ Maroon | 8.50 | .70 | .22 | .16 |

## 1960-1961. CREDO OF AMERICA SERIES

| | | | | |
|---|---|---|---|---|
| ☐ 1139 4¢ Dark Violet, Blue & Carmine | | | | |
| | 6.50 | .70 | .22 | .16 |
| ☐ 1140 4¢ Olive Bistre & Green | | | | |
| | 6.50 | .70 | .22 | .16 |
| ☐ 1141 4¢ Gray & Red | 7.50 | .70 | .22 | .16 |
| ☐ 1142 4¢ Red & Blue | 7.50 | .70 | .22 | .16 |
| ☐ 1143 4¢ Violet & Green | 10.00 | .70 | .22 | .16 |
| ☐ 1144 4¢ Green & Brown | 11.00 | .70 | .22 | .16 |

## COMMEMORATIVES
## 1960. BOY SCOUTS GOLDEN JUBILEE

| | | | | |
|---|---|---|---|---|
| ☐ 1145 4¢ Red, Khaki & Blue | 6.50 | .72 | .22 | .16 |

*No hinge pricing from 1941 to date is figured at (N-H ADD 15%)

| Scott No. | Mint Sheet | Plate Block | Fine Unused Each | Fine Used Each |
|---|---|---|---|---|

**1960. WINTER OLYMPIC GAMES**

| ☐1146 4¢ Blue | 7.50 | .70 | .22 | .16 |

**1960. CZECHOSLOVAKIA—CHAMPION OF LIBERTY**

| ☐1147 4¢ Blue | 8.50 | .70 | .22 | .16 |
| ☐1148 8¢ Yellow, Blue & Red | | | | |
| | 15.00 | 1.60 | .26 | .16 |

**1960. WORLD REFUGEE YEAR**

| ☐1149 4¢ Gray Black | 6.50 | .70 | .22 | .16 |

**1960. WATER CONSERVATION**

| ☐1150 4¢ Blue, Green & Orange Brown | | | | |
| | 6.50 | .70 | .22 | .16 |

**1960. SOUTHEAST ASIA TREATY ORGANIZATION**

| ☐1151 4¢ Blue | 8.50 | .70 | .22 | .16 |

**1960. HONORING AMERICAN WOMEN**

| ☐1152 4¢ Violet | 6.50 | .70 | .22 | .16 |

**1960. 50-STAR FLAG ISSUE**

| ☐1153 4¢ Red & Blue | 6.50 | .70 | .22 | .16 |

**1960. PONY EXPRESS CENTENNIAL**

| ☐1154 4¢ Sepia | 6.50 | .70 | .22 | .16 |

**1960. EMPLOY THE HANDICAPPED**

| ☐1155 4¢ Blue | 6.50 | .70 | .22 | .16 |

**1960. WORLD FORESTRY CONGRESS**

| ☐1156 4¢ Green | 6.50 | .70 | .22 | .16 |

**1960. MEXICAN INDEPENDENCE SESQUICENTENNIAL**

| ☐1157 4¢ Red & Green | 6.50 | .70 | .22 | .16 |

**1960. UNITED STATES—JAPAN TREATY CENTENNIAL**

| ☐1158 4¢ Blue & Pink | 6.50 | .70 | .22 | .16 |

*No hinge pricing from 1941 to date is figured at (N-H ADD 15%)

| Scott No. | Mint Sheet | Plate Block | Fine Unused Each | Fine Used Each |
|---|---|---|---|---|

## 1960. POLAND—CHAMPION OF LIBERTY

| | | | | |
|---|---|---|---|---|
| ☐ 1159 4¢ Blue | 8.50 | .70 | .22 | .16 |
| ☐ 1160 8¢ Red, Blue & Gold | 15.00 | 1.60 | .26 | .16 |

## 1960. ROBERT A. TAFT MEMORIAL ISSUE

| | | | | |
|---|---|---|---|---|
| ☐ 1161 4¢ Dull Violet | 8.50 | .70 | .22 | .16 |

## 1960. WHEELS OF FREEDOM

| | | | | |
|---|---|---|---|---|
| ☐ 1162 4¢ Dark Blue | 6.50 | .70 | .22 | .16 |

## 1960. BOYS' CLUBS OF AMERICA

| | | | | |
|---|---|---|---|---|
| ☐ 1163 4¢ Indigo, Slate & Red | | | | |
| | 6.50 | .70 | .22 | .16 |

## 1960. FIRST AUTOMATED POST OFFICE

| | | | | |
|---|---|---|---|---|
| ☐ 1164 4¢ Dark Blue & Carmine | | | | |
| | 6.50 | .70 | .22 | .16 |

## 1960. FINLAND—CHAMPION OF LIBERTY

| | | | | |
|---|---|---|---|---|
| ☐ 1165 4¢ Blue | 8.50 | .70 | .22 | .16 |
| ☐ 1166 8¢ Red, Blue & Gold | 15.00 | 1.20 | .26 | .16 |

## 1960. CAMP FIRE GIRLS

| | | | | |
|---|---|---|---|---|
| ☐ 1167 4¢ Dark Blue & Red | 6.50 | .70 | .22 | .16 |

## 1960. ITALY—CHAMPION OF LIBERTY

| | | | | |
|---|---|---|---|---|
| ☐ 1168 4¢ Green | 8.75 | .70 | .22 | .16 |
| ☐ 1169 8¢ Red, Blue & Gold | 16.00 | 1.15 | .28 | .16 |

## 1960. WALTER F. GEORGE MEMORIAL ISSUE

| | | | | |
|---|---|---|---|---|
| ☐ 1170 4¢ Dull Violet | 8.50 | .70 | .22 | .16 |

## 1960. ANDREW CARNEGIE

| | | | | |
|---|---|---|---|---|
| ☐ 1171 4¢ Deep Claret | 8.50 | .70 | .22 | .16 |

## 1960. JOHN FOSTER DULLES MEMORIAL ISSUE

| | | | | |
|---|---|---|---|---|
| ☐ 1172 4¢ Dull Violet | 8.50 | .70 | .22 | .16 |

*No hinge pricing from 1941 to date is figured at (N-H ADD 15%)

| Scott No. | Mint Sheet | Plate Block | Fine Unused Each | Fine Used Each |
|---|---|---|---|---|

## 1960. "ECHO I" SATELLITE
| | | | | |
|---|---|---|---|---|
| ☐1173 4¢ Deep Violet | 11.00 | .95 | .28 | .16 |

## 1961. COMMEMORATIVES
## 1961. INDIA—CHAMPION OF LIBERTY
| | | | | |
|---|---|---|---|---|
| ☐1174 4¢ Red Orange | 8.50 | .70 | .22 | .16 |
| ☐1175 8¢ Red, Blue & Gold | 15.00 | 1.40 | .28 | .16 |

## 1961. RANGE CONSERVATION
| | | | | |
|---|---|---|---|---|
| ☐1176 4¢ Blue, Slate & Brown Orange | | | | |
| | 7.50 | .70 | .22 | .16 |

## 1961. HORACE GREELEY
| | | | | |
|---|---|---|---|---|
| ☐1177 4¢ Dull Violet | 8.50 | .70 | .22 | .16 |

## 1961-1965. CIVIL WAR CENTENNIAL SERIES
## 1961. FORT SUMTER
| | | | | |
|---|---|---|---|---|
| ☐1178 4¢ Light Green | 11.50 | 1.00 | .28 | .16 |

## 1962. BATTLE OF SHILOH
| | | | | |
|---|---|---|---|---|
| ☐1179 4¢ Black on Peach | 7.50 | .70 | .22 | .16 |

## 1963. BATTLE OF GETTYSBURG
| | | | | |
|---|---|---|---|---|
| ☐1180 5¢ Blue & Gray | 9.50 | .95 | .22 | .16 |

## 1964. BATTLE OF THE WILDERNESS
| | | | | |
|---|---|---|---|---|
| ☐1181 5¢ Dark Red & Black | 9.50 | .95 | .22 | .16 |

## 1965. APPOMATTOX
| | | | | |
|---|---|---|---|---|
| ☐1182 5¢ Black & Blue | 21.00 | 2.00 | .36 | .18 |

## 1961. KANSAS STATEHOOD
| | | | | |
|---|---|---|---|---|
| ☐1183 4¢ Brown, Dark Red & Green on Yellow Paper | | | | |
| | 6.75 | .70 | .22 | .16 |

## 1961. GEORGE W. NORRIS BIRTH CENTENARY
| | | | | |
|---|---|---|---|---|
| ☐1184 4¢ Blue Green | 6.50 | .70 | .22 | .16 |

*No hinge pricing from 1941 to date is figured at (N-H ADD 15%)

| Scott No. | Mint Sheet | Plate Block | Fine Unused Each | Fine Used Each |
|---|---|---|---|---|
| **1961. NAVAL AVIATION GOLDEN JUBILEE** | | | | |
| ☐1185 4¢ Blue | 7.00 | .70 | .22 | .16 |
| **1961. WORKMEN'S COMPENSATION LAW** | | | | |
| ☐1186 4¢ Ultramarine | 6.50 | .70 | .22 | .16 |
| **1961. F. REMINGTON BIRTH CENTENNIAL** | | | | |
| ☐1187 4¢ Blue, Red & Yellow | | | | |
| | 6.50 | .70 | .22 | .16 |
| **1961. REPUBLIC OF CHINA ISSUE** | | | | |
| ☐1188 4¢ Blue | 7.25 | .80 | .22 | .16 |
| **1961. DR. J. NAISMITH—BASKETBALL FOUNDER** | | | | |
| ☐1189 4¢ Brown | 8.00 | .70 | .22 | .16 |
| **1961. NURSING PROFESSION** | | | | |
| ☐1190 4¢ Blue, Red, Black & Green | | | | |
| | 10.00 | .70 | .22 | .16 |
| **1962. COMMEMORATIVES** | | | | |
| **1962. NEW MEXICO STATEHOOD** | | | | |
| ☐1191 4¢ Blue, Maroon, Bistre | | | | |
| | 6.50 | .70 | .22 | .16 |
| **1961. ARIZONA STATEHOOD** | | | | |
| ☐1192 4¢ Red, Deep Blue, Green | | | | |
| | 7.50 | .70 | .22 | .16 |
| **1962. PROJECT MERCURY** | | | | |
| ☐1193 4¢ Dark Blue & Yellow | | | | |
| | 7.50 | .70 | .22 | .16 |
| **1962. MALARIA ERADICATION** | | | | |
| ☐1194 4¢ Blue & Bistre | 6.50 | .70 | .22 | .16 |

*No hinge pricing from 1941 to date is figured at (N-H ADD 15%)

| Scott No. | Mint Sheet | Plate Block | Fine Unused Each | Fine Used Each |
|---|---|---|---|---|

## 1962. CHARLES EVANS HUGHES BIRTH CENTENNIAL

| | | | | |
|---|---|---|---|---|
| ☐1195 4¢ Black on Buff | 6.50 | .70 | .22 | .16 |

## 1962. SEATTLE WORLD'S FAIR

| | | | | |
|---|---|---|---|---|
| ☐1196 4¢ Red & Dark Blue | 6.50 | .70 | .22 | .16 |

## 1962. LOUISIANA STATEHOOD

| | | | | |
|---|---|---|---|---|
| ☐1197 4¢ Blue, Green, Red | 6.50 | .70 | .22 | .16 |

## 1962. THE HOMESTEAD ACT

| | | | | |
|---|---|---|---|---|
| ☐1198 4¢ Slate | 6.50 | .70 | .22 | .16 |

## 1962. GIRL SCOUTS 50TH ANNIVERSARY

| | | | | |
|---|---|---|---|---|
| ☐1199 4¢ Red | 7.00 | .70 | .22 | .16 |

## 1962. BRIEN MCMAHON MEMORIAL ISSUE

| | | | | |
|---|---|---|---|---|
| ☐1200 4¢ Purple | 6.50 | .70 | .22 | .16 |

## 1962. NATIONAL APPRENTICESHIP ACT

| | | | | |
|---|---|---|---|---|
| ☐1201 4¢ Black on Buff | 6.50 | .70 | .22 | .16 |

## 1962. SAM RAYBURN MEMORIAL ISSUE

| | | | | |
|---|---|---|---|---|
| ☐1202 4¢ Brown & Blue | 6.50 | .70 | .22 | .16 |

## 1962. DAG HAMMARSKJOLD MEMORIAL

| | | | | |
|---|---|---|---|---|
| ☐1203 4¢ Yellow, Brown & Black | 6.50 | .70 | .22 | .16 |
| ☐1204 4¢ Yellow Color Inverted | 7.50 | 1.60 | .24 | .16 |

## 1962. CHRISTMAS WREATH

| | | | | |
|---|---|---|---|---|
| ☐1205 4¢ Green & Red | 11.00 | .70 | .22 | .16 |

## 1962. HIGHER EDUCATION

| | | | | |
|---|---|---|---|---|
| ☐1206 4¢ Green & Black | 6.50 | .70 | .22 | .16 |

*No hinge pricing from 1941 to date is figured at (N-H ADD 15%)

| Scott No. | Mint Sheet | Plate block | Fine Unused Each | Fine Used Each |
|---|---|---|---|---|

## 1962. WINSLOW HOMER
☐1207 4¢ Brown & Blue — 7.00 — .70 — .22 — .16

## 1963. 50-STAR FLAG
☐1208 5¢ Red & Blue — 14.00 — .75 — .22 — .16

## 1962-1963. REGULAR ISSUE
☐1209 1¢ Green — 6.50 — .70 — .22 — .16
☐1213 5¢ Dark Blue Gray — 12.00 — .80 — .22 — .16

## 1962-1963. ROTARY PRESS COIL STAMPS PERF. 10 VERTICALLY

| Scott No. | Fine Unused Plate Blk | Ave. Unused Plate Blk | Fine Unused Each | Ave. Unused Each | Fine Used Each | Ave. Used Each |
|---|---|---|---|---|---|---|
| ☐1225 1¢ Green | | | | | | |
| | 2.60 | 2.10 | 1.45 | .28 | .22 | .16 |
| ☐1229 5¢ Dark Blue Gray | | | | | | |
| | 4.00 | 3.00 | 1.25 | 1.00 | .22 | .16 |

| Scott No. | Mint Sheet | Plate Block | Fine Unused Each | Fine Used Each |
|---|---|---|---|---|

## 1963. COMMEMORATIVES
## 1963. CAROLINA CHARTER TERCENTENARY
☐1230 5¢ Dark Carmine & Brown
— 7.50 — .70 — .22 — .16

## 1963. FOOD FOR PEACE—FREEDOM FROM HUNGER
☐1231 5¢ Green, Buff & Red
— 7.50 — .70 — .22 — .16

## 1963. WEST VIRGINIA STATEHOOD
☐1232 5¢ Green, Red & Black
— 7.50 — .70 — .22 — .16

*No hinge pricing from 1941 to date is figured at (N-H ADD 15%)

| Scott No. | Mint Sheet | Plate block | Fine Unused Each | Fine Used Each |
|---|---|---|---|---|

**1963. EMANCIPATION PROCLAMATION**

| ☐1233 5¢ Black, Blue & Red | 7.50 | .70 | .22 | .16 |

**1963. ALLIANCE FOR PROGRESS**

☐1234 5¢ Bright Blue & Green

| | 7.50 | .70 | .22 | .16 |

**1963. CORDELL HULL**

| ☐1235 5¢ Blue Green | 7.50 | .70 | .22 | .16 |

**1963. ELEANOR ROOSEVELT**

| ☐1236 5¢ Light Purple | 8.00 | .70 | .22 | .16 |

**1963. THE SCIENCES**

| ☐1237 5¢ Blue & Black | 7.25 | .70 | .22 | .16 |

**1963. CITY MAIL DELIVERY**

| ☐1238 5¢ Red, Blue & Gray | 7.25 | .70 | .22 | .16 |

**1963. INTERNATIONAL RED CROSS CENTENARY**

| ☐1239 5¢ Slate & Carmine | 7.00 | .70 | .22 | .16 |

**1963. CHRISTMAS ISSUE**

☐1240 5¢ Dark Blue, Blue Black & Red

| | 12.00 | .70 | .22 | .16 |

**1963. JOHN JAMES AUDUBON**

☐1241 5¢ Blue, Brown, Bistre

| | 8.50 | .80 | .22 | .16 |

**1964. COMMEMORATIVES**
**1964. SAM HOUSTON**

| ☐1242 5¢ Black | 8.50 | .80 | .22 | .16 |

**1964. CHARLES M. RUSSELL**

☐1243 5¢ Indigo, Red Brown & Olive

| | 8.50 | .80 | .22 | .16 |

*No hinge pricing from 1941 to date is figured at (N-H ADD 15%)

| Scott No. | Mint Sheet | Plate block | Fine Unused Each | Fine Used Each |
|---|---|---|---|---|

## 1964. NEW YORK WORLD'S FAIR
| | | | | |
|---|---|---|---|---|
| ☐1244 5¢ Green | 7.50 | .70 | .22 | .16 |

## 1964. JOHN MUIR—CONSERVATIONIST
| | | | | |
|---|---|---|---|---|
| ☐1245 5¢ Brown, Green & Olive | 7.50 | .70 | .22 | .16 |

## 1964. JOHN F. KENNEDY MEMORIAL
| | | | | |
|---|---|---|---|---|
| ☐1246 5¢ Blue Gray | 8.50 | .80 | .22 | .16 |

## 1964. NEW JERSEY TERCENTENARY
| | | | | |
|---|---|---|---|---|
| ☐1247 5¢ Ultramarine | 8.50 | .80 | .22 | .16 |

## 1964. NEVADA STATEHOOD
| | | | | |
|---|---|---|---|---|
| ☐1248 5¢ Red, Yellow & Blue | 7.50 | .70 | .22 | .16 |

## 1964. REGISTER AND VOTE
| | | | | |
|---|---|---|---|---|
| ☐1249 5¢ Dark Blue & Red | 7.50 | .70 | .22 | .16 |

## 1964. WILLIAM SHAKESPEARE
| | | | | |
|---|---|---|---|---|
| ☐1250 5¢ Brown on Tan | 7.50 | .70 | .22 | .16 |

## 1964. DOCTORS MAYO
| | | | | |
|---|---|---|---|---|
| ☐1251 5¢ Green | 10.00 | 1.20 | .22 | .16 |

## 1964. AMERICAN MUSIC
| | | | | |
|---|---|---|---|---|
| ☐1252 5¢ Red, Black & Blue | 7.50 | .70 | .22 | .16 |

## 1964. AMERICAN HOMEMAKERS
| | | | | |
|---|---|---|---|---|
| ☐1253 5¢ Multicolored | 7.50 | .70 | .22 | .16 |

## 1964. CHRISTMAS ISSUE
| | | | | |
|---|---|---|---|---|
| ☐1254 5¢ Red & Green | — | — | 1.35 | .16 |
| ☐1255 5¢ Red & Green | — | — | 1.35 | .16 |
| ☐1256 5¢ Red & Green | — | — | 1.00 | .16 |
| ☐1257 5¢ Red & Green | — | — | .22 | .16 |

*No hinge pricing from 1941 to date is figured at (N-H ADD 15%)

| Scott No. | Mint Sheet | Plate block | Fine Unused Each | Fine Used Each |
|---|---|---|---|---|

## 1964. VERRAZANO–NARROWS BRIDGE

| ☐ 1258 5¢ Green | 7.50 | .70 | .22 | .16 |

## 1964. STUART DAVIS—MODERN ART

☐ 1259 5¢ Ultramarine, Black & Red

|  | 7.50 | .70 | .22 | .16 |

## 1964. RADIO AMATEURS

| ☐ 1260 5¢ Red Lilac | 7.50 | .70 | .22 | .16 |

## 1964. COMMEMORATIVES
## 1965. BATTLE OF NEW ORLEANS

☐ 1261 5¢ Carmine, Blue & Gray

|  | 7.50 | .70 | .22 | .16 |

## 1965. PHYSICAL FITNESS—SOKOL CENTENNIAL

| ☐ 1262 5¢ Maroon & Black | 7.50 | .70 | .22 | .16 |

## 1965. CRUSADE AGAINST CANCER

☐ 1263 5¢ Black, Purple, Orange

|  | 7.50 | .70 | .22 | .16 |

## 1965. SIR WINSTON CHURCHILL MEMORIAL

| ☐ 1264 5¢ Black | 7.50 | .70 | .22 | .16 |

## 1965. MAGNA CARTA 750TH ANNIVERSARY

☐ 1265 5¢ Black, Ochre, Red Lilac

|  | 7.50 | .70 | .22 | .16 |

## 1965. INTERNATIONAL COOPERATION YEAR

| ☐ 1266 5¢ Dull Blue & Black | 7.50 | .70 | .22 | .16 |

## 1965. SALVATION ARMY

| ☐ 1267 5¢ Red, Black & Blue | 7.50 | .70 | .22 | .16 |

## 1965. DANTE ALIGHIERI

| ☐ 1268 5¢ Maroon on Tan | 7.50 | .70 | .22 | .16 |

*No hinge pricing from 1941 to date is figured at (N-H ADD 15%)

| Scott No. | Mint Sheet | Plate block | Fine Unused Each | Fine Used Each |
|---|---|---|---|---|

## 1965. HERBERT HOOVER

| ☐ 1269 5¢ Red Rose | 7.50 | .70 | .22 | .16 |
|---|---|---|---|---|

## 1965. ROBERT FULTON BIRTH BICENTENNIAL

| ☐ 1270 5¢ Black & Blue | 7.50 | .70 | .22 | .16 |
|---|---|---|---|---|

## 1965. FLORIDA SETTLEMENT QUADRICENTENNIAL

☐ 1271 5¢ Red, Yellow & Black

| | 7.50 | .70 | .22 | .16 |
|---|---|---|---|---|

## 1965. TRAFFIC SAFETY

| ☐ 1272 5¢ Green, Black, Red | 7.50 | .70 | .22 | .16 |
|---|---|---|---|---|

## 1965. JOHN SINGLETON COPLEY—ARTIST

☐ 1273 5¢ Black, Brown, Olive

| | 7.50 | .70 | .22 | .16 |
|---|---|---|---|---|

## 1965. INTERNATIONAL TELECOMMUNICATION UNION

☐ 1274 11¢ Black, Carmine, Bistre

| | 26.00 | 8.00 | .50 | .16 |
|---|---|---|---|---|

## 1965. ADLAI E. STEVENSON MEMORIAL

☐ 1275 5¢ Light & Dark Blue, Black & Red

| | 7.50 | .70 | .22 | .16 |
|---|---|---|---|---|

## 1965. CHRISTMAS ISSUE

☐ 1276 5¢ Red, Green & Yellow

| | 13.00 | .70 | .22 | .16 |
|---|---|---|---|---|

## 1965–1968. PROMINENT AMERICANS SERIES

| ☐ 1278 1¢ Green | 6.00 | .60 | .22 | .16 |
|---|---|---|---|---|
| ☐ 1279 1¼¢ Green | 20.00 | 12.00 | .22 | .16 |
| ☐ 1280 2¢ Slate Blue | 6.00 | .65 | .22 | .16 |
| ☐ 1281 3¢ Purple | 8.00 | .70 | .22 | .16 |
| ☐ 1282 4¢ Black | 11.00 | .70 | .22 | .16 |
| ☐ 1283 5¢ Blue | 13.00 | .70 | .22 | .16 |

*No hinge pricing from 1941 to date is figured at (N-H ADD 15%)

| Scott No. | Mint Sheet | Plate block | Fine Unused Each | Fine Used Each |
|---|---|---|---|---|
| ☐1283B 5¢ Blue | 12.00 | .85 | .22 | .16 |
| ☐1284 6¢ Gray Brown | 20.00 | .80 | .22 | .16 |
| ☐1285 8¢ Violet | 23.00 | 1.20 | .30 | .16 |
| ☐1286 10¢ Lilac | 26.00 | 1.40 | .28 | .16 |
| ☐1286A 12¢ Black | 32.00 | 1.50 | .31 | .16 |
| ☐1287 13¢ Brown | 40.00 | 2.00 | .45 | .16 |
| ☐1288 15¢ Rose Claret | 39.00 | 2.10 | .40 | .16 |
| ☐1288A 15¢ Rose Claret II | 34.00 | 4.50 | .36 | .16 |
| ☐1289 20¢ Olive Green | 55.00 | 2.60 | .65 | .16 |
| ☐1290 25¢ Rose Lake | 65.00 | 3.00 | .60 | .16 |
| ☐1291 30¢ Light Purple | 76.00 | 3.50 | .70 | .16 |
| ☐1292 40¢ Dark Blue | 92.00 | 4.90 | 1.00 | .16 |
| ☐1293 50¢ Maroon | 100.00 | 5.00 | 1.25 | .16 |
| ☐1294 $1 Purple | 160.00 | 11.00 | 2.25 | .16 |
| ☐1295 $5 Gray | 800.00 | 50.00 | 11.00 | 2.50 |

| Scott No. | Fine Unused Line Pair | Ave. Unused Line Pair | Fine Unused Each | Ave. Unused Each | Fine Used Each | Ave. Used Each |
|---|---|---|---|---|---|---|
| **PERF. 10 HORIZONTALLY** | | | | | | |
| ☐1297 3¢ Purple | | | | | | |
| | .75 | .65 | .24 | .22 | .21 | .16 |
| ☐1298 6¢ Gray Brown | | | | | | |
| | 1.60 | 1.45 | .24 | .22 | .21 | .16 |
| **PERF. 10 VERTICALLY** | | | | | | |
| ☐1299 1¢ Green | | | | | | |
| | .60 | .45 | .24 | .22 | .21 | .16 |
| ☐1303 4¢ Black | | | | | | |
| | .90 | .75 | .24 | .22 | .21 | .16 |
| ☐1304 5¢ Blue | | | | | | |
| | .70 | .60 | .24 | .22 | .21 | .16 |
| ☐1305 6¢ Gray Brown | | | | | | |
| | .85 | .80 | .24 | .22 | .21 | .16 |
| ☐1305C $1 Purple | | | | | | |
| | 6.00 | 4.50 | 2.00 | 1.90 | 1.75 | 1.10 |

*No hinge pricing from 1941 to date is figured at (N-H ADD 15%)

| Scott No. | Mint Sheet | Plate Block | Fine Unused Each | Fine Used Each |
|---|---|---|---|---|

## 1966. COMMEMORATIVES
## 1966. MIGRATORY BIRD TREATY
☐1306 5¢ Red, Blue, Black    7.50    .70    .20    .16

## 1966. HUMANE TREATMENT OF ANIMALS
☐1307 5¢ Orange Brown & Black
   7.50    .70    .20    .16

## 1966. INDIANA STATEHOOD
☐1308 5¢ Ochre, Brown & Violet Blue
   7.50    .70    .20    .16

## 1966. AMERICAN CIRCUS
☐1309 5¢ Red, Blue, Pink, Black
   8.00    .70    .22    .16

## 1966. SIXTH INTL. PHILATELIC EXHIBITION "SIPEX"
☐1310 5¢ Multicolored    7.50    .90    .22    .16

## 1966. IMPERFORATE SOUVENIR SHEET
☐1311 5¢ Multicolored    —    .70    .22    .16

## 1966. BILL OF RIGHTS
☐1312 5¢ Red, Dark & Light Blue
   8.50    .85    .22    .16

## 1966. POLISH MILLENNIUM
☐1313 5¢ Red    7.50    .70    .22    .16

## 1966. NATIONAL PARK SERVICE
☐1314 5¢ Yellow, Black & Green
   7.50    .70    .22    .16

## 1966. MARINE CORPS RESERVE
☐1315 5¢ Black, Red, Blue, Olive
   7.50    .70    .22    .16

*No hinge pricing from 1941 to date is figured at (N-H ADD 15%)

| Scott No. | Mint Sheet | Plate block | Fine Unused Each | Fine Used Each |
|---|---|---|---|---|

## 1966. GENERAL FEDERATION OF WOMEN'S CLUBS
☐1316 5¢ Blue, Pink, Black — 7.50 / .70 / .22 / .16

## 1966. AMERICAN FOLKLORE—JOHNNY APPLESEED
☐1317 5¢ Red, Black, Green — 7.50 / .70 / .22 / .16

## 1966. BEAUTIFICATION OF AMERICA
☐1318 5¢ Emerald, Pink, Black — 7.50 / .70 / .22 / .16

## 1966. GREAT RIVER ROAD
☐1319 5¢ Yellow, Red, Blue, Green — 7.50 / .70 / .22 / .16

## 1966. SERVICEMEN & SAVINGS BONDS
☐1320 5¢ Red, Light Blue, Dark Blue — 7.50 / .70 / .22 / .16

## 1966. CHRISTMAS ISSUE
☐1321 5¢ Multicolored — 13.00 / .70 / .22 / .16

## 1966. MARY CASSATT—ARTIST
☐1322 5¢ Multicolored — 9.00 / .90 / .22 / .16

## 1967. COMMEMORATIVES
## 1967. NATIONAL GRANGE CENTENARY
☐1323 5¢ Orange, Yellow, Black, Brown & Green — 8.50 / .80 / .22 / .16

## 1967. CANADA CENTENNIAL
☐1324 5¢ Green, Light & Dark Blue, Black — 7.50 / .70 / .22 / .16

## 1967. ERIE CANAL SESQUICENTENNIAL
☐1325 5¢ Light & Dark Blue, Red & Black — 7.50 / .70 / .22 / .16

*No hinge pricing from 1941 to date is figured at (N-H ADD 15%)

| Scott No. | Mint Sheet | Plate block | Fine Unused Each | Fine Used Each |
|---|---|---|---|---|

## 1967. SEARCH FOR PEACE—LIONS INTL.
☐ 1326 5¢ Red, Blue & Black   8.50   .80   .22   .16

## 1967. HENRY DAVID THOREAU
☐ 1327 5¢ Black, Red & Green

8.00   .80   .22   .16

## 1967. NEBRASKA STATEHOOD CENTENNIAL
☐ 1328 5¢ Yellow Green & Brown

8.00   .85   .22   .16

## 1967. VOICE OF AMERICA
☐ 1329 5¢ Red, Blue & Black   8.00   .70   .22   .16

## 1967. AMERICAN FOLKLORE—DAVY CROCKETT
☐ 1330 5¢ Green & Black   8.00   .70   .22   .16

## 1967. SPACE ACCOMPLISHMENTS
☐ 1331 5¢ Light & Dark Blue, Red, Black

—   .80   1.00   .30

☐ 1332 5¢ Light & Dark Blue, Red, Black

—   .80   1.00   .30

## 1967. URBAN PLANNING
☐ 1333 5¢ Blue & Black   8.00   .80   .22   .16

## 1967. FINNISH INDEPENDENCE
☐ 1334 5¢ Blue   8.00   .80   .22   .16

## 1967. THOMAS EAKINS—ARTIST
☐ 1335 5¢ Gold & Multicolored

8.00   .80   .22   .16

## 1967. CHRISTMAS ISSUE
☐ 1336 5¢ Multicolored   7.50   .70   .22   .16

## 1967. MISSISSIPPI STATEHOOD
☐ 1337 5¢ Multicolored   9.00   .90   .22   .16

*No hinge pricing from 1941 to date is figured at (N-H ADD 15%)

| Scott No. | Mint Sheet | Plate block | Fine Unused Each | Fine Used Each |
|---|---|---|---|---|
| **1968–1971. REGULAR ISSUES** | | | | |
| **1968. FLAG ISSUE** | | | | |
| ☐ 1338 6¢ Red, Blue, Green | 15.00 | .80 | .22 | .16 |
| **1968. COMMEMORATIVES** | | | | |
| **1968. ILLINOIS STATEHOOD** | | | | |
| ☐ 1339 6¢ Black, Gold, Pink | 8.50 | .80 | .22 | .16 |
| **1968. HEMISFAIR '68** | | | | |
| ☐ 1340 6¢ Indigo, Carmine, White | | | | |
| | 8.50 | .80 | .22 | .16 |
| **1968. AIRLIFT TO SERVICEMEN** | | | | |
| ☐ 1341 $1 Multicolored | 140.00 | 10.00 | 4.00 | 2.00 |
| **1968. SUPPORT OUR YOUTH (ELKS)** | | | | |
| ☐ 1342 6¢ Blue & Black | 8.00 | .80 | .22 | .16 |
| **1968. LAW AND ORDER** | | | | |
| ☐ 1343 6¢ Blue & Black | 10.00 | 1.00 | .22 | .16 |
| **1968. REGISTER & VOTE** | | | | |
| ☐ 1344 6¢ Black & Gold | 8.50 | .80 | .22 | .16 |
| **1968. HISTORIC AMERICAN FLAGS** | | | | |
| ☐ 1345 6¢ Dark Blue | — | — | .50 | .40 |
| ☐ 1346 6¢ Red & Dark Blue | — | — | .45 | .40 |
| ☐ 1347 6¢ Dark, Blue, Olive Green | | | | |
| | — | — | .35 | .25 |
| ☐ 1348 6¢ Dark Blue & Red | — | — | .35 | .25 |
| ☐ 1349 6¢ Black, Yellow, Red | | | | |
| | — | — | .35 | .25 |
| ☐ 1350 6¢ Dark Blue & Red | — | — | .35 | .25 |
| ☐ 1351 6¢ Blue, Olive Green, Red | | | | |
| | — | — | .35 | .25 |
| ☐ 1352 6¢ Dark Blue & Red | — | — | .35 | .25 |
| ☐ 1353 6¢ Blue, Yellow, Red | — | — | .35 | .25 |
| ☐ 1354 6¢ Blue Red, Yellow | — | — | .35 | .25 |

*No hinge pricing from 1941 to date is figured at (N-H ADD 15%)

| Scott No. | Mint Sheet | Plate block | Fine Unused Each | Fine Used Each |
|---|---|---|---|---|
| **1968. WALT DISNEY** | | | | |
| ☐1355 6¢ Multicolored | 24.00 | 2.40 | .60 | .16 |
| **1968. FATHER MARQUETTE—EXPLORATIONS** | | | | |
| ☐1356 6¢ Black, Brown, Green | | | | |
| | 10.00 | 1.00 | .22 | .16 |
| **1968. AMERICAN FOLKLORE—DANIEL BOONE** | | | | |
| ☐1357 6¢ Brown, Yellow, Black, Red | | | | |
| | 8.50 | .80 | .22 | .16 |
| **1968. ARKANSAS RIVER NAVIGATION** | | | | |
| ☐1358 6¢ Black & Blue | 8.50 | .80 | .21 | .16 |
| **1968. LEIF ERIKSON** | | | | |
| ☐1359 6¢ Dark Brown on Brown | | | | |
| | 8.50 | .80 | .22 | .16 |
| **1968. CHEROKEE STRIP LAND RUSH** | | | | |
| ☐1360 6¢ Brown | 11.00 | .90 | .24 | .16 |
| **1968. JOHN TRUMBULL PAINTING** | | | | |
| ☐1361 6¢ Yellow Red, Black | 10.00 | 1.10 | .24 | .16 |
| **1968. WILDLIFE CONSERVATION—DUCKS** | | | | |
| ☐1362 6¢ Multicolored | 11.00 | 1.15 | .24 | .16 |
| **1968. CHRISTMAS ISSUE** | | | | |
| ☐1363 6¢ Multicolored | 8.00 | 1.75 | .22 | .16 |
| **1968. AMERICAN INDIAN** | | | | |
| ☐1364 6¢ Multicolored | 11.00 | 1.15 | .24 | .16 |
| **1969. COMMEMORATIVES** | | | | |
| **1969. BEAUTIFICATION OF AMERICA** | | | | |
| ☐1365 6¢ Multicolored | — | — | .70 | .18 |
| ☐1366 6¢ Multicolored | — | — | .70 | .18 |

*No hinge pricing from 1941 to date is figured at (N-H ADD 15%)

| Scott No. | Mint Sheet | Plate block | Fine Unused Each | Fine Used Each |
|---|---|---|---|---|
| ☐1367 6¢ Multicolored | — | — | .70 | .18 |
| ☐1368 6¢ Multicolored | — | — | .70 | .18 |

## 1969. AMERICAN LEGION

| | | | | |
|---|---|---|---|---|
| ☐1369 6¢ Red, Blue, Black | 7.50 | .80 | .22 | .16 |

## 1969. GRANDMA MOSES PAINTING

| | | | | |
|---|---|---|---|---|
| ☐1370 6¢ Multicolored | 7.50 | .90 | .22 | .16 |

## 1969. APOLLO 8 MOON ORBIT

| | | | | |
|---|---|---|---|---|
| ☐1371 6¢ Black, Blue, Ochre | 11.50 | 1.15 | .22 | .16 |

## 1969. W. C. HANDY—MUSICIAN

| | | | | |
|---|---|---|---|---|
| ☐1372 6¢ Multicolored | 10.00 | 1.00 | .22 | .16 |

## 1969. SETTLEMENT OF CALIFORNIA

| | | | | |
|---|---|---|---|---|
| ☐1373 6¢ Multicolored | 8.00 | .70 | .22 | .16 |

## 1969. MAJOR JOHN WESLEY POWELL—GEOLOGIST

| | | | | |
|---|---|---|---|---|
| ☐1374 6¢ Multicolored | 8.50 | .80 | .22 | .16 |

## 1969. ALABAMA STATEHOOD

| | | | | |
|---|---|---|---|---|
| ☐1375 6¢ Red, Yellow, Brown | 8.50 | .80 | .22 | .16 |

## 1969. XI INTL. BOTANICAL CONGRESS

| | | | | |
|---|---|---|---|---|
| ☐1376 6¢ Multicolored | — | — | 1.60 | .35 |
| ☐1377 6¢ Multicolored | — | — | 1.60 | .35 |
| ☐1378 6¢ Multicolored | — | — | 1.60 | .35 |
| ☐1379 6¢ Multicolored | — | — | 1.60 | .35 |

## 1969. DARTMOUTH COLLEGE CASE

| | | | | |
|---|---|---|---|---|
| ☐1380 6¢ Green | 9.00 | 1.00 | .22 | .16 |

## 1969. PROFESSIONAL BASEBALL CENTENARY

| | | | | |
|---|---|---|---|---|
| ☐1381 6¢ Multicolored | 41.00 | 4.70 | .90 | .16 |

*No hinge pricing from 1941 to date is figured at (N-H ADD 15%)

| Scott No. | Mint Sheet | Plate block | Fine Unused Each | Fine Used Each |
|---|---|---|---|---|

## 1969. INTERCOLLEGIATE FOOTBALL CENTENARY

| ☐1382 6¢ Red & Green | 13.00 | 1.50 | .40 | .16 |

## 1969. DWIGHT D. EISENHOWER MEMORIAL

| ☐1383 6¢ Blue, Black & Red | 6.00 | .80 | .22 | .16 |

## 1969. CHRISTMAS ISSUE

| ☐1384 6¢ Multicolored | 8.50 | 1.90 | .22 | .16 |

## 1969. HOPE FOR THE CRIPPLED

| ☐1385 6¢ Multicolored | 8.50 | .90 | .22 | .16 |

## 1969. WILLIAM M. HARNETT PAINTING

| ☐1386 6¢ Multicolored | 6.00 | .90 | .22 | .16 |

## 1970. COMMEMORATIVES
## 1970. NATURAL HISTORY

| ☐1387 6¢ Multicolored | — | — | .30 | .16 |
| ☐1388 6¢ Multicolored | — | — | .30 | .16 |
| ☐1389 6¢ Multicolored | — | — | .30 | .16 |
| ☐1390 6¢ Multicolored | — | — | .30 | .16 |

## 1970. MAINE STATEHOOD SESQUICENTENNIAL

| ☐1391 6¢ Multicolored | 8.50 | .85 | .22 | 16 |

## 1970. WILDLIFE CONSERVATION—BUFFALO

| ☐1392 6¢ Black on Tan | 8.50 | .85 | .22 | .16 |

## 1970–1974. REGULAR ISSUE

| ☐1393 6¢ Blue Gray | 16.00 | .85 | .22 | .16 |
| ☐1393D 7¢ Light Blue | 18.00 | 1.20 | .22 | .16 |
| ☐1394 8¢ Black, Blue, Red | 20.00 | 1.00 | .25 | .16 |
| ☐1395 8¢ Rose Violet | — | — | .25 | .16 |
| ☐1396 8¢ Multicolored | 20.00 | 4.00 | .26 | .16 |
| ☐1397 14¢ Brown | 40.00 | 1.50 | .36 | .16 |
| ☐1398 16¢ Orange Brown | 40.00 | 1.80 | .40 | .16 |
| ☐1399 18¢ Purple | 46.50 | 2.10 | .50 | .16 |

*No hinge pricing from 1941 to date is figured at (N-H ADD 15%)

| Scott No. | Mint Sheet | Plate block | Fine Unused Each | Fine Used Each |
|---|---|---|---|---|
| ☐1400 21¢ Green | 50.00 | 2.15 | .50 | .35 |

| Scott No. | Fine Unused Line Pair | Ave. Unused Line Pair | Fine Unused Each | Ave. Unused Each | Fine Used Each | Ave. Used Each |
|---|---|---|---|---|---|---|

## 1970–1971. ROTARY PRESS COIL STAMPS— PERF. 10 VERTICALLY

| Scott No. | Fine Unused Line Pair | Ave. Unused Line Pair | Fine Unused Each | Ave. Unused Each | Fine Used Each | Ave. Used Each |
|---|---|---|---|---|---|---|
| ☐1401 6¢ Blue Gray | .70 | .60 | .24 | .22 | .21 | .16 |
| ☐1402 8¢ Rose Violet | .70 | .60 | .24 | .22 | .21 | .16 |

| Scott No. | Mint Sheet | Plate Block | Fine Unused Each | Fine Used Each |
|---|---|---|---|---|

## 1970. EDGAR LEE MASTERS—POET

| | Mint Sheet | Plate Block | Fine Unused Each | Fine Used Each |
|---|---|---|---|---|
| ☐1405 6¢ Black & Olive Bistre | 8.50 | .80 | .22 | .16 |

## 1970. 50TH ANNIVERSARY WOMEN'S SUFFRAGE

| | Mint Sheet | Plate Block | Fine Unused Each | Fine Used Each |
|---|---|---|---|---|
| ☐1406 6¢ Blue | 8.50 | .80 | .22 | .16 |

## 1970. SOUTH CAROLINA TERCENTENARY

| | Mint Sheet | Plate Block | Fine Unused Each | Fine Used Each |
|---|---|---|---|---|
| ☐1407 6¢ Multicolored | 8.50 | .80 | .22 | .16 |

## 1970. STONE MOUNTAIN MEMORIAL

| | Mint Sheet | Plate Block | Fine Unused Each | Fine Used Each |
|---|---|---|---|---|
| ☐1408 6¢ Gray Black | 8.50 | .80 | .22 | .16 |

## 1970. FORT SNELLING

| | Mint Sheet | Plate Block | Fine Unused Each | Fine Used Each |
|---|---|---|---|---|
| ☐1409 6¢ Multicolored | 8.50 | .80 | .22 | .16 |

## 1970. ANTI-POLLUTION

| | Mint Sheet | Plate Block | Fine Unused Each | Fine Used Each |
|---|---|---|---|---|
| ☐1410 6¢ Multicolored | — | — | .35 | .16 |
| ☐1411 6¢ Multicolored | — | — | .35 | .16 |
| ☐1412 6¢ Multicolored | — | — | .35 | .16 |
| ☐1413 6¢ Multicolored | — | — | .35 | .16 |

| Scott No. | Mint Sheet | Plate block | Fine Unused Each | Fine Used Each |
|---|---|---|---|---|
| **1970. CHRISTMAS ISSUE** | | | | |
| ☐ 1414 6¢ Multicolored | 8.50 | 1.75 | .26 | .16 |
| ☐ 1415 6¢ Multicolored | — | — | .46 | .16 |
| ☐ 1416 6¢ Multicolored | — | — | .46 | .16 |
| ☐ 1417 6¢ Multicolored | — | — | .46 | .16 |
| ☐ 1418 6¢ Multicolored | — | — | .46 | .16 |
| **1970. PRECANCELLED CHRISTMAS ISSUE** | | | | |
| ☐ 1414a 6¢ Multicolored | 8.50 | 3.00 | .40 | .16 |
| ☐ 1415a 6¢ Multicolored | — | — | .90 | .16 |
| ☐ 1416a 6¢ Multicolored | — | — | .90 | .16 |
| ☐ 1417a 6¢ Multicolored | — | — | .90 | .16 |
| ☐ 1418a 6¢ Multicolored | — | — | .90 | .16 |
| **1970. UNITED NATIONS 25TH ANNIVERSARY** | | | | |
| ☐ 1419 6¢ Black, Red, Blue | 8.50 | .80 | .22 | .16 |
| **1970. PILGRIM LANDING 350TH ANNIVERSARY** | | | | |
| ☐ 1420 6¢ Multicolored | 8.50 | .80 | .22 | .16 |
| **1970. DISABLED AMERICAN VETERANS AND SERVICEMEN ISSUE** | | | | |
| ☐ 1421 6¢ Blue, Black, Red | — | — | .28 | .16 |
| ☐ 1422 6¢ Blue, Black, Red | — | — | .28 | .16 |
| **1971. COMMEMORATIVES** | | | | |
| **1971. ADVENT OF SHEEP TO AMERICA** | | | | |
| ☐ 1423 6¢ Multicolored | 8.50 | .80 | .22 | .16 |
| **1971. GENERAL DOUGLAS MacARTHUR** | | | | |
| ☐ 1424 6¢ Red, Blue, Black | 8.50 | .80 | .22 | .16 |
| **1971. BLOOD DONORS PROGRAM** | | | | |
| ☐ 1425 6¢ Light Blue, Scarlet, Indigo | | | | |
| | 8.50 | .80 | .22 | .16 |
| **1971. MISSOURI STATEHOOD** | | | | |
| ☐ 1426 8¢ Multicolored | 10.00 | 3.00 | .26 | .18 |

*No hinge pricing from 1941 to date is figured at (N-H ADD 15%)

| Scott No. | Mint Sheet | Plate Block | Fine Unused Each | Fine Used Each |
|---|---|---|---|---|

## 1971. WILDLIFE CONSERVATION

| Scott No. | Mint Sheet | Plate Block | Fine Unused Each | Fine Used Each |
|---|---|---|---|---|
| ☐1427 8¢ Multicolored | — | — | .26 | .16 |
| ☐1428 8¢ Multicolored | — | — | .26 | .16 |
| ☐1429 8¢ Multicolored | — | — | .26 | .16 |
| ☐1430 8¢ Multicolored | — | — | .26 | .16 |

## 1971. ANTARCTIC TREATY

| ☐1431 8¢ Red & Blue | 10.00 | 1.10 | .24 | .16 |
|---|---|---|---|---|

## 1971. AMERICAN REVOLUTION BICENTENNIAL

| ☐1432 8¢ Red, Blue, Black | 11.00 | 1.25 | .24 | .16 |
|---|---|---|---|---|

## 1971. JOHN SLOAN PAINTING

| ☐1433 8¢ Multicolored | 11.00 | 1.10 | .24 | .16 |
|---|---|---|---|---|

## 1971. DECADE OF SPACE ACHIEVEMENTS

| ☐1434 8¢ Multicolored | — | — | .26 | .16 |
|---|---|---|---|---|
| ☐1435 8¢ Multicolored | — | — | .26 | .16 |

## 1971. EMILY DICKINSON—POET

| ☐1436 8¢ Multicolored | 11.00 | 1.00 | .26 | .16 |
|---|---|---|---|---|

## 1971. SAN JUAN 450TH ANNIVERSARY

| ☐1437 8¢ Brown, Carmine, Blk. | | | | |
|---|---|---|---|---|
| | 11.00 | 1.00 | .26 | .16 |

## 1971. DRUG ADDICTION

| ☐1438 8¢ Blue & Black | 11.00 | 1.50 | .26 | .16 |
|---|---|---|---|---|

## 1971. CARE ANNIVERSARY

| ☐1439 8¢ Multicolored | 11.00 | 2.00 | .26 | .16 |
|---|---|---|---|---|

## 1971. HISTORIC PRESERVATION

| ☐1440 8¢ Dark Brown & Ochre | | | | |
|---|---|---|---|---|
| | — | — | .26 | 16 |
| ☐1441 8¢ Dark Brown & Ochre | | | | |
| | — | — | .26 | .16 |

*No hinge pricing from 1941 to date is figured at (N-H ADD 15%)

| Scott No. | Mint Sheet | Plate Block | Fine Unused Each | Fine Used Each |
|---|---|---|---|---|
| ☐1442 8¢ Dark Brown & Ochre | — | — | .26 | .16 |
| ☐1443 8¢ Dark Brown & Ochre | — | — | .26 | .16 |

## 1971. CHRISTMAS
| | | | | |
|---|---|---|---|---|
| ☐1444 8¢ Multicolored | 11.00 | 3.00 | .22 | .16 |
| ☐1445 8¢ Multicolored | 11.00 | 3.00 | .22 | .16 |

## 1972. COMMEMORATIVES
## 1972. SIDNEY LANIER—POET
| | | | | |
|---|---|---|---|---|
| ☐1446 8¢ Multicolored | 11.00 | 1.15 | .26 | .16 |

## 1972. PEACE CORPS
| | | | | |
|---|---|---|---|---|
| ☐1447 8¢ Red & Blue | 11.00 | 1.50 | .26 | .16 |

## 1972. NATIONAL PARKS CENTENNIAL
| | | | | |
|---|---|---|---|---|
| ☐1448 2¢ Multicolored | — | — | .22 | .16 |
| ☐1449 2¢ Multicolored | — | — | .22 | .16 |
| ☐1450 2¢ Multicolored | — | — | .22 | .16 |
| ☐1451 2¢ Multicolored | — | — | .22 | .16 |
| ☐1452 6¢ Multicolored | 8.50 | .80 | .22 | .16 |
| ☐1453 8¢ Multicolored | 7.50 | 1.00 | .26 | .16 |
| ☐1454 15¢ Multicolored | 20.00 | 2.00 | .40 | .35 |

## 1972. FAMILY PLANNING
| | | | | |
|---|---|---|---|---|
| ☐1455 8¢ Multicolored | 11.00 | 1.10 | .22 | .16 |

## 1972. AMERICAN REVOLUTION BICENTENNIAL—COLONIAL CRAFTSMEN
| | | | | |
|---|---|---|---|---|
| ☐1456 8¢ Deep Brown, Yellow | — | — | .26 | .16 |
| ☐1457 8¢ Deep Brown, Yellow | — | — | .26 | .16 |
| ☐1458 8¢ Deep Brown, Yellow | — | — | .26 | .16 |
| ☐1459 8¢ Deep Brown, Yellow | — | — | .26 | .16 |

| Scott No. | Mint Sheet | Plate Block | Fine Unused Each | Fine Used Each |
|---|---|---|---|---|

## 1972. OLYMPIC GAMES

| | Mint Sheet | Plate Block | Fine Unused Each | Fine Used Each |
|---|---|---|---|---|
| ☐1460 6¢ Multicolored | 10.00 | 2.00 | .22 | .16 |
| ☐1461 8¢ Multicolored | 10.00 | 2.60 | .22 | .16 |
| ☐1462 15¢ Multicolored | 17.00 | 4.50 | .40 | .35 |

## 1972. PARENT TEACHER ASSOCIATION

| | | | | |
|---|---|---|---|---|
| ☐1463 8¢ Black & Yellow | 10.00 | 1.00 | .22 | .16 |
| ☐1463a 8¢ Black & Yellow, Reversed Pl. No. | | | | |
| | — | 1.10 | — | — |

## 1972. WILDLIFE CONSERVATION

| | | | | |
|---|---|---|---|---|
| ☐1464 8¢ Multicolored | — | — | .26 | .16 |
| ☐1465 8¢ Multicolored | — | — | .26 | .16 |
| ☐1466 8¢ Multicolored | — | — | .26 | .16 |
| ☐1467 8¢ Multicolored | — | — | .26 | .16 |

## 1972. MAIL ORDER BUSINESS

| | | | | |
|---|---|---|---|---|
| ☐1468 8¢ Multicolored | 11.00 | 3.00 | .26 | .16 |

## 1972. OSTEOPATHIC MEDICINE

| | | | | |
|---|---|---|---|---|
| ☐1469 8¢ Yellow Orange, Brown | | | | |
| | 11.00 | 1.50 | .26 | .16 |

## 1972. TOM SAWYER—AMERICAN FOLKLORE

| | | | | |
|---|---|---|---|---|
| ☐1470 8¢ Multicolored | 11.00 | 1.10 | .26 | .16 |

## 1972. CHRISTMAS

| | | | | |
|---|---|---|---|---|
| ☐1471 8¢ Multicolored | 11.00 | 3.00 | .26 | .16 |
| ☐1472 8¢ Multicolored | 11.00 | 3.00 | .26 | .16 |

## 1972. PHARMACY

| | | | | |
|---|---|---|---|---|
| ☐1473 8¢ Multicolored | 12.00 | 1.30 | .26 | .16 |

## 1972. STAMP COLLECTING

| | | | | |
|---|---|---|---|---|
| ☐1474 8¢ Multicolored | 8.50 | 1.10 | .26 | .16 |

*No hinge pricing from 1941 to date is figured at (N-H ADD 15%)

| Scott No. | Mint Sheet | Plate Block | Fine Unused Each | Fine Used Each |
|---|---|---|---|---|

## 1973. COMMEMORATIVES
## 1973. LOVE—"FOR SOMEONE SPECIAL"

| | | | | |
|---|---|---|---|---|
| ☐1475 8¢ Red, Green, Blue | 11.00 | 1.40 | .26 | .16 |

## 1973. COLONIAL COMMUNICATIONS

| | | | | |
|---|---|---|---|---|
| ☐1476 8¢ Black, Red, Blue | 11.00 | 1.10 | .27 | .16 |
| ☐1477 8¢ Blue, Red, Brown | 11.00 | 1.10 | .27 | .16 |
| ☐1478 8¢ Multicolored | 11.00 | 1.10 | .27 | .16 |
| ☐1479 8¢ Multicolored | 11.00 | 1.10 | .27 | .16 |

## 1973. BOSTON TEA PARTY

| | | | | |
|---|---|---|---|---|
| ☐1480 8¢ Multicolored | — | — | .26 | .16 |
| ☐1481 8¢ Multicolored | — | — | .26 | .16 |
| ☐1482 8¢ Multicolored | — | — | .26 | .16 |
| ☐1483 8¢ Multicolored | — | — | .26 | .16 |

## 1973. GEORGE GERSHWIN—COMPOSER

| | | | | |
|---|---|---|---|---|
| ☐1484 8¢ Multicolored | 10.00 | 3.50 | .26 | .16 |

## 1973. ROBINSON JEFFERS—POET

| | | | | |
|---|---|---|---|---|
| ☐1485 8¢ Multicolored | 8.50 | 3.00 | .26 | .16 |

## 1973. HENRY OSSAWA TANNER—ARTIST

| | | | | |
|---|---|---|---|---|
| ☐1486 6¢ Multicolored | 8.50 | 3.00 | .26 | .16 |

## 1973. WILLA CATHER—NOVELIST

| | | | | |
|---|---|---|---|---|
| ☐1487 8¢ Multicolored | 8.50 | 3.00 | .26 | .16 |

## 1973. NICOLAUS COPERNICUS

| | | | | |
|---|---|---|---|---|
| ☐1488 8¢ Black & Orange | 11.00 | 1.00 | .26 | .16 |

## 1973. POSTAL PEOPLE

| | | | | |
|---|---|---|---|---|
| ☐1489 8¢ Multicolored | — | — | .26 | .16 |
| ☐1490 8¢ Multicolored | — | — | .26 | .16 |
| ☐1491 8¢ Multicolored | — | — | .26 | .16 |
| ☐1492 8¢ Multicolored | — | — | .26 | .16 |
| ☐1493 8¢ Multicolored | — | — | .26 | .16 |
| ☐1494 8¢ Multicolored | — | — | .26 | .16 |

*No hinge pricing from 1941 to date is figured at (N-H ADD 15%)

| Scott No. | Mint Sheet | Plate Block | Fine Unused Each | Fine Used Each |
|---|---|---|---|---|
| ☐1495 8¢ Multicolored | — | — | .26 | .16 |
| ☐1496 8¢ Multicolored | — | — | .26 | .16 |
| ☐1497 8¢ Multicolored | — | — | .26 | .16 |
| ☐1498 8¢ Multicolored | — | — | .26 | .16 |

## 1973. HARRY S. TRUMAN MEMORIAL

| | | | | |
|---|---|---|---|---|
| ☐1499 8¢ Black, Red, Blue | 7.00 | 1.00 | .26 | .16 |

## 1973. PROGRESS IN ELECTRONICS

| | | | | |
|---|---|---|---|---|
| ☐1500 6¢ Multicolored | 8.50 | .95 | .26 | .16 |
| ☐1501 8¢ Multicolored | 11.00 | 1.00 | .26 | .16 |
| ☐1502 15¢ Multicolored | 21.00 | 1.65 | .40 | .24 |

## 1973. LYNDON B. JOHNSON MEMORIAL

| | | | | |
|---|---|---|---|---|
| ☐1503 8¢ Multicolored | 8.50 | 3.00 | .26 | .24 |

## 1973. ANGUS CATTLE—RURAL AMERICA

| | | | | |
|---|---|---|---|---|
| ☐1504 8¢ Multicolored | 10.00 | 1.00 | .26 | .24 |

## 1974. CHAUTAUQUA—RURAL AMERICA

| | | | | |
|---|---|---|---|---|
| ☐1505 10¢ Multicolored | 12.00 | 1.20 | .29 | .24 |

## 1974. WINTER WHEAT—RURAL AMERICA

| | | | | |
|---|---|---|---|---|
| ☐1506 10¢ Multicolored | 12.00 | 1.20 | .20 | .24 |

## 1973. CHRISTMAS

| | | | | |
|---|---|---|---|---|
| ☐1507 8¢ Multicolored | 11.00 | 3.00 | .26 | .24 |
| ☐1508 8¢ Multicolored | 11.00 | 3.00 | .26 | .24 |

## 1973–1974. REGULAR ISSUES

| | | | | |
|---|---|---|---|---|
| ☐1509 10¢ Red & Blue | 31.00 | 7.00 | .34 | .24 |
| ☐1510 10¢ Blue | 26.00 | 1.25 | .32 | .24 |
| ☐1511 10¢ Multicolored | 25.00 | 2.10 | .29 | .24 |

| Scott No. | Fine Unused Line Pair | Ave. Unused Line Pair | Fine Unused Each | Ave. Unused Each | Fine Used Each | Ave. Used Each |
|---|---|---|---|---|---|---|

## 1973–1974. COIL STAMPS—PERF. 10 VERTICALLY

☐1518 63¢ Orange

| | | | | | |
|---|---|---|---|---|---|
| 1.10 | .90 | .26 | .22 | .24 | .16 |

*No hinge pricing from 1941 to date is figured at (N-H ADD 15%)

| Scott No. | Fine Unused Line Pair | Ave. Unused Line Pair | Fine Unused Each | Ave. Unused Each | Fine Used Each | Ave. Used Each |
|---|---|---|---|---|---|---|
| ☐1519 10¢ Red & Blue | | | | | | |
| | — | — | .28 | .25 | .24 | .16 |
| ☐1520 10¢ Blue | | | | | | |
| | 1.20 | .90 | .28 | .25 | .24 | .16 |

| Scott No. | Mint Sheet | Plate Block | Fine Unused Each | Fine Used Each |
|---|---|---|---|---|

## 1974. COMMEMORATIVES
## 1974. VETERANS OF FOREIGN WARS

| | Mint Sheet | Plate Block | Fine Unused Each | Fine Used Each |
|---|---|---|---|---|
| ☐1525 10¢ Carmine & Blue | 12.00 | 1.25 | .30 | .16 |

## 1974. ROBERT FROST—POET

| | Mint Sheet | Plate Block | Fine Unused Each | Fine Used Each |
|---|---|---|---|---|
| ☐1526 10¢ Black | 12.00 | 1.25 | .30 | .16 |

## 1975. EXPO '74—PRESERVE THE ENVIRONMENT

| | Mint Sheet | Plate Block | Fine Unused Each | Fine Used Each |
|---|---|---|---|---|
| ☐1527 10¢ Multicolored | 11.00 | 3.50 | .30 | .16 |

## 1974. HORSE RACING

| | Mint Sheet | Plate Block | Fine Unused Each | Fine Used Each |
|---|---|---|---|---|
| ☐1528 10¢ Multicolored | 12.00 | 3.40 | .30 | .16 |

## 1975. SKYLAB PROJECT

| | Mint Sheet | Plate Block | Fine Unused Each | Fine Used Each |
|---|---|---|---|---|
| ☐1529 10¢ Multicolored | 12.00 | 1.25 | .30 | .16 |

## 1974. UNIVERSAL POSTAL UNION CENTENARY

| | Mint Sheet | Plate Block | Fine Unused Each | Fine Used Each |
|---|---|---|---|---|
| ☐1530 10¢ Multicolored | — | — | .32 | .18 |
| ☐1531 10¢ Multicolored | — | — | .32 | .18 |
| ☐1532 10¢ Multicolored | — | — | .32 | .18 |
| ☐1533 10¢ Multicolored | — | — | .32 | .18 |
| ☐1534 10¢ Multicolored | — | — | .32 | .18 |
| ☐1535 10¢ Multicolored | — | — | .32 | .18 |
| ☐1536 10¢ Multicolored | — | — | .32 | .18 |
| ☐1537 10¢ Multicolored | — | — | .32 | .18 |

## 1974. MINERALS HERITAGE ISSUE

| | Mint Sheet | Plate Block | Fine Unused Each | Fine Used Each |
|---|---|---|---|---|
| ☐1538 10¢ Multicolored | — | — | .30 | .16 |

*No hinge pricing from 1941 to date is figured at (N-H ADD 15%)

| Scott No. | Mint Sheet | Plate Block | Fine Unused Each | Fine Used Each |
|---|---|---|---|---|
| ☐ 1539 10¢ Multicolored | — | — | .30 | .16 |
| ☐ 1540 10¢ Multicolored | — | — | .30 | .16 |
| ☐ 1541 10¢ Multicolored | — | — | .30 | .16 |

## 1974. FORT HARROD BICENTENNIAL
| | | | | |
|---|---|---|---|---|
| ☐ 1542 10¢ Multicolored | 12.75 | 1.25 | .31 | .16 |

## 1974. CONTINENTAL CONGRESS
| | | | | |
|---|---|---|---|---|
| ☐ 1543 10¢ Red, Blue, Gray | — | — | .30 | .16 |
| ☐ 1544 10¢ Red, Blue, Gray | — | — | .30 | .16 |
| ☐ 1545 10¢ Red, Blue, Gray | — | — | .30 | .16 |
| ☐ 1546 10¢ Red, Blue, Gray | — | — | .30 | .16 |

## 1974. ENERGY CONSERVATION
| | | | | |
|---|---|---|---|---|
| ☐ 1547 10¢ Multicolored | 13.00 | 1.10 | .30 | .16 |

## 1974. LEGEND OF SLEEPY HOLLOW
| | | | | |
|---|---|---|---|---|
| ☐ 1548 10¢ Multicolored | 13.00 | 1.10 | .30 | .16 |

## 1974. RETARDED CHILDREN
| | | | | |
|---|---|---|---|---|
| ☐ 1549 10¢ Light & Dark Brown | | | | |
| | 13.00 | 1.10 | .30 | .16 |

## 1974. CHRISTMAS
| | | | | |
|---|---|---|---|---|
| ☐ 1550 10¢ Multicolored | 13.00 | 3.00 | .31 | .16 |
| ☐ 1551 10¢ Multicolored | 13.00 | 3.20 | .31 | .16 |
| ☐ 1552 10¢ Multicolored | 13.00 | 3.75 | .31 | .16 |
| ☐ 1552A 10¢ Multicolored, Plate Block of 12 | | | | |
| | 13.00 | 4.00 | — | — |

## 1975. COMMEMORATIVES—AMERICAN ARTS
## 1975. BENJAMIN WEST—ARTIST
| | | | | |
|---|---|---|---|---|
| ☐ 1553 10¢ Multicolored | 13.00 | 3.10 | .31 | .16 |

## 1975. PAUL LAURENCE DUNBAR—POET
| | | | | |
|---|---|---|---|---|
| ☐ 1554 10¢ Multicolored | 13.00 | 3.10 | .31 | .16 |

*No hinge pricing from 1941 to date is figured at (N-H ADD 15%)

| Scott No. | Mint Sheet | Plate Block | Fine Unused Each | Fine Used Each |
|---|---|---|---|---|
| **1975. D. W. GRIFFITH—MOTION PICTURES** | | | | |
| ☐ 1555 10¢ Multicolored | 14.00 | 1.30 | .32 | .16 |
| **1975. PIONEER 10 SPACE MISSION** | | | | |
| ☐ 1556 10¢ Multicolored | 14.00 | 1.35 | .36 | .16 |
| **1975. MARINER 10 SPACE MISSION** | | | | |
| ☐ 1557 10¢ Multicolored | 14.00 | 1.35 | .36 | .16 |
| **1975. COLLECTIVE BARGAINING** | | | | |
| ☐ 1558 10¢ Blue, Red, Purple | | | | |
| | 12.00 | 2.50 | .30 | .16 |
| **1975. CONTRIBUTORS TO THE CAUSE** | | | | |
| ☐ 1559 8¢ Multicolored | 10.00 | 2.25 | .26 | .16 |
| ☐ 1560 10¢ Multicolored | 12.00 | 2.40 | .32 | .16 |
| ☐ 1561 10¢ Multicolored | 12.00 | 2.40 | .32 | .16 |
| ☐ 1562 18¢ Multicolored | 22.00 | 6.00 | .50 | .21 |
| **1975. LEXINGTON AND CONCORD BATTLES BICENTENNIAL** | | | | |
| ☐ 1563 10¢ Multicolored | 8.50 | 3.25 | .30 | .16 |
| **1975. BATTLE OF BUNKER HILL** | | | | |
| ☐ 1564 10¢ Multicolored | 8.50 | 3.25 | .30 | .16 |
| **1975. CONTINENTAL MILITARY SERVICE UNIFORMS** | | | | |
| ☐ 1565 10¢ Multicolored | — | — | .30 | .16 |
| ☐ 1566 10¢ Multicolored | — | — | .30 | .16 |
| ☐ 1567 10¢ Multicolored | — | — | .30 | .16 |
| ☐ 1568 10¢ Multicolored | — | — | .30 | .16 |
| **1975. U.S.-SOVIET JOINT SPACE MISSION** | | | | |
| ☐ 1569 10¢ Multicolored | — | — | .30 | .16 |
| ☐ 1570 10¢ Multicolored | — | — | .30 | .16 |
| **1975. INTERNATIONAL WOMEN'S YEAR** | | | | |
| ☐ 1571 10¢ Multicolored | 12.00 | 1.75 | .30 | .16 |

*No hinge pricing from 1941 to date is figured at (N-H ADD 15%)

| Scott No. | Mint Sheet | Plate Block | Fine Unused Each | Fine Used Each |
|---|---|---|---|---|
| **1975. U.S. POSTAL SERVICE BICENTENNIAL** | | | | |
| ☐1572 10¢ Multicolored | — | — | .30 | .16 |
| ☐1573 10¢ Multicolored | — | — | .30 | .16 |
| ☐1574 10¢ Multicolored | — | — | .30 | .16 |
| ☐1575 10¢ Multicolored | — | — | .30 | .16 |
| **1975. WORLD PEACE THROUGH LAW** | | | | |
| ☐1576 10¢ Blue, Green, Brown | | | | |
| | 15.00 | 1.50 | .30 | .16 |
| **1975. BANKING AND COMMERCE** | | | | |
| ☐1577 10¢ Multicolored | — | — | .30 | .16 |
| ☐1578 10¢ Multicolored | — | — | .30 | .16 |
| **1975. CHRISTMAS** | | | | |
| ☐1579 10¢ Multicolored | 12.00 | 3.50 | .30 | .16 |
| ☐1580 10¢ Multicolored | 12.00 | 3.50 | .30 | .16 |
| **1975–1980. AMERICANA SERIES** | | | | |
| ☐1581 1¢ Blue on Green | 8.00 | .70 | .22 | .16 |
| ☐1582 2¢ Brown on Green | 8.00 | .70 | .22 | .16 |
| ☐1584 3¢ Olive on Green | 9.50 | .70 | .22 | .16 |
| ☐1585 4¢ Maroon on Green | 11.00 | .65 | .22 | .16 |
| ☐1590 9¢ Slate on Green | — | — | .45 | .30 |
| ☐1591 9¢ Green on Gray | 20.00 | 1.00 | .26 | .16 |
| ☐1592 10¢ Purple | 25.00 | 1.40 | .30 | .16 |
| ☐1593 11¢ Orange on Gray | 26.00 | 1.20 | .30 | .16 |
| ☐1594 12¢ Maroon | 29.00 | 1.85 | .30 | .16 |
| ☐1595 13¢ Brown | — | — | .36 | .16 |
| ☐1596 13¢ Multicolored | 31.00 | 4.35 | .36 | .16 |
| ☐1597 15¢ Multicolored | 36.00 | 9.00 | .42 | .16 |
| ☐1598 15¢ Multicolored | — | — | .60 | .16 |
| ☐1599 16¢ Blue & Black | 46.00 | 2.20 | .56 | .16 |
| ☐1603 24¢ Red on Blue | 52.00 | 2.60 | .60 | .16 |
| ☐1604 28¢ Brown & Blue | 65.00 | 3.10 | .70 | .16 |
| ☐1605 29¢ Blue & Blue | 62.00 | 3.35 | .80 | .16 |
| ☐1606 30¢ Green on Blue | 62.00 | 4.00 | .80 | .16 |

*No hinge pricing from 1941 to date is figured at (N-H ADD 15%)

| Scott No. | Mint Sheet | Plate Block | Fine Unused Each | Fine Used Each |
|---|---|---|---|---|
| ☐1608 50¢ Black & Orange | 100.00 | 6.00 | 1.25 | .16 |
| ☐1610 $1 Multicolored | 230.00 | 11.00 | 3.00 | .16 |
| ☐1611 $2 Multicolored | 420.00 | 22.00 | 5.00 | .65 |
| ☐1612 $5 Multicolored | 1000.00 | 45.00 | 10.00 | 3.40 |

| Scott No. | Fine Unused Line Pair | Ave. Unused Line Pair | Fine Unused Each | Ave. Unused Each | Fine Used Each | Ave. Used Each |
|---|---|---|---|---|---|---|
| **1975–1978. COIL STAMPS** | | | | | | |
| ☐1613 3 .1¢ Brown on Yellow | | | | | | |
| | 1.00 | .90 | .30 | .24 | .22 | .16 |
| ☐1614 7.7¢ Gold on Yellow | | | | | | |
| | 1.50 | 1.25 | .35 | .24 | .22 | .16 |
| ☐1615 7.9¢ Red on Yellow | | | | | | |
| | 1.00 | .90 | .32 | .24 | .22 | .16 |
| ☐1615C 8.4¢ Blue on White | | | | | | |
| | 2.50 | 2.00 | .32 | .24 | .22 | .16 |
| ☐1616 9¢ Green on Gray | | | | | | |
| | 1.00 | .95 | .32 | .24 | .22 | .16 |
| ☐1617 10¢ Purple on Gray | | | | | | |
| | 1.00 | .95 | .32 | .24 | .22 | .16 |
| ☐1618 13¢ Brown | | | | | | |
| | 1.00 | .95 | .35 | .24 | .22 | .16 |

| Scott No. | Mint Sheet | Plate Block | Fine Unused Each | Fine Used Each |
|---|---|---|---|---|
| **1975–1977. REGULAR ISSUES** | | | | |
| ☐1622 13¢ Red, Brown, Blue | 30.00 | 8.50 | .36 | .16 |
| ☐1623 13¢ Blue, Red | 26.00 | 9.00 | .36 | .16 |
| ☐1623c 13¢ Blue, Red, pf 10 | — | — | 2.25 | .16 |

| Scott No. | Fine Unused Each | Ave. Unused Each | Fine Used Each | Ave. Used Each |
|---|---|---|---|---|
| **1975. COIL STAMPS** | | | | |
| ☐1625 13¢ Red, Brown, Blue | .50 | .30 | .24 | .16 |

*No hinge pricing from 1941 to date is figured at (N-H ADD 15%)

| Scott No. | Mint Sheet | Plate Block | Fine Unused Each | Fine Used Each |
|---|---|---|---|---|

## 1976. COMMEMORATIVES—AMERICAN BICENTENNIAL
## 1976. SPIRIT OF '76

| | | | | |
|---|---|---|---|---|
| ☐1629 3¢ Multicolored | — | — | .35 | .16 |
| ☐1630 13¢ Multicolored | — | — | .35 | .16 |
| ☐1631 13¢ Multicolored | — | — | .35 | .16 |

## 1976. INTERPHIL '76

| | | | | |
|---|---|---|---|---|
| ☐1632 13¢ Dark Blue, Red, Ultramarine | | | | |
| | 18.00 | 1.60 | .42 | .16 |

## 1976. STATE FLAGS

| | | | | |
|---|---|---|---|---|
| ☐ 13¢ All 50 States | | | | |
| | 23.00 | 6.00 | — | — |
| ☐ 13¢ Individual States | — | — | .50 | .34 |

| | |
|---|---|
| ☐1633 Delaware | ☐1655 Maine |
| ☐1634 Pennsylvania | ☐1656 Missouri |
| ☐1635 New Jersey | ☐1657 Arkansas |
| ☐1636 Georgia | ☐1658 Michigan |
| ☐1637 Connecticut | ☐1659 Florida |
| ☐1638 Massachusetts | ☐1660 Texas |
| ☐1639 Maryland | ☐1661 Iowa |
| ☐1640 South Carolina | ☐1662 Wisconsin |
| ☐1641 New Hampshire | ☐1663 California |
| ☐1642 Virginia | ☐1664 Minnesota |
| ☐1643 New York | ☐1665 Oregon |
| ☐1644 North Carolina | ☐1666 Kansas |
| ☐1645 Rhode Island | ☐1667 West Virginia |
| ☐1646 Vermont | ☐1668 Nevada |
| ☐1647 Kentucky | ☐1669 Nebraska |
| ☐1648 Tennessee | ☐1670 Colorado |
| ☐1649 Ohio | ☐1671 North Dakota |
| ☐1650 Louisiana | ☐1672 South Dakota |
| ☐1651 Indiana | ☐1673 Montana |
| ☐1652 Mississippi | ☐1674 Washington |
| ☐1653 Illinois | ☐1675 Idaho |
| ☐1654 Alabama | ☐1676 Wyoming |

*No hinge pricing from 1941 to date is figured at (N-H ADD 15%)

☐1677 Utah      ☐1680 Arizona
☐1678 Oklahoma      ☐1681 Alaska
☐1679 New Mexico      ☐1682 Hawaii

| Scott No. | Mint Sheet | Plate Block | Fine Unused Each | Fine Used Each |
|---|---|---|---|---|
| **1976. TELEPHONE CENTENNIAL** | | | | |
| ☐1683 13¢ Black, Purple, Red | | | | |
| | 18.00 | 1.65 | .40 | .16 |
| **1976. COMMERCIAL AVIATION** | | | | |
| ☐1684 13¢ Multicolored | 18.00 | 3.90 | .40 | .16 |
| **1976. CHEMISTRY** | | | | |
| ☐1685 13¢ Multicolored | 18.00 | 4.50 | .40 | .16 |
| **1976. BICENTENNIAL SOUVENIR SHEETS** | | | | |
| ☐1686 65¢ Sheet of 5 | — | — | 4.50 | 3.50 |
| ☐1686a 13¢ Multicolored | — | — | .95 | .75 |
| ☐1686b 13¢ Multicolored | — | — | .95 | .75 |
| ☐1686c 13¢ Multicolored | — | — | .95 | .75 |
| ☐1686d 13¢ Multicolored | — | — | .95 | .75 |
| ☐1686e 13¢ Multicolored | — | — | .95 | .75 |
| ☐1687 90¢ Sheet of 5 | — | — | 7.50 | 6.00 |
| ☐1687a 18¢ Multicolored | — | — | 1.40 | 1.10 |
| ☐1687b 18¢ Multicolored | — | — | 1.40 | 1.10 |
| ☐1687c 18¢ Multicolored | — | — | 1.40 | 1.10 |
| ☐1687d 18¢ Multicolored | — | — | 1.40 | 1.10 |
| ☐1687e 18¢ Multicolored | — | — | 1.75 | 1.40 |
| ☐1688 1.20 Sheet of 5 | — | — | 8.50 | 8.00 |
| ☐1688a 24¢ Multicolored | — | — | 2.00 | 1.60 |
| ☐1688b 24¢ Multicolored | — | — | 2.00 | 1.60 |
| ☐1688c 24¢ Multicolored | — | — | 2.00 | 1.60 |
| ☐1688d 24¢ Multicolored | — | — | 2.00 | 1.60 |
| ☐1688e 24¢ Multicolored | — | — | 2.00 | 1.60 |
| ☐1689 1.55 Sheet of 5 | — | — | 10.50 | 9.50 |

*No hinge pricing from 1941 to date is figured at (N-H ADD 15%)

| Scott No. | Mint Sheet | Plate Block | Fine Unused Each | Fine Used Each |
|---|---|---|---|---|
| ☐ 1689a 31¢ Multicolored | — | — | 2.10 | 1.85 |
| ☐ 1689b 31¢ Multicolored | — | — | 2.10 | 1.85 |
| ☐ 1689c 31¢ Multicolored | — | — | 2.10 | 1.85 |
| ☐ 1689d 31¢ Multicolored | — | — | 2.10 | 1.85 |
| ☐ 1689e 31¢ Multicolored | — | — | 2.10 | 1.85 |

## 1976. BENJAMIN FRANKLIN
| | | | | |
|---|---|---|---|---|
| ☐ 1690 13¢ Blue & Multicolored | | | | |
| | 17.00 | 1.70 | .42 | .16 |

## 1976. DECLARATION OF INDEPENDENCE
| | | | | |
|---|---|---|---|---|
| ☐ 1691 13¢ Multicolored | — | — | .40 | .16 |
| ☐ 1692 13¢ Multicolored | — | — | .40 | .16 |
| ☐ 1693 13¢ Multicolored | — | — | .40 | .16 |
| ☐ 1694 13¢ Multicolored | — | — | .40 | .16 |

## 1976. OLYMPIC GAMES
| | | | | |
|---|---|---|---|---|
| ☐ 1695 13¢ Multicolored | — | — | .42 | .16 |
| ☐ 1696 13¢ Multicolored | — | — | .42 | .16 |
| ☐ 1697 13¢ Multicolored | — | — | .42 | .16 |
| ☐ 1698 13¢ Multicolored | — | — | .42 | .16 |

## 1976. CLARA MAASS
| | | | | |
|---|---|---|---|---|
| ☐ 1699 13¢ Multicolored | 13.00 | 4.75 | .42 | .16 |

## 1976. ADOLPH S. OCHS
| | | | | |
|---|---|---|---|---|
| ☐ 1700 13¢ Black, Green & White | | | | |
| | 11.00 | 1.60 | .42 | .16 |

## 1976. CHRISTMAS
| | | | | |
|---|---|---|---|---|
| ☐ 1701 13¢ Multicolored | 17.00 | 5.00 | .42 | .16 |
| ☐ 1702 13¢ Multicolored | 17.00 | 4.00 | .42 | .16 |
| ☐ 1703 13¢ Multicolored | 17.00 | 7.00 | .42 | .16 |

## 1977. COMMEMORATIVES
## 1977. WASHINGTON
| | | | | |
|---|---|---|---|---|
| ☐ 1704 13¢ Multicolored | 14.00 | 3.90 | .42 | .16 |

*No hinge pricing from 1941 to date is figured at (N-H ADD 15%)

| Scott No. | Mint Sheet | Plate Block | Fine Unused Each | Fine Used Each |
|---|---|---|---|---|
| **1977. SOUND RECORDING CENTENARY** | | | | |
| ☐1705 13¢ Multicolored | 16.00 | 1.50 | .42 | .16 |
| **1977. PUEBLO ART** | | | | |
| ☐1706 13¢ Multicolored | — | — | .38 | .16 |
| ☐1707 13¢ Multicolored | — | — | .38 | .16 |
| ☐1708 13¢ Multicolored | — | — | .38 | .16 |
| ☐1709 13¢ Multicolored | — | — | .38 | .16 |
| **1977. TRANSATLANTIC FLIGHT** | | | | |
| ☐1710 13¢ Multicolored | 18.00 | 4.60 | .40 | .16 |
| **1977. COLORADO** | | | | |
| ☐1711 13¢ Multicolored | 18.00 | 4.60 | .40 | .16 |
| **1977. BUTTERFLIES** | | | | |
| ☐1712 13¢ Multicolored | — | — | .40 | .16 |
| ☐1713 13¢ Multicolored | — | — | .40 | .16 |
| ☐1714 13¢ Multicolored | — | — | .40 | .16 |
| ☐1715 13¢ Multicolored | — | — | .40 | .16 |
| **1977. LAFAYETTE** | | | | |
| ☐1716 13¢ Multicolored | 13.50 | 1.60 | .40 | .16 |
| **1977. SKILLED HANDS** | | | | |
| ☐1717 13¢ Multicolored | — | — | .40 | .16 |
| ☐1718 13¢ Multicolored | — | — | .40 | .16 |
| ☐1719 13¢ Multicolored | — | — | .40 | .16 |
| ☐1720 13¢ Multicolored | — | — | .40 | .16 |
| **1977. PEACE BRIDGE** | | | | |
| ☐1721 13¢ Blue & White | 17.00 | 1.60 | .40 | .16 |
| **1977. BATTLE OF ORISKANY** | | | | |
| ☐1722 13¢ Multicolored | 13.00 | 3.75 | .40 | .16 |

*No hinge pricing from 1941 to date is figured at (N-H ADD 15%)

| Scott No. | Mint Sheet | Plate Block | Fine Unused Each | Fine Used Each |
|---|---|---|---|---|
| **1977. ENERGY CONSERVATION AND DEVELOPMENT** | | | | |
| ☐1723 13¢ Multicolored | — | — | .40 | .16 |
| ☐1724 13¢ Multicolored | — | — | .40 | .16 |
| **1977. ALTA, CALIFORNIA BICENTENNIAL** | | | | |
| ☐1725 13¢ Multicolored | 17.50 | 1.50 | .40 | .16 |
| **1977. ARTICLES OF CONFEDERATION** | | | | |
| ☐1726 13¢ Red & Brown on Tan | | | | |
| | 17.50 | 1.60 | .40 | .16 |
| **1977. TALKING PICTURES** | | | | |
| ☐1727 13¢ Multicolored | 17.50 | 1.60 | .40 | .16 |
| **1977. SURRENDER AT SARATOGA** | | | | |
| ☐1728 13¢ Multicolored | 13.50 | 4.15 | .40 | .16 |
| **1977. CHRISTMAS** | | | | |
| ☐1729 13¢ Multicolored | 34.00 | 8.00 | .38 | .16 |
| ☐1730 13¢ Multicolored | 32.00 | 4.00 | .38 | .16 |
| **1978. CARL SANDBURG** | | | | |
| ☐1731 13¢ Brown, Black, White | | | | |
| | 18.00 | 1.50 | .36 | .16 |
| **1978. CAPTAIN COOK ISSUES** | | | | |
| ☐1732 13¢ Dark Blue | — | 1.55 | .36 | .16 |
| ☐1733 13¢ Green | — | 1.50 | .36 | 16 |
| **1978. INDIAN HEAD PENNY** | | | | |
| ☐1734 13¢ Brown & Blue Green | | | | |
| | 48.00 | 1.80 | .38 | .16 |
| **1978. NONDENOMINATED "A"** | | | | |
| ☐1735 15¢ Orange | 32.00 | 1.80 | .38 | .16 |
| **1978. ROSES** | | | | |
| ☐1737 15¢ Multicolored | — | — | .38 | .16 |

| Scott No. | Mint Sheet | Plate Block | Fine Unused Each | Fine Used Each |
|---|---|---|---|---|

## 1980. WINDMILL—VIRGINIA

| | | | | |
|---|---|---|---|---|
| ☐1738 15¢ Black | — | — | .38 | .16 |

## 1980. WINDMILL—RHODE ISLAND

| | | | | |
|---|---|---|---|---|
| ☐1739 15¢ Black | — | — | .38 | .16 |

## 1980. WINDMILL—MASSACHUSETTS

| | | | | |
|---|---|---|---|---|
| ☐1740 15¢ Black | — | — | .38 | .16 |

## 1980. WINDMILL—ILLINOIS

| | | | | |
|---|---|---|---|---|
| ☐1741 15¢ Black | — | — | .38 | .16 |

## 1980. WINDMILL—TEXAS

| | | | | |
|---|---|---|---|---|
| ☐1742 15¢ Black | — | — | .38 | .16 |

## 1978. HARRIET TUBMAN

| | | | | |
|---|---|---|---|---|
| ☐1744 13¢ Multicolored | 25.00 | 7.00 | .38 | .16 |

## 1978. AMERICAN FOLK ART ISSUE

| | | | | |
|---|---|---|---|---|
| ☐1745 13¢ Multicolored | — | — | .38 | .16 |
| ☐1746 13¢ Multicolored | — | — | .38 | .16 |
| ☐1747 13¢ Multicolored | — | — | .38 | .16 |
| ☐1748 13¢ Multicolored | — | — | .38 | .16 |

## 1978. AMERICAN DANCE ISSUE

| | | | | |
|---|---|---|---|---|
| ☐1749 13¢ Multicolored | — | — | .38 | .16 |
| ☐1750 13¢ Multicolored | — | — | .38 | .16 |
| ☐1751 13¢ Multicolored | — | — | .38 | .16 |
| ☐1752 13¢ Multicolored | — | — | .38 | .16 |

## 1978. FRENCH ALLIANCE

| | | | | |
|---|---|---|---|---|
| ☐1753 13¢ Blue, Black & Red | 14.00 | 1.50 | .38 | .16 |

## 1978. EARLY CANCER DETECTION

| | | | | |
|---|---|---|---|---|
| ☐1754 13¢ Brown | 19.00 | 1.80 | .38 | .16 |

*No hinge pricing from 1941 to date is figured at (N-H ADD 15%)

| Scott No. | Mint Sheet | Plate Block | Fine Unused Each | Fine Used Each |
|---|---|---|---|---|

### 1978. JIMMIE RODGERS

| ☐1755 13¢ Multicolored | 17.25 | 5.00 | .38 | .16 |

### 1978. GEORGE M. COHAN

| ☐1756 15¢ Multicolored | 21.00 | 6.00 | .46 | 16 |

### 1978. "CAPAX" '78 SOUVENIR SHEET

☐1757 13¢ Multicolored, set of 6

| | 15.00 | — | 2.90 | 2.65 |

### 1978. PHOTOGRAPHY

| ☐1758 15¢ Multicolored | 14.00 | 6.00 | .38 | .16 |

### 1978. VIKING MISSION TO MARS

| ☐1759 15¢ Multicolored | 21.00 | 1.85 | .45 | .16 |

### 1978. AMERICAN OWL ISSUE

| ☐1760 15¢ Multicolored | — | — | .36 | .16 |
| ☐1761 15¢ Multicolored | — | — | .36 | .16 |
| ☐1762 15¢ Multicolored | — | — | .36 | .16 |
| ☐1763 15¢ Multicolored | — | — | .36 | .16 |

### 1978. AMERICAN TREES ISSUE

| ☐1764 15¢ Multicolored | — | — | .38 | .16 |
| ☐1765 15¢ Multicolored | — | — | .38 | .16 |
| ☐1766 15¢ Multicolored | — | — | .38 | .16 |
| ☐1767 15¢ Multicolored | — | — | .38 | .16 |

### 1978. CHRISTMAS ISSUES

| ☐1768 15¢ Multicolored | 40.00 | 6.00 | .38 | .16 |
| ☐1769 15¢ Multicolored | 40.00 | 6.00 | .38 | .16 |

### 1979. ROBERT F. KENNEDY ISSUE

| ☐1770 15¢ Blue | 18.00 | 1.90 | .38 | .16 |

### 1979. MARTIN LUTHER KING ISSUE

| ☐1771 15¢ Multicolored | 21.00 | 5.00 | .38 | .16 |

*No hinge pricing from 1941 to date is figured at (N-H ADD 15%)

| Scott No. | Mint Sheet | Plate Block | Fine Unused Each | Fine Used Each |
|---|---|---|---|---|

## 1979. INTERNATIONAL YEAR OF THE CHILD
| ☐1772 15¢ Light Brown | 20.00 | 1.85 | .38 | .16 |

## 1979. JOHN STEINBECK ISSUE
| ☐1773 15¢ Dark Blue | 20.00 | 1.85 | .38 | .16 |

## 1979. ALBERT EINSTEIN ISSUE
| ☐1774 15¢ Brown | 20.00 | 1.85 | .38 | .16 |

## 1979. PENNSYLVANIA TOLEWARE ISSUE
| ☐1775 15¢ Multicolored | — | — | .39 | .16 |
| ☐1776 15¢ Multicolored | — | — | .39 | .16 |
| ☐1777 15¢ Multicolored | — | — | .39 | .16 |
| ☐1778 15¢ Multicolored | — | — | .39 | .16 |

## 1979. ARCHITECTURE U.S.A. ISSUE
| ☐1779 15¢ Light Blue & Brown | — | — | .39 | .16 |
| ☐1780 15¢ Light Blue & Brown | — | — | .39 | .16 |
| ☐1781 15¢ Light Blue & Brown | — | — | .39 | .16 |
| ☐1782 15¢ Light Blue & Brown | — | — | .39 | .16 |

## 1979. ENDANGERED FLORA ISSUE
| ☐1783 15¢ Multicolored | — | — | .39 | .16 |
| ☐1784 15¢ Multicolored | — | — | .39 | .16 |
| ☐1785 15¢ Multicolored | — | — | .39 | .16 |
| ☐1786 15¢ Multicolored | — | — | .39 | .16 |

## 1979. SEEING FOR ME ISSUE
| ☐1787 15¢ Multicolored | 19.00 | 8.00 | .39 | .16 |

## 1979. SPECIAL OLYMPICS
| ☐1788 15¢ Multicolored | 19.00 | 5.00 | .38 | .16 |

*No hinge pricing from 1941 to date is figured at (N-H ADD 15%)

| Scott No. | Mint Sheet | Plate Block | Fine Unused Each | Fine Used Each |
|---|---|---|---|---|
| **1979. JOHN PAUL JONES** | | | | |
| ☐1789 15¢ Multicolored | 19.00 | 5.00 | .38 | .16 |
| **1979. OLYMPIC DECATHALON** | | | | |
| ☐1790 10¢ Multicolored | 14.00 | 5.00 | .28 | .16 |
| **1979. OLYMPIC RUNNERS** | | | | |
| ☐1791 15¢ Multicolored | — | — | .38 | .16 |
| **1979. OLYMPIC SWIMMERS** | | | | |
| ☐1792 15¢ Multicolored | — | — | .38 | .16 |
| **1979. OLYMPIC ROWERS** | | | | |
| ☐1793 15¢ Multicolored | — | — | .38 | .16 |
| **1979. OLYMPIC EQUESTRIAN** | | | | |
| ☐1794 15¢ Multicolored | — | — | .38 | .16 |
| **1979. OLYMPIC SKATER** | | | | |
| ☐1795 15¢ Multicolored | — | — | .38 | .16 |
| **1979. OLYMPIC SKIER** | | | | |
| ☐1796 15¢ Multicolored | — | — | .38 | .16 |
| **1979. OLYMPIC SKI JUMPER** | | | | |
| ☐1797 15¢ Multicolored | — | — | .38 | .16 |
| **1979. OLYMPIC GOALTENDER** | | | | |
| ☐1798 15¢ Multicolored | — | — | .38 | .16 |
| **1979. MADONNA** | | | | |
| ☐1799 15¢ Multicolored | 40.00 | 6.00 | .38 | .16 |
| **1979. CHRISTMAS** | | | | |
| ☐1800 15¢ Multicolored | 40.00 | 6.00 | .38 | .16 |
| **1979. WILL ROGERS** | | | | |
| ☐1801 15¢ Multicolored | 20.00 | 5.50 | .38 | .16 |

*No hinge pricing from 1941 to date is figured at (N-H ADD) 15%

| Scott No. | Mint Sheet | Plate Block | Fine Unused Each | Fine Used Each |
|---|---|---|---|---|
| **1979. VIETNAM VETERANS** | | | | |
| ☐1802 15¢ Multicolored | 22.00 | 6.00 | .46 | .16 |
| **1980. W. C. FIELDS** | | | | |
| ☐1803 15¢ Multicolored | 20.00 | 6.50 | .46 | .16 |
| **1980. BENJAMIN BANNEKER** | | | | |
| ☐1804 15¢ Multicolored | 20.00 | 6.00 | .46 | .16 |
| **1980. LETTERS PRESERVE MEMORIES** | | | | |
| ☐1805 15¢ Violet & Bistre | — | — | .38 | .16 |
| **1980. PRESERVE MEMORIES—P.S. WRITE SOON** | | | | |
| ☐1806 15¢ Violet & Pink | — | — | .38 | .16 |
| **1980. LETTERS LIFT SPIRITS** | | | | |
| ☐1807 15¢ Green, Pink & Orange | | | | |
| | — | — | .38 | .16 |
| **1980. LIFT SPIRITS—P.S. WRITE SOON** | | | | |
| ☐1808 15¢ Green & Yellow Green | | | | |
| | — | — | .38 | .16 |
| **1980. LETTERS SHAPE OPINIONS** | | | | |
| ☐1809 15¢ Scarlet & Blue | — | — | .38 | .16 |
| **1980. SHAPE OPINIONS—P.S. WRITE SOON** | | | | |
| ☐1810 15¢ Scarlet & Blue | — | — | .38 | .16 |
| **1980. AMERICANA SERIES** | | | | |
| ☐1811 1¢ Dark Blue & Green | | | | |
| | — | .65 | .22 | .16 |
| ☐1813 3.5¢ Purple & Yellow | — | 1.40 | .22 | .16 |
| ☐1816 12¢ Green | — | 1.75 | .34 | .16 |
| **1980. NONDENOMINATED "B"** | | | | |
| ☐1818 18¢ Purple | — | 2.10 | .48 | .16 |

*No hinge pricing from 1941 to date is figured at (N-H ADD 15%)

| Scott No. | Mint Sheet | Plate Block | Fine Unused Each | Fine Used Each |
|---|---|---|---|---|
| **1980. FRANCIS PERKINS** | | | | |
| ☐1821 15¢ Blue | 20.00 | 2.00 | .38 | .16 |
| **1980. DOLLY MADISON** | | | | |
| ☐1822 15¢ Multicolored | 55.00 | 1.80 | .38 | .16 |
| **1980. EMILY BISSELL** | | | | |
| ☐1823 15¢ Scarlet & Black | 20.00 | 1.80 | .38 | .16 |
| **1980. HELLEN KELLER—ANNE SULLIVAN** | | | | |
| ☐1824 15¢ Multicolored | 20.00 | 1.80 | .38 | .16 |
| **1980. VETERANS ADMINISTRATION** | | | | |
| ☐1825 15¢ Carmine & Blue | — | — | .38 | .16 |
| **1980. GENERAL BERNARDO de GALVEZ** | | | | |
| ☐1826 15¢ Multicolored | — | — | .38 | .16 |
| **1980. CORAL REEFS—VIRGIN ISLANDS** | | | | |
| ☐1827 15¢ Multicolored | — | — | .38 | .16 |
| **1980. CORAL REEFS—FLORIDA** | | | | |
| ☐1828 15¢ Multicolored | — | — | .38 | .16 |
| **1980. CORAL REEFS—AMERICAN SAMOA** | | | | |
| ☐1829 15¢ Multicolored | — | — | .38 | .16 |
| **1980. CORAL REEFS—HAWAII** | | | | |
| ☐1830 15¢ Multicolored | — | — | .38 | .16 |
| **1980. ORGANIZED LABOR** | | | | |
| ☐1831 15¢ Multicolored | 20.00 | 6.00 | .38 | .16 |
| **1980. EDITH WHARTON** | | | | |
| ☐1832 15¢ Violet | 39.00 | 4.00 | .38 | .16 |
| **1980. EDUCATION** | | | | |
| ☐1833 15¢ Multicolored | 28.00 | 7.00 | .38 | .16 |

*No hinge pricing from 1941 to date is figured at (N-H ADD 15%)

| Scott No. | Mint Sheet | Plate Block | Fine Unused Each | Fine Used Each |
|---|---|---|---|---|
| **1980. INDIAN ARTS** | | | | |
| ☐1834 15¢ Multicolored | — | — | .38 | .16 |
| ☐1835 15¢ Multicolored | — | — | .38 | .16 |
| ☐1836 15¢ Multicolored | — | — | .38 | .16 |
| ☐1837 15¢ Multicolored | — | — | .38 | .16 |
| **1980. ARCHITECTURE** | | | | |
| ☐1838 15¢ Black & Red | — | — | .38 | .16 |
| ☐1839 15¢ Black & Red | — | — | .38 | .16 |
| ☐1840 15¢ Black & Red | — | — | .38 | .16 |
| ☐1841 15¢ Black & Red | — | — | .38 | .16 |
| **1980. CHRISTMAS ISSUE** | | | | |
| ☐1842 15¢ Multicolored | 20.00 | 6.00 | .38 | .16 |
| ☐1843 15¢ Multicolored | 20.00 | 9.00 | .38 | .16 |
| **1982. DOROTHEA DIX** | | | | |
| ☐1844 1¢ Black | 11.00 | 3.00 | .22 | .16 |
| **1983. IGOR STRAVINSKY** | | | | |
| ☐1845 2¢ Brown | 8.00 | .70 | .22 | .16 |
| **1983. HENRY CLAY** | | | | |
| ☐1846 3¢ Green | 11.00 | .70 | .22 | .16 |
| **1983. CARL SCHURZ** | | | | |
| ☐1847 4¢ Purple | 12.00 | .70 | .22 | .16 |
| **1985. PEARL BUCK** | | | | |
| ☐1848 5¢ Reddish Brown | 13.00 | .85 | .22 | .16 |
| **1985. WALTER LIPPMANN** | | | | |
| ☐1849 6¢ Orange | 16.00 | 4.00 | .22 | .16 |
| **1985. ABRAHAM BALDWIN** | | | | |
| ☐1850 7¢ Red | 17.00 | 5.00 | .22 | .16 |
| **1985. HENRY KNOX** | | | | |
| ☐1851 8¢ Black | 21.00 | 1.30 | .26 | .16 |

*No hinge pricing from 1941 to date is figured at (N-H ADD 15%)

| Scott No. | Mint Sheet | Plate Block | Fine Unused Each | Fine Used Each |
|---|---|---|---|---|

**1985. SYLVANUS THAYER**

| ☐1852 9¢ Green | 24.00 | 6.00 | .26 | .16 |

**1984. RICHARD RUSSELL**

| ☐1853 10¢ Blue | 26.00 | 7.00 | .28 | .16 |

**1985. ALDEN PARTRIDGE**

| ☐1854 11¢ Blue | 29.00 | 1.70 | .28 | .16 |

**1982. CRAZY HORSE**

| ☐1855 13¢ Brown | 35.00 | 2.00 | .42 | .16 |

**1985. SINCLAIR LEWIS**

| ☐1856 14¢ Green | 40.00 | 9.00 | .42 | .16 |

**1981. RACHEL CARSON**

| ☐1857 17¢ Blue Green | 39.00 | 2.00 | .43 | .16 |

**1981. GEORGE MASON**

| ☐1958 18¢ Dark Blue | 46.00 | 3.50 | .50 | .16 |

**1980. SEQUOYAH**

| ☐1859 19¢ Light Brown | 49.00 | 3.00 | .60 | .16 |

**1982. RALPH BUNCHE**

| ☐1860 20¢ Carmine | 52.00 | 3.60 | .65 | .16 |

**1983. THOMAS H. GALLAUDET**

| ☐1861 20¢ Green | 58.00 | 4.50 | .60 | .16 |

**1984. HARRY S. TRUMAN**

| ☐1862 20¢ Black & White | 54.00 | 12.50 | .65 | .16 |

**1985. JOHN J. AUDUBON**

| ☐1863 22¢ Blue | 55.00 | 13.00 | .70 | .16 |

**1984. FRANK C. LAUBACH**

| ☐1864 30¢ Dark Green | 70.00 | 17.00 | .85 | .16 |

*No hinge pricing from 1941 to date is figured at (N-H ADD 15%)

| Scott No. | Mint Sheet | Plate Block | Fine Unused Each | Fine Used Each |
|---|---|---|---|---|
| **1981. CHARLES DREW** | | | | |
| ☐1865 35¢ Gray | 85.00 | 5.00 | 1.10 | .16 |
| **1982. ROBERT MILLIKAN** | | | | |
| ☐1866 37¢ Blue | 90.00 | 5.00 | 1.10 | .16 |
| **1985. GRENVILLE CLARK** | | | | |
| ☐1867 39¢ Reddish Purple | 95.00 | 21.00 | 1.00 | .16 |
| **1984. LILLIAN M. GILBRETH** | | | | |
| ☐1868 40¢ Green | 90.00 | 20.00 | 1.00 | .16 |
| **1985. CHESTER W. NIMITZ** | | | | |
| ☐1869 50¢ Dark Brown | 115.00 | 7.00 | 1.40 | .16 |
| **1981. EVERETT M. DIRKSEN** | | | | |
| ☐1874 15¢ Dark Green | 19.00 | 1.90 | .40 | .16 |
| **1981. WHITNEY M. YOUNG** | | | | |
| ☐1875 15¢ Multicolored | 19.00 | 1.90 | .40 | .16 |
| **1981. FLOWERS** | | | | |
| ☐1876 18¢ Multicolored | — | — | .55 | .16 |
| ☐1877 18¢ Multicolored | — | — | .55 | .16 |
| ☐1878 18¢ Multicolored | — | — | .55 | .16 |
| ☐1879 18¢ Multicolored | — | — | .55 | .16 |
| **1981. AMERICAN WILDLIFE** | | | | |
| ☐1880 18¢ Light Brown | — | — | 1.00 | .16 |
| ☐1881 18¢ Light Brown | — | — | 1.00 | .16 |
| ☐1882 18¢ Light Brown | — | — | 1.00 | .16 |
| ☐1883 18¢ Light Brown | — | — | 1.00 | .16 |
| ☐1884 18¢ Light Brown | — | — | 1.00 | .16 |
| ☐1885 18¢ Light Brown | — | — | 1.00 | .16 |
| ☐1886 18¢ Light Brown | — | — | 1.00 | .16 |
| ☐1887 18¢ Light Brown | — | — | 1.00 | .16 |
| ☐1888 18¢ Light Brown | — | — | 1.00 | .16 |
| ☐1889 18¢ Light Brown | — | — | 1.00 | .16 |

*No hinge pricing from 1941 to date is figured at (N-H ADD 15%)

| Scott No. | Mint Sheet | Plate Block | Fine Unused Each | Fine Used Each |
|---|---|---|---|---|

### 1981. FLAG—FOR AMBER WAVES OF GRAIN
| ☐1890 18¢ Multicolored | 50.00 | 12.00 | .50 | .16 |

### 1981. FLAG—FROM SEA TO SHINING SEA
| ☐1891 18¢ Multicolored | —PR. | 7.00 | .50 | .16 |

### 1981. U.S.A.
☐1892 6¢ Carmine & Dark Blue

| | — | — | .70 | .16 |

### 1981. FLAG—FOR PURPLE MOUNTAIN MAJESTIES
| ☐1893 18¢ Multicolored | — | — | .48 | .16 |

### 1982. FLAG OVER SUPREME COURT
☐1894 20¢ Carmine & Dark Blue

| | 50.00 | 12.00 | .55 | .16 |

### 1983. OMNIBUS
| ☐1897 1¢ Violet | — | — | .23 | .16 |

### 1982. LOCOMOTIVE
| ☐1897A 2¢ Black | — | — | .23 | .16 |

### 1983. HANDCAR
| ☐1898 3¢ Dark Green | — | — | .23 | .16 |

### 1982. STAGECOACH
| ☐1898A 4¢ Red Brown | — | — | .23 | .16 |

### 1983. MOTORCYCLE
| ☐1899 5¢ Gray Green | — | — | .23 | .16 |

### 1983. SLEIGH
| ☐1900 5.2¢ Carmine | — | — | .28 | .16 |

### 1982. BICYCLE
| ☐1901 5.9¢ Blue | — | — | .28 | .16 |

*No hinge pricing from 1941 to date is figured at (N-H ADD 15%)

| Scott No. | Mint Sheet | Plate Block | Fine Unused Each | Fine Used Each |
|---|---|---|---|---|
| **1984. BABY BUGGY** | | | | |
| ☐1902 7.4¢ Brown | — | — | .28 | .16 |
| **1982. MAIL WAGON** | | | | |
| ☐1903 9.3¢ Carmine | — | — | .28 | .16 |
| **1982. HANSOM CAB** | | | | |
| ☐1904 10.9¢ Purple | — | — | .50 | .16 |
| **1984. RAILROAD CABOOSE** | | | | |
| ☐1905 11¢ Red | — | — | .28 | .16 |
| **1981. ELECTRIC CAR** | | | | |
| ☐1906 17¢ Ultramarine | —LP. | 5.50 | .48 | .16 |
| **1981. SURREY** | | | | |
| ☐1907 18¢ Brown | —LP. | 6.00 | .40 | .16 |
| **1982. FIRE PUMPER** | | | | |
| ☐1908 20¢ Vermilion | — | — | .55 | .16 |
| **1981. AMERICAN RED CROSS** | | | | |
| ☐1910 18¢ Multicolored | — | 2.75 | .50 | .16 |
| **1981. SAVINGS AND LOAN** | | | | |
| ☐1911 19¢ Multicolored | — | 2.75 | .50 | .16 |
| **1981. SPACE ACHIEVEMENT** | | | | |
| ☐1912 18¢ Multicolored | — | — | .60 | .16 |
| ☐1913 18¢ Multicolored | — | — | .60 | .16 |
| ☐1914 18¢ Multicolored | — | — | .60 | .16 |
| ☐1915 18¢ Multicolored | — | — | .60 | .16 |
| ☐1916 18¢ Multicolored | — | — | .60 | .16 |
| ☐1917 18¢ Multicolored | — | — | .60 | .16 |
| ☐1918 18¢ Multicolored | — | — | .60 | .16 |
| ☐1919 18¢ Multicolored | — | — | .60 | .16 |

*No hinge pricing from 1941 to date is figured at (N-H ADD 15%)

| Scott No. | Mint Sheet | Plate Block | Fine Unused Each | Fine Used Each |
|---|---|---|---|---|

## 1981. PROFESSIONAL MANAGEMENT

| | | | | |
|---|---|---|---|---|
| ☐1920 18¢ Dark Blue & Black | 24.00 | 2.50 | .55 | .16 |

## 1981. PRESERVATION OF WILDLIFE HABITATS

| | | | | |
|---|---|---|---|---|
| ☐1921 18¢ Multicolored | — | — | .48 | .16 |
| ☐1922 18¢ Multicolored | — | — | .48 | .16 |
| ☐1923 18¢ Multicolored | — | — | .48 | .16 |
| ☐1924 18¢ Multicolored | — | — | .48 | .16 |

## 1981. DISABLED PERSONS

| | | | | |
|---|---|---|---|---|
| ☐1925 18¢ Multicolored | 24.00 | 2.50 | .50 | .16 |

## 1981. EDNA ST. VINCENT MILLAY

| | | | | |
|---|---|---|---|---|
| ☐1926 18¢ Multicolored | 24.00 | 2.50 | .50 | .16 |

## 1981. ALCOHOLISM

| | | | | |
|---|---|---|---|---|
| ☐1927 18¢ Dark Blue | 65.00 | 48.00 | .80 | .16 |

## 1981. ARCHITECTURE

| | | | | |
|---|---|---|---|---|
| ☐1928 18¢ Brown & Black | — | — | .60 | .16 |
| ☐1929 18¢ Brown & Black | — | — | .60 | .16 |
| ☐1930 18¢ Brown & Black | — | — | .60 | .16 |
| ☐1931 18¢ Brown & Black | — | — | .60 | .16 |

## 1981. BABE ZAHARIAS

| | | | | |
|---|---|---|---|---|
| ☐1932 18¢ Purple | | 3.00 | .50 | .16 |

## 1981. BOBBY JONES

| | | | | |
|---|---|---|---|---|
| ☐1933 18¢ Dark Green | — | 4.00 | .50 | .16 |

## 1981. FREDERIC REMINGTON

| | | | | |
|---|---|---|---|---|
| ☐1934 18¢ Light Brown & Green | | | | |
| | 22.00 | 2.30 | .55 | .16 |

## 1981. JAMES HOBAN

| | | | | |
|---|---|---|---|---|
| ☐1935 18¢ Multicolored | 23.00 | 2.30 | .55 | .16 |

*No hinge pricing from 1941 to date is figured at (N-H ADD 15%)

| Scott No. | Mint Sheet | Plate Block | Fine Unused Each | Fine Used Each |
|---|---|---|---|---|
| **1981. JAMES HOBAN** | | | | |
| ☐1936 20¢ Multicolored | 25.00 | 2.60 | .55 | .16 |
| **1981. YORKTOWN MAP** | | | | |
| ☐1937 18¢ Multicolored | — | — | .55 | .16 |
| **1981. VIRGINIA CAPES MAP** | | | | |
| ☐1938 18¢ Multicolored | — | — | .55 | .16 |
| **1981. CHRISTMAS—BOTTICELLI** | | | | |
| ☐1939 20¢ Multicolored | 49.00 | 2.40 | .55 | .16 |
| **1981. SEASONS GREETINGS** | | | | |
| ☐1940 20¢ Multicolored | 25.00 | 2.40 | .55 | .16 |
| **1981. JOHN HANSON** | | | | |
| ☐1941 20¢ Multicolored | 26.00 | 2.60 | .55 | .16 |
| **1981. DESERT PLANTS** | | | | |
| ☐1942 20¢ Multicolored | — | — | .55 | .16 |
| ☐1943 20¢ Multicolored | — | — | .55 | .16 |
| ☐1944 20¢ Multicolored | — | — | .55 | .16 |
| ☐1945 20¢ Multicolored | — | — | .55 | .16 |
| **1981. "C" EAGLE—SINGLE** | | | | |
| ☐1946 20¢ Light Brown | 50.00 | 2.60 | .55 | .16 |
| **1981. "C" EAGLE—COIL SINGLE** | | | | |
| ☐1947 20¢ Light Brown | — | — | .55 | .16 |
| **1981. "C" EAGLE—BOOKLET SINGLE** | | | | |
| ☐1948 20¢ Light Brown | — | — | .55 | .16 |
| **1981. BIGHORN SHEEP** | | | | |
| ☐1949 20¢ Dark Blue | — | — | .60 | .16 |
| **1982. FRANKLIN ROOSEVELT** | | | | |
| ☐1950 20¢ Dark Blue | 28.00 | 3.00 | .60 | .16 |

| Scott No. | Mint Sheet | Plate Block | Fine Unused Each | Fine Used Each |
|---|---|---|---|---|
| **1982. "LOVE" FLOWERS** | | | | |
| ☐1951 20¢ Multicolored | 48.00 | 6.00 | 1.00 | .16 |
| **1982. GEORGE WASHINGTON** | | | | |
| ☐1952 20¢ Multicolored | 28.00 | 3.00 | .60 | .16 |
| **1982. STATE BIRDS AND FLOWERS** | | | | |
| ☐1953– | | | | |
| 2002 20¢ Multicolored | 34.00 | — | .50 | .16 |
| **1982. THE NETHERLANDS** | | | | |
| ☐2003 20¢ Dark Blue & Red | 34.00 | 17.50 | .65 | .16 |
| **1982. LIBRARY OF CONGRESS** | | | | |
| ☐2004 20¢ Rose & Dark Gray | 26.00 | 2.60 | .58 | .16 |
| **1982. CONSUMER EDUCATION** | | | | |
| ☐2005 20¢ Light Blue & Dark Blue | | | | |
| | — | 40.00 | 1.25 | .16 |
| **1982. KNOXVILLE WORLD'S FAIR** | | | | |
| ☐2006 20¢ Multicolored | 30.00 | 4.00 | .65 | .16 |
| ☐2007 20¢ Multicolored | 30.00 | 4.00 | .65 | .16 |
| ☐2008 20¢ Multicolored | 30.00 | 4.00 | .65 | .16 |
| ☐2009 20¢ Multicolored | 30.00 | 4.00 | .65 | .16 |
| **1982. HORATIO ALGER** | | | | |
| ☐2010 20¢ Carmine & Black | 26.00 | 2.60 | .55 | .16 |
| **1982. AGING TOGETHER** | | | | |
| ☐2011 20¢ Light Rose | 26.00 | 2.60 | .55 | .16 |
| **1982. THE BARRYMORES** | | | | |
| ☐2012 20¢ Multicolored | 26.00 | 2.70 | .60 | .16 |
| **1982. DR. MARY WALKER** | | | | |
| ☐2013 20¢ Multicolored | 26.00 | 2.70 | .55 | .16 |

*No hinge pricing from 1941 to date is figured at (N-H ADD 15%)

| Scott No. | Mint Sheet | Plate Block | Fine Unused Each | Fine Used Each |
|---|---|---|---|---|
| **1982. INTERNATIONAL PEACE GARDEN** | | | | |
| ☐2014 20¢ Multicolored | 26.00 | 2.60 | .58 | .16 |
| **1982. AMERICA'S LIBRARIES** | | | | |
| ☐2015 20¢ Orange-Red & Black | | | | |
| | 26.00 | 2.60 | .58 | .16 |
| **1982. JACKIE ROBINSON** | | | | |
| ☐2016 20¢ Multicolored | 85.00 | 10.00 | 2.00 | .16 |
| **1982. TOURO SYNAGOGUE** | | | | |
| ☐2017 20¢ Multicolored | 38.00 | 18.00 | 1.00 | .16 |
| **1982. WOLF TRAP FARM PARK** | | | | |
| ☐2018 20¢ Multicolored | 27.00 | 2.60 | .60 | .16 |
| **1982. ARCHITECTURE—WRIGHT** | | | | |
| ☐2019 20¢ Black and Brown | — | — | .60 | .16 |
| **1982. ARCHITECTURE—VAN DER ROHE** | | | | |
| ☐2020 20¢ Black and Brown | — | — | .60 | .16 |
| **1982. ARCHITECTURE—GROPIUS** | | | | |
| ☐2021 20¢ Black and Brown | — | — | .60 | .16 |
| **1982. ARCHITECTURE—SAARINEN** | | | | |
| ☐2022 20¢ Black and Brown | — | — | .60 | .16 |
| ☐Architecture, above four attached | | | | |
| | 36.00 | 4.25 | .60 | .16 |
| **1982. FRANCIS OF ASSISI** | | | | |
| ☐2023 20¢ Multicolored | 28.00 | 3.00 | .65 | .16 |
| **1982. PONCE DE LEON** | | | | |
| ☐2024 20¢ Multicolored | 38.00 | 19.00 | .95 | 16 |
| **1982. CHRISTMAS ISSUE, CAT AND DOG** | | | | |
| ☐2025 13¢ Multicolored | 19.00 | 2.00 | .42 | .16 |

*No hinge pricing from 1941 to date is figured at (N-H ADD 15%)

| Scott No. | Mint Sheet | Plate Block | Fine Unused Each | Fine Used Each |
|---|---|---|---|---|

## 1982. CHRISTMAS ISSUE, TIEPOLO'S "MADONNA AND CHILD"

| | | | | |
|---|---|---|---|---|
| ☐2026 20¢ Multicolored | 30.00 | 16.00 | .65 | .16 |

## 1982. SEASON'S GREETINGS, SLEDDING

| | | | | |
|---|---|---|---|---|
| ☐2027 20¢ Multicolored | — | — | .75 | .16 |

## 1982. SEASON'S GREETINGS, BUILDING SNOWMAN

| | | | | |
|---|---|---|---|---|
| ☐2028 20¢ Multicolored | — | — | .75 | .16 |

## 1982. SEASON'S GREETINGS, ICE SKATING

| | | | | |
|---|---|---|---|---|
| ☐2029 20¢ Multicolored | — | — | .75 | .16 |

## 1982. SEASON'S GREETINGS, TRIMMING TREE

| | | | | |
|---|---|---|---|---|
| ☐2030 20¢ Multicolored | — | — | .75 | .16 |
| ☐Season's Greetings, above four attached | 41.00 | 4.00 | .75 | .16 |

## 1982. SCIENCE AND INDUSTRY

| | | | | |
|---|---|---|---|---|
| ☐2031 20¢ Multicolored | 26.00 | 2.60 | .60 | .16 |

## 1983. BALLOONING

| | | | | |
|---|---|---|---|---|
| ☐2032 20¢ Multicolored | — | — | .60 | .16 |

## 1982. BALLOONING

| | | | | |
|---|---|---|---|---|
| ☐2033 20¢ Multicolored | — | — | .60 | .16 |

## 1982. BALLOONING

| | | | | |
|---|---|---|---|---|
| ☐2034 20¢ Multicolored | — | — | .60 | .16 |

## 1982. BALLOONING

| | | | | |
|---|---|---|---|---|
| ☐2035 20¢ Multicolored | — | — | .60 | .16 |
| ☐Ballooning, above four attached | 26.00 | 3.00 | .60 | .16 |

## 1983. TREATY OF AMITY

| | | | | |
|---|---|---|---|---|
| ☐2036 20¢ Blue and Black | 26.00 | 2.60 | .62 | .16 |

*No hinge pricing from 1941 to date is figured at (N-H ADD 15%)

| Scott No. | Mint Sheet | Plate Block | Fine Unused Each | Fine Used Each |
|---|---|---|---|---|
| **1983. CIVILIAN CONSERVATION CORPS** | | | | |
| ☐2037 20¢ Multicolored | 27.00 | 2.60 | .62 | .16 |
| **1983. JOSEPH PRIESTLEY** | | | | |
| ☐2038 20¢ Rust Brown | 30.00 | 2.60 | .62 | .16 |
| **1983. VOLUNTEER** | | | | |
| ☐2039 20¢ Black and Red | 40.00 | 19.00 | .80 | .16 |
| **1983. CONCORD** | | | | |
| ☐2040 20¢ Beige | 26.00 | 2.60 | .62 | .16 |
| **1983. BROOKLYN BRIDGE** | | | | |
| ☐2041 20¢ Blue | 27.00 | 2.60 | .60 | .16 |
| **1983. TENNESSEE VALLEY AUTHORITY** | | | | |
| ☐2042 20¢ Multicolored | 40.00 | 19.00 | .90 | .16 |
| **1983. PHYSICAL FITNESS** | | | | |
| ☐2043 20¢ Multicolored | 40.00 | 19.00 | .80 | .16 |
| **1982. SCOTT JOPLIN** | | | | |
| ☐2044 20¢ Multicolored | 29.00 | 3.00 | .80 | .16 |
| **1983. MEDAL OF HONOR** | | | | |
| ☐2045 20¢ Multicolored | 26.00 | 3.00 | .65 | .16 |
| **1983. BABE RUTH** | | | | |
| ☐2046 20¢ Blue | 85.00 | 9.00 | 2.10 | .16 |
| **1983. NATHANIEL HAWTHORNE** | | | | |
| ☐2047 20¢ Multicolored | 27.00 | 2.60 | .60 | .16 |
| **1983. SUMMER OLYMPICS 1984** | | | | |
| ☐2048 13¢ Multicolored | — | — | .42 | .16 |
| **1983. SUMMER OLYMPICS 1984** | | | | |
| ☐2049 13¢ Multicolored | — | — | .42 | .16 |

*No hinge pricing from 1941 to date is figured at (N-H ADD 15%)

| Scott No. | Mint Sheet | Plate Block | Fine Unused Each | Fine Used Each |
|---|---|---|---|---|
| **1983. SUMMER OLYMPICS 1984** | | | | |
| ☐2050 13¢ Multicolored | — | — | .42 | .16 |
| **1983. SUMMER OLYMPICS 1984** | | | | |
| ☐2051 13¢ Multicolored | — | — | .42 | .16 |
| **1983. TREATY OF PARIS** | | | | |
| ☐2052 20¢ Multicolored | 22.00 | 2.90 | .65 | .16 |
| **1983. CIVIL SERVICE** | | | | |
| ☐2053 20¢ Multicolored | 39.00 | 12.00 | .80 | .16 |
| **1983. METROPOLITAN OPERA** | | | | |
| ☐2054 20¢ Yellow & Brown | 35.00 | 3.50 | .75 | .16 |
| **1983. INVENTORS** | | | | |
| ☐2055 20¢ Multicolored | 36.00 | 4.50 | .65 | .16 |
| **1983. INVENTORS** | | | | |
| ☐2056 20¢ Multicolored | 36.00 | 4.50 | .65 | .16 |
| **1983. INVENTORS** | | | | |
| ☐2057 20¢ Multicolored | 36.00 | 4.50 | .65 | .16 |
| **1983. INVENTORS** | | | | |
| ☐2058 20¢ Multicolored | 36.00 | 4.50 | .65 | .16 |
| **1983. STREETCARS** | | | | |
| ☐2059 20¢ Multicolored | 34.00 | 4.00 | .65 | .16 |
| **1983. STREETCARS** | | | | |
| ☐2060 20¢ Multicolored | 34.00 | 2.75 | .60 | .16 |
| **1983. STREETCARS** | | | | |
| ☐2061 20¢ Multicolored | 34.00 | 2.75 | .60 | .16 |
| **1983. STREETCARS** | | | | |
| ☐2062 20¢ Multicolored | 34.00 | 2.75 | .60 | .16 |

*No hinge pricing from 1941 to date is figured at (N-H ADD 15%)

| Scott No. | Mint Sheet | Plate Block | Fine Unused Each | Fine Used Each |
|---|---|---|---|---|
| **1983. CHRISTMAS, MADONNA** | | | | |
| ☐2063 20¢ Multicolored | 27.00 | 2.60 | .60 | .16 |
| **1983. CHRISTMAS, SEASON'S GREETINGS** | | | | |
| ☐2064 20¢ Multicolored | 32.00 | 2.60 | .60 | .16 |
| **1983. MARTIN LUTHER** | | | | |
| ☐2065 20¢ Multicolored | 26.00 | 2.60 | .60 | .16 |
| **1984. ALASKA STATEHOOD** | | | | |
| ☐2066 20¢ Multicolored | 26.00 | 2.40 | .60 | .16 |
| **1984. WINTER OLYMPICS 1984** | | | | |
| ☐2067 20¢ Multicolored | 30.00 | 3.60 | .60 | .16 |
| **1984. WINTER OLYMPICS 1984** | | | | |
| ☐2068 20¢ Multicolored | 30.00 | 3.60 | .60 | .16 |
| **1984. WINTER OLYMPICS 1984** | | | | |
| ☐2069 20¢ Multicolored | 30.00 | 3.60 | .60 | .16 |
| **1984. WINTER OLYMPICS 1984** | | | | |
| ☐2070 20¢ Multicolored | 30.00 | 3.60 | .60 | .16 |
| **1984. FEDERAL DEPOSIT INSURANCE CORPORATION** | | | | |
| ☐2071 20¢ Red & Yellow | 26.00 | 2.60 | .60 | .16 |
| **1984. LOVE** | | | | |
| ☐2072 20¢ Multicolored | 34.00 | 2.60 | .60 | .16 |
| **1984. CARTER G. WOODSON** | | | | |
| ☐2073 20¢ Multicolored | 30.00 | 2.70 | .58 | .16 |
| **1984. SOIL AND WATER CONSERVATION** | | | | |
| ☐2074 20¢ Multicolored | 26.00 | 2.40 | .58 | .16 |
| **1984. CREDIT UNION** | | | | |
| ☐2075 20¢ Multicolored | 26.00 | 2.40 | .58 | .16 |

*No hinge pricing from 1941 to date is figured at (N-H ADD 15%)

| Scott No. | Mint Sheet | Plate Block | Fine Unused Each | Fine Used Each |
|---|---|---|---|---|
| **1984. ORCHIDS** | | | | |
| ☐2076 20¢ Multicolored | 32.00 | 3.60 | .65 | .16 |
| **1984. ORCHIDS** | | | | |
| ☐2077 20¢ Multicolored | 32.00 | 3.60 | .65 | .16 |
| **1984. ORCHIDS** | | | | |
| ☐2078 20¢ Multicolored | 32.00 | 3.60 | .65 | .16 |
| **1984. ORCHIDS** | | | | |
| ☐2079 20¢ Multicolored | 32.00 | 3.00 | .65 | .16 |
| **1984. HAWAII STATEHOOD** | | | | |
| ☐2080 20¢ Blue & Yellow | 31.00 | 3.10 | .70 | .16 |
| **1984. NATIONAL ARCHIVES** | | | | |
| ☐2081 20¢ Brown & Black | 32.00 | 3.00 | .70 | .16 |
| **1984. SUMMER OLYMPICS 1984** | | | | |
| ☐2082 20¢ Multicolored | 41.00 | 4.00 | 1.00 | .16 |
| **1984. SUMMER OLYMPICS 1984** | | | | |
| ☐2083 20¢ Multicolored | 41.00 | 4.00 | 1.00 | .16 |
| **1984. SUMMER OLYMPICS 1984** | | | | |
| ☐2084 20¢ Multicolored | 41.00 | 4.00 | 1.00 | .16 |
| **1984. SUMMER OLYMPICS 1984** | | | | |
| ☐2085 20¢ Multicolored | 41.00 | 4.00 | 1.00 | .16 |
| **1984. LOUISIANA WORLD'S FAIR** | | | | |
| ☐2086 20¢ Multicolored | 23.00 | 2.80 | .65 | .16 |
| **1984. HEALTH RESEARCH** | | | | |
| ☐2087 20¢ Multicolored | 30.00 | 3.10 | .70 | .16 |
| **1984. DOUGLAS FAIRBANKS** | | | | |
| ☐2088 20¢ Black & White | 36.00 | 18.50 | .70 | .16 |

*No hinge pricing from 1941 to date is figured at (N-H ADD 15%)

| Scott No. | Mint Sheet | Plate Block | Fine Unused Each | Fine Used Each |
|---|---|---|---|---|
| **1984. JIM THORPE** | | | | |
| ☐2089 20¢ Black & White | 30.00 | 3.00 | .70 | .16 |
| **1984. JOHN McCORMACK** | | | | |
| ☐2090 20¢ Multicolored | 27.00 | 2.50 | .60 | .16 |
| **1984. ST. LAWRENCE SEAWAY** | | | | |
| ☐2091 20¢ Multicolored | 27.00 | 2.80 | .60 | .16 |
| **1984. WATERFOWL PRESERVATION** | | | | |
| ☐2092 20¢ Multicolored | 40.00 | 3.50 | 1.00 | .16 |
| **1984. ROANOKE VOYAGES 1584** | | | | |
| ☐2093 20¢ Multicolored | 30.00 | 2.80 | .58 | .16 |
| **1984. HERMAN MELVILLE** | | | | |
| ☐2094 20¢ Green | 26.00 | 2.60 | .58 | .16 |
| **1984. HORACE MOSES** | | | | |
| ☐2095 20¢ Orange & Brown | 58.00 | 20.00 | .58 | .16 |
| **1984. SMOKEY THE BEAR** | | | | |
| ☐2096 20¢ Multicolored | 30.00 | 3.00 | .58 | .16 |
| **1984. ROBERTO CLEMENTE** | | | | |
| ☐2097 20¢ Multicolored | 100.00 | 12.00 | 2.00 | .16 |
| **1984. DOGS: BEAGLE** | | | | |
| ☐2098 20¢ Multicolored | 28.00 | 4.50 | .65 | .16 |
| **1984. DOGS: RETRIEVER** | | | | |
| ☐2099 20¢ Multicolored | 28.00 | 4.50 | .65 | .16 |
| **1984. DOGS: MALAMUTE** | | | | |
| ☐2100 20¢ Multicolored | 28.00 | 4.50 | .65 | .16 |
| **1984. DOGS: COONHOUND** | | | | |
| ☐2101 20¢ Multicolored | 28.00 | 4.50 | .65 | .16 |

*No hinge pricing from 1941 to date is figured at (N-H ADD 15%)

| Scott No. | Mint Sheet | Plate Block | Fine Unused Each | Fine Used Each |
|---|---|---|---|---|
| **1984. CRIME PREVENTION** | | | | |
| ☐2102 20¢ Multicolored | 26.00 | 2.60 | .60 | .16 |
| **1984. HISPANIC AMERICANS** | | | | |
| ☐2103 20¢ Multicolored | 20.00 | 2.60 | .60 | .16 |
| **1984. FAMILY UNITY** | | | | |
| ☐2104 20¢ Multicolored | 44.00 | 20.00 | .60 | .16 |
| **1984. ELEANOR ROOSEVELT** | | | | |
| ☐2105 20¢ Blue | 24.00 | 2.60 | .60 | .16 |
| **1984. NATION OF READERS** | | | | |
| ☐2106 20¢ Brown & Maroon | 25.00 | 2.60 | .60 | .16 |
| **1984. MADONNA AND CHILD** | | | | |
| ☐2107 20¢ Multicolored | 26.00 | 2.60 | .60 | .16 |
| **1984. SANTA CLAUS** | | | | |
| ☐2108 20¢ Multicolored | 27.00 | 2.60 | .60 | .16 |
| **1984. VIETNAM MEMORIAL** | | | | |
| ☐2109 20¢ Multicolored | 29.00 | 3.60 | .60 | .16 |
| **1985. JEROME KERN** | | | | |
| ☐2110 22¢ Multicolored | 30.00 | 3.10 | .65 | .16 |
| **1985. "D" NON-DENOMINATIONAL** | | | | |
| ☐2111 22¢ Green | 95.00 | 36.00 | .75 | .16 |
| **1985. "D" NON-DENOMINATIONAL COIL** | | | | |
| ☐2112 22¢ Green | — | 6.00 | .70 | .16 |
| **1985. "D" NON-DENOMINATIONAL BOOKLET** | | | | |
| ☐2113 22¢ Green | — | — | .70 | .16 |
| **1985. FLAG OVER DOME** | | | | |
| ☐2114 22¢ Multicolored | 50.00 | 2.80 | .65 | .16 |

*No hinge pricing from 1941 to date is figured at (N-H ADD 15%)

| Scott No. | Mint Sheet | Plate Block | Fine Unused Each | Fine Used Each |
|---|---|---|---|---|
| **1985. FLAG OVER DOME COIL** | | | | |
| ☐2115 22¢ Multicolored | — | — | .65 | .16 |
| **1985. FLAG OVER DOME BOOKLET** | | | | |
| ☐2116 22¢ Multicolored | — | — | .85 | .16 |
| **1985. SEASHELLS: DOGWINKLE** | | | | |
| ☐2117 22¢ Brown | — | — | .70 | .16 |
| **1985. SEASHELLS: HELMET** | | | | |
| ☐2118 22¢ Brown | — | — | .70 | .16 |
| **1985. SEASHELLS: NEPTUNE** | | | | |
| ☐2119 22¢ Brown | — | — | .70 | .16 |
| **1985. SEASHELLS: SCALLOP** | | | | |
| ☐2120 22¢ Pink | — | — | .70 | .16 |
| **1985. SEASHELLS: WHELK** | | | | |
| ☐2121 22¢ Brown | — | — | .70 | .16 |
| **1985. EXPRESS MAIL U.S.A.** | | | | |
| ☐2122 $10.75 Multicolored | — | — | 26.00 | 10.00 |
| **1985. SCHOOL BUS** | | | | |
| ☐2123 3.4¢ Dark Brown | — | — | .23 | .16 |
| **1985. BUCKBOARD** | | | | |
| ☐2124 4.9¢ Dark Brown | — | — | .23 | .16 |
| **1986. STAR ROUTE TRUCK** | | | | |
| ☐2125 5.5¢ Carmine | — | — | .23 | .16 |
| **1985. TRICYCLE 1880s** | | | | |
| ☐2126 6¢ Red | — | — | .23 | .16 |
| **1985. TRACTOR** | | | | |
| ☐2127 7.1¢ Lake | — | — | .23 | .16 |

*No hinge pricing from 1941 to date is figured at (N-H ADD 15%)

| Scott No. | Mint Sheet | Plate Block | Fine Unused Each | Fine Used Each |
|---|---|---|---|---|

**1985. AMBULANCE**

| ☐2128 8.3¢ Green | — | — | .23 | .16 |

**1985. TOW TRUCK**

| ☐2129 8.5¢ Dark Green | — | — | .23 | .16 |

**1985. OIL WAGON 1890s**

| ☐2130 10.1¢ Black | — | — | .30 | .16 |

**1985. STUTZ AUTO**

| ☐2131 11¢ Blue | — | — | .28 | .16 |

**1985. STANLEY STEAMER 1909**

| ☐2132 12¢ Blue | — | — | .30 | .16 |

**1985. PUSHCART 1880s**

| ☐2133 12.5¢ Black | — | — | .32 | .16 |

**1985. ICEBOAT 1880s**

| ☐2134 14¢ Blue | — | — | .40 | .16 |

**1986. DOG SLED 1920s**

| ☐2135 17¢ Blue | — | — | .46 | .16 |

**1986. BREAD WAGON 1880s**

| ☐2136 25¢ Brown | — | — | .65 | .16 |

**1985. MARY McCLEOD BETHUNE**

| ☐2137 22¢ Multicolored | 32.00 | 3.50 | .75 | .16 |

**1985. DUCKS: BROADBILL**

| ☐2138 22¢ Multicolored | 55.00 | 8.50 | .90 | .16 |

**1985. DUCKS: MALLARD**

| ☐2139 22¢ Multicolored | 55.00 | 8.50 | .90 | .16 |

**1985. DUCKS: CANVASBACK**

| ☐2140 22¢ Multicolored | 55.00 | 8.50 | .90 | .16 |

*No hinge pricing from 1941 to date is figured at (N-H ADD 15%)

| Scott No. | Mint Sheet | Plate Block | Fine Unused Each | Fine Used Each |
|---|---|---|---|---|
| **1985. DUCKS: REDHEAD** | | | | |
| ☐2141 22¢ Multicolored | 55.00 | 8.50 | .90 | .16 |
| **1985. WINTER SPECIAL OLYMPICS** | | | | |
| ☐2142 22¢ Multicolored | 22.00 | 3.00 | .65 | .16 |
| **1985. LOVE** | | | | |
| ☐2143 22¢ Multicolored | 28.00 | 3.00 | .65 | .16 |
| **1985. RURAL ELECTRIFICATION ADMINISTRATION** | | | | |
| ☐2144 22¢ Multicolored | 54.00 | 25.00 | .90 | .16 |
| **1985. AMERIPEX SHOW** | | | | |
| ☐2145 22¢ Multicolored | 28.00 | 3.00 | .65 | .16 |
| **1985. ABIGAIL ADAMS** | | | | |
| ☐2146 22¢ Multicolored | 28.00 | 3.10 | .65 | .16 |
| **1985. BARTHOLDI, STATUE OF LIBERTY** | | | | |
| ☐2147 22¢ Multicolored | 28.00 | 3.10 | .65 | .16 |
| **1985. GEORGE WASHINGTON** | | | | |
| ☐2149 18¢ Multicolored | — | — | .46 | .16 |
| **1985. ENVELOPES** | | | | |
| ☐2150 2.1¢ Multicolored | — | — | .46 | .16 |
| **1985. KOREAN VETERANS** | | | | |
| ☐2152 22¢ Red & Green | 32.50 | 3.50 | .65 | .16 |
| **1985. SOCIAL SECURITY** | | | | |
| ☐2153 22¢ Blue | 28.00 | 3.35 | .65 | .16 |
| **1985. WORLD WAR I VETERANS** | | | | |
| ☐2154 22¢ Red & Green | 33.00 | 4.00 | .75 | .16 |
| **1985. HORSES: QUARTER HORSE** | | | | |
| ☐2155 22¢ Multicolored | 80.00 | 10.00 | .80 | .16 |

*No hinge pricing from 1941 to date is figured at (N-H ADD 15%)

| Scott No. | Mint Sheet | Plate Block | Fine Unused Each | Fine Used Each |
|---|---|---|---|---|
| **1985. HORSES: MORGAN** | | | | |
| ☐2156 22¢ Multicolored | 80.00 | 10.00 | .80 | .16 |
| **1985. HORSES: SADDLEBRED** | | | | |
| ☐2157 22¢ Multicolored | 80.00 | 10.00 | 1.00 | .16 |
| **1985. HORSES: APPALOOSA** | | | | |
| ☐2158 22¢ Multicolored | 80.00 | 10.00 | 1.00 | .16 |
| **1985. PUBLIC EDUCATION** | | | | |
| ☐2159 22¢ Multicolored | 58.00 | 6.00 | 1.30 | .16 |
| **1985. YOUTH YEAR: Y.M.C.A.** | | | | |
| ☐2160 22¢ Multicolored | 54.00 | 6.00 | 1.00 | .16 |
| **1985. YOUTH YEAR: BOY SCOUTS** | | | | |
| ☐2161 22¢ Multicolored | 54.00 | 6.00 | 1.00 | .16 |
| **1985. YOUTH YEAR: BIG BROTHERS** | | | | |
| ☐2162 22¢ Multicolored | 54.00 | 6.00 | 1.00 | 16 |
| **1985. YOUTH YEAR: CAMPFIRE** | | | | |
| ☐2163 22¢ Multicolored | 54.00 | 6.00 | 1.00 | .16 |
| **1985. HELP END HUNGER** | | | | |
| ☐2164 22¢ Multicolored | 31.00 | 3.25 | .70 | .16 |
| **1985. MADONNA** | | | | |
| ☐2165 22¢ Multicolored | 28.00 | 2.85 | .65 | .16 |
| **1985. POINSETTIA** | | | | |
| ☐2166 22¢ Multicolored | 28.00 | 2.85 | .65 | .16 |
| **1986. ARKANSAS** | | | | |
| ☐2167 22¢ Multicolored | 30.00 | 3.10 | .70 | .16 |
| **1986. MARGARET MITCHELL** | | | | |
| ☐2168 1¢ Brown | 6.00 | — | .23 | .16 |

*No hinge pricing from 1941 to date is figured at (N-H ADD 15%)

| Scott No. | Mint Sheet | Plate Block | Fine Unused Each | Fine Used Each |
|---|---|---|---|---|
| **1987. MARY LYON** | | | | |
| ☐2169 2¢ Blue | 6.00 | — | .23 | .16 |
| **1986. PAUL DUDLEY WHITE M.D.** | | | | |
| ☐2170 3¢ Blue | 8.00 | — | .23 | .16 |
| **1986. FATHER FLANAGAN** | | | | |
| ☐2171 4¢ Blue | 9.00 | — | .23 | .16 |
| **1986. HUGO L. BLACK** | | | | |
| ☐2172 5¢ Olive Green | 12.00 | .80 | .23 | .16 |
| **1990. LUIS MUNOZ MARIN** | | | | |
| ☐2173 5¢ Carmine | 11.00 | — | .23 | .16 |
| **1988. RED CLOUD** | | | | |
| ☐2176 10¢ Lake | 22.00 | — | .23 | .16 |
| **1987. JULIA WARD HOWE** | | | | |
| ☐2177 14¢ Red | 31.00 | 2.00 | .32 | .16 |
| **1988. BUFFALO BILL CODY** | | | | |
| ☐2178 15¢ Claret | 30.00 | — | .40 | .16 |
| **1986. BELVA ANN LOCKWOOD** | | | | |
| ☐2179 17¢ Blue Green | 40.00 | 2.50 | .46 | .16 |
| **1988. CHESTER CARLSON** | | | | |
| ☐2180 21¢ Blue Violet | 52.00 | — | .60 | .16 |
| **1988. MARY CASSATT** | | | | |
| ☐2182 23¢ Purple | 42.00 | — | .55 | .16 |
| **1986. JACK LONDON** | | | | |
| ☐2183 25¢ Blue | 56.00 | 3.25 | .70 | .16 |
| **1989. SITTING BULL** | | | | |
| ☐2184 28¢ Myrtle Green | 50.00 | — | .60 | .16 |

*No hinge pricing from 1941 to date is figured at (N-H ADD 15%)

| Scott No. | Mint Sheet | Plate Block | Fine Unused Each | Fine Used Each |
|---|---|---|---|---|
| **1992. EARL WARREN** | | | | |
| ☐2184A 29¢ Blue | 60.00 | — | .70 | .18 |
| **1986. DENNIS CHAVEZ** | | | | |
| ☐2185 35¢ Black | 68.00 | — | .75 | .18 |
| **1990. CLAIRE CHENAULT** | | | | |
| ☐2186 40¢ Dark Blue | 72.00 | — | .85 | .18 |
| **1988. DR. HARVEY CUSHING** | | | | |
| ☐2188 45¢ Blue | 100.00 | — | 1.00 | .18 |
| **1987. HUBERT HUMPHREY** | | | | |
| ☐2190 52¢ Purple | 92.00 | — | 1.10 | .18 |
| **1986. JOHN HARVARD** | | | | |
| ☐2191 56¢ Brown | 125.00 | — | 1.35 | .16 |
| **1988. H.H. ARNOLD** | | | | |
| ☐2192 65¢ Blue/Gray | 110.00 | — | 1.50 | .16 |
| **1987. WENDELL WILLKIE** | | | | |
| ☐2193 75¢ Magenta | 145.00 | — | 1.65 | .16 |
| **1986. BERNARD REVEL** | | | | |
| ☐2194 $1.00 Green | 190.00 | — | 3.10 | .30 |
| **1988. JOHNS HOPKINS** | | | | |
| ☐2194A $1.00 Dark Green | 39.00 | — | 8.00 | .42 |
| **1986. WILLIAM JENNINGS BRYAN** | | | | |
| ☐2195 $2.00 Violet | 360.00 | — | 4.50 | .50 |
| **1987. BRET HARTE** | | | | |
| ☐2196 $5.00 Brown | 170.00 | — | 10.00 | 1.50 |
| **1986. STAMP COLLECTING: AMERICAN PHILATELIC ASSOC.** | | | | |
| ☐2198 22¢ Multicolored | — | — | .78 | .16 |

*No hinge from 1941 to date is figured at (N-H ADD 15%)

| Scott No. | Mint Sheet | Plate Block | Fine Unused Each | Fine Used Each |
|---|---|---|---|---|
| **1986. STAMP COLLECTING: LITTLE BOY** | | | | |
| ☐2199 22¢ Multicolored | — | — | .60 | .16 |
| **1986. STAMP COLLECTING: MAGNIFIER** | | | | |
| ☐2200 22¢ Multicolored | — | — | .60 | .16 |
| **1986. STAMP COLLECTING: RUBBER STAMP** | | | | |
| ☐2201 22¢ Multicolored | — | — | .60 | .16 |
| **1986. LOVE** | | | | |
| ☐2202 22¢ Multicolored | 28.00 | 3.50 | .60 | .16 |
| **1986. SOJOURNER TRUTH** | | | | |
| ☐2203 22¢ Multicolored | 31.00 | 3.50 | .70 | .16 |
| **1986. TEXAS—SAN JACINTO 1836** | | | | |
| ☐2204 22¢ Multicolored | 31.00 | 3.50 | .70 | .16 |
| **1986. FISH: MUSKELLUNGE** | | | | |
| ☐2205 22¢ Multicolored | — | — | .75 | .16 |
| **1986. FISH: ATLANTIC COD** | | | | |
| ☐2206 22¢ Multicolored | — | — | .75 | .16 |
| **1986. FISH: LARGEMOUTH BASS** | | | | |
| ☐2207 22¢ Multicolored | — | — | .75 | .16 |
| **1986. FISH: BLUEFIN TUNA** | | | | |
| ☐2208 22¢ Multicolored | — | — | .75 | .16 |
| **1986. FISH: CATFISH** | | | | |
| ☐2209 22¢ Multicolored | — | — | .75 | .16 |
| **1986. PUBLIC HOSPITALS** | | | | |
| ☐2210 22¢ Multicolored | 27.00 | 3.00 | .60 | .16 |
| **1986. DUKE ELLINGTON** | | | | |
| ☐2211 22¢ Multicolored | 31.00 | 3.15 | .70 | .16 |

| Scott No. | Mint Sheet | Plate Block | Fine Unused Each | Fine Used Each |
|---|---|---|---|---|
| **1986. AMERIPEX '86-PRESIDENTS I** | | | | |
| ☐2216 22¢ Brown & Black | — | — | .50 | .16 |
| **1986. AMERIPEX '86-PRESIDENTS II** | | | | |
| ☐2217 22¢ Brown & Black | — | — | .50 | .16 |
| **1986. AMERIPEX '86-PRESIDENTS III** | | | | |
| ☐2218 22¢ Brown & Black | — | — | .50 | .16 |
| **1986. AMERIPEX '86-PRESIDENTS IV** | | | | |
| ☐2219 22¢ Brown & Black | — | — | .50 | .16 |
| **1986. POLAR EXPLORERS: KANE** | | | | |
| ☐2220 22¢ Multicolored | — | — | 1.00 | .16 |
| **1986. POLAR EXPLORERS: GREELY** | | | | |
| ☐2221 22¢ Multicolored | — | — | 1.00 | .16 |
| **1986. POLAR EXPLORERS: STEFANSSON** | | | | |
| ☐2222 22¢ Multicolored | — | — | 1.00 | .16 |
| **1986. POLAR EXPLORERS: HENSON** | | | | |
| ☐2223 22¢ Multicolored | — | — | 1.00 | .16 |
| **1986. LIBERTY** | | | | |
| ☐2224 22¢ Carmine & Blue | 28.00 | 3.00 | .65 | .16 |
| **1986. NAVAJO ART** | | | | |
| ☐2235 22¢ Multicolored | 34.00 | 3.60 | .65 | .16 |
| **1986. NAVAJO ART** | | | | |
| ☐2236 22¢ Multicolored | — | — | .65 | .16 |
| **1986. NAVAJO ART** | | | | |
| ☐2237 22¢ Multicolored | — | — | .65 | .16 |
| **1986. NAVAJO ART** | | | | |
| ☐2238 22¢ Multicolored | — | — | .65 | .16 |

*No hinge pricing from 1941 to date is figured at (N-H ADD 15%)

| Scott No. | Mint Sheet | Plate Block | Fine Unused Each | Fine Used Each |
|---|---|---|---|---|
| **1986. T.S. ELIOT** | | | | |
| ☐2239 22¢ Brown | 26.00 | 3.00 | .65 | .16 |
| **1986. FOLK ART: HIGHLANDER** | | | | |
| ☐2240 22¢ Multicolored | 32.00 | 4.00 | .65 | .16 |
| **1986. FOLK ART: SHIP** | | | | |
| ☐2241 22¢ Multicolored | — | — | .65 | .16 |
| **1986. FOLK ART: NAUTICAL** | | | | |
| ☐2242 22¢ Multicolored | — | — | .65 | .16 |
| **1986. FOLK ART: CIGAR STORE** | | | | |
| ☐2243 22¢ Multicolored | — | — | .65 | .16 |
| **1986. CHRISTMAS: PEROGINO GALLERY** | | | | |
| ☐2244 22¢ Multicolored | 52.00 | 2.90 | .65 | .16 |
| **1986. CHRISTMAS: GREETINGS** | | | | |
| ☐2245 22¢ Multicolored | 52.00 | 2.90 | .65 | .16 |
| **1987. MICHIGAN STATEHOOD** | | | | |
| ☐2246 22¢ Multicolored | 28.00 | 3.00 | .65 | .16 |
| **1987. PAN AMERICAN GAMES** | | | | |
| ☐2247 22¢ Multicolored | 28.00 | 3.00 | .65 | .16 |
| **1987. LOVE** | | | | |
| ☐2248 22¢ Multicolored | — | — | .65 | .16 |
| **1987. JEAN BAPTISTE POINTE DU SABLE** | | | | |
| ☐2249 22¢ Multicolored | 28.00 | 3.00 | .65 | .16 |
| **1987. ENRICO CARUSO** | | | | |
| ☐2250 22¢ Multicolored | 28.00 | 2.50 | .65 | .16 |
| **1987. GIRL SCOUTS** | | | | |
| ☐2251 22¢ Multicolored | 28.00 | 3.00 | .65 | .16 |

*No hinge pricing from 1941 to date is figured at (N-H ADD 15%)

| Scott No. | Mint Sheet | Plate Block | Fine Unused Each | Fine Used Each |
|---|---|---|---|---|

### 1988. CONESTOGA WAGON
☐2252 3¢ Claret — — .23 .16

### 1988. MILK WAGON
☐2253 5¢ Black — — .23 .16

### 1988. ELEVATOR
☐2254 5.3¢ Black — — .23 .16

### 1988. CARRETA
☐2255 7.6¢ Brown — — .23 .16

### 1988. WHEELCHAIR
☐2256 8.4¢ Claret — — .23 .16

### 1988. CANAL BOAT
☐2257 10¢ Sky Blue — — .28 .16

### 1988. POLICE WAGON
☐2258 13¢ Black — — .28 .16

### 1988. RAILROAD COALCAR
☐2259 13.2¢ Slate Green — — .38 .16

### 1988. TUG BOAT
☐2260 15¢ Violet — — .38 .16

### 1988. POPCORN WAGON
☐2261 16.7¢ Rose — — .50 .16

### 1988. RACING CAR
☐2262 17.5¢ Violet — — .50 .16

### 1988. CABLE CAR
☐2263 20¢ Blue Violet — — .55 .16

### 1988. FIRE ENGINE
☐2264 20.5¢ Rose — — .60 .16

*No hinge pricing from 1941 to date is figured at (N-H ADD 15%)

| Scott No. | Mint Sheet | Plate Block | Fine Unused Each | Fine Used Each |
|---|---|---|---|---|
| **1988. RAILROAD MAILCAR** | | | | |
| ☐2265 21¢ Green | — | — | .60 | .16 |
| **1988. TANDEM BICYCLE** | | | | |
| ☐2266 24.1¢ Ultramarine | — | — | .65 | .16 |
| **1987. SPECIAL OCCASIONS** | | | | |
| ☐2267– | | | | |
| 2274 22¢ Multicolored | — | — | .65 | .16 |
| **1987. UNITED WAY UNITING COMMUNITIES** | | | | |
| ☐2275 22¢ Multicolored | 28.00 | 2.90 | .65 | .16 |
| **1987. AMERICAN FLAG** | | | | |
| ☐2276 22¢ Multicolored | — | — | .65 | .16 |
| **1987. "E" EARTH** | | | | |
| ☐2277 25¢ Multicolored | 62.00 | 3.40 | .75 | .16 |
| **1987. FLAG ON CLOUDS** | | | | |
| ☐2278 25¢ Multicolored | 60.00 | 3.10 | .70 | .16 |
| **1987. FLAG YOSEMITE** | | | | |
| ☐2280 25¢ Multicolored | — | — | .70 | .16 |
| **1987. HONEY BEE** | | | | |
| ☐2281 25¢ Multicolored | — | — | .70 | .16 |
| **1987. PHEASANT** | | | | |
| ☐2283 25¢ Multicolored | — | — | .70 | .16 |
| **1987. GROSBEAK** | | | | |
| ☐2284 25¢ Multicolored | — | — | .70 | .16 |
| **1987. OWL** | | | | |
| ☐2285 25¢ Multicolored | — | — | .70 | .16 |

*No hinge pricing from 1941 to date is figured at (N-H ADD 15%)

| Scott No. | Mint Sheet | Plate Block | Fine Unused Each | Fine Used Each |
|---|---|---|---|---|
| **1987. AMERICAN WILDLIFE** | | | | |
| ☐2286– | | | | |
| 2335 22¢ Multicolored | 68.00 | — | .70 | .16 |
| **1987. DELAWARE** | | | | |
| ☐2336 22¢ Multicolored | 30.00 | 3.00 | .60 | .16 |
| **1987. PENNSYLVANIA** | | | | |
| ☐2337 22¢ Multicolored | 34.00 | 3.75 | .80 | .16 |
| **1987. NEW JERSEY** | | | | |
| ☐2338– | | | | |
| 2348 22¢ Multicolored | 32.00 | 3.40 | .75 | .16 |
| **1987. FRIENDSHIP WITH MOROCCO** | | | | |
| ☐2349 22¢ Multicolored | 28.00 | 2.90 | .65 | .16 |
| **1987. WILLIAM FAULKNER** | | | | |
| ☐2350 22¢ Green | 28.00 | 2.90 | .65 | .16 |
| **1987. LACEMAKING** | | | | |
| ☐2351– | | | | |
| 2354 22¢ Blue | 35.00 | 4.00 | .65 | .16 |
| **1987. CONSTITUTION (BICENTENNIAL)** | | | | |
| ☐2355 22¢ Multicolored | — | — | .65 | .16 |
| **1987. CONSTITUTION (WE THE PEOPLE)** | | | | |
| ☐2356 22¢ Multicolored | — | — | .65 | .16 |
| **1987. CONSTITUTION (ESTABLISH JUSTICE)** | | | | |
| ☐2357 22¢ Multicolored | — | — | .65 | .16 |
| **1987. CONSTITUTION (AND SECURE)** | | | | |
| ☐2358 22¢ Multicolored | — | — | .65 | .16 |
| **1987. CONSTITUTION (DO ORDAIN)** | | | | |
| ☐2359 22¢ Multicolored | — | — | .70 | .16 |

*No hinge pricing from 1941 to date is figured at (N-H ADD 15%)

| Scott No. | Mint Sheet | Plate Block | Fine Unused Each | Fine Used Each |
|---|---|---|---|---|

## 1987. U.S. CONSTITUTION
☐2360 22¢ Multicolored 30.00 3.10 .70 .16

## 1987. C.P.A. CERTIFIED PUBLIC ACCOUNTANTS
☐2361 22¢ multicolored 168.00 14.00 .75 .16

## 1987. LOCOMOTIVES
☐2362–
2366 22¢ Multicolored — — .65 .16

## 1987. CHRISTMAS: MARONI, NATIONAL GALLERY
☐2367 22¢ Multicolored 52.00 3.00 .65 .16

## 1987. GREETINGS
☐2368 22¢ Multicolored 52.00 3.00 .65 .16

## 1988. OLYMPICS (WINTER)
☐2369 22¢ Multicolored 30.00 3.50 .70 .16

## 1988. AUSTRALIA BICENTENNIAL
☐2370 22¢ Multicolored 25.00 3.00 .65 .16

## 1988. J.W. JOHNSON
☐2371 22¢ Multicolored 28.00 3.00 .65 .16

## 1988. CATS (SHORT HAIR)
☐2372 22¢ Multicolored 29.00 4.75 .65 .16

## 1988. CATS (HIMALAYAN)
☐2373 22¢ Multicolored — — .65 .16

## 1988. CATS (BURMESE)
☐2374 22¢ Multicolored — — .65 .16

## 1988. CATS (PERSIAN)
☐2375 22¢ Multicolored — — .65 .16

## 1988. KNUTE ROCKNE
☐2376 22¢ Multicolored 32.00 3.50 .75 .16

| Scott No. | Mint Sheet | Plate Block | Fine Unused Each | Fine Used Each |
|---|---|---|---|---|
| **1988. FRANCIS OUIMET** | | | | |
| ☐2377 25¢ Multicolored | 42.00 | 5.00 | .90 | .16 |
| **1988. LOVE** | | | | |
| ☐2378 25¢ Multicolored | 65.00 | 3.50 | .75 | .16 |
| **1988. LOVE** | | | | |
| ☐2379 45¢ Multicolored | 58.00 | 6.00 | 1.00 | .16 |
| **1988. OLYMPICS (SUMMER)** | | | | |
| ☐2380 25¢ Multicolored | 32.00 | 3.50 | .75 | .16 |
| **1988. CARS (LOCOMOBILE)** | | | | |
| ☐2381 25¢ Multicolored | — | — | .70 | .16 |
| **1988. CARS (PIERCE-ARROW)** | | | | |
| ☐2382 25¢ Multicolored | — | — | .70 | .16 |
| **1988. CARS (CORD)** | | | | |
| ☐2383 25¢ Multicolored | — | — | .70 | .16 |
| **1988. CARS (PACKARD)** | | | | |
| ☐2384 25¢ Multicolored | — | — | .70 | .16 |
| **1988. CARS (DUESENBERG)** | | | | |
| ☐2385 25¢ Multicolored | — | — | .70 | .16 |
| **1988. ANTARCTIC: NATHANIEL PALMER** | | | | |
| ☐2386 25¢ Multicolored | 50.00 | 5.50 | .70 | .16 |
| **1988. ANTARCTIC: LT. CHARLES WILKES** | | | | |
| ☐2387 25¢ Multicolored | 50.00 | 5.50 | .75 | .16 |
| **1988. ANTARCTIC: RICHARD E. BYRD** | | | | |
| ☐2388 25¢ Multicolored | 50.00 | 5.50 | .75 | .16 |
| **1988. ANTARCTIC: LINCOLN ELLSWORTH** | | | | |
| ☐2389 25¢ Multicolored | 50.00 | 5.50 | .75 | .16 |

*No hinge pricing from 1941 to date is figured at (N-H ADD 15%)

# HOW TO FIND YOUR STAMP

This new stamp catalog takes the confusion out of finding and identifying individual stamps. A complete, new FULL-COLOR FAST-FIND PHOTO INDEX is illustrated on the following pages. All of the stamp photographs are arranged in Scott numerical order and date of issue. Below each stamp picture is the Scott number and the page number on which the stamp listing appears.

| Scott No. | Date | Page | Scott No. | Date | Page |
|---|---|---|---|---|---|
| 1–138 | 1847–1870 | A–1 | 1038–1065 | 1954–1955 | A–22 |
| 139–236 | 1870–1893 | A–2 | 1066–1076 | 1955–1956 | A–23 |
| 237–287 | 1893–1898 | A–3 | 1077–1093 | 1956–1957 | A–24 |
| 288–323 | 1898–1904 | A–4 | 1094–1113 | 1957–1958 | A–25 |
| 324–551 | 1904–1922 | A–5 | 1114–1127 | 1958–1959 | A–26 |
| 552–620 | 1922–1925 | A–6 | 1128–1143 | 1959–1960 | A–27 |
| 621–689 | 1925–1930 | A–7 | 1144–1158 | 1960 | A–28 |
| 690–733 | 1931–1933 | A–8 | 1159–1174 | 1960–1961 | A–29 |
| 734–777 | 1933–1936 | A–9 | 1175–1186 | 1961 | A–30 |
| 782–801 | 1936–1937 | A–10 | 1187–1199 | 1961–1962 | A–31 |
| 802–830 | 1937–1938 | A–11 | 1200–1234 | 1962–1963 | A–32 |
| 831–867 | 1938–1940 | A–12 | 1235–1248 | 1963–1964 | A–33 |
| 868–896 | 1940 | A–13 | 1249–1265 | 1964–1965 | A–34 |
| 897–927 | 1940–1945 | A–14 | 1266–1287 | 1965 | A–35 |
| 928–942 | 1945–1946 | A–15 | 1288–1313 | 1965–1966 | A–36 |
| 943–954 | 1946–1948 | A–16 | 1314–1330 | 1966–1967 | A–37 |
| 955–970 | 1948 | A–17 | 1331–1354 | 1967–1968 | A–38 |
| 971–986 | 1948–1950 | A–18 | 1355–1370 | 1968–1969 | A–39 |
| 987–1005 | 1950–1952 | A–19 | 1371–1390 | 1969–1970 | A–40 |
| 1006–1020 | 1952–1953 | A–20 | 1391–1414 | 1970 | A–41 |
| 1021–1037 | 1953–1954 | A–21 | 1415–1432 | 1970–1971 | A–42 |

| Scott No. | Date | Page | Scott No. | Date | Page |
|-----------|------|------|-----------|------|------|
| 1433–1451 | 1971–1972 | A–43 | 2108–2136 | 1984–1986 | A–74 |
| 1452–1467 | 1972 | A–44 | 2137–2158 | 1985 | A–75 |
| 1468–1483 | 1972–1973 | A–45 | 2159–2196 | 1985–1987 | A–76 |
| 1484–1497 | 1973 | A–46 | 2198–2218 | 1986 | A–77 |
| 1498–1518 | 1973 | A–47 | 2219–2246 | 1986–1987 | A–78 |
| 1525–1541 | 1974 | A–48 | 2247–2336 | 1987 | A–79 |
| 1542–1556 | 1974–1975 | A–49 | 2337–2375 | 1987–1988 | A–80 |
| 1557–1571 | 1975 | A–50 | 2376–2398 | 1988 | A–81 |
| 1572–1597 | 1975 | A–51 | 2399–2418 | 1988–1989 | A–82 |
| 1599–1685 | 1975–1976 | A–52 | 2419–2444 | 1989–1990 | A–83 |
| 1686–1699 | 1976 | A–53 | 2445–2507 | 1990 | A–84 |
| 1700–1714 | 1976–1977 | A–54 | 2508–2539 | 1990–1991 | A–85 |
| 1715–1730 | 1977 | A–55 | 2540–2566 | 1991 | A–86 |
| 1731–1755 | 1978 | A–56 | 2567–2609 | 1991–1992 | A–87 |
| 1756–1766 | 1978 | A–57 | 2611–2636 | 1992 | A–88 |
| 1767–1782 | 1978–1979 | A–58 | 2637–2696 | 1992 | A–89 |
| 1783–1796 | 1979 | A–59 | 2697–2709 | 1992 | A–90 |
| 1797–1824 | 1979–1980 | A–60 | 2710–2727 | 1992–1993 | A–91 |
| 1825–1839 | 1980 | A–61 | 2728–2759 | 1993 | A–92 |
| 1840–1857 | 1980–1981 | A–62 | 2760–2770 | 1993 | A–93 |
| 1858–1886 | 1981 | A–63 | 2779–2813 | 1993–1994 | A–94 |
| 1887–1919 | 1981 | A–64 | 2814–2837 | 1994 | A–95 |
| 1920–1932 | 1981 | A–65 | 2838–2847 | 1994 | A–96 |
| 1933–1952 | 1981–1982 | A–66 | | | |
| 1953–2009 | 1982 | A–67 | | | |
| 2010–2025 | 1982 | A–68 | | | |
| 2026–2043 | 1982–1983 | A–69 | | | |
| 2044–2058 | 1982–1983 | A–70 | | | |
| 2059–2072 | 1983–1984 | A–71 | | | |
| 2073–2091 | 1984 | A–72 | | | |
| 2092–2107 | 1984 | A–73 | | | |

1, 39, 48A
PG 39

2, 4, 948B
PG 39

5, 9, 18-24,
40–PG 39

10, 11, 25, 26,
41–PG 39

12, 27-30A,
42–PG 39

13-16, 31-
35, 43
PG 39

17, 36, 44
PG 39

37, 45
PG 40

38, 46
PG 40

39, 47
PG 40

56, 63, 85,
86, 92, 102
PG 40

64-66, 74, 79,
88, 94, 104
PG 40

57-67, 75, 76,
80, 95,
195–PG 40

58-62B, 68,
85D, 89, 96,
106–PG 40

59, 69, 85E,
90 97, 107
PG 40

60, 70, 78,
99, 109–PG
40

61, 71, 81,
100, 110
PG 40

62, 72, 101,
111–PG 40

73, 84, 85B,
87, 93, 103
PG 41

77, 85F, 91,
98, 108
PG 41

112, 123, 133
PG 42

113, 124
PG 42

114, 125
PG 42

115, 126
PG 42

116, 127
PG 42

117, 128
PG 42

118,119, 129
PG 42

120, 130
PG 43

121, 131
PG 43

122, 132
PG 43

134, 156, 167,
182, 206
PG 43

135, 157, 168,
203
PG 43

136, 158, 169,
214
PG 43

137, 148, 159,
195, 208
PG 43

138, 149, 160,
171, 196
PG 43

139, 150, 161,
197, 209
PG 43

140-151, 162,
173, 198
PG 43

141, 152, 163,
189, 199
PG 43

142, 153, 164,
175, 200
PG 43

143, 154, 165,
190, 201, 217
PG 43

144, 155, 166,
202, 218
PG 43

179, 181, 185,
204–PG 44

205, 205C, 216
PG 45

210, 211B, 213
PG 45

211, 211D, 215
PG 45

212
PG 45

219
PG 46

219D, 220
PG 46

221
PG 46

222
PG 46

223
PG 46

224
PG 46

225
PG 46

226
PG 46

227
PG 46

228
PG 46

229
PG 46

230
PG 46

231
PG 46

232
PG 46

233
PG 47

234
PG 47

235
PG 47

236
PG 47

# GENERAL ISSUE—SCOTT NO. 237–287 (1893–1898)

237
PG 47

238
PG 47

239
PG 47

240
PG 47

241
PG 47

242
PG 47

243
PG 47

244
PG 47

245
PG 47

246, 247,
264, 279
PG 47

248-252, 265-
267, 279B
PG 47

253, 268
PG 48

254, 269, 280
PG 48

255, 270, 281
PG 48

256, 271, 282
PG 48

257, 272
PG 48

258, 273
282C, 283
PG 48

259, 273, 284
PG 48

260, 275
PG 48

261-261A,
276, 276A
PG 48

262, 277
PG 48

263, 278
PG 48

285
PG 50

286
PG 50

287
PG 50

A-3

288
PG 50

289
PG 50

290
PG 50

291
PG 50

292
PG 50

293
PG 50

294
PG 50

295
PG 50

296
PG 50

297
PG 51

298
PG 51

299
PG 51

300, 314, 316,
318–PG 51

301
PG 51

302
PG 51

303, 314A
PG 51

304, 315, 317
PG 51

305
PG 51

306
PG 51

307
PG 51

308
PG 51

309
PG 51

310
PG 51

311
PG 51

312, 479
PG 51

313, 480
PG 51

319-322
PG 51

323
PG 52

# GENERAL ISSUE—SCOTT NO. 324–551 (1904–1922)

324
PG 52

325
PG 52

326
PG 52

327
PG 52

328
PG 52

329
PG 52

330
PG 52

331, 392
PG 53

332-393, 519
PG 53

333-541
PG 53

367, 369
PG 55

370, 371
PG 55

372, 373
PG 55

397, 401
PG 57

398, 402
PG 57

399, 403
PG 57

400, 400A, 404
PG 57

405-545
PG 58

406-546
PG 58

414-518
PG 59

523, 524, 547
PG 65

537
PG 67

548
PG 68

549
PG 68

550
PG 68

551, 653
PG 68

552, 575, 578, 604, 632
PG 68

553, 576, 598, 605, 633
PG 68

555, 584, 600, 635
PG 68

556–585, 601, 636
PG 68

557, 586, 602, 637
PG 68

558, 587, 638, 723
PG 68

559, 588, 639
PG 68

560, 589, 640
PG 68

561, 590, 641
PG 68

562, 591, 603, 641–PG 69

563, 692
PG 69

564, 693
PG 69

565, 695
PG 69

566–696
PG 69

567, 698
PG 69

568, 699
PG 69

569, 700
PG 69

570, 701
PG 69

571
PG 69

572
PG 69

573
PG 69

583, 599-99A 634-34A–PG 70

610-613
PG 71

614
PG 71

615
PG 71

616
PG 71

617
PG 72

618
PG 72

619
PG 72

620
PG 72

# GENERAL ISSUE—SCOTT NO. 621–689 (1925–1930)

621
PG 72

622, 694
PG 72

623, 697
PG 72

627
PG 72

628
PG 72

629
PG 72

643
PG 73

644
PG 73

645
PG 74

646
PG 74

647
PG 74

648
PG 74

649
PG 74

650
PG 74

651
PG 74

654-656
PG 74

657
PG 75

680
PG 76

681
PG 76

682
PG 76

683
PG 77

684, 686
PG 77

685, 687
PG 77

688
PG 77

689
PG 77

A-7

690
PG 77

702
PG 78

703
PG 78

704
PG 78

705
PG 78

706
PG 79

707
PG 79

708
PG 79

709
PG 79

710
PG 79

711
PG 79

712
PG 79

713
PG 79

714
PG 79

715
PG 79

716
PG 79

717
PG 79

718
PG 79

719
PG 79

720-722
PG 80

724
PG 80

725
PG 80

726
PG 80

727, 752
PG 80

728, 730, 766
PG 81

729, 731, 767
PG 81

732
PG 81

733, 735, 753
PG 81

734
PG 81

736
PG 82

737, 738, 754
PG 82

739, 755
PG 82

740, 751, 756,
769–PG 82

741, 757
PG 82

742, 750, 758, 770
PG 82

743, 759
PG 82

744, 760
PG 82

745, 761
PG 82

746, 762
PG 82

747, 763
PG 82

748, 764
PG 82

749, 765, 797
PG 82

772, 778A
PG 84

773, 778B
PG 84

774
PG 84

775, 778C
PG 84

776, 778D
PG 84

777
PG 85

782
PG 85

783
PG 85

784
PG 85

785
PG 85

786
PG 85

787
PG 85

788
PG 86

789
PG 86

790
PG 86

791
PG 86

792
PG 86

793
PG 86

794
PG 86

795
PG 86

796
PG 86

798
PG 86

799
PG 87

800
PG 87

801
PG 87

802
PG 87

803
PG 87

804, 848
PG 87

805, 849
PG 87

806
PG 87

807
PG 87

808, 843
PG 87

809, 844
PG 87

810,845
PG 87

811, 846
PG 87

812
PG 87

813
PG 87

814
PG 87

815, 847
PG 87

816
PG 88

817
PG 88

818
PG 88

819
PG 88

820
PG 88

821
PG 88

822
PG 88

823
PG 88

824
PG 88

825
PG 88

826
PG 88

827
PG 88

828
PG 88

829
PG 88

830
PG 88

831
PG 88

832
PG 88

833
PG 89

834
PG 89

835
PG 89

836
PG 89

837
PG 89

838
PG 89

852
PG 90

853
PG 90

854
PG 90

855
PG 91

856
PG 91

857
PG 91

858
PG 91

859
PG 91

860
PG 91

861
PG 91

862
PG 91

863
PG 91

864
PG 91

865
PG 92

866
PG 92

867
PG 92

# GENERAL ISSUE—SCOTT NO. 868–896 (1940)

868–PG 92

869–PG 92

870–PG 92

871–PG 92

872–PG 92

873–PG 92

874–PG 92

875–PG 92

876–PG 92

877–PG 92

878–PG 92

879–PG 92

880–PG 92

881–PG 92

882–PG 93

883–PG 93

884–PG 93

885–PG 93

886–PG 93

887–PG 93

888–PG 93

889–PG 93

890–PG 93

891–PG 93

892–PG 93

893–PG 93

894–PG 93

895–PG 93

896–PG 94

A-13

897–PG 94

898–PG 94

899–PG 94

900–PG 94

901–PG 94

902–PG 94

903–PG 94

904–PG 95

905–PG 95

906–PG 95

907–PG 95

908–PG 95

909–PG 95

921–PG 95

922–PG 95

923–PG 95

924–PG 96

925–PG 96

926–PG 96

927–PG 96

# GENERAL ISSUE—SCOTT NO. 928–942 (1945–1946)

928
PG 96

929
PG 96

930
PG 96

931
PG 96

932
PG 96

933
PG 96

934
PG 96

935
PG 96

936
PG 96

937
PG 96

938
PG 96

939
PG 97

940–PG 97

941–PG 97

942–PG 97

A-15

943
PG 97

944
PG 97

945
PG 97

946
PG 97

948
PG 97

947
PG 97

949
PG 97

950
PG 97

951
PG 98

952–PG 98

953–PG 98

954–PG 98

# GENERAL ISSUE—SCOTT NO. 955–970 (1948)

955
PG 98

956
PG 98

957
PG 98

958
PG 98

959
PG 98

960
PG 98

961
PG 98

962
PG 98

963
PG 99

964
PG 99

965
PG 99

966
PG 99

967
PG 99

968–PG 99

969–PG 99

970–PG 99

A-17

# GENERAL ISSUE—SCOTT NO. 971–986 (1948–1950)

971
PG 99

972
PG 99

973
PG 99

974
PG 99

975
PG 100

976
PG 100

977
PG 100

978
PG 100

979
PG 100

980
PG 100

981
PG 100

982
PG 100

983
PG 100

984–PG 100

985–PG 100

986–PG 100

# GENERAL ISSUE—SCOTT NO. 987–1005 (1950–1952)

987
PG 100

988
PG 101

989
PG 101

990
PG 101

991
PG 101

992
PG 101

993
PG 101

994
PG 101

995
PG 101

996
PG 101

997
PG 101

998
PG 101

999
PG 101

1000
PG 101

1001
PG 101

1002
PG 102

1003–PG 102

1004–PG 102

1005–PG 102

1006
PG 102

1007
PG 102

1008–PG 102

1009
PG 102

1010
PG 102

1011
PG 102

1012
PG 102

1013
PG 102

1014
PG 103

1015
PG 103

1016
PG 103

1017
PG 103

1018
PG 103

1019
PG 103

1020
PG 103

1021
PG 103

1022
PG 103

1023
PG 103

1024
PG 103

1025
PG 103

1026
PG 103

1027
PG 104

1028
PG 104

1029
PG 104

1030
PG 104

1031, 1054
PG 104

1031A, 1054A
PG 104

1032
PG 104

1033, 1055
PG 104

1034, 1056
PG 104

1035-1075
PG 104

1036-1058
PG 104

1037, 1059
PG 104

1038
PG 104

1039
PG 104

1040
PG 104

1041, 1075B
PG 104

1042A
PG 104

1043
PG 104

1044A
PG 104

1044
PG 104

1045
PG 104

1046
PG 104

1047
PG 104

1048
PG 104

1049
PG 104

1050
PG 104

1051
PG 105

1052
PG 105

1053
PG 105

1060
PG 105

1061
PG 105

1062–PG 105

1063–PG 106

1064–PG 106

1065–PG 106

1066
PG 106

1067
PG 106

1068
PG 106

1069
PG 106

1070
PG 106

1071
PG 106

1072
PG 106

1073
PG 106

1074
PG 106

1076
PG 107

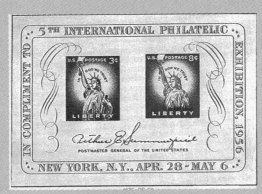

1075–PG 107

1077
PG 107

1078
PG 107

1079
PG 107

1080
PG 107

1081
PG 107

1082
PG 107

1083
PG 107

1084
PG 107

1085
PG 107

1086
PG 107

1087
PG 107

1088
PG 108

1089
PG 108

1090
PG 108

1091
PG 108

1092
PG 108

1093
PG 108

1094–PG 108

1095–PG 108

1096–PG 108

1097–PG 108

1098–PG 108

1099–PG 108

1100–PG 109

1104
PG 109

1105
PG 109

1106
PG 109

1107
PG 109

1108
PG 109

1109
PG 109

1110
PG 109

1111
PG 109

1112
PG 109

1113
PG 109

1114
PG 109

1115
PG 109

1116
PG 109

1117
PG 109

1118
PG 109

1119
PG 110

1120
PG 110

1121
PG 110

1122
PG 110

1123
PG 110

1124
PG 110

1125
PG 110

1126
PG 110

1127
PG 110

# GENERAL ISSUE—SCOTT NO. 1128–1143 (1959–1960)

1128
PG 110

1129
PG 110

1130
PG 110

1131
PG 111

1132
PG 111

1133
PG 111

1134
PG 111

1135
PG 111

1136
PG 111

1137
PG 111

1138
PG 111

1139
PG 111

1140
PG 111

1141
PG 111

1142
PG 111

1143
PG 111

1144
PG 111

1145
PG 111

1146
PG 112

1147
PG 112

1148
PG 112

1149
PG 112

1150
PG 112

1151
PG 112

1152
PG 112

1153
PG 112

1154
PG 112

1155
PG 112

1156
PG 112

1157
PG 112

1158
PG 112

1159
PG 113

1160
PG 113

1161
PG 113

1162
PG 113

1163
PG 113

1164
PG 113

1165
PG 113

1166
PG 113

1167
PG 113

1168
PG 113

1169
PG 113

1170
PG 113

1171
PG 113

1172
PG 113

1173
PG 114

1174
PG 114

1175
PG 114

1176
PG 114

1177
PG 114

1178
PG 114

1179
PG 114

1180
PG 114

1181
PG 114

1182
PG 114

1183
PG 114

1184
PG 114

1185
PG 115

1186
PG 115

1187
PG 115

1188
PG 115

1189
PG 115

1190
PG 115

1191
PG 115

1192
PG 115

1193
PG 115

1194
PG 115

1195
PG 116

1196
PG 116

1197
PG 116

1198
PG 116

1199
PG 116

# GENERAL ISSUE—SCOTT NO. 1200–1234 (1962–1963)

1200
PG 116

1201
PG 116

1202
PG 116

1203
PG 116

1204
PG 116

1205
PG 116

1206
PG 116

1207
PG 117

1208
PG 117

1209, 1225
PG 117

1213
PG 117

1230
PG 117

1231
PG 117

1232
PG 117

1233
PG 118

1234
PG 118

A-32

1235
PG 118

1236
PG 118

1237
PG 118

1238
PG 118

1239
PG 118

1240
PG 118

1241
PG 118

1242
PG 118

1243
PG 118

1244
PG 119

1245
PG 119

1246
PG 119

1247
PG 119

1248
PG 119

# GENERAL ISSUE—SCOTT NO. 1249–1265 (1964–1965)

1249
PG 119

1250
PG 119

1251
PG 119

1252
PG 119

1253
PG 119

1254
PG 119

1255
PG 119

1256
PG 119

1257
PG 119

1258
PG 120

1259
PG 120

1260
PG 120

1261
PG 120

1262
PG 120

1263
PG 120

1264
PG 120

1265
PG 120

A-34

1266
PG 120

1267
PG 120

1268
PG 120

1269
PG 121

1270
PG 121

1271
PG 121

1272
PG 121

1273
PG 121

1274
PG 121

1275
PG 121

1276
PG 121

1278
PG 121

1279
PG 121

1280
PG 121

1281, 1297
PG 121

1282, 1303
PG 121

1283, 1304
PG 121

1283B
PG 122

1284, 1298
PG 122

1285
PG 122

1286
PG 122

1286A
PG 122

1287
PG 122

# GENERAL ISSUE—SCOTT NO. 1288–1313 (1965–1966)

1288
PG 122

1289
PG 122

1290
PG 122

1291
PG 122

1292
PG 122

1293
PG 122

1294, 1305C
PG 122

1295
PG 122

1305
PG 122

1306
PG 123

1307
PG 123

1308
PG 123

1309
PG 123

1310
PG 123

1312
PG 123

1311
PG 123

1313
PG 123

A-36

# GENERAL ISSUE—SCOTT NO. 1314–1330 (1966–1967)

1314
PG 123

1315
PG 123

1316
PG 124

1317
PG 124

1318
PG 124

1319
PG 124

1320
PG 124

1321
PG 124

1322
PG 124

1323—PG 124

1324—PG 124

1325
PG 124

1326—PG 125

1327
PG 125

1328
PG 125

1329
PG 125

1330
PG 125

A-37

1331–PG 125     1332–PG 125

1333
PG 125

1334
PG 125

1335–PG 125

1336–PG 125

1337–PG 125

1338, 1338A
PG 126

1338F, G
PG 126

1339
PG 126

1340
PG 126

1341–PG 126

1342
PG 126

1343–PG 126

1344
PG 126

1345
PG 126

1354
PG 126

1355
PG 127

1356
PG 127

1357
PG 127

1358
PG 127

1359
PG 127

1360
PG 127

1361
PG 127

1362
PG 127

1363
PG 127

1364
PG 127

1365-1368
PG 127-128

1369
PG 128

1370
PG 128

# GENERAL ISSUE—SCOTT NO. 1371–1390 (1969–1970)

1371
PG 128

1372–PG 128

1373–PG 128

1374
PG 128

1375–PG 128

1376-1379
PG 128

1380
PG 128

1381–PG 129

1382–PG 129

1383
PG 129

1384
PG 129

1385
PG 129

1386
PG 129

1387-1390
PG 129

A-40

1391
PG 129

1392
PG 129

1393
PG 129

1393D
PG 129

1394
PG 129

1395
PG 129

1396
PG 129

1397
PG 129

1398
PG 129

1399
PG 129

1400
PG 130

1405
PG 130

1406
PG 130

1407
PG 130

1408
PG 130

1409
PG 130

1410-1413
PG 130

1414
PG 131

# GENERAL ISSUE—SCOTT NO. 1415–1432 (1970–1971)

1415-1418
PG 131

1419
PG 131

1420
PG 131

1421
PG 131

1422
PG 131

1423
PG 131

1424
PG 131

1425
PG 131

1426
PG 131

1431
PG 132

1427-1430
PG 132

1432
PG 132

A-42

# GENERAL ISSUE—SCOTT NO. 1433–1451 (1971–1972)

1433
PG 132

1434
PG 132

1435
PG 132

1436
PG 132

1437
PG 132

1438
PG 132

1439
PG 132

1440-1443
PG 132-133

1444
PG 133

1445
PG 133

1446
PG 133

1447
PG 133

1448-1451
PG 133

A-43

1452
PG 133

1453
PG 133

1454
PG 133

1455
PG 133

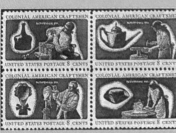

1456-1459
PG 133

1460
PG 134

1461
PG 134

1462
PG 134

1463
PG 134

1464-1467
PG 134

A-44

# GENERAL ISSUE—SCOTT NO. 1468–1483 (1972–1973)

1468
PG 134

1469
PG 134

1470
PG 134

1471
PG 134

1472
PG 134

1473
PG 134

1474
PG 134

1475
PG 135

1476
PG 135

1477
PG 135

1478
PG 135

1479
PG 135

1480-1483
PG 135

A-45

1484
PG 135

1485
PG 135

1486
PG 135

1487
PG 135

1488
PG 135

1489
PG 135

1490
PG 135

1491
PG 135

1492
PG 135

1493
PG 135

1494
PG 135

1495
PG 136

1496
PG 136

1497
PG 136

1498
PG 136

1499
PG 136

1500
PG 136

1501
PG 136

1502
PG 136

1503
PG 136

1504
PG 136

1505
PG 136

1506F
PG 136

1507
PG 136

1508
PG 136

1509, 1519
PG 136

1510
PG 136

1511
PG 136

1518
PG 136

# GENERAL ISSUE—SCOTT NO. 1525–1541 (1974)

1525
PG 137

1526
PG 137

1527
PG 137

1528
PG 137

1529
PG 137

1530
PG 137

1531
PG 137

1532
PG 137

1533
PG 137

1534
PG 137

1535
PG 137

1536
PG 137

1537
PG 137

1538–1539
1540–1541—PG 137-138

1543-1546
PG 138

1542
PG 138

1547
PG 138

1548
PG 138

1549
PG 138

1550
PG 138

1551
PG 138

1552
PG 138

1553
PG 138

1554
PG 138

1555
PG 139

1556
PG 139

1557
PG 139

1558
PG 139

1559
PG 139

1560
PG 139

1561
PG 139

1562
PG 139

1563
PG 139

1564
PG 139

1565
PG 139

1566
PG 139

1567
PG 139

1568
PG 139

1569
PG 139

1570
PG 139

1571
PG 139

# GENERAL ISSUE—SCOTT NO. 1572–1597 (1975)

1572
PG 140

1573
PG 140

1574
PG 140

1575
PG 140

1577-1578
PG 140

1576
PG 140

1579
PG 140

1580
PG 140

1581
PG 140

1582
PG 140

1584
PG 140

1585
PG 140

1590
PG 140

1592
PG 140

1593
PG 140

1594
PG 140

1595
PG 140

1596
PG 140

1597
PG 140

1599
PG 140

1603
PG 140

1604
PG 140

1605
PG 140

1606
PG 140

1608
PG 141

1610
PG 141

1611
PG 141

1612
PG 141

1613
PG 141

1614
PG 141

1615
PG 141

1615C
PG 141

1622
PG 141

1623
PG 141

1629-1630-1631
PG 142

1632–PG 141

1633-1682–PG 142

1683
PG 143

1684
PG 143

1685
PG 143

1686
PG 143

1687
PG 143

1688
PG 143

1689
PG 143

1690
PG 144

1691-1692-1693-1694
PG 144

1695
PG 144

1696
PG 144

1697
PG 144

1698
PG 144

1699
PG 144

1700
PG 144

1701
PG 144

1702-1703
PG 144

1704
PG 144

1705
PG 145

1706
PG 145

1707
PG 145

1708
PG 145

1709
PG 145

1710
PG 145

1711
PG 145

1712
PG 145

1713
PG 145

1714
PG 145

1715
PG 145

1716
PG 145

1717
PG 145

1718
PG 145

1719
PG 145

1720
PG 145

1721
PG 145

1722
PG 145

1723
PG 146

1724
PG 146

1725
PG 146

1726
PG 146

1727
PG 146

1728
PG 146

1729
PG 146

1730
PG 146

# GENERAL ISSUE—SCOTT NO. 1731–1755 (1978)

1731
PG 146

1732
PG 146

1733
PG 146

1734
PG 146

1735
PG 146

1737
PG 146

1738-1739-1740-1741-1742
PG 147

1744
PG 147

1745
PG 147

1746
PG 147

1747
PG 147

1748
PG 147

1749
PG 147

1750
PG 147

1751
PG 147

1752
PG 147

1753
PG 147

1754
PG 147

1755
PG 148

1757–PG 148

1756
PG 148

PG 1481758

1759
PG 148

1760
PG 148

1761
PG 148

1762
PG 148

1763
PG 148

1764
PG 148

1765
PG 148

1766
PG 148

1767
PG 148

1768
PG 148

1769
PG 148

1770
PG 148

1771
PG 148

1772
PG 149

1773
PG 149

1774
PG 149

1775
PG 149

1776
PG 149

1777
PG 149

1778
PG 149

1779
PG 149

1780
PG 149

1781
PG 149

1782
PG 149

# GENERAL ISSUE—SCOTT NO. 1783–1796 (1979)

1783
PG 149

1784
PG 149

1785
PG 149

1786
PG 149

1787
PG 149

1788
PG 149

1789
PG 150

1790
PG 150

1791
PG 150

1792
PG 150

1793
PG 150

1794
PG 150

1795
PG 150

1796
PG 150

# GENERAL ISSUE—SCOTT NO. 1797–1824 (1979–1980)

1797
PG 150

1798
PG 150

1799
PG 150

1800
PG 150

1801
PG 150

1802
PG 151

1803
PG 151

1804
PG 151

1805-1806
PG 151

1807-1808
PG 151

1809-1810
PG 151

1811
PG 151

1813
PG 151

1818
PG 151

1821
PG 152

1822
PG 152

1823
PG 152

1824
PG 152

# GENERAL ISSUE—SCOTT NO. 1825–1839 (1980)

1825
PG 152

1826
PG 152

1827
PG 152

1828
PG 152

1829
PG 152

1830
PG 152

1831
PG 152

1832
PG 152

1833
PG 152

1834
PG 153

1835
PG 153

1836
PG 153

1837
PG 153

1838
PG 153

1839
PG 153

# GENERAL ISSUE—SCOTT NO. 1840–1857 (1980–1981)

1840
PG 153

1841
PG 153

1842
PG 153

1843
PG 153

1844
PG 153

1845
PG 153

1846
PG 153

1847
PG 153

1848
PG 153

1849
PG 153

1850
PG 153

1851
PG 153

1852
PG 154

1853
PG 154

1854
PG 154

1855
PG 154

1856
PG 154

1857
PG 154

1858
PG 154

1859
PG 154

1860
PG 154

1861
PG 154

1862
PG 154

1863
PG 154

1864
PG 154

1865
PG 155

1866
PG 155

1867
PG 155

1868
PG 155

1869
PG 155

1874
PG 155

1875
PG 155

1876
PG 155

1877
PG 155

1878
PG 155

1879
PG 155

1880
PG 155

1881
PG 155

1882
PG 155

1883
PG 155

1884
PG 155

1885
PG 155

1886
PG 155

1887
PG 155

1888
PG 155

1889
PG 155

1890
PG 156

1891
PG 156

1892
PG 156

1893
PG 156

1894
PG 156

1903
PG 157

1905
PG 157

1906
PG 157

1907
PG 157

1908
PG 157

1910
PG 157

1911
PG 157

1912-1919
PG 157

1920
PG 158

1921
PG 158

1922
PG 158

1923
PG 158

1924
PG 158

1925
PG 158

1926
PG 158

1927
PG 158

1928
PG 158

1929
PG 158

1930
PG 158

1931
PG 158

1932
PG 158

# GENERAL ISSUE—SCOTT NO. 1933–1952 (1981–1982)

1933–PG 158

1934–PG 158

1935–PG 158

1936–PG 159

1937-1938–PG 159

1939–PG 159

1940–PG 159

1941–PG 159

1942-1945–PG 159

1946-1948
PG 159

1949
PG 159

1950
PG 159

1951
PG 160

1952
PG 160

1953-2002
PG 160

2003
PG 160

2004
PG 160

2005
PG 160

2006-2009–PG 160

# GENERAL ISSUE—SCOTT NO. 2010–2025 (1982)

2010
PG 160

2011
PG 160

2012
PG 160

2013
PG 160

2014
PG 161

2015
PG 161

2016
PG 161

2017
PG 161

2018
PG 161

2019-2022
PG 161

2023
PG 161

2024
PG 161

2025
PG 161

A-68

# GENERAL ISSUE—SCOTT NO. 2026–2043 (1982–1983)

2026
PG 162

2027-2030
PG 162

2031
PG 162

2032-2035
PG 162

2036
PG 162

2037
PG 163

2038
PG 163

2039
PG 163

2040
PG 163

2041
PG 163

2042
PG 163

2043
PG 163

2044
PG 163

2045
PG 163

2046
PG 163

2047
PG 163

2048-2051
PG 163-164

2052
PG 164

2053
PG 164

2054
PG 164

2055
PG 164

2056
PG 164

2057
PG 164

2058
PG 164

**2059**
PG 164

**2060**
PG 164

**2061**
PG 164

**2062**
PG 164

**2063**
PG 165

**2064**
PG 165

**2065**
PG 165

**2066**
PG 165

**2067-2070**
PG 165

**2071**
PG 165

**2072**
PG 165

# GENERAL ISSUE—SCOTT NO. 2073–2091 (1984)

2073
PG 165

2074
PG 165

2075
PG 165

2076-2079
PG 166

2082-2085
PG 166

2080
PG 166

2081
PG 166

2086
PG 166

2087
PG 166

2088
PG 166

2089
PG 167

2090
PG 167

2091
PG 167

A-72

# GENERAL ISSUE—SCOTT NO. 2092–2107 (1984)

2092
PG 167

2093
PG 167

2094
PG 167

2095
PG 167

2096
PG 167

2097
PG 167

2098
PG 167

2099
PG 167

2100
PG 167

2101
PG 167

2102
PG 168

2103
PG 168

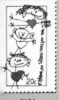

2104
PG 168

2105
PG 168

2106
PG 168

2107
PG 168

2108
PG 168

2109
PG 168

2110
PG 168

2111-2113
PG 168

2114-2116
PG 168

2122
PG 169

2117-212
PG 169

2123
PG 169

2124
PG 169

2125
PG 169

2126
PG 169

2128
PG 170

2130
PG 170

2131
PG 170

2132
PG 170

2133
PG 170

2134
PG 170

2135
PG 170

2136
PG 170

# GENERAL ISSUE—SCOTT NO. 2137–2158 (1985)

2137
PG 170

2138-2141
PG 170

2142
PG 171

2144
PG 171

2143
PG 171

2145
PG 171

2146
PG 171

2147
PG 171

2149
PG 171

2150
PG 171

2152
PG 171

2153
PG 171

2154
PG 171

2155-2158
PG 171-172

A-75

# GENERAL ISSUE—SCOTT NO. 2159–2196 (1985–1987)

2159
PG 172

2160-2163
PG 172

2164
PG 172

2165
PG 172

2166
PG 172

2167
PG 172

2168
PG 172

2169
PG 173

2170
PG 173

2171
PG 173

2172
PG 173

2177
PG 173

2179
PG 173

2183
PG 173

2191
PG 174

2194
PG 174

2195
PG 174

2196
PG 174

A-76

2198-2201–PG 174-175

2202
PG 175

2203
PG 175

2204
PG 175

2205-2209
PG 175

2210
PG 175

2211
PG 175

2216
PG 176

2217
PG 176

2218
PG 176

2219
PG 176

2220-2223
PG 176

2235-2238
PG 176

2224
PG 176

2239
PG 177

2240-2243
PG 177

2244
PG 177

2245
PG 177

2246
PG 177

# GENERAL ISSUE—SCOTT NO. 2247–2336 (1987)

2247
PG 177

2248
PG 177

2249
PG 177

2250
PG 177

2251
PG 177

2275
PG 179

2276
PG 179

2336
PG 180

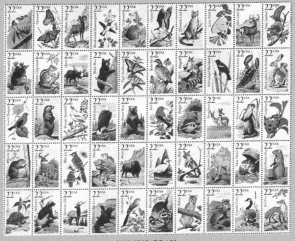

2286-2335–PG 180

2337
PG 180

2338
PG 180

2349
PG 180

2350
PG 180

2351-2354
PG 180

2355-2359
PG 180

2360
PG 181

2368
PG 181

2369
PG 181

2361
PG 181

2367
PG 181

2370
PG 181

2371
PG 181

2372-2375
PG 181

2376
PG 181

2377
PG 182

2378–PG 182

2379–PG 182

2380–PG 182

2381-2385–PG 182

2390-2393
PG 183

2386-2389–PG 182

2394
PG 185

2395
PG 185

2396
PG 185

2397
PG 185

2398
PG 185

A-81

2399
PG 185

2400
PG 185

2401
PG 185

2402
PG 185

2403
PG 186

2404
PG 186

2405-2409
PG 186

2410
PG 186

2411
PG 186

2412
PG 186

2413
PG 186

2414
PG 186

2416
PG 187

2417
PG 187

2418
PG 187

A-82

# GENERAL ISSUE—SCOTT NO. 2419–2444 (1989–1990)

2420
PG 187

2419
PG 187

2421
PG 187

2422-2425–PG 187

2426–PG 187

2427–PG 187

2428
PG 187

2434-2437
PG 188

2439
PG 188

2440
PG 188

2442
PG 188

2443
PG 188

2444
PG 188

# GENERAL ISSUE—SCOTT NO. 2445–2507 (1990)

2445-2448
PG 188

2449–PG 189

2452
PG 189

2496-2500
PG 190

2470-2474–PG 189

2501–PG 190

2506-2507–PG 190

A-84

# GENERAL ISSUE—SCOTT NO. 2508–2539 (1990–1991)

2508-2511–PG 190-191

2512
PG 191

2513–PG 191

2514–PG 191

2515–PG 191

2517–PG 191

2521–PG 191

2523–PG 191

2524–PG 191

2528–PG 191

2530–PG 192

2531–PG 192

2532–PG 192

2533–PG 192

2534–PG 192

2535–PG 192

2537–PG 192

2538–PG 192

2539–PG 192

A-85

# GENERAL ISSUE—SCOTT NO. 2540–2566 (1991)

2540
PG 192

2541
PG 192

2542
PG 192

2545-2549
PG 192-193

2550
PG 193

2551
PG 193

2558
PG 193

2553-2557
PG 193

2560
PG 193

2561
PG 193

2562-2566
PG 193

A-86

2568-2577
PG 194

2567
PG 194

2578
PG 194

2579
PG 194

2582
PG 194

2583
PG 194

2584
PG 194

2585
PG 194

2604
PG 194

2607
PG 194

2608
PG 194

2609
PG 194

# GENERAL ISSUE—SCOTT NO. 2611–2636 (1992)

2611-2615
PG 194

2616
PG 194

2620-2623
PG 195

2618
PG 195

2630
PG 195

2631-2634–PG 195

2635
PG 195

2636–PG 195

A-88

2637-2641—PG 195

2642-2646—PG 196

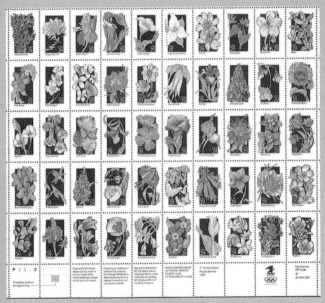

2647-2696—PG 196-197

2697
PG 197

2698
PG 197

2699
PG 197

2700-2703
PG 197

2704
PG 197

2705-2709
PG 197

# GENERAL ISSUE—SCOTT NO. 2710–2727 (1992–1993)

2710
PG 197

2711
PG 197

2712
PG 198

2713
PG 198

2714
PG 198

2719
PG 198

2721
PG 198

2722
PG 198

2723
PG 198

2724
PG 198

2725
PG 198

2726
PG 198

2727
PG 198

# GENERAL ISSUE—SCOTT NO. 2728–2759 (1993)

2728–PG 198

2729–PG 198

2730–PG 199

2746–PG 199

2741-2745–PG 199

2747–PG 199

2748–PG 199

2754–PG 199

2749–PG 199

2755–PG 199

2570-2753–PG 199

2756-2759–PG 199-200

A-92

# GENERAL ISSUE—SCOTT NO. 2760–2770 (1993)

2765
PG 200

2760-2764
PG 200

2766–PG 200

2767-2770–PG 200

# GENERAL ISSUE—SCOTT NO. 2779–2813 (1993–1994)

2779-2782
PG 200

2804
PG 200

2805
PG 200

2806
PG 200

2807-2811
PG 201

2812
PG 201

2813
PG 201

# GENERAL ISSUE—SCOTT NO. 2814–2837 (1994)

2814
PG 201

2815
PG 201

2818
PG 201

2829-2833
PG 201-202

2834-2837–PG 202

A-95

2838
PG 202

2840
PG 202

2843-2847
PG 202

2841
PG 202

2848
PG 202

| Scott No. | Mint Sheet | Plate Block | Fine Unused Each | Fine Used Each |
|---|---|---|---|---|
| **1988. CAROUSEL: DEER** | | | | |
| ☐2390 25¢ Multicolored | 50.00 | 5.50 | .75 | .16 |
| **1988. CAROUSEL: HORSE** | | | | |
| ☐2391 25¢ Multicolored | 52.00 | 5.50 | .75 | .16 |
| **1988. CAROUSEL: CAMEL** | | | | |
| ☐2392 25¢ Multicolored | 52.00 | 5.50 | .75 | .16 |
| **1988. CAROUSEL: GOAT** | | | | |
| ☐2393 25¢ Multicolored | 52.00 | 5.50 | .75 | .16 |
| **1988. EXPRESS MAIL** | | | | |
| ☐2394 $8.75 Multicolored | — | 85.00 | 20.00 | 9.00 |
| **1988. OCCASIONS: HAPPY BIRTHDAY** | | | | |
| ☐2395 25¢ Multicolored | — | — | .70 | .16 |
| **1988. OCCASIONS: BEST WISHES** | | | | |
| ☐2396 25¢ Multicolored | — | — | .70 | .16 |
| **1988. OCCASIONS: THINKING OF YOU** | | | | |
| ☐2397 25¢ Multicolored | — | — | .70 | .16 |
| **1988. OCCASIONS: LOVE YOU** | | | | |
| ☐2398 25¢ Multicolored | — | — | .70 | .16 |
| **1988. CHRISTMAS (BOTTICELLI)** | | | | |
| ☐2399 25¢ Multicolored | 30.00 | 3.10 | .70 | .16 |
| **1988. GREETINGS (CHRISTMAS)** | | | | |
| ☐2400 25¢ Multicolored | 30.00 | 3.10 | .70 | .16 |
| **1989. MONTANA** | | | | |
| ☐2401 25¢ Multicolored | 32.00 | 3.80 | .80 | .16 |
| **1989. A. PHILIPP RANDOLPH** | | | | |
| ☐2402 25¢ Multicolored | 30.00 | 3.00 | .70 | .16 |

*No hinge pricing from 1941 to date is figured at (N-H ADD 15%)

| Scott No. | Mint Sheet | Plate Block | Fine Unused Each | Fine Used Each |
|---|---|---|---|---|
| **1989. NORTH DAKOTA** | | | | |
| ☐2403 25¢ Multicolored | 30.00 | 3.00 | .70 | .16 |
| **1989. WASHINGTON** | | | | |
| ☐2404 25¢ Multicolored | 32.00 | 3.00 | .70 | .16 |
| **1989. STEAMBOATS: EXPERIMENT** | | | | |
| ☐2405 25¢ Multicolored | — | — | .70 | 16 |
| **1989. STEAMBOATS: PHOENIX** | | | | |
| ☐2406 25¢ Multicolored | — | — | .70 | .16 |
| **1989. STEAMBOATS: NEW ORLEANS** | | | | |
| ☐2407 25¢ Multicolored | — | — | .70 | .16 |
| **1989. STEAMBOATS: WASHINGTON** | | | | |
| ☐2408 25¢ Multicolored | — | — | .70 | .16 |
| **1989. STEAMBOATS: WALK IN THE WATER** | | | | |
| ☐2409 25¢ Multicolored | — | — | .70 | .16 |
| **1989. WORLD STAMP EXPO '89** | | | | |
| ☐2410 25¢ Black & Carmine | 30.00 | 3.50 | .70 | .16 |
| **1989. ARTURO TOSCANINI** | | | | |
| ☐2411 25¢ Multicolored | 32.00 | 3.50 | .70 | .16 |
| **1989. BICENTENNIAL: HOUSE OF REPRESENTATIVES** | | | | |
| ☐2412 25¢ Multicolored | 32.00 | 3.75 | .80 | .16 |
| **1989. BICENTENNIAL: UNITED STATES SENATE** | | | | |
| ☐2413 25¢ Multicolored | 32.00 | 3.60 | .80 | .16 |
| **1989. BICENTENNIAL: EXECUTIVE BRANCH** | | | | |
| ☐2414 25¢ Multicolored | 36.00 | 4.50 | 1.00 | .16 |
| **1989. U.S. SUPREME COURT** | | | | |
| ☐2415 25¢ Multicolored | 34.00 | 4.00 | .80 | .16 |

*No hinge pricing from 1941 to date is figured at (N-H ADD 15%)

| Scott No. | Mint Sheet | Plate Block | Fine Unused Each | Fine Used Each |
|---|---|---|---|---|
| **1989. SOUTH DAKOTA 1889: STATEHOOD** | | | | |
| ☐2416 25¢ Multicolored | 30.00 | 3.75 | .80 | .16 |
| **1989. LOU GEHRIG** | | | | |
| ☐2417 25¢ Multicolored | 34.00 | 3.75 | .80 | .16 |
| **1989. ERNEST HEMINGWAY** | | | | |
| ☐2418 25¢ Multicolored | 30.00 | 3.75 | .80 | .16 |
| **1989. MOON LANDING** | | | | |
| ☐2419 $2.40 Multicolored | 100.00 | 25.00 | 6.00 | .16 |
| **1989. LETTER CARRIERS** | | | | |
| ☐2420 25¢ Multicolored | 24.00 | 3.00 | .70 | .16 |
| **1989. BILL OF RIGHTS** | | | | |
| ☐2421 25¢ Multicolored | 50.00 | 7.00 | 1.80 | .16 |
| **1989. DINOSAURS: TYRANNOSAURUS** | | | | |
| ☐2422 25¢ Multicolored | 40.00 | 7.50 | .80 | .16 |
| **1989. DINOSAURS: PTERANODON** | | | | |
| ☐2423 25¢ Multicolored | 40.00 | 7.50 | .80 | .16 |
| **1989. DINOSAURS: STEGOSAURUS** | | | | |
| ☐2424 25¢ Multicolored | 40.00 | 7.50 | .80 | .16 |
| **1989. DINOSAURS: BRONTOSAURUS** | | | | |
| ☐2425 25¢ Multicolored | 40.00 | 7.50 | .80 | .16 |
| **1989. COLUMBIAN ARTIFACTS** | | | | |
| ☐2426 25¢ Multicolored | 32.00 | 4.00 | .70 | .16 |
| **1989. CHRISTMAS: MADONNA** | | | | |
| ☐2427 25¢ Multicolored | 30.00 | 4.00 | .70 | .16 |
| **1989. CHRISTMAS: SLEIGH** | | | | |
| ☐2428 25¢ Multicolored | 30.00 | 4.00 | .70 | .16 |

*No hinge pricing from 1941 to date is figured at (N-H ADD 15%)

| Scott No. | Mint Sheet | Plate Block | Fine Unused Each | Fine Used Each |
|---|---|---|---|---|
| **1989. MAIL DELIVERY: STAGECOACH** | | | | |
| ☐2434 25¢ Multicolored | 38.00 | 4.50 | .70 | .16 |
| **1989. MAIL DELIVERY: PADDLEWHEEL** | | | | |
| ☐2435 25¢ Multicolored | 38.00 | 4.50 | .70 | .16 |
| **1989. MAIL DELIVERY: BIPLANE** | | | | |
| ☐2436 25¢ Multicolored | 38.00 | 4.50 | .70 | .16 |
| **1989. MAIL DELIVERY: AUTOMOBILE** | | | | |
| ☐2437 25¢ Multicolored | 38.00 | 4.50 | .70 | .16 |
| **1990. IDAHO CENTENARY: BLUEBIRD** | | | | |
| ☐2439 25¢ Multicolored | 30.00 | 4.00 | .70 | .16 |
| **1990. LOVE** | | | | |
| ☐2440 25¢ Multicolored | 30.00 | 4.00 | .72 | .16 |
| **1990. BLACK HERITAGE. IDA B. WELLS** | | | | |
| ☐2442 25¢ Multicolored | 30.00 | 4.00 | .72 | .16 |
| **1990. BEACH UMBRELLA** | | | | |
| ☐2443 25¢ Multicolored | — | 4.50 | .50 | .16 |
| **1990. WYOMING CENTENARY—MOUNTAIN** | | | | |
| ☐2444 25¢ Multicolored | 30.00 | 8.00 | 1.50 | .16 |
| **1990. CLASSIC FILMS: WIZARD OF OZ** | | | | |
| ☐2445 25¢ Multicolored | 70.00 | 8.00 | 1.50 | .16 |
| **1990. CLASSIC FILMS: GONE WITH THE WIND** | | | | |
| ☐2446 25¢ Multicolored | 70.00 | 8.00 | 1.50 | .16 |
| **1990. CLASSIC FILMS: BEAU GESTE** | | | | |
| ☐2447 25¢ Multicolored | 70.00 | 10.00 | 1.00 | .16 |
| **1990. CLASSIC FILMS: STAGECOACH** | | | | |
| ☐2448 25¢ Multicolored | 70.00 | 10.00 | 1.00 | .16 |

*No hinge pricing from 1941 to date is figured at (N-H ADD 15%)

| Scott No. | Mint Sheet | Plate Block | Fine Unused Each | Fine Used Each |
|---|---|---|---|---|

**1990. LITERARY ARTS: MARIANNE MOORE**

| | | | | |
|---|---|---|---|---|
| ☐2449 25¢ Multicolored | 30.00 | 3.10 | .70 | .16 |

**1990. TRANSPORTATION**

☐2451–2464 4¢, 5¢, 10¢, 23¢ Multicolored

| | | | | |
|---|---|---|---|---|
| | — | 2.75 | .30 | .16 |

**1990. LIGHTHOUSES: ADMIRALTY HEAD**

| | | | | |
|---|---|---|---|---|
| ☐2470 25¢ Multicolored | — | — | .30 | .16 |

**1990. LIGHTHOUSES: CAPE HATTERAS**

| | | | | |
|---|---|---|---|---|
| ☐2471 25¢ Multicolored | — | — | .30 | .16 |

**1990. LIGHTHOUSES: WEST QUODDY HEAD**

| | | | | |
|---|---|---|---|---|
| ☐2472 25¢ Multicolored | — | — | .30 | .16 |

**1990. LIGHTHOUSES: AMERICAN SHOALS**

| | | | | |
|---|---|---|---|---|
| ☐2473 25¢ Multicolored | — | — | .30 | .16 |

**1990. LIGHTHOUSES: SANDY HOOK**

| | | | | |
|---|---|---|---|---|
| ☐2474 25¢ Multicolored | — | — | .30 | .16 |

**1990. BOBCAT**

| | | | | |
|---|---|---|---|---|
| ☐2476 $2.00 Multicolored | 80.00 | 18.00 | 4.00 | .60 |

**1990. KESTRAL**

| | | | | |
|---|---|---|---|---|
| ☐2481 1¢ Multicolored | 8.00 | .70 | .25 | .16 |

**1990. BLUEBIRD**

| | | | | |
|---|---|---|---|---|
| ☐2482 3¢ Multicolored | 9.00 | .75 | .25 | .16 |

**1990. FAWN**

| | | | | |
|---|---|---|---|---|
| ☐2487 19¢ Multicolored | 35.00 | 2.50 | .45 | .16 |

**1990. CARDINAL**

| | | | | |
|---|---|---|---|---|
| ☐2489 30¢ Multicolored | 52.00 | 3.60 | .65 | .16 |

**1990. WOOD DUCK**

| | | | | |
|---|---|---|---|---|
| ☐2493 29¢ Black & Multicolored — | | — | .85 | .16 |

*No hinge pricing from 1941 to date is figured at (N-H ADD 15%)

| Scott No. | Mint Sheet | Plate Block | Fine Unused Each | Fine Used Each |
|---|---|---|---|---|
| **1990. OLYMPIANS: JESSE OWENS** | | | | |
| ☐2496 25¢ Multicolored | 32.00 | 9.00 | .80 | .16 |
| **1990. OLYMPIANS: RAY EWRY** | | | | |
| ☐2497 25¢ Multicolored | 32.00 | 9.00 | .80 | .16 |
| **1990. OLYMPIANS: HAZEL WIGHTMAN** | | | | |
| ☐2498 25¢ Multicolored | 32.00 | 9.00 | .80 | .16 |
| **1990. OLYMPIANS: EDDIE EAGAN** | | | | |
| ☐2499 25¢ Multicolored | 32.00 | 9.00 | .80 | .16 |
| **1990. OLYMPIANS: HELENE MADISON** | | | | |
| ☐2500 25¢ Multicolored | 32.00 | 9.00 | .75 | .16 |
| **1990. INDIAN: ASSINIBOINE** | | | | |
| ☐2501 25¢ Multicolored | — | — | — | .16 |
| **1990. INDIAN: CHEYENNE** | | | | |
| ☐2502 25¢ Multicolored | — | — | — | .16 |
| **1990. INDIAN: COMANCHE** | | | | |
| ☐2503 25¢ Multicolored | — | — | — | .16 |
| **1990. INDIAN: FLATHEAD** | | | | |
| ☐2505 25¢ Multicolored | — | — | .75 | .16 |
| **1990. INDIAN: SHOSHONE** | | | | |
| ☐2505 25¢ Multicolored | — | — | .75 | .16 |
| **1990. MICRONESIA** | | | | |
| ☐2506 25¢ Multicolored | 38.00 | 4.00 | 1.00 | .16 |
| **1990. MARSHALL ISLANDS** | | | | |
| ☐2507 25¢ Multicolored | 38.00 | 4.00 | 1.00 | .16 |
| **1990. SEA CREATURES: KILLER WHALE** | | | | |
| ☐2508 25¢ Multicolored | 32.00 | 4.00 | 1.00 | .16 |

*No hinge pricing from 1941 to date is figured at (N-H ADD 15%)

| Scott No. | Mint Sheet | Plate Block | Fine Unused Each | Fine Used Each |
|---|---|---|---|---|
| **1990. SEA CREATURES: NORTHERN SEA LION** | | | | |
| ☐2509 25¢ Multicolored | 32.00 | 4.00 | 1.00 | .16 |
| **1990. SEA CREATURES: SEA OTTER** | | | | |
| ☐2510 25¢ Multicolored | 30.00 | 4.00 | 1.00 | .16 |
| **1990. SEA CREATURES: DOLPHIN** | | | | |
| ☐2511 25¢ Multicolored | 30.00 | 4.00 | 1.00 | .16 |
| **1990. GRAND CANYON** | | | | |
| ☐2512 25¢ Multicolored | 29.00 | 3.00 | 1.00 | .16 |
| **1990. DWIGHT D. EISENHOWER** | | | | |
| ☐2513 25¢ Multicolored | 25.00 | 3.00 | 1.00 | .16 |
| **1990. CHRISTMAS: MADONNA** | | | | |
| ☐2514 25¢ Multicolored | 30.00 | 3.00 | .70 | .16 |
| **1990. CHRISTMAS: CHRISTMAS TREE** | | | | |
| ☐2515 25¢ Multicolored | 30.00 | 3.00 | .70 | .16 |
| **1991. "F" FLOWER: TULIP** | | | | |
| ☐2517 29¢ Multicolored | 62.00 | 4.00 | .65 | .16 |
| **1991. "F" STAMP RATE: EXTRA POSTAGE** | | | | |
| ☐2521 4 ¢ Multicolored | 10.00 | .80 | .50 | .16 |
| **1991. FLAG: MT. RUSHMORE** | | | | |
| ☐2523 29¢ Multicolored | — | 6.00 | .70 | .16 |
| **1991. FLOWER: TULIP** | | | | |
| ☐2524 29¢ Multicolored | 65.00 | 4.00 | .70 | .16 |
| **1991. FLAG: OLYMPIC RINGS** | | | | |
| ☐2528 29¢ Multicolored | — | — | .80 | .16 |
| **1991. FISHING BOAT** | | | | |
| ☐2529 19¢ Multicolored | — | — | .45 | .16 |

*No hinge pricing from 1941 to date is figured at (N-H ADD 15%)

| Scott No. | Mint Sheet | Plate Block | Fine Unused Each | Fine Used Each |
|---|---|---|---|---|
| **1991. BALLOONING** | | | | |
| ☐2530 19¢ Multicolored | — | — | .45 | .16 |
| **1991. FLAGS: ON PARADE** | | | | |
| ☐2531 29¢ Multicolored | 52.00 | 3.00 | .65 | .16 |
| **1991. SWITZERLAND: 700TH ANNIVERSARY** | | | | |
| ☐2532 50¢ Multicolored | 42.00 | 5.00 | 1.30 | .18 |
| **1991. VERMONT: BICENTENNIAL** | | | | |
| ☐2533 29¢ Multicolored | 32.00 | 3.50 | .75 | .16 |
| **1991. SAVINGS BONDS: 50TH ANNIVERSARY** | | | | |
| ☐2534 29¢ Multicolored | 32.00 | 3.50 | .75 | .16 |
| **1991. LOVE: HEART** | | | | |
| ☐2535 29¢ Multicolored | 36.00 | 4.00 | .80 | .16 |
| **1991. LOVE: LOVE BIRDS** | | | | |
| ☐2537 52¢ Multicolored | 60.00 | 6.00 | 1.15 | .16 |
| **1991. LITERARY ARTS: WILLIAM SAROYAN** | | | | |
| ☐2538 29¢ Multicolored | 30.00 | 3.50 | .65 | .16 |
| **1991. USPS: OLYMPIC RINGS** | | | | |
| ☐2539 $1.00 Multicolored | 46.00 | 10.00 | 2.15 | .30 |
| **1991. EAGLE: OLYMPIC RINGS** | | | | |
| ☐2540 $2.90 Multicolored | 120.00 | 29.00 | 7.00 | 2.00 |
| **1991. DOMESTIC: EXPRESS MAIL** | | | | |
| ☐2541 9.95 Multicolored | 350.00 | 85.00 | 19.00 | 7.00 |
| **1991. INTERNATIONAL: EXPRESS MAIL** | | | | |
| ☐2542 $14.00 Multicolored | 450.00 | 115.00 | 26.00 | 15.00 |
| **1991. FISHING FLIES** | | | | |
| ☐2545 29¢ Multicolored | — | — | .75 | .16 |
| ☐2546 29¢ Multicolored | — | — | .75 | .16 |

*No hinge pricing from 1941 to date is figured at (N-H ADD 15%)

| Scott No. | Mint Sheet | Plate Block | Fine Unused Each | Fine Used Each |
|---|---|---|---|---|
| □2547 29¢ Multicolored | — | — | .75 | .16 |
| □2548 29¢ Multicolored | — | — | .75 | .16 |
| □2549 29¢ Multicolored | — | — | .75 | .16 |

## 1991. PERFORMING ARTS: COLE PORTER
| □2550 29¢ Multicolored | 31.00 | 3.50 | .75 | .16 |

## 1991. DESERT STORM: SOUTHWEST ASIA
| □2551 29¢ Multicolored | 31.00 | 3.50 | .75 | .16 |

## 1991. 1992 SUMMER OLYMPICS: BARCELONA
| □2553 29¢ Multicolored | — | — | .85 | .16 |
| □2554 29¢ Multicolored | — | — | .85 | .16 |
| □2555 29¢ Multicolored | — | — | .70 | .16 |
| □2556 29¢ Multicolored | — | — | .70 | .16 |
| □2557 29¢ Multicolored | — | — | .70 | .16 |

## 1991. NUMISMATICS: COINS AND NOTES
| □2558 29¢ Multicolored | — | 3.75 | .80 | .16 |

## 1991. WORLD WAR II
| □2559 29¢ Multicolored | — | 8.50 | .85 | .60 |

## 1991. BASKETBALL: 100TH ANNIVERSARY
| □2560 29¢ Multicolored | 34.00 | 3.75 | .80 | .16 |

## 1991. DISTRICT OF COLUMBIA: BICENTENNIAL
| □2561 29¢ Multicolored | 31.00 | 3.50 | .70 | .16 |

## 1991. COMEDIANS
| □2562 29¢ Multicolored | — | — | .70 | .14 |
| □2563 29¢ Multicolored | — | — | .70 | .14 |
| □2564 29¢ Multicolored | — | — | .70 | .14 |
| □2565 29¢ Multicolored | — | — | .70 | .14 |
| □2566 29¢ Multicolored | — | — | .70 | .14 |

## 1991. BLACK HERITAGE
| □2567 29¢ Multicolored | 31.00 | 3.75 | .75 | .14 |

*No hinge pricing from 1941 to date is figured at (N-H ADD 15%)

| Scott No. | Mint Sheet | Plate Block | Fine Unused Each | Fine Used Each |
|---|---|---|---|---|
| **1991. SPACE EXPLORATION** | | | | |
| ☐2568 29¢ Multicolored | — | — | .75 | .14 |
| ☐2569 29¢ Multicolored | — | — | .75 | .14 |
| ☐2570 29¢ Multicolored | — | — | .75 | .14 |
| ☐2571 29¢ Multicolored | — | — | .75 | .14 |
| ☐2572 29¢ Multicolored | — | — | .75 | .14 |
| ☐2573 29¢ Multicolored | — | — | .75 | .14 |
| ☐2574 29¢ Multicolored | — | — | .75 | .14 |
| ☐2575 29¢ Multicolored | — | — | .75 | .14 |
| ☐2576 29¢ Multicolored | — | — | .75 | .14 |
| ☐2577 29¢ Multicolored | — | — | .75 | .14 |
| **1991. CHRISTMAS** | | | | |
| ☐2578 29¢ Multicolored | 31.00 | 3.75 | .75 | .14 |
| ☐2579 29¢ Multicolored | 31.00 | 3.75 | .75 | .14 |
| ☐2582 29¢ Multicolored | — | — | .75 | .14 |
| ☐2583 29¢ Multicolored | — | — | .75 | .14 |
| ☐2584 29¢ Multicolored | — | — | .75 | .14 |
| ☐2585 29¢ Multicolored | — | — | .75 | .14 |
| **1992. BULK RATE** | | | | |
| ☐2604 10¢ Multicolored | — | — | .30 | .14 |
| ☐2607 23¢ Multicolored | — | — | .65 | .14 |
| ☐2608 23¢ Multicolored | — | — | .65 | .14 |
| ☐2609 29¢ Multicolored | — | — | .65 | .14 |
| **1992. WINTER OLYMPICS** | | | | |
| ☐2611 29¢ Multicolored | 30.00 | 9.00 | .70 | .14 |
| ☐2612 29¢ Multicolored | — | — | .70 | .14 |
| ☐2613 29¢ Multicolored | — | — | .70 | .14 |
| ☐2613 29¢ Multicolored | — | — | .70 | .14 |
| ☐2614 29¢ Multicolored | — | — | .70 | .14 |
| ☐2615 29¢ Multicolored | — | — | .70 | .14 |
| **1992. WORLD COLUMBIAN STAMP EXPO** | | | | |
| ☐2616 29¢ Multicolored | 31.00 | 2.90 | .65 | .14 |

*No hinge pricing from 1941 to date is figured at (N-H ADD 15%)

| Scott No. | Mint Sheet | Plate Block | Fine Unused Each | Fine Used Each |
|---|---|---|---|---|
| **1992. BLACK HERITAGE** | | | | |
| ☐2617 29¢ Multicolored | 31.00 | 2.90 | .65 | .14 |
| **1992. LOVE** | | | | |
| ☐2618 29¢ Multicolored | 31.00 | 2.90 | .65 | .14 |
| **1992. OLYMPIC BASEBALL** | | | | |
| ☐2619 29¢ Multicolored | 48.00 | 5.00 | .90 | .14 |
| **1992. VOYAGES OF COLUMBUS** | | | | |
| ☐2620 29¢ Multicolored | 31.00 | 4.00 | .65 | .14 |
| ☐2621 29¢ Multicolored | — | — | .65 | .14 |
| ☐2622 29¢ Multicolored | — | — | .65 | .14 |
| ☐2623 29¢ Multicolored | — | — | .65 | .14 |
| **1992. NEW YORK STOCK EXCHANGE BICENTENNIAL** | | | | |
| ☐2630 29¢ Green, Red & Black | 28.00 | 3.50 | .65 | .14 |
| **1992. SPACE ACCOMPLISHMENTS** | | | | |
| ☐2631 29¢ Multicolored | 40.00 | 3.50 | .65 | .14 |
| ☐2632 29¢ Multicolored | — | — | .65 | .14 |
| ☐2633 29¢ Multicolored | — | — | .65 | .14 |
| ☐2634 29¢ Multicolored | — | — | .65 | .14 |
| **1992. ALASKA HIGHWAY—5OTH ANNIVERSARY** | | | | |
| ☐2635 29¢ Multicolored | 31.00 | 3.00 | .65 | .14 |
| **1992. KENTUCKY STATEHOOD BICENTENNIAL** | | | | |
| ☐2636 29¢ Multicolored | 31.00 | 3.00 | .65 | .14 |
| **1992. SUMMER OLYMPICS** | | | | |
| ☐2637 29¢ Multicolored | — | — | .65 | .14 |
| ☐2638 29¢ Multicolored | — | — | .65 | .14 |
| ☐2639 29¢ Multicolored | — | — | .65 | .14 |
| ☐2640 29¢ Multicolored | — | — | .65 | .14 |
| ☐2641 29¢ Multicolored | — | — | .65 | .14 |

*No hinge pricing from 1941 to date is figured at (N-H ADD 15%)

| Scott No. | Mint Sheet | Plate Block | Fine Unused Each | Fine Used Each |
|---|---|---|---|---|

## 1992. HUMMINGBIRDS

| | | | | |
|---|---|---|---|---|
| ☐2642 29¢ Muticolored | — | — | .65 | .14 |
| ☐2643 29¢ Multicolored | — | — | .65 | .14 |
| ☐2644 29¢ Multicolored | — | — | .65 | .14 |
| ☐2645 29¢ Multicolored | — | — | .65 | .14 |
| ☐2646 29¢ Multicolored | — | — | .70 | .14 |
| ☐2646A Five Above Attached | — | | 4.75 | — |

## 1992. WILD FLOWERS

| | | | | |
|---|---|---|---|---|
| ☐ 29¢ Multicolored, 50 Vari. Attached | 35.00 | — | — | — |
| ☐ 29¢ Multicolored, Individual Flowers | — | — | .70 | .14 |

☐2647 Indian Paintbrush
☐2648 Fragrant Water Lily
☐2649 Meadow Beauty
☐2650 Jack-in-the-Pulpit
☐2651 California Poppy
☐2652 Large Flower Trillium
☐2653 Tickseed
☐2654 Shooting Star
☐2655 Stream Violet
☐2656 Bluets
☐2657 Herb Robert
☐2658 Marsh Marigold
☐2659 Sweet White Violet
☐2660 Claret Cup Cactus
☐2661 White Mountain Avens
☐2662 Sessile Bellwort
☐2663 Blue Flag
☐2664 Harlequin Lupine
☐2665 Twin Flower
☐2666 Common Sunflower
☐2667 Sego Lily
☐2668 Virginia Bluebells
☐2669 Ohi'a Lehua
☐2670 Rosebud Orchid
☐2671 Showy Evening Primrose
☐2672 Fringed Gentian
☐2673 Yellow Lady's Slipper
☐2674 Passion Flower
☐2675 Bunch Berry
☐2676 Pasque Flower
☐2677 Round-Lobed Hepatica
☐2678 Wild Columbine
☐2679 Firewood
☐2680 Indian Pond Lily
☐2681 Turk's Cap Lily
☐2682 Dutchman's Breeches
☐2683 Trumpet Honeysuckle
☐2684 Jacob's Ladder
☐2685 Plains Prickly Pear
☐2686 Mots Campion
☐2687 Bearberry
☐2688 Mexican Hat
☐2689 Harebell
☐2690 Desert Five Spot
☐2691 Smooth Solomon's Seal
☐2692 Red Maids

*No hinge pricing from 1941 to date is figured at (N-H ADD 15%)

☐2693 Yellow Skunk Cabbage    ☐2695 Standing Cypress
☐2694 Rue Anemone            ☐2696 Wild Flax

| Scott No. | Mint Sheet | Plate Block | Fine Unused Each | Fine Used Each |
|---|---|---|---|---|
| **1992. WORLD WAR II** | | | | |
| ☐2697     Souvenir Sheet Multicolored | | | | |
| | 12.00 | — | 7.00 | .14 |
| 29¢ Single Stamps | — | — | .65 | .14 |
| **1992. LITERARY ART SERIES** | | | | |
| ☐2698 29¢ Multicolored | 31.00 | 3.40 | .65 | .14 |
| **1992. THEODORE VON KÁRMÁN** | | | | |
| ☐2699 29¢ Multicolored | 31.00 | 3.40 | .65 | .14 |
| **1992. MINERALS** | | | | |
| ☐2700 29¢ Multicolored | 31.00 | 4.00 | .65 | .14 |
| ☐2701 29¢ Multicolored | — | — | .65 | .14 |
| ☐2702 29¢ Multicolored | — | — | .65 | .14 |
| ☐2703 29¢ Multicolored | — | — | .65 | .14 |
| **1992. JUAN RODRÍGUEZ CABRILLO** | | | | |
| ☐2704 29¢ Multicolored | — | 3.50 | .65 | .14 |
| **1992. WILD ANIMALS** | | | | |
| ☐2705  29¢ Multicolored | — | — | .70 | .14 |
| ☐2706  29¢ Multicolored | — | — | .70 | .14 |
| ☐2707  29¢ Multicolored | — | — | .70 | .14 |
| ☐2708  29¢ Multicolored | — | — | .70 | .14 |
| ☐2709  29¢ Multicolored | — | — | .70 | .14 |
| ☐2709A 29¢ Multicolored Five Above Attached | | | | |
| | — | — | 4.00 | .14 |
| **1992. MADONNA AND CHILD** | | | | |
| ☐2710 29¢ Multicolored | 31.00 | 3.50 | .70 | .14 |
| **1992. HORSE AND RIDER** | | | | |
| ☐2711 29¢ Multicolored | — | 3.75 | .70 | .14 |

*No hinge pricing from 1941 to date is figured at (N-H ADD 15%)

| Scott No. | Mint Sheet | Plate Block | Fine Unused Each | Fine Used Each |
|---|---|---|---|---|
| **1992. TOY LOCOMOTIVE** | | | | |
| ☐2712 29¢ Multicolored | — | 3.75 | .70 | .14 |
| **1992. TOY FIRE PUMPER** | | | | |
| ☐2713 29¢ Multicolored | — | 3.75 | .70 | .14 |
| **1992. RIVERBOAT ON WHEELS** | | | | |
| ☐2714 29¢ Multicolored | — | 3.75 | .70 | .14 |
| **1992. HAPPY NEW YEAR** | | | | |
| ☐2720 29¢ Multicolored | 24.00 | 3.75 | .70 | .14 |
| **1993. ELVIS** | | | | |
| ☐2721 29¢ Multicolored | 26.00 | 3.75 | .70 | .14 |
| **1993. OKLAHOMA** | | | | |
| ☐2722 29¢ Multicolored | 26.00 | 3.75 | .70 | .14 |
| **1993. HANK WILLIAMS** | | | | |
| ☐2723 29¢ Multicolored | 26.00 | 3.75 | .70 | .14 |
| **1993. AMERICAN MUSIC—ELVIS PRESLEY** | | | | |
| ☐2724 29¢ Multicolored | 26.00 | 3.75 | .70 | .14 |
| **1993. AMERICAN MUSIC—BILL HALEY** | | | | |
| ☐2725 29¢ Multicolored | 26.00 | 4.50 | .70 | .14 |
| **1993. AMERICAN MUSIC—CLYDE McPHATTER** | | | | |
| ☐2726 29¢ Multicolored | 25.00 | 4.50 | .70 | .14 |
| **1993. AMERICAN MUSIC—RITCHIE VALENS** | | | | |
| ☐2727 29¢ Multicolored | 25.00 | 4.50 | .70 | .14 |
| **1993. AMERICAN MUSIC—OTIS REDDING** | | | | |
| ☐2728 29¢ Multicolored | 25.00 | 4.50 | .70 | .14 |
| **1993. AMERICAN MUSIC—BUDDY HOLLY** | | | | |
| ☐2729 29¢ Multicolored | 25.00 | 4.50 | .70 | .14 |

| Scott No. | Mint Sheet | Plate Block | Fine Unused Each | Fine Used Each |
|---|---|---|---|---|

## 1993. AMERICAN MUSIC—DINAH WASHINGTON

| | | | | |
|---|---|---|---|---|
| ☐ 2730 29¢ Multicolored | 25.00 | 4.50 | .70 | .14 |

## 1993. SPACE FANTASY

| | | | | |
|---|---|---|---|---|
| ☐ 2741 29¢ Multicolored | — | — | .70 | .14 |
| ☐ 2742 29¢ Multicolored | — | — | .70 | .14 |
| ☐ 2743 29¢ Multicolored | — | — | .70 | .14 |
| ☐ 2744 29¢ Multicolored | — | — | .70 | .14 |
| ☐ 2745 29¢ Multicolored | — | — | .70 | .14 |

## 1993. PERCY LAVON JULIAN

| | | | | |
|---|---|---|---|---|
| ☐ 2746 29¢ Multicolored | 31.00 | 3.10 | .70 | .14 |

## 1993. OREGON TRAIL

| | | | | |
|---|---|---|---|---|
| ☐ 2747 29¢ Multicolored | 31.00 | 3.10 | .70 | .14 |

## 1993. WORLD UNIVERSITY GAMES

| | | | | |
|---|---|---|---|---|
| ☐ 2748 29¢ Multicolored | 31.00 | 3.10 | .70 | .14 |

## 1993. GRACE KELLY

| | | | | |
|---|---|---|---|---|
| ☐ 2749 29¢ Multicolored | 31.00 | 3.10 | .70 | .14 |

## 1993. CIRCUS

| | | | | |
|---|---|---|---|---|
| ☐ 2750 29¢ Multicolored | 29.00 | 3.10 | .70 | .14 |
| ☐ 2751 29¢ Multicolored | — | — | .70 | .14 |
| ☐ 2752 29¢ Multicolored | — | — | .70 | .14 |
| ☐ 2753 29¢ Multicolored | — | — | .70 | .14 |

## 1993. CHEROKEE STRIP LAND RUN

| | | | | |
|---|---|---|---|---|
| ☐ 2754 29¢ Multicolored | 29.00 | 3.10 | .70 | .14 |

## 1993. DEAN ACHESON

| | | | | |
|---|---|---|---|---|
| ☐ 2755 29¢ Multicolored | 29.00 | 3.10 | .70 | .14 |

## 1993. SPORTING HORSES

| | | | | |
|---|---|---|---|---|
| ☐ 2756 29¢ Multicolored | 29.00 | 3.10 | .70 | .14 |
| ☐ 2757 29¢ Multicolored | — | — | .70 | .14 |

* No hinge pricing from 1941 to date is figured at (N-H ADD 15%)

| | Mint Sheet | Plate Block | Fine Unused Each | Fine Used Each |
|---|---|---|---|---|
| ☐2758 29¢ Multicolored | — | — | .70 | .14 |
| ☐2759 29¢ Multicolored | — | — | .70 | .14 |

## 1993. GARDEN FLOWERS

| | | | | |
|---|---|---|---|---|
| ☐2760 29¢ Multicolored | — | — | .65 | .14 |
| ☐2761 29¢ Multicolored | — | — | .65 | .14 |
| ☐2762 29¢ Multicolored | — | — | .65 | .14 |
| ☐2763 29¢ Multicolored | — | — | .65 | .14 |
| ☐2764 29¢ Multicolored | — | — | .65 | .14 |

## 1993. WORLD WAR II 1943

| | | | | |
|---|---|---|---|---|
| ☐2765 29¢ Multicolored | — | 7.00 | .65 | .14 |

## 1993. JOE LOUIS

| | | | | |
|---|---|---|---|---|
| ☐2766 Multicolored | 28.00 | 3.00 | .65 | .14 |

## 1993. BROADWAY MUSICALS

| | | | | |
|---|---|---|---|---|
| ☐2767 29¢ Multicolored | — | — | .65 | .14 |
| ☐2768 29¢ Multicolored | — | — | .65 | .14 |
| ☐2769 29¢ Multicolored | — | — | .65 | .14 |
| ☐2770 29¢ Multicolored | — | — | .65 | .14 |

## 1993. NATIONAL POSTAL MUSEUM

| | | | | |
|---|---|---|---|---|
| ☐2779 29¢ Multicolored | — | — | .65 | .14 |
| ☐2780 29¢ Multicolored | — | — | .65 | .14 |
| ☐2781 29¢ Multicolored | — | — | .65 | .14 |
| ☐2782 29¢ Multicolored | — | — | .65 | .14 |

## 1993. MARIANA ISLANDS

| | | | | |
|---|---|---|---|---|
| ☐2804 29¢ Multicolored | 28.00 | 3.10 | .70 | .14 |

## 1993. COLUMBUS LANDING

| | | | | |
|---|---|---|---|---|
| ☐2805 29¢ Multicolored | 28.00 | 3.10 | .70 | .14 |

## 1993. AIDS AWARENESS

| | | | | |
|---|---|---|---|---|
| ☐2806 29¢ Multicolored | 28.00 | 3.10 | .70 | .14 |

* No hinge pricing from 1941 to date is figured at (N-H ADD 15%)

| | Mint Sheet | Plate Block | Fine Unused Each | Fine Used Each |
|---|---|---|---|---|
| **1994. WINTER OLYMPICS** | | | | |
| ☐2807 29¢ Multicolored | — | — | .55 | .14 |
| ☐2808 29¢ Multicolored | — | — | .55 | .14 |
| ☐2809 29¢ Multicolored | — | — | .55 | .14 |
| ☐2810 29¢ Multicolored | — | — | .55 | .14 |
| ☐2811 29¢ Multicolored | — | — | .55 | .14 |
| **1994. EDWARD R. MURROW** | | | | |
| ☐2812 29¢ Brown | 30.00 | 3.10 | .70 | .14 |
| **1994. LOVE** | | | | |
| ☐2813 29¢ Multicolored | — | — | .70 | .14 |
| ☐2814 29¢ Multicolored | — | — | .70 | .14 |
| ☐2815 29¢ Multicolored | 45.00 | 4.50 | .70 | .14 |
| **1994. BLACK HERITAGE** | | | | |
| ☐2816 29¢ Multicolored | 13.00 | 3.50 | .70 | .14 |
| **1994. CHINESE NEW YEAR** | | | | |
| ☐2817 29¢ Multicolored | 13.00 | 3.50 | .70 | .14 |
| **1994. BUFFALO SOLDIERS** | | | | |
| ☐2818 29¢ Multicolored | 13.00 | 3.50 | .70 | .14 |
| **1994. SILENT SCREEN STARS** | | | | |
| ☐2819 29¢ Multicolored | — | — | .65 | .14 |
| ☐2820 29¢ Multicolored | — | — | .65 | .14 |
| ☐2821 29¢ Multicolored | — | — | .65 | .14 |
| ☐2822 29¢ Multicolored | — | — | .65 | .14 |
| ☐2823 29¢ Multicolored | — | — | .65 | .14 |
| ☐2824 29¢ Multicolored | — | — | .65 | .14 |
| ☐2825 29¢ Multicolored | — | — | .65 | .14 |
| ☐2826 29¢ Multicolored | — | — | .65 | .14 |
| ☐2827 29¢ Multicolored | — | — | .65 | .14 |
| ☐2828 29¢ Multicolored | — | — | .65 | .14 |
| ☐2828A 29¢ Multicolored | 24.00 | 9.00 | .65 | .14 |
| **1994. GARDEN FLOWERS** | | | | |
| ☐2829 29¢ Multicolored | — | — | .65 | .14 |

* No hinge pricing from 1941 to date is figured at (N-H ADD 15%)

| | Mint Sheet | Plate Block | Fine Unused Each | Fine Used Each |
|---|---|---|---|---|
| ☐2830 29¢ Multicolored | — | — | .65 | .14 |
| ☐2831 29¢ Multicolored | — | — | .65 | .14 |
| ☐2832 29¢ Multicolored | — | — | .65 | .14 |
| ☐2833 29¢ Multicolored | — | — | .65 | .14 |

## 1994. WORLD CUP SOCCER

| | Mint Sheet | Plate Block | Fine Unused Each | Fine Used Each |
|---|---|---|---|---|
| ☐2834 29¢ Multicolored | 11.00 | 3.10 | .65 | .14 |
| ☐2835 40¢ Multicolored | 15.00 | 5.00 | .85 | .14 |
| ☐2836 50¢ Multicolored | 20.00 | 6.00 | .90 | .14 |
| ☐2837 29¢ -40¢ -50¢ Multicolored | — | — | 3.25 | 2.00 |

## 1994. WORLD WAR II

| | Mint Sheet | Plate Block | Fine Unused Each | Fine Used Each |
|---|---|---|---|---|
| ☐2838 29¢ Multicolored | 12.00 | 7.00 | 6.00 | 6.00 |

## 1994. NORMAN ROCKWELL

| | Mint Sheet | Plate Block | Fine Unused Each | Fine Used Each |
|---|---|---|---|---|
| ☐2839 29¢ Multicolored | 30.00 | 3.50 | .65 | .14 |
| ☐2840 50¢ Multicolored | — | — | 4.50 | 4.50 |

## 1994. MOON LANDING ANNIVERSARY

| | Mint Sheet | Plate Block | Fine Unused Each | Fine Used Each |
|---|---|---|---|---|
| ☐2841 29¢ Multicolored | 12.50 | 3.50 | .85 | .14 |
| ☐2842 $9.95 Multicolored | 345.00 | 90.00 | 12.00 | 4.50 |

## 1994. LOCOMOTIVES

| | Mint Sheet | Plate Block | Fine Unused Each | Fine Used Each |
|---|---|---|---|---|
| ☐2843 29¢ Multicolored | — | — | .65 | .14 |
| ☐2844 29¢ Multicolored | — | — | .65 | .14 |
| ☐2845 29¢ Multicolored | — | — | .65 | .14 |
| ☐2846 29¢ Multicolored | — | — | .65 | .14 |
| ☐2847 29¢ Multicolored | — | — | .65 | .14 |

## 1994. GEORGE MEANY

| | Mint Sheet | Plate Block | Fine Unused Each | Fine Used Each |
|---|---|---|---|---|
| ☐2848 29¢ Multicolored | — | — | .65 | .14 |

| Scott No. | Fine Unused Plate Blk | Ave. Unused Plate Blk | Fine Unused Each | Ave. Unused Each | Fine Used Each | Ave. Used Each |
|---|---|---|---|---|---|---|
| **AIRMAIL STAMPS** | | | | | | |
| **1918. FIRST ISSUE—(N-H ADD 45%)** | | | | | | |
| ☐C1 6¢ Orange | 700.00 | 600.00 | 85.00 | 60.00 | 33.00 | 22.00 |

* No hinge pricing from 1941 to date is figured at (N-H ADD 15%)

| Scott No. | Fine Unused Plate Blk | Ave. Unused Plate Blk | Fine Unused Each | Ave. Unused Each | Fine Used Each | Ave. Used Each |
|---|---|---|---|---|---|---|
| □C2 16¢ Green | | | | | | |
| | 1200.00 | 1000.00 | 115.00 | 85.00 | 36.00 | 26.00 |
| □C3 24¢ Carmine & Blue | | | | | | |
| | 1400.00 | 1200.00 | 115.00 | 85.00 | 39.00 | 26.00 |

## 1923. SECOND ISSUE—(N-H ADD 35%)

| | | | | | | |
|---|---|---|---|---|---|---|
| □C4 8¢ Dark Green | | | | | | |
| | 310.00 | 275.00 | 29.00 | 24.00 | 14.00 | 10.00 |
| □C5 16¢ Dark Blue | | | | | | |
| | 1800.00 | 1500.00 | 100.00 | 75.00 | 38.00 | 32.00 |
| □C6 24¢ Carmine | | | | | | |
| | 2300.00 | 1900.00 | 110.00 | 85.00 | 31.00 | 26.00 |

## 1926–1927. LONG MAP (N-H ADD 35%)

| | | | | | | |
|---|---|---|---|---|---|---|
| □C7 10¢ Dark Blue | | | | | | |
| | 40.00 | 30.00 | 3.25 | 2.50 | .45 | .30 |
| □C8 15¢ Olive Brown | | | | | | |
| | 50.00 | 36.00 | 4.00 | 3.00 | 2.30 | 1.90 |
| □C9 20¢ Yellow Green | | | | | | |
| | 130.00 | 80.00 | 10.00 | 7.50 | 1.90 | 1.60 |

## 1927. LINDBERGH TRIBUTE ISSUE (N-H ADD 25%)

| | | | | | | |
|---|---|---|---|---|---|---|
| □C10 10¢ Dark Blue | | | | | | |
| | 165.00 | 120.00 | 8.75 | 6.00 | 2.30 | 1.40 |

## 1928. BEACON (N-H ADD 20%)

| | | | | | | |
|---|---|---|---|---|---|---|
| □C11 5¢ Carmine & Blue | | | | | | |
| | 70.00 | 50.00 | 4.00 | 3.00 | .60 | .30 |

## 1930. WINGED GLOBE—FLAT PRESS (N-H ADD 35%)

| | | | | | | |
|---|---|---|---|---|---|---|
| □C12 5¢ Violet | | | | | | |
| | 180.00 | 120.00 | 10.00 | 8.00 | .45 | .30 |

## 1930. GRAF ZEPPELIN ISSUE (N-H ADD 20%)

| | | | | | | |
|---|---|---|---|---|---|---|
| □C13 65¢ Green | | | | | | |
| | 2400.00 | 2000.00 | 280.00 | 225.00 | 230.00 | 180.00 |
| □C14 $1.30 Brown | | | | | | |
| | 5500.00 | 4800.00 | 700.00 | 500.00 | 500.00 | 380.00 |
| □C15 $2.60 Blue | | | | | | |
| | 8600.00 | 7000.00 | 1050.00 | 800.00 | 700.00 | 500.00 |

* No hinge pricing from 1941 to date is figured at (N-H ADD 15%)

| Scott No. | Fine Unused Plate Blk | Ave. Unused Plate Blk | Fine Unused Each | Ave. Unused Each | Fine Used Each | Ave. Used Each |
|---|---|---|---|---|---|---|

## 1931–1932.
## WINGED GLOBE—ROTARY PRESS (N-H ADD 25%)

| | | | | | | |
|---|---|---|---|---|---|---|
| □C16 5¢ Violet | | | | | | |
| | 95.00 | 80.00 | 6.00 | 3.80 | .60 | .35 |
| □C17 8¢ Olive Bistre | | | | | | |
| | 34.00 | 27.00 | 2.40 | 1.80 | .30 | .22 |

## 1933. CENTURY OF PROGRESS ISSUE
## (N-H ADD 25%)

| | | | | | | |
|---|---|---|---|---|---|---|
| □C18 50¢ Green | | | | | | |
| | 700.00 | 600.00 | 94.00 | 80.00 | 82.00 | 55.00 |

## 1934. DESIGN OF 1930 (N-H ADD 25%)

| | | | | | | |
|---|---|---|---|---|---|---|
| □C19 6¢ Orange | | | | | | |
| | 26.00 | 23.00 | 2.90 | 2.10 | .20 | .15 |

## 1935–1937. TRANSPACIFIC ISSUE (N-H ADD 10%)

| | | | | | | |
|---|---|---|---|---|---|---|
| □C20 25¢ Blue | | | | | | |
| | 24.00 | 20.00 | 1.30 | 1.00 | .95 | .75 |
| □C21 20¢ Green | | | | | | |
| | 130.00 | 100.00 | 9.00 | 7.00 | 1.80 | 1.10 |
| □C22 50¢ Carmine | | | | | | |
| | 130.00 | 100.00 | 9.00 | 7.50 | 5.00 | 3.20 |

## 1938. EAGLE (N-H ADD 20%)

| | | | | | | |
|---|---|---|---|---|---|---|
| □C23 6¢ Blue & Carmine | | | | | | |
| | 8.00 | 6.50 | .50 | .36 | .20 | .15 |

## 1939. TRANSATLANTIC (N-H ADD 20%)

| | | | | | | |
|---|---|---|---|---|---|---|
| □C24 30¢ Dull Blue | | | | | | |
| | 170.00 | 135.00 | 8.50 | 7.00 | 1.60 | 1.00 |

## 1941–1944. TRANSPORT PLANE (N-H ADD 20%)

| | | | | | | |
|---|---|---|---|---|---|---|
| □C25 6¢ Carmine | | | | | | |
| | 1.15 | .90 | .25 | .20 | .18 | .14 |
| □C26 8¢ Olive Green | | | | | | |
| | 2.10 | 1.75 | .25 | .20 | .18 | .14 |

*No hinge pricing from 1941 to date is figured at (N-H ADD 15%)

| Scott No. | Fine Unused Plate Blk | Ave. Unused Plate Blk | Fine Unused Each | Ave. Unused Each | Fine Used Each | Ave. Used Each |
|---|---|---|---|---|---|---|
| ☐C27 10¢ Violet | | | | | | |
| | 11.00 | 9.00 | 1.40 | 1.00 | .21 | .14 |
| ☐C28 15¢ Brown Carmine | | | | | | |
| | 13.00 | 10.00 | 2.80 | 2.30 | .38 | .28 |
| ☐C29 20¢ Bright Green | | | | | | |
| | 13.00 | 10.00 | 2.40 | 1.90 | .36 | .28 |
| ☐C30 30¢ Blue | | | | | | |
| | 14.00 | 11.00 | 2.80 | 2.00 | .46 | .28 |
| ☐C31 50¢ Orange | | | | | | |
| | 90.00 | 78.00 | 12.50 | 9.00 | 4.00 | 3.00 |

| Scott No. | Mint Sheet | Plate Block | Fine Unused Each | Fine Used Each |
|---|---|---|---|---|

## 1946–1947. DC-4 SKYMASTER

| Scott No. | Mint Sheet | Plate Block | Fine Unused Each | Fine Used Each |
|---|---|---|---|---|
| ☐C32 5¢ Carmine | 7.00 | .75 | .22 | .14 |
| ☐C33 5¢ Carmine | 14.00 | .75 | .22 | .14 |

## 1947. REGULAR ISSUE

| Scott No. | Mint Sheet | Plate Block | Fine Unused Each | Fine Used Each |
|---|---|---|---|---|
| ☐C34 10¢ Black | 14.00 | 1.40 | .30 | .14 |
| ☐C35 15¢ Bright Blue Green | 23.00 | 2.10 | .46 | .14 |
| ☐C36 25¢ Blue | 51.00 | 5.00 | 1.00 | .14 |

| Scott No. | Fine Unused Line Pair | Ave. Unused Line Pair | Fine Unused Each | Ave. Unused Each | Fine Used Each | Ave. Used Each |
|---|---|---|---|---|---|---|

## 1948. DESIGN OF 1947

| Scott No. | Fine Unused Line Pair | Ave. Unused Line Pair | Fine Unused Each | Ave. Unused Each | Fine Used Each | Ave. Used Each |
|---|---|---|---|---|---|---|
| ☐C37 5¢ Carmine | | | | | | |
| | 9.00 | 10.00 | 1.00 | .85 | .95 | .60 |

| Scott No. | Mint Sheet | Plate Block | Fine Unused Each | Fine Used Each |
|---|---|---|---|---|

## 1948. NEW YORK CITY JUBILEE ISSUE

| Scott No. | Mint Sheet | Plate Block | Fine Unused Each | Fine Used Each |
|---|---|---|---|---|
| ☐C38 5¢ Red | 18.00 | 6.00 | .22 | .16 |

* No hinge pricing from 1941 to date is figured at (N-H ADD 15%)

| Scott No. | Mint Sheet | Plate Block | Fine Unused Each | Fine Used Each |
|---|---|---|---|---|

## 1949. DESIGN OF 1947
| | | | | |
|---|---|---|---|---|
| ☐C39 6¢ Carmine | 15.00 | .75 | .22 | .16 |

## 1949. ALEXANDRIA BICENTENNIAL
| | | | | |
|---|---|---|---|---|
| ☐C40 6¢ Carmine | 8.00 | .70 | .22 | .16 |

| Scott No. | Fine Unused Line Pair | Ave. Unused Line Pair | Fine Unused Each | Ave. Unused Each | Fine Used Each | Ave. Used Each |
|---|---|---|---|---|---|---|

## 1949. DESIGN OF 1947
| | | | | | | |
|---|---|---|---|---|---|---|
| ☐C41 6¢ Carmine | 14.00 | 12.00 | 3.40 | 2.90 | .20 | .16 |

| Scott No. | Mint Sheet | Plate Block | Fine Unused Each | Fine Used Each |
|---|---|---|---|---|

## 1949. U.P.U.—UNIVERSAL POSTAL UNION ISSUE
| | | | | |
|---|---|---|---|---|
| ☐C42 10¢ Purple | 15.00 | 1.75 | .35 | .30 |
| ☐C43 15¢ Ultramarine | 18.00 | 1.90 | .40 | .35 |
| ☐C44 25¢ Carmine | 34.00 | 8.00 | .70 | .60 |

## 1949. WRIGHT BROTHERS ISSUE
| | | | | |
|---|---|---|---|---|
| ☐C45 6¢ Magenta | 10.00 | .85 | .25 | .16 |

## 1952. HAWAII—DIAMOND HEAD
| | | | | |
|---|---|---|---|---|
| ☐C46 80¢ Bright Red Violet | 340.00 | 32.00 | 7.50 | 1.40 |

## 1953. 50TH ANNIVERSARY POWERED FLIGHT
| | | | | |
|---|---|---|---|---|
| ☐C47 6¢ Carmine | 8.00 | .85 | .22 | .16 |

## 1954. EAGLE IN FLIGHT
| | | | | |
|---|---|---|---|---|
| ☐C48 4¢ Bright Blue | 13.00 | 2.10 | .22 | .16 |

## 1957. 50TH ANNIVERSARY AIR FORCE
| | | | | |
|---|---|---|---|---|
| ☐C49 6¢ Blue | 8.00 | .75 | .22 | .16 |

## 1958. DESIGN OF 1954
| | | | | |
|---|---|---|---|---|
| ☐C50 5¢ Red | 15.00 | 1.90 | .22 | .16 |

* No hinge pricing from 1941 to date is figured at (N-H ADD 15%)

| Scott No. | Mint Sheet | Plate Block | Fine Unused Each | Fine Used Each |
|---|---|---|---|---|
| **1958. JETLINER SILHOUETTE** | | | | |
| ☐C51 7¢ Blue | 17.00 | .80 | .22 | .16 |

| Scott No. | Fine Unused Line Pair | Ave. Unused Line Pair | Fine Unused Each | Ave. Unused Each | Fine Used Each | Ave. Used Each |
|---|---|---|---|---|---|---|
| ☐C52 7¢ Blue | 17.00 | 14.00 | 2.30 | 1.75 | .20 | .16 |

| Scott No. | Mint Sheet | Plate Block | Fine Unused Each | Fine Used Each |
|---|---|---|---|---|
| **1959. COMMEMORATIVES** | | | | |
| **1959. ALASKA STATEHOOD** | | | | |
| ☐C53 7¢ Dark Blue | 10.00 | .90 | .25 | .16 |
| **1959. BALLOON JUPITER FLIGHT** | | | | |
| ☐C54 7¢ Dark Blue & Red | 11.00 | .90 | .25 | .16 |
| **1959. HAWAII STATEHOOD** | | | | |
| ☐C55 7¢ Rose Red | 9.00 | .90 | .25 | .16 |
| **1959. PAN AMERICAN GAMES** | | | | |
| ☐C56 10¢ Red & Blue | 12.00 | 1.60 | .28 | .16 |
| **1959–1961. REGULAR ISSUE** | | | | |
| ☐C57 10¢ Black & Green | 76.00 | 7.75 | 1.25 | .85 |
| ☐C58 15¢ Black & Orange | 26.00 | 2.50 | .48 | .16 |
| ☐C59 25¢ Black & Maroon | 34.00 | 3.50 | .75 | .16 |
| **1960. DESIGN OF 1958** | | | | |
| ☐C60 7¢ Carmine | 17.00 | .80 | .25 | .16 |

*No hinge pricing from 1941 to date is figured at (N-H ADD 15%)

| Scott No. | Fine Unused Line Pair | Ave. Unused Line Pair | Fine Unused Each | Ave. Unused Each | Fine Used Each | Ave. Used Each |
|---|---|---|---|---|---|---|
| ☐C61 7¢ Carmine | | | | | | |
| | 42.00 | 36.00 | 5.50 | 4.00 | .34 | .24 |

| Scott No. | Mint Sheet | Plate Block | Fine Unused Each | Fine Used Each |
|---|---|---|---|---|

## 1961. DESIGNS OF 1959–1960

| Scott No. | Mint Sheet | Plate Block | Fine Unused Each | Fine Used Each |
|---|---|---|---|---|
| ☐C62 13¢ Black & Red | 24.00 | 2.50 | .60 | .16 |
| ☐C63 15¢ Black & Orange | 20.00 | 1.90 | .40 | .16 |

## 1962. JETLINER OVER CAPITOL

| Scott No. | Mint Sheet | Plate Block | Fine Unused Each | Fine Used Each |
|---|---|---|---|---|
| ☐C64 8¢ Carmine | 23.00 | 1.10 | .25 | .16 |

| Scott No. | Fine Unused Line Pair | Ave. Unused Line Pair | Fine Unused Each | Ave. Unused Each | Fine Used Each | Ave. Used Each |
|---|---|---|---|---|---|---|
| ☐C65 8¢ Carmine | | | | | | |
| | 7.00 | 5.50 | .51 | .35 | .20 | .14 |

| Scott No. | Mint Sheet | Plate Block | Fine Unused Each | Fine Used Each |
|---|---|---|---|---|

## 1963. FIRST INTERNATIONAL POSTAL CONFERENCE CENTENARY

| Scott No. | Mint Sheet | Plate Block | Fine Unused Each | Fine Used Each |
|---|---|---|---|---|
| ☐C66 15¢ Dull Red, Dark Brown & Blue | | | | |
| | 34.00 | 4.00 | .80 | .60 |

## 1963. POSTAL CARD RATE

| Scott No. | Mint Sheet | Plate Block | Fine Unused Each | Fine Used Each |
|---|---|---|---|---|
| ☐C67 6¢ Red | 20.00 | 2.40 | .24 | .15 |

## 1963. AMELIA EARHART

| Scott No. | Mint Sheet | Plate Block | Fine Unused Each | Fine Used Each |
|---|---|---|---|---|
| ☐C68 8¢ Carmine & Maroon | | | | |
| | 13.00 | 1.50 | .28 | .16 |

## 1964. DR. ROBERT H. GODDARD

| Scott No. | Mint Sheet | Plate Block | Fine Unused Each | Fine Used Each |
|---|---|---|---|---|
| ☐C69 8¢ Blue, Red, Bistre | 24.00 | 2.30 | .55 | .19 |

*No hinge pricing from 1941 to date is figured at (N-H ADD 15%)

| Scott No. | Mint Sheet | Plate Block | Fine Unused Each | Fine Used Each |
|---|---|---|---|---|

## 1967–1969.
## 1967. ALASKA PURCHASE CENTENARY

| Scott No. | Mint Sheet | Plate Block | Fine Unused Each | Fine Used Each |
|---|---|---|---|---|
| ☐C70 8¢ Dark Brown | 14.00 | 1.90 | .35 | .19 |

## 1967.

| | Mint Sheet | Plate Block | Fine Unused Each | Fine Used Each |
|---|---|---|---|---|
| ☐C71 20¢ Blue, Brown, Bistre | | | | |
| | 48.00 | 5.00 | 1.15 | .16 |

## 1968.

| | Mint Sheet | Plate Block | Fine Unused Each | Fine Used Each |
|---|---|---|---|---|
| ☐C72 10¢ Carmine | 29.00 | 1.40 | .32 | .16 |

| Scott No. | Fine Unused Line Pair | Ave. Unused Line Pair | Fine Unused Each | Ave. Unused Each | Fine Used Each | Ave. Used Each |
|---|---|---|---|---|---|---|
| ☐C73 10¢ Carmine | | | | | | |
| | 2.50 | 2.00 | .45 | .30 | .18 | .15 |

| Scott No. | Mint Sheet | Plate Block | Fine Unused Each | Fine Used Each |
|---|---|---|---|---|

## 1968. 50TH ANNIVERSARY AIRMAIL SERVICE

| | Mint Sheet | Plate Block | Fine Unused Each | Fine Used Each |
|---|---|---|---|---|
| ☐C74 10¢ Black, Blue, Red | 16.00 | 3.50 | .36 | .16 |

## 1968.

| | Mint Sheet | Plate Block | Fine Unused Each | Fine Used Each |
|---|---|---|---|---|
| ☐C75 20¢ Red, Blue, Black | 28.00 | 3.00 | .65 | .18 |

## 1969. FIRST MAN ON THE MOON

| | Mint Sheet | Plate Block | Fine Unused Each | Fine Used Each |
|---|---|---|---|---|
| ☐C76 10¢ Red, Blue, Brown | 11.00 | 2.00 | .42 | .18 |

## 1971–1973.

| | Mint Sheet | Plate Block | Fine Unused Each | Fine Used Each |
|---|---|---|---|---|
| ☐C77 9¢ Red | 22.00 | 1.25 | .28 | .22 |
| ☐C78 11¢ Carmine | 31.00 | 1.40 | .36 | .16 |
| ☐C79 13¢ Carmine | 32.00 | 1.70 | .38 | .16 |
| ☐C80 17¢ Green, Blue, Red | 25.00 | 2.60 | .50 | .16 |
| ☐C81 21¢ Blue, Red, Black | 24.00 | 2.60 | .60 | .16 |

* No hinge pricing from 1941 to date is figured at (N-H ADD 15%)

| Scott No. | Fine Unused Line Pair | Ave. Unused Line Pair | Fine Unused Each | Ave. Unused Each | Fine Used Each | Ave. Used Each |
|---|---|---|---|---|---|---|
| ☐C82 11¢ Carmine | | | | | | |
| | 1.25 | 1.10 | .40 | .32 | .18 | .16 |
| ☐C83 13¢ Carmine | | | | | | |
| | 1.30 | 1.15 | .46 | .35 | .18 | .16 |

| Scott No. | Mint Sheet | Plate Block | Fine Unused Each | Fine Used Each |
|---|---|---|---|---|

## 1972. NATIONAL PARKS CENTENNIAL

| | | | | |
|---|---|---|---|---|
| ☐C84 11¢ Multicolored | 14.00 | 1.50 | .33 | .16 |

## 1972. OLYMPIC GAMES

| | | | | |
|---|---|---|---|---|
| ☐C85 11¢ Multicolored | 13.00 | 4.00 | .33 | .16 |

## 1973. PROGRESS IN ELECTRONICS

| | | | | |
|---|---|---|---|---|
| ☐C86 11¢ Multicolored | 13.00 | 1.40 | .33 | .16 |

## 1974.

| | | | | |
|---|---|---|---|---|
| ☐C87 18¢ Red, Blue, Black | 25.00 | 2.50 | .60 | .40 |
| ☐C88 26¢ Red, Blue, Black | 30.00 | 3.00 | .65 | .16 |

## 1976.

| | | | | |
|---|---|---|---|---|
| ☐C89 25¢ Red, Blue, Black | 30.00 | 3.00 | .65 | .16 |
| ☐C90 31¢ Red, Blue, Black | 35.00 | 4.00 | .75 | .16 |

## 1979.

| | | | | |
|---|---|---|---|---|
| ☐C91 31¢ Blue, Brown, Red | 100.00 | 5.00 | 2.10 | .50 |
| ☐C92 31¢ Blue, Brown, Red | 100.00 | 5.00 | 2.10 | .50 |

## 1979.

| | | | | |
|---|---|---|---|---|
| ☐C93 21¢ Blue, Brown, Red | 96.00 | 6.00 | 1.00 | .35 |
| ☐C94 21¢ Blue, Brown, Red | 96.00 | 6.00 | 1.00 | .35 |

## 1980.

| | | | | |
|---|---|---|---|---|
| ☐C95 25¢ Multicolored | 175.00 | 11.00 | 2.10 | .24 |
| ☐C96 25¢ Multicolored | 175.00 | 11.00 | 2.10 | .24 |

*No hinge pricing from 1941 to date is figured at (N-H ADD 15%)

| Scott No. | Mint Sheet | Plate Block | Fine Unused Each | Fine Used Each |
|---|---|---|---|---|
| ☐C97 31¢ Multicolored | 40.00 | 13.00 | .80 | .34 |
| **1981.** | | | | |
| ☐C98 40¢ Multicolored | 50.00 | 12.50 | 1.00 | .17 |
| ☐C99 28¢ Multicolored | 36.00 | 9.00 | .85 | .19 |
| ☐C100 35¢ Multicolored | 45.00 | 11.00 | 1.00 | .19 |
| **1983.** | | | | |
| ☐C101 28¢ Multicolored | 52.00 | 6.00 | 1.50 | .30 |
| ☐C102 28¢ Multicolored | 52.00 | 6.00 | 1.50 | .30 |
| ☐C103 28¢ Multicolored | 52.00 | 6.00 | 1.50 | .30 |
| ☐C104 28¢ Multicolored | 52.00 | 6.00 | 1.50 | .30 |
| ☐C105 40¢ Multicolored | 64.00 | 7.00 | 1.30 | .30 |
| ☐C106 40¢ Multicolored | 64.00 | 7.00 | 1.30 | .30 |
| ☐C107 40¢ Multicolored | 64.00 | 7.00 | 1.30 | .30 |
| ☐C108 40¢ Multicolored | 64.00 | 7.00 | 1.30 | .30 |
| ☐C109 35¢ Multicolored | 70.00 | 9.50 | 1.20 | .32 |
| ☐C110 35¢ Multicolored | 70.00 | 9.50 | 1.20 | .32 |
| ☐C111 35¢ Multicolored | 70.00 | 9.50 | 1.20 | .32 |
| ☐C112 35¢ Multicolored | 70.00 | 9.50 | 1.20 | .32 |
| **1985.** | | | | |
| ☐C113 33¢ Multicolored | 42.00 | 5.00 | 1.00 | .28 |
| ☐C114 39¢ Multicolored | 48.00 | 6.00 | 1.20 | .28 |
| ☐C115 44¢ Multicolored | 56.00 | 6.00 | 1.30 | .28 |
| ☐C116 44¢ Multicolored | 72.00 | 11.00 | 1.40 | .28 |
| **1988.** | | | | |
| ☐C117 44¢ Multicolored | 62.00 | 9.00 | 1.10 | .28 |
| ☐C118 45¢ Multicolored | 55.00 | 6.00 | 1.10 | .28 |
| ☐C119 36¢ Multicolored | 45.00 | 5.00 | 1.00 | .28 |
| **1989.** | | | | |
| ☐C120 45¢ Multicolored | 34.00 | 6.00 | 1.40 | .28 |
| ☐C121 45¢ Multicolored | 56.00 | 6.00 | 1.40 | .28 |
| ☐C122 45¢ Multicolored | 68.00 | 7.50 | 2.00 | .28 |
| ☐C123 45¢ Multicolored | 68.00 | 7.50 | 2.00 | .28 |

*No hinge pricing from 1941 to date is figured at (N-H ADD 15%)

| Scott No. | Mint Sheet | Plate Block | Fine Unused Each | Fine Used Each |
|---|---|---|---|---|
| ☐C124 45¢ Multicolored | 68.00 | 7.50 | 2.00 | .28 |
| ☐C125 45¢ Multicolored | 68.00 | 7.50 | 2.00 | .28 |
| ☐C126 45¢ Multicolored | 68.00 | 7.50 | 5.00 | .28 |
| **1990.** | | | | |
| ☐C127 45¢ Multicolored | 60.00 | 7.00 | 1.40 | .26 |
| ☐C128 50¢ Multicolored | 62.00 | 7.50 | 1.40 | .26 |
| ☐C129 40¢ Multicolored | 46.00 | 6.00 | 1.00 | .26 |
| ☐C130 50¢ Multicolored | 64.00 | 7.00 | 1.00 | .26 |
| **1991.** | | | | |
| ☐C131 50¢ Multicolored | 62.00 | 7.00 | 1.25 | .26 |
| **1993.** | | | | |
| ☐C132 40¢ Multicolored | 36.00 | 5.00 | 1.00 | .25 |

| Scott No. | Fine Unused Plate Blk | Ave. Unused Plate Blk | Fine Unused Each | Ave. Unused Each | Fine Used Each | Ave. Used Each |
|---|---|---|---|---|---|---|
| **AIRMAIL SPECIAL DELIVERY** | | | | | | |
| ☐CE1 16¢ Dark Blue | | | | | | |
| | 22.00 | 17.00 | .90 | .75 | .75 | .50 |
| ☐CE2 16¢ Red & Blue | | | | | | |
| | 9.00 | 7.00 | .60 | .45 | .40 | .16 |
| **SPECIAL DELIVERY STAMPS** | | | | | | |
| **1885.** | | | | | | |
| ☐E1 10¢ Blue | | | | | | |
| | — | — | 220.00 | 128.00 | 34.00 | 20.00 |
| **1888.** | | | | | | |
| ☐E2 10¢ Blue | | | | | | |
| | — | — | 220.00 | 124.00 | 8.50 | 6.00 |
| **1893. (N-H ADD 80%)** | | | | | | |
| ☐E3 10¢ Orange | | | | | | |
| | — | — | 190.00 | 85.00 | 14.00 | 9.00 |

* No hinge pricing from 1941 to date is figured at (N-H ADD 15%)

| Scott No. | Fine Unused Plate Blk | Ave. Unused Plate Blk | Fine Unused Each | Ave. Unused Each | Fine Used Each | Ave. Used Each |
|---|---|---|---|---|---|---|
| **1894. (N-H ADD 80%)** | | | | | | |
| ☐E4 10¢ Blue | — | — | 600.00 | 330.00 | 19.00 | 11.00 |
| **1895. (N-H ADD 80%)** | | | | | | |
| ☐E5 10¢ Blue | — | — | 105.00 | 67.00 | 2.60 | 1.70 |
| **1902. (N-H ADD 55%)** | | | | | | |
| ☐E6 10¢ Ultramarine | — | — | 72.00 | 60.00 | 3.00 | 2.00 |
| **1908. (N-H ADD 55%)** | | | | | | |
| ☐E7 10¢ Green | — | — | 48.00 | 38.00 | 29.00 | 16.00 |
| **1911. (N-H ADD 40%)** | | | | | | |
| ☐E8 10¢ Ultramarine | — | — | 72.00 | 60.00 | 4.10 | 2.50 |
| **1914. (N-H ADD 40%)** | | | | | | |
| ☐E9 10¢ Ultramarine | — | — | 130.00 | 95.00 | 6.00 | 3.00 |
| **1916. (N-H ADD 40%)** | | | | | | |
| ☐E10 10¢ Pale Ultramarine | — | — | 230.00 | 180.00 | 17.00 | 12.00 |
| **1917. (N-H ADD 40%)** | | | | | | |
| ☐E11 10¢ Ultramarine | — | — | 13.50 | 9.00 | .50 | .36 |
| **1922–1925. (N-H ADD 30%)** | | | | | | |
| ☐E12 10¢ Deep Ultramarine | 260.00 | 200.00 | 20.00 | 15.00 | .26 | .18 |
| ☐E13 10¢ Deep Orange | 200.00 | 140.00 | 19.00 | 16.00 | 1.10 | .50 |

*No hinge pricing from 1941 to date is figured at (N-H ADD 15%)

| Scott No. | Fine Unused Plate Blk | Ave. Unused Plate Blk | Fine Unused Each | Ave. Unused Each | Fine Used Each | Ave. Used Each |
|---|---|---|---|---|---|---|
| ☐E14 20¢ Black | | | | | | |
| | 40.00 | 30.00 | 3.00 | 2.25 | 1.60 | .65 |

## 1927–1951. (N-H ADD 30%)

| Scott No. | Fine Unused Plate Blk | Ave. Unused Plate Blk | Fine Unused Each | Ave. Unused Each | Fine Used Each | Ave. Used Each |
|---|---|---|---|---|---|---|
| ☐E15 10¢ Gray Violet | | | | | | |
| | 8.00 | 6.00 | .80 | .60 | .21 | .16 |
| ☐E16 15¢ Orange | | | | | | |
| | 6.00 | 5.00 | .95 | .75 | .21 | .16 |
| ☐E17 13¢ Blue | | | | | | |
| | 5.50 | 4.10 | .80 | .45 | .21 | .16 |
| ☐E18 17¢ Yellow | | | | | | |
| | 34.00 | 26.00 | 3.70 | 2.50 | 1.50 | 1.40 |
| ☐E19 20¢ Black | | | | | | |
| | 10.50 | 8.00 | 2.10 | 1.40 | .21 | .14 |

| Scott No. | Mint Sheet | Plate Block | Fine Unused Each | Fine Used Each |
|---|---|---|---|---|
| **1954.** | | | | |
| ☐E20 20¢ Blue | 30.00 | 3.10 | .75 | .15 |
| **1957.** | | | | |
| ☐E21 30¢ Maroon | 32.00 | 3.40 | .80 | .15 |
| **1969.** | | | | |
| ☐E22 45¢ Red & Blue | 62.00 | 7.00 | 1.50 | .15 |
| **1971.** | | | | |
| ☐E23 60¢ Blue & Red | 60.00 | 7.00 | 1.40 | .15 |

| Scott No. | Fine Unused Plate Blk | Ave. Unused Plate Blk | Fine Unused Each | Ave. Unused Each | Fine Used Each | Ave. Used Each |
|---|---|---|---|---|---|---|
| **1911. REGISTRATION STAMPS (N-H ADD 30%)** | | | | | | |
| ☐F1 10¢ Ultramarine | | | | | | |
| | 1100.00 | 900.00 | 58.00 | 42.00 | 5.00 | 3.00 |

*No hinge pricing from 1941 to date is figured at (N-H ADD 15%)

| Scott No. | | Mint Sheet | Plate Block | Fine Unused Each | Fine Used Each |
|---|---|---|---|---|---|
| ☐FA1 | 15¢ Postman | 21.00 | 5.50 | .50 | .26 |

| Scott No. | | Name Block 6 | Name Block 4 | Plain Block 4 | Unused Each | Used Each |
|---|---|---|---|---|---|---|

# UNITED NATIONS
## 1951.

| Scott No. | | Name Block 6 | Name Block 4 | Plain Block 4 | Unused Each | Used Each |
|---|---|---|---|---|---|---|
| ☐1 | 1¢ Magenta | .90 | .65 | .40 | .23 | .16 |
| ☐2 | 1½¢ Blue Green | .90 | .65 | .40 | .23 | .16 |
| ☐2a | 1½¢ Precancelled | — | — | — | — | 31.00 |
| ☐3 | 2¢ Purple | 1.10 | .65 | .55 | .22 | .16 |
| ☐4 | 3¢ Magenta & Blue | .90 | .65 | .55 | .22 | .16 |
| ☐5 | 5¢ Blue | 1.10 | .75 | .65 | .22 | .16 |
| ☐6 | 10¢ Chocolate | 3.00 | 1.50 | 1.30 | .28 | .21 |
| ☐7 | 15¢ Violet & Blue | 3.00 | 1.60 | 1.40 | .32 | .21 |
| ☐8 | 20¢ Dark Brown | 10.00 | 5.00 | 4.00 | .72 | .48 |
| ☐9 | 25¢ Olive Gray & Blue | 13.00 | 4.00 | 3.00 | .65 | .48 |
| ☐10 | 50¢ Indigo | 68.00 | 40.00 | 23.00 | 6.00 | 3.50 |
| ☐11 | $1 Red | 26.00 | 17.00 | 10.00 | 2.10 | 1.20 |
| ☐1–11 | First Postage Set Complete | | | | | |
| | | — | 75.00 | 40.00 | 8.50 | 6.00 |

## 1952.

| Scott No. | | Name Block 6 | Name Block 4 | Plain Block 4 | Unused Each | Used Each |
|---|---|---|---|---|---|---|
| ☐12 | 5¢ War Memorial Bldg. | 7.00 | 4.50 | 1.80 | .60 | .25 |
| ☐13–14 | 3¢, 5¢ Fourth H.R. Day | 18.00 | 9.00 | 4.00 | .80 | .45 |

## 1953.

| Scott No. | | Name Block 6 | Name Block 4 | Plain Block 4 | Unused Each | Used Each |
|---|---|---|---|---|---|---|
| ☐15–16 | 3¢, 5¢ Refugees | 19.00 | 11.00 | 6.00 | 1.00 | .85 |
| ☐17–18 | 3¢, 5¢ U.P.U. | 18.00 | 12.00 | 7.00 | 1.50 | .90 |
| ☐19–20 | 3¢, 5¢ Technical Assist | 16.50 | 11.00 | 5.00 | 1.10 | .90 |
| ☐21–22 | 3¢, 5¢ Human Rights | 20.00 | 16.00 | 10.00 | 2.00 | .90 |

## 1954.

| Scott No. | | Name Block 6 | Name Block 4 | Plain Block 4 | Unused Each | Used Each |
|---|---|---|---|---|---|---|
| ☐23–24 | 3¢, FAO (Agriculture) | 15.00 | 11.00 | 7.00 | 1.90 | 1.00 |
| ☐25–26 | 3¢, 8¢ OIT (Labor Org.) | | | | | |
| | | 32.00 | 18.00 | 12.00 | 3.00 | 1.30 |
| ☐27–28 | 3¢, 8¢ UN Day | 42.00 | 30.00 | 19.00 | 4.50 | 2.50 |
| ☐29–30 | 3¢, 8¢ H.R. Day | 95.00 | 78.00 | 58.00 | 12.00 | 4.00 |

*No hinge pricing from 1941 to date is figured at (N-H ADD 15%)

| Scott No. | Name Block 6 | Name Block 4 | Plain Block 4 | Unused Each | Used Each |
|---|---|---|---|---|---|
| **1955.** | | | | | |
| ☐31–32 3¢, 8¢ I.C.A.O | 40.00 | 31.00 | 21.00 | 5.00 | 2.10 |
| ☐33–34 3¢, 8¢ UNESCO | 15.00 | 8.00 | 4.00 | 1.00 | .75 |
| ☐35–37 3¢, 4¢, 8¢ UN Day | 36.00 | 29.00 | 15.50 | 4.00 | 1.50 |
| ☐38 3¢, 4¢, 8¢ UN Day Sheet | — | — | — | 180.00 | 55.00 |
| ☐39–40 3¢, 8¢ Human Rights | 15.00 | 11.00 | 5.00 | 1.00 | .80 |
| **1956.** | | | | | |
| ☐41–42 3¢, 8¢ Telecommunication | | | | | |
| | 12.00 | 8.00 | 5.50 | 1.10 | .85 |
| ☐43–44 3¢, 8¢ World Health | 12.00 | 8.00 | 4.50 | 1.00 | .85 |
| ☐45–46 3¢, 8¢ UN Day | 3.00 | 1.75 | 1.25 | .36 | .25 |
| ☐47–48 3¢, 8¢ Human Rights | 2.60 | 1.75 | 1.10 | .36 | .25 |
| **1957.** | | | | | |
| ☐49–50 3¢, 8¢ W.M.O. Meteorological | | | | | |
| | 2.40 | 1.80 | 1.35 | .35 | .25 |
| ☐51–52 3¢, 8¢ U.N.E.F. 1st Printing | | | | | |
| | 2.40 | 1.80 | 1.35 | .35 | .25 |
| ☐53–54 3¢, 8¢ U.N.E.F. 2nd Printing | | | | | |
| | 3.10 | 1.90 | 1.50 | .36 | .25 |
| ☐55–56 3¢, 8¢ Security Council | 2.00 | 1.80 | 1.25 | .35 | .25 |
| ☐57–58 3¢, 8¢ Human Rights | 2.00 | 1.80 | 1.25 | .35 | .25 |
| **1958.** | | | | | |
| ☐59–60 3¢, 8¢ Atomic Energy | 2.00 | 1.75 | 1.25 | .35 | .25 |
| ☐61–62 3¢, 8¢ General Assembly | | | | | |
| | 2.00 | 1.75 | 1.25 | .35 | .25 |
| ☐63–64 4¢, 8¢ Regular Issues | 2.00 | 1.75 | 1.25 | .36 | .24 |
| ☐65–66 4¢, 8¢ Economic Council | | | | | |
| | 2.00 | 1.75 | 1.25 | .36 | .24 |
| ☐67–68 4¢, 8¢ Human Rights | 2.00 | 1.75 | 1.25 | .36 | .24 |
| ☐69–70 4¢, 8¢ Flushing Meadows | | | | | |
| | 2.00 | 1.75 | 1.25 | .36 | .24 |
| ☐71–72 4¢, 8¢ E.C.E. | 4.00 | 3.00 | 2.60 | .55 | .40 |
| ☐73–74 4¢, 8¢ Trusteeship | 2.10 | 1.90 | 1.25 | .36 | .24 |
| ☐75–76 4¢, 8¢ World Refugee Year | | | | | |
| | 2.10 | 1.90 | 1.40 | .36 | .24 |

*No hinge pricing from 1941 to date is figured at (N-H ADD 15%)

| Scott No. | Name Block 6 | Name Block 4 | Plain Block 4 | Unused Each | Used Each |
|---|---|---|---|---|---|

**1960.**

☐77–78  4¢,8¢ Palais de Chaillot

| | 2.10 | 1.75 | 1.35 | .36 | .24 |

☐79–80  4¢,8¢ Forestry Congress

| | 2.10 | 1.75 | 1.35 | .36 | .24 |

☐83–84  4¢,8¢ 15th Anniversary | 2.10 | 1.75 | 1.35 | .36 | .24 |

☐85  4¢,8¢ 15th Ann. Souv. Sheet

| | — | — | — | 2.10 | 1.85 |

☐86–87  4¢,8¢ International | 2.10 | 1.75 | 1.40 | .36 | .25 |

**1961.**

| ☐88–89 | 4¢,8¢ Court of Justice | 2.10 | 1.80 | 1.40 | .38 | .30 |
| ☐90–91 | 4¢,7¢ Monetary Fund | 2.10 | 1.80 | 1.40 | .38 | .30 |
| ☐92 | 30¢ Regular Issue | 5.00 | 4.00 | 2.50 | .60 | .32 |

☐93–94  4¢,11¢ E.C. for Latin Am.

| | 5.00 | 4.00 | 2.50 | .60 | .32 |

| ☐95–96 | 4¢,11¢ E.C. for Africa | 3.50 | 2.25 | 2.50 | .38 | .30 |

☐97–99  3¢,4¢,13¢ Children's Fund

| | 4.10 | 3.50 | 2.80 | .60 | .30 |

**1962.**

| ☐100–01 | 4¢ 7¢ Housing | 3.25 | 2.50 | 1.90 | .38 | .26 |
| ☐102–03 | 4¢ 11¢ Malaria | 4.10 | 3.00 | 2.75 | .50 | .32 |

☐104–07  1¢,3¢, 5¢, 11¢ Reg. Issue

| | 6.00 | 4.50 | 3.75 | .80 | .45 |

| ☐108–09 | 5¢, 15¢ Hammarskjold | 9.50 | 7.50 | 4.00 | .70 | .50 |
| ☐110–11 | 4¢, 11¢ U.N. Congo | 7.50 | 6.50 | 3.00 | .60 | .50 |

☐112–13  4¢, 11¢ Peaceful Space Use

| | 4.00 | 2.75 | 2.00 | .46 | .30 |

**1963.**

☐114–15  5¢,11¢ Econ. Development

| | 3.40 | 2.60 | 1.85 | .45 | .32 |

☐116–17  5¢,11¢ Freedom—Hunger

| | 3.40 | 2.60 | 1.85 | .45 | .32 |

| ☐118 | 25¢ UNTEA W. Irian | 4.50 | 3.50 | 3.00 | .62 | .38 |

☐119–20  5¢,11¢, 10th Hdqrs. Anniv.

| | 3.40 | 2.60 | 1.85 | .42 | .32 |

☐121–22  5¢,11¢, 15th Anniv. H. Rights

| | 3.40 | 2.60 | 2.00 | .48 | .32 |

| Scott No. | Name Block 6 | Name Block 4 | Plain Block 4 | Unused Each | Used Each |
|---|---|---|---|---|---|
| **1964.** | | | | | |
| ☐123–24 5¢, 11¢ Maritime | 3.10 | 2.40 | 1.95 | .45 | .32 |
| ☐125–27 2¢, 7¢, 10¢ Reg. Issue | 3.10 | 2.40 | 2.10 | .60 | .45 |
| ☐128 50¢ New Regular | 7.50 | 6.00 | 5.00 | 1.50 | .70 |
| ☐129–30 5¢, 11¢ Trade & Develop | | | | | |
| | 3.00 | 2.40 | 1.95 | .40 | .35 |
| ☐131–32 5¢, 11¢ Narcotics Control | | | | | |
| | 3.00 | 2.40 | 1.95 | .40 | .35 |
| ☐133 5¢ Nuclear Tests End | 1.25 | 1.00 | .80 | .26 | .24 |
| ☐134–36 4¢, 5¢, 11¢ Education | 2.30 | 2.35 | 1.90 | .45 | .38 |
| **1965.** | | | | | |
| ☐137–38 5¢, 11¢ Special Fund | 2.65 | 2.15 | 1.50 | .38 | .28 |
| ☐139–40 5¢, 11¢ U.N. in Cyprus | 2.65 | 2.15 | 1.50 | .38 | .28 |
| ☐141–42 5¢, 11¢ I.T.U. (Satellite) | | | | | |
| | 2.65 | 2.15 | 1.50 | .38 | .28 |
| ☐143–44 5¢, 15¢ Co-operation | 2.90 | 2.40 | 1.85 | .40 | .40 |
| ☐145 5¢, 15¢ Min. Sheet | — | — | — | .75 | .65 |
| ☐146–49 1¢, 15¢, 20¢, 25¢ Regular | | | | | |
| | 15.00 | 10.00 | 7.00 | 1.90 | 1.10 |
| ☐150 $1 Regular Issue (1966) | | | | | |
| | 21.00 | 14.00 | 10.00 | 2.25 | 1.90 |
| ☐151–53 4¢, 5¢, 11¢ Population Trends | | | | | |
| | 3.00 | 2.25 | 2.00 | .50 | .40 |
| **1966.** | | | | | |
| ☐154–55 5¢, 15¢ World Federation | | | | | |
| | 3.00 | 2.00 | 1.60 | .38 | .28 |
| ☐156–57 5¢, 11¢ W.H.O. Building | | | | | |
| | 3.00 | 2.15 | 1.80 | .40 | .28 |
| ☐158–59 5¢, 11¢ Coffee Agreement | | | | | |
| | 3.00 | 2.00 | 1.60 | .38 | .28 |
| ☐160 15¢ Peacekeeping | 2.90 | 1.90 | 1.50 | .40 | .28 |
| ☐161–63 4¢, 5¢, 11¢ UNICEF Anniv. | | | | | |
| | 3.00 | 2.50 | 1.80 | .45 | .30 |
| **1967.** | | | | | |
| ☐164–65 5¢, 11¢ Development | 3.00 | 2.00 | 1.65 | .36 | .29 |
| ☐166–67 1½¢, 5¢ Regular Issue | 2.50 | 1.85 | 1.20 | .36 | .29 |
| ☐168–69 5¢, 11¢ Independence | 3.00 | 2.00 | 1.50 | .36 | .29 |

| Scott<br>No. | Name<br>Block 6 | Name<br>Block 4 | Plain<br>Block 4 | Unused<br>Each | Used<br>Each |
|---|---|---|---|---|---|
| **1967.** | | | | | |
| ☐170–74 4¢, 5¢, 8¢, 10¢, 15¢ EXPO | | | | | |
| | 8.00 | 6.50 | 4.50 | .95 | .75 |
| ☐175–76 5¢, 15¢ Intl. Tourist Year | | | | | |
| | 2.85 | 2.40 | 2.00 | .36 | .30 |
| ☐177–78 6¢, 13¢ Toward Disarm | 3.25 | 2.75 | 2.10 | .40 | .36 |
| ☐179    6¢ Chagall Sheet of Six | — | — | — | .65 | .60 |
| ☐180    6¢ Chagall Window | 1.50 | 1.00 | .80 | .28 | .20 |
| **1968.** | | | | | |
| ☐181–82 6¢, 13¢, Secretariat | 3.25 | 2.70 | 2.00 | .45 | .36 |
| ☐183–84 6¢, 75¢ Starcke Statue | 20.00 | 17.00 | 10.00 | 1.90 | 1.75 |
| ☐185–86 6¢, 13¢ ONUDI | 3.00 | 2.30 | 1.90 | .36 | .32 |
| ☐187    6¢ Regular Issue | 1.75 | 1.00 | .85 | .26 | .20 |
| ☐188–89 6¢, 20¢ Weather Watch | 4.00 | 3.00 | 2.40 | .45 | .40 |
| ☐190–91 6¢, 13¢ Int'l. Year Human Rts. | | | | | |
| | 3.75 | 3.10 | 2.40 | .45 | .40 |
| **1969.** | | | | | |
| ☐192–93 6¢, 13¢ UNITAR | 3.00 | 2.40 | 1.85 | .43 | .36 |
| ☐194–95 6¢, 15¢ ECLA Bldg | 3.25 | 2.65 | 2.25 | .48 | .40 |
| ☐196    13¢, Regular Issue | 2.75 | 2.00 | 1.85 | .34 | .26 |
| ☐197–98 6¢, 13¢ Peace thru Law | 3.00 | 2.40 | 2.10 | .45 | .36 |
| ☐199–00 6¢, 20¢ Labor & Devl | 4.00 | 3.10 | 2.65 | .48 | .45 |
| ☐201–02 6¢, 13¢ Art Series | 3.75 | 2.70 | 1.95 | .46 | .34 |
| ☐203–04 6¢, 25¢ Japan Peace Bell | | | | | |
| | 4.25 | 3.50 | 2.75 | .60 | .52 |
| ☐205–06 6¢, 13¢ Mekong Basin | 3.75 | 2.50 | 1.90 | .45 | .33 |
| ☐207–08 6¢, 13¢ Cancer | 3.10 | 2.40 | 1.90 | .40 | .33 |
| ☐209–11 6¢, 13¢, 25¢ 25th U.V. Anniv. | | | | | |
| | 8.00 | 6.50 | 4.50 | 1.00 | .87 |
| ☐212    Same, Souvenir Sheet | | | | | |
| | — | — | — | 1.00 | 1.15 |
| ☐213–14 6¢, 13¢ Peace, Just. Prog. | | | | | |
| | 3.10 | 2.50 | 2.10 | .45 | .35 |
| **1971.** | | | | | |
| ☐215    6¢ Sea Bed | 1.75 | 1.00 | .80 | .25 | .18 |
| ☐216–17 6¢, 13¢ Refugees | 3.40 | 2.50 | 1.85 | .35 | .32 |
| ☐218    13¢ World Food Prog. | 2.60 | 2.00 | 1.40 | .30 | .24 |

| Scott No. | | Name Block 6 | Name Block 4 | Plain Block 4 | Unused Each | Used Each |
|---|---|---|---|---|---|---|
| ☐219 | 20¢ U.P.U. Building | 3.50 | 2.50 | 1.85 | .34 | .32 |
| ☐220–21 | 3¢, 13¢ Anti-Discrim. | 3.80 | 3.00 | 2.00 | .42 | .36 |
| ☐222–23 | 8¢, 60¢ Regular Issue | 10.00 | 7.00 | 6.00 | 1.25 | 1.25 |
| ☐224–25 | 8¢, 21¢ Intl. Schools | 6.00 | 4.25 | 3.00 | .70 | .60 |

**1972.**

| | | | | | | |
|---|---|---|---|---|---|---|
| ☐226 | 95¢ Regular Issue | 12.00 | 11.00 | 9.00 | 2.00 | 1.50 |
| ☐227 | 8¢, Non-Proliferation | 2.00 | 1.60 | .90 | .22 | .20 |
| ☐228 | 15¢ World Health | 3.00 | 2.25 | 1.40 | .34 | .28 |
| ☐229–30 | 8¢, 15¢ Environment | 4.00 | 3.00 | 2.50 | .48 | .42 |
| ☐231 | 21¢ E.C. Europe | 4.00 | 3.15 | 2.40 | .45 | .40 |
| ☐232–33 | 8¢, 15¢ U.N. Art Sert. | 4.15 | 3.25 | 2.40 | .46 | .40 |

**1973.**

| | | | | | | |
|---|---|---|---|---|---|---|
| ☐234–35 | 8¢, 15¢ Disarmament | 4.50 | 3.00 | 2.80 | .55 | .40 |
| ☐236–37 | 8¢, 15¢ Drug Abuse | 4.50 | 3.50 | 2.75 | .60 | .52 |
| ☐238–39 | 8¢, 21¢ U.N. Volunteers | 5.00 | 4.00 | 3.00 | .62 | .58 |
| ☐240–41 | 8¢, 15¢ Namibia | 5.00 | 3.40 | 3.00 | .60 | .50 |
| ☐242–43 | 8¢, 21¢ Human Rights | 5.00 | 3.80 | 3.00 | .68 | .55 |

**1974.**

| | | | | | | |
|---|---|---|---|---|---|---|
| ☐244–45 | 10¢, 21¢ ILO Hdqr. | 6.50 | 5.00 | 4.00 | .76 | .67 |
| ☐246 | 10¢ UPU Centenary | 2.25 | 1.75 | 1.25 | .24 | .20 |
| ☐247–48 | 10¢, 18¢ Brazil Mural | 4.75 | 3.80 | 3.40 | .65 | .55 |
| ☐249–51 | 2¢, 10¢, 18¢ Regular | 5.00 | 4.00 | 3.00 | .65 | .56 |
| ☐252–53 | 10¢, 18¢ Population | 5.50 | 4.00 | 3.25 | .58 | .50 |
| ☐254–55 | 10¢, 26¢ Law of Sea | 6.50 | 5.00 | 3.75 | 1.90 | .70 |

**1975.**

| | | | | | | |
|---|---|---|---|---|---|---|
| ☐256–57 | 10¢, 26¢ Space Usage | 7.50 | 4.50 | 3.75 | .90 | .70 |
| ☐258–59 | 10¢, 18¢ Women's Year | 4.50 | 4.00 | 3.60 | .75 | .55 |
| ☐260–61 | 10¢, 26¢ UN 30th Anniv | 7.50 | 6.00 | 3.60 | .75 | .62 |
| ☐262 | 36¢ Same Souv. Sheet | — | — | — | 1.00 | .82 |
| ☐263–64 | 10¢, 18¢ Namibia | 5.50 | 4.00 | 2.90 | .60 | .50 |
| ☐265–66 | 13¢, 26¢ Peacekeeping | 8.00 | 5.00 | 4.00 | .90 | .70 |

**1976.**

| | | | | | | |
|---|---|---|---|---|---|---|
| ☐267–71 | 3¢,4¢, 9¢, 30¢, 50¢ Regular | | | | | |
| | | 15.00 | 10.00 | 9.00 | 1.80 | 1.65 |
| ☐272–73 | 13¢, 26¢ WFUNA | 7.50 | 6.00 | 4.50 | .80 | .70 |

| Scott No. | | Name Block 6 | Name Block 4 | Plain Block 4 | Unused Each | Used Each |
|---|---|---|---|---|---|---|
| ☐274–75 | 13¢, 31¢ UNCTAD | 8.00 | 6.00 | 4.90 | .85 | .80 |
| ☐276–77 | 13¢, 25¢ HABITAT | 7.50 | 6.00 | 4.25 | .85 | .75 |
| ☐278–79 | 13¢, 31¢ 25th Postal Anniv. | | | | | |
| | | 26.00 | 21.00 | 19.00 | 4.00 | 2.50 |
| ☐280 | 13¢ Food Council | 3.40 | 2.80 | 2.40 | .38 | .26 |

**1977.**

| | | | | | | |
|---|---|---|---|---|---|---|
| ☐281–82 | 13¢, 31¢ WIPO | 8.10 | 6.00 | 4.10 | .90 | .82 |
| ☐283–84 | 13¢, 25¢ Water Conf. | 8.00 | 6.00 | 4.00 | .90 | .75 |
| ☐285–86 | 13¢, 31¢ Security Council | | | | | |
| | | 7.50 | 6.50 | 4.50 | .75 | .65 |
| ☐287–88 | 13¢, 25¢ Combat Racism | | | | | |
| | | 6.50 | 5.00 | 3.80 | .75 | .80 |
| ☐289–90 | 13¢,18¢ Atomic Energy | 6.00 | 5.00 | 3.60 | .75 | .60 |

**1978.**

| | | | | | | |
|---|---|---|---|---|---|---|
| ☐291–93 | 1¢, 25¢, $1 Regular | 20.00 | 15.00 | 12.00 | 2.60 | 2.00 |
| ☐294–95 | 13¢, 31¢ Small Pox | 9.00 | 7.50 | 4.50 | 1.00 | .85 |
| ☐296–97 | 13¢, 18¢ Namibia | 6.50 | 5.00 | 3.25 | .75 | .60 |
| ☐298–99 | 13¢, 25¢ ICAO-Air Safety | | | | | |
| | | 7.40 | 6.10 | 4.10 | .90 | .70 |
| ☐300–01 | 13¢, 18¢ General Assembly | | | | | |
| | | 6.50 | 4.50 | 3.80 | .70 | .56 |
| ☐302–03 | 13¢, 31¢ Technical Cooperation | | | | | |
| | | 10.00 | 8.00 | 6.00 | 1.20 | .95 |

**1979.**

| | | | | | | |
|---|---|---|---|---|---|---|
| ☐304–07 | 5¢, 14¢, 15¢, 20¢ Regular Issues | | | | | |
| | | 9.00 | 7.00 | 6.00 | 1.25 | .90 |
| ☐308–09 | 15¢, 20¢ UNDRO | 7.00 | 5.50 | 5.00 | .80 | .70 |
| ☐310–11 | 15¢, 31¢ Intl. Year of Child | | | | | |
| | | 9.00 | 7.50 | 5.50 | 1.25 | 1.00 |
| ☐312–13 | 15¢, 31¢ Namibia | 8.00 | 6.00 | 4.25 | 1.00 | .80 |
| ☐314–15 | 15¢, 31¢ Court of Justice | | | | | |
| | | 7.50 | 5.50 | 4.00 | .85 | .70 |

**1980.**

| | | | | | | |
|---|---|---|---|---|---|---|
| ☐316–17 | 15¢, 31¢ Economic Order | 8.00 | 6.50 | 5.00 | .95 | .75 |
| ☐318–19 | 15¢, 20¢, Women's Decade | | | | | |
| | | 6.50 | 5.50 | 4.50 | .85 | .70 |

| Scott No. | | Name Block 6 | Name Block 4 | Plain Block 4 | Unused Each | Used Each |
|---|---|---|---|---|---|---|
| ☐320–21 | 15¢, 31¢ Peacekeeping | 8.50 | 7.00 | 5.00 | 1.00 | 1.00 |
| ☐322–23 | 15¢, 31¢ 35th Anniversary | | | | | |
| | | 8.50 | 7.00 | 4.50 | .90 | .86 |
| ☐324 | 15¢ Same, Souvenir Sheet | | | | | |
| | | — | — | — | .90 | .95 |
| ☐325–40 | 15¢ World Flags | — | 16.00 | — | 4.00 | 3.50 |
| ☐325–28 | 15¢ World Flags | — | 6.00 | — | 1.10 | 1.00 |
| ☐329–32 | 15¢ World Flags | — | 6.00 | — | 1.10 | 1.00 |
| ☐333–36 | 15¢ World Flags | — | 6.00 | — | 1.10 | 1.00 |
| ☐337–40 | 15¢ World Flags | — | 6.00 | — | 1.10 | 1.00 |
| ☐341–42 | 15¢ 20¢ Economic and Social Council | | | | | |
| | | 6.50 | 5.50 | 4.00 | .90 | .85 |

## 1981.

| Scott No. | | Name Block 6 | Name Block 4 | Plain Block 4 | Unused Each | Used Each |
|---|---|---|---|---|---|---|
| ☐343 | 15¢ Palestinian People | 3.60 | 2.50 | 1.90 | .40 | .30 |
| ☐344–45 | 20¢, 35¢ Disabled Persons | | | | | |
| | | 10.00 | 7.50 | 6.00 | 1.25 | 1.00 |
| ☐346–47 | 20¢, 31¢ Fresco | — | 7.50 | 6.00 | 1.50 | .90 |
| ☐348–49 | 20¢, 40¢ Sources of Energy | | | | | |
| | | 12.00 | 9.00 | 6.50 | 1.60 | 1.20 |
| ☐350–65 | 1981 World Flags | — | 28.00 | — | 6.50 | 4.50 |
| ☐350–53 | 20¢ World Flags | — | 10.00 | — | 2.00 | 1.00 |
| ☐358–61 | 20¢ World Flags | — | 10.00 | — | 2.00 | 1.00 |
| ☐354–57 | 15¢, 20¢ World Flags | — | 10.00 | — | 2.00 | 1.00 |
| ☐362–65 | 20¢ World Flags | — | 10.00 | — | 2.00 | 1.00 |
| ☐366–67 | 18¢, 28¢ Volunteers Program | | | | | |
| | | — | 8.50 | 7.00 | 1.40 | .80 |

## 1982.

| Scott No. | | Name Block 6 | Name Block 4 | Plain Block 4 | Unused Each | Used Each |
|---|---|---|---|---|---|---|
| ☐368–70 | 17¢, 28¢, 40¢ Definitives | | | | | |
| | | 12.00 | 9.00 | 10.00 | 2.25 | 1.50 |
| ☐371–72 | 20¢, 40¢ Human Environment | | | | | |
| | | 11.00 | 8.00 | 8.50 | 1.60 | 1.20 |
| ☐373 | 20¢ Space Exploration | 5.00 | 4.00 | 4.50 | .70 | .40 |
| ☐374–89 | World Flags | 38.00 | 30.00 | 26.00 | 6.50 | 6.10 |
| ☐390–91 | 20¢, 28¢ Nature Conservation | | | | | |
| | | 10.00 | 7.00 | 5.00 | 1.50 | 1.00 |

## 1983.

| Scott No. | | Name Block 6 | Name Block 4 | Plain Block 4 | Unused Each | Used Each |
|---|---|---|---|---|---|---|
| ☐392–93 | 20¢, 40¢ Communication | | | | | |
| | | 11.00 | 8.50 | 7.00 | 1.50 | 1.15 |

| Scott No. | | Name Block 6 | Name Block 4 | Plain Block 4 | Unused Each | Used Each |
|---|---|---|---|---|---|---|
| ☐394–95 | 20¢, 37¢ Safety at Sea | | | | | |
| | | 12.00 | 9.00 | 8.00 | 1.65 | 1.40 |
| ☐396 | 20¢ World Food | 6.25 | 5.00 | 4.00 | .90 | .45 |
| ☐397–98 | 20¢, 28¢ Trade | 11.00 | 8.50 | 7.00 | 1.75 | .90 |
| ☐399–14 | World Flags | 35.00 | 30.00 | 24.00 | 7.00 | 6.00 |
| ☐415–16 | 20¢, 40¢ Human Rights | 16.00 | 11.00 | 8.50 | 2.50 | 1.65 |

**1984.**

| | | | | | | |
|---|---|---|---|---|---|---|
| ☐417–18 | 20¢, 40¢ Population Conference | | | | | |
| | | 12.00 | 9.50 | 8.00 | 2.00 | 1.15 |
| ☐419–20 | 20¢, 40¢ World Food Day | | | | | |
| | | 12.00 | 9.50 | 8.00 | 2.00 | 1.15 |
| ☐421–22 | 20¢, 50¢ Heritage | 12.00 | 9.50 | 9.00 | 2.00 | 1.20 |
| ☐423–24 | 20¢, 50¢ Refugees | 12.00 | 10.00 | 8.50 | 2.10 | 1.25 |
| ☐425–40 | World Flags | 60.00 | 50.00 | 40.00 | 15.00 | 2.00 |
| ☐441–42 | 20¢, 35¢ Youth Year | 29.00 | 11.00 | 9.00 | 2.50 | 1.50 |

**1985.**

| | | | | | | |
|---|---|---|---|---|---|---|
| ☐443 | 23¢ Turin Centre | 10.00 | 6.50 | 4.00 | .80 | .45 |
| ☐444 | 50¢ U.N. University | 14.00 | 11.00 | 6.50 | 1.30 | 1.20 |
| ☐445–46 | 22¢, $3.00 People of the World | | | | | |
| | | 38.00 | 32.00 | 27.00 | 6.50 | 4.00 |
| ☐447–48 | 22¢, 45¢ 40th U.N. Anniversary | | | | | |
| | | 18.00 | 10.00 | 8.00 | 1.50 | 1.35 |
| ☐449 | 22¢, 45¢ 40th Anniversary Souvenir Sheet | | | | | |
| | | — | — | — | 3.00 | 1.50 |
| ☐450–65 | 22¢ World Flags | — | — | 8.50 | 4.00 | 1.50 |
| ☐466–67 | 22¢, 33¢ UNICEF | 11.00 | 9.50 | 7.50 | 1.85 | 1.25 |

**1986.**

| | | | | | | |
|---|---|---|---|---|---|---|
| ☐468 | 22¢ Africa in Crisis | 7.00 | 6.50 | 4.50 | .85 | .50 |
| ☐469–72 | 22¢ U.N. Resources | 15.00 | 13.00 | 11.00 | — | 5.00 |
| ☐473–74 | 22¢, 44¢ Philately | 12.00 | 10.00 | 8.00 | 1.70 | 1.15 |
| ☐475–76 | 22¢, 33¢ Peace Year | 12.00 | 11.00 | 9.00 | 2.00 | 1.30 |
| ☐477–92 | 22¢ World Flags | 11.00 | 10.00 | 8.50 | 3.00 | 1.75 |
| ☐493 | 22¢, 44¢ WFUNA Souvenir Sheet | | | | | |
| | | — | — | — | 7.00 | 4.50 |

**1987.**

| | | | | | | |
|---|---|---|---|---|---|---|
| ☐494 | 22¢ Trygve H. Lie | 9.00 | 7.00 | 6.00 | 1.30 | .38 |

| Scott No. | | Name Block 6 | Name Block 4 | Plain Block 4 | Unused Each | Used Each |
|---|---|---|---|---|---|---|
| ☐495–96 | 22¢, 44¢ Shelter Homeless | | | | | |
| | | 14.00 | 12.00 | 10.00 | 1.50 | 1.00 |
| ☐497–98 | 22¢, 33¢ Fight Drugs | 14.00 | 11.00 | 9.00 | 1.60 | 1.00 |
| ☐499–514 | 22¢ World Flags | 14.00 | 11.00 | 9.00 | 2.10 | 1.25 |
| ☐515–16 | 22¢, 39¢ United Nations Day | | | | | |
| | | 13.00 | 9.00 | 7.00 | 1.65 | 1.15 |
| ☐516–18 | 22¢, 44¢ Child Immunizations | | | | | |
| | | 16.00 | 13.00 | 11.00 | 2.00 | 1.15 |

## 1988.

| | | | | | | |
|---|---|---|---|---|---|---|
| ☐519–20 | 22¢, 33¢ World Hunger | | | | | |
| | | 18.00 | 15.00 | 12.00 | 2.50 | .95 |
| ☐521 | 3¢ U.N. A Better World | | | | | |
| | | 6.00 | 4.00 | 2.00 | .26 | .25 |
| ☐522–23 | 25¢, 44¢ Forest Survival | | | | | |
| | | 24.00 | 19.00 | 16.00 | 2.50 | 1.50 |
| ☐524–25 | 25¢, 50¢ Int. Volunteers | | | | | |
| | | 16.00 | 14.00 | 11.00 | 2.50 | 1.40 |
| ☐526–27 | 25¢, 38¢ Health Sports | | | | | |
| | | 18.00 | 15.00 | 12.00 | 3.00 | 1.25 |
| ☐528–43 | 25¢ World Flags | 10.00 | 8.00 | 6.00 | 3.50 | 2.10 |
| ☐544 | 25¢ Human Rights | — | — | — | — | — |
| ☐545 | 25¢ Human Rights Souvenir Sheet | | | | | |
| | | — | — | — | 4.00 | 1.95 |

## 1989.

| | | | | | | |
|---|---|---|---|---|---|---|
| ☐546–47 | 25¢, 45¢ World Bank | 9.50 | 7.50 | 14.00 | 3.10 | 1.10 |
| ☐548 | 25¢ Nobel Peace Prize | 7.50 | 5.50 | 8.00 | 1.80 | .40 |
| ☐549 | 45¢ U.N. Building | 7.50 | 5.50 | 6.00 | 1.50 | .40 |
| ☐550–51 | 25¢, 36¢ World Weather | | | | | |
| | | 7.50 | 6.50 | 14.00 | 3.50 | 1.00 |
| ☐552–53 | 25¢, 90¢ U.N. Vienna | 12.00 | 9.00 | 27.00 | 6.00 | 1.25 |
| ☐554–69 | World Flags | 12.00 | 9.00 | 7.00 | 2.50 | 1.80 |
| ☐570–71 | Human Rights | 13.00 | 12.50 | 2.50 | 4.00 | 1.00 |

## 1990.

| | | | | | | |
|---|---|---|---|---|---|---|
| ☐572 | 25¢ Int'l Trade Center | 5.50 | 4.50 | 11.00 | 2.40 | .35 |
| ☐573–74 | 25¢, 40¢ AIDS | 7.00 | 6.00 | 13.00 | 3.10 | .85 |
| ☐575–76 | 25¢, 90¢ Medicinal Plants | | | | | |
| | | 12.50 | 9.00 | 17.00 | 4.00 | 1.60 |

| Scott No. | Name Block 6 | Name Block 4 | Plain Block 4 | Unused Each | Used Each |
|---|---|---|---|---|---|
| ☐577–78 25¢,45¢ U.N. 45th Anniversary | | | | | |
| | 9.50 | 8.50 | 20.00 | 4.50 | 1.00 |
| ☐579 25¢, 45¢ U.N. 45th Anniversary Souvenir Sheet | | | | | |
| | — | — | — | 4.50 | .90 |
| ☐580–81 25¢, 96¢ Crime Prevention | | | | | |
| | 7.50 | 6.00 | 20.00 | 4.50 | .90 |
| ☐582–83 25¢, 45¢ Human Rights | | | | | |
| | 9.00 | 7.50 | 6.50 | 1.75 | .85 |

## 1991.

| | | | | | |
|---|---|---|---|---|---|
| ☐584–87 30¢ Economic Comm. Europe | | | | | |
| | 9.00 | 6.00 | 6.00 | 3.50 | 1.60 |
| ☐588–89 30¢, 36¢ Namibia | 9.50 | 7.50 | 13.00 | 3.00 | 1.00 |
| ☐590–91 30¢, 50¢ U.N. Golden Rule | | | | | |
| | 9.50 | 7.50 | 13.00 | 3.00 | 1.00 |
| ☐592 $2.00 U.N. Building | 10.00 | 8.50 | 20.00 | 4.00 | 2.10 |
| ☐593–94 30¢, 70¢ Children's Rights | | | | | |
| | 10.00 | 8.50 | 16.00 | 3.50 | 2.00 |
| ☐595–96 30¢, 90¢ Banning Chem. Weapons | | | | | |
| | 10.00 | 8.50 | 20.00 | 3.10 | 2.00 |
| ☐597–98 30¢, 40¢ UNPA 40th Anniversary | | | | | |
| | 9.50 | 8.00 | 13.00 | 2.50 | 1.00 |
| ☐599–600 30¢, 50¢ Human Rights — | — | — | 2.50 | 1.25 |

## 1992.

| | | | | | |
|---|---|---|---|---|---|
| ☐601–02 29¢, 50¢ UNESCO Heritage | | | | | |
| | 17.00 | 15.00 | 13.00 | 3.00 | 1.00 |
| ☐603–04 29¢ Clean Oceans | 9.50 | 7.50 | 6.00 | 1.60 | .75 |
| ☐605–08 29¢ UNICEF Summit | 7.50 | 6.50 | 4.50 | 3.00 | 1.75 |
| ☐609–10 29¢ Mission to Earth | 21.00 | 18.00 | 16.00 | 7.00 | 2.50 |
| ☐611–12 29¢, 59¢ Science and Technology | | | | | |
| | 12.00 | 10.00 | 8.50 | 2.00 | 1.00 |
| ☐613–15 4¢, 40¢ Definitives | 14.00 | 12.00 | 11.00 | 2.50 | 1.00 |
| ☐616–17 29¢, 50¢ Human Rights | | | | | |
| | 12.00 | 9.50 | 8.00 | 2.00 | 1.00 |

## UNITED NATIONS AIRMAILS
## 1951–1957.

| | | | | | |
|---|---|---|---|---|---|
| ☐C1 6¢ Airmail (1951) | 20.00 | 15.00 | 9.00 | 2.00 | 1.65 |
| ☐C2 10¢ Airmail | 20.00 | 15.00 | 9.00 | 2.00 | 1.65 |

| Scott No. | | Name Block 6 | Name Block 4 | Plain Block 4 | Unused Each | Used Each |
|---|---|---|---|---|---|---|
| ☐C3 | 15¢ Airmail | 20.00 | 15.00 | 9.00 | 2.00 | 1.65 |
| ☐C4 | 25¢ Airmail | 20.00 | 15.00 | 9.00 | 2.00 | 1.65 |
| ☐C1–4 | First Issue Airmails | | | | | |
| | | 65.00 | 55.00 | 38.00 | 8.50 | 1.65 |
| ☐C5–7 | 4¢, 5¢, 7¢ Airmail (1957) | | | | | |
| | | 4.00 | 3.50 | 3.00 | .60 | .50 |

**1963–1964.**

| Scott No. | | Name Block 6 | Name Block 4 | Plain Block 4 | Unused Each | Used Each |
|---|---|---|---|---|---|---|
| ☐C8–10 | 6¢, 8¢, 13¢ Airmail (1963) | | | | | |
| | | 14.00 | 6.00 | 3.00 | .75 | .50 |
| ☐C11–12 | 15¢, 25¢ Airmail (1964) | | | | | |
| | | 17.00 | 11.00 | 7.00 | 1.75 | .75 |

**1968–1972.**

| Scott No. | | Name Block 6 | Name Block 4 | Plain Block 4 | Unused Each | Used Each |
|---|---|---|---|---|---|---|
| ☐C13 | 20¢ Airmail (1968) | 6.00 | 4.00 | 3.50 | .65 | .40 |
| ☐C14 | 10¢ Airmail (1969) | 6.00 | 4.00 | 3.50 | .65 | .40 |
| ☐C15–18 | 9¢, 11¢, 17¢, 21¢ (1972) | | | | | |
| | | 10.00 | 7.00 | 5.00 | .85 | .90 |

**1974–1977.**

| Scott No. | | Name Block 6 | Name Block 4 | Plain Block 4 | Unused Each | Used Each |
|---|---|---|---|---|---|---|
| ☐C19–21 | 13¢, 18¢, 26¢ (1974) | 9.00 | 8.00 | 5.50 | 1.20 | 1.00 |
| ☐C22–23 | 25¢, 31¢ (1977) | 9.50 | 7.50 | 5.50 | 1.20 | 1.00 |

## UNITED NATIONS SOUVENIR CARDS

| | | Unused Each | Used Each |
|---|---|---|---|
| ☐1 | WHO, First Printing | 4.00 | — |
| ☐1a | WHO, Second Printing | 3.00 | — |
| ☐2 | Art at U.N. | 3.50 | — |
| ☐3 | Disarmament | 3.50 | — |
| ☐4 | Human Rights | 4.00 | — |
| ☐5 | Universal Postal Union | 5.00 | — |
| ☐6 | World Population | 16.00 | — |
| ☐7 | Outer Space | 6.00 | — |
| ☐8 | Peacekeeping | 8.00 | — |
| ☐9 | World Federation of U.N. | 8.00 | — |
| ☐10 | World Food Council | 3.50 | — |
| ☐11 | World Intellectual Property | 4.00 | — |
| ☐12 | Combat Racism | 4.00 | — |

| | | | | | Unused Each | Used Each |
|---|---|---|---|---|---|---|
| ☐13 | Namibia | | | | 3.00 | — |
| ☐14 | ICAO-Air Safety | | | | 3.00 | — |
| ☐15 | International Year of the Child | | | | 2.50 | — |
| ☐16 | Court of Justice | | | | 4.50 | — |
| ☐17 | Women's Decade | | | | 18.00 | — |
| ☐18 | Economic and Social Council | | | | 3.00 | — |
| ☐19 | Disabled Persons | | | | 3.00 | — |
| ☐20 | Energy Sources | | | | 3.00 | — |

| Scott No. | | Name Block 6 | Name Block 4 | Plain Block 4 | Unused Each | Used Each |
|---|---|---|---|---|---|---|

## UNITED NATIONS—GENEVA, SWITZERLAND, ISSUES DENOMINATIONS ARE GIVEN IN SWISS CURRENCY DESIGNS ARE SIMILAR TO U.N. NEW YORK ISSUES

**1969–1970.**

| ☐1–14 | 5¢ to 10 franc | 140.00 | 100.00 | 50.00 | 11.50 | 10.00 |
|---|---|---|---|---|---|---|

**1971.**

| ☐15 | 30¢ Sea Bed | 2.00 | 1.75 | 1.25 | .36 | .30 |
|---|---|---|---|---|---|---|
| ☐16 | 50¢ Refugees | 4.00 | 3.00 | 2.00 | .50 | .40 |
| ☐17 | 50¢ World Food Prog. | 5.00 | 4.00 | 2.00 | .45 | .45 |
| ☐18 | 75¢ U.P.U. Building | 10.00 | 8.50 | 4.00 | .75 | .80 |
| ☐19–20 | 30¢,50¢ Anti-Discrim | 9.50 | 8.00 | 5.00 | .80 | .60 |
| ☐21 | 1.10 fr. Intl. Schools | 14.00 | 10.00 | 5.00 | 1.15 | 1.10 |

**1972.**

| ☐22 | 40¢ Regular Issue | 3.80 | 3.00 | 2.10 | .40 | .36 |
|---|---|---|---|---|---|---|
| ☐23 | 40¢ Non-Proliferation | 9.50 | 7.00 | 3.00 | .75 | .70 |
| ☐24 | 80¢ World Health | 9.50 | 7.00 | 4.00 | .75 | .80 |
| ☐25–26 | 40¢,80¢ Environment | 15.00 | 9.00 | 7.00 | 1.25 | 1.30 |
| ☐27 | 1.10 fr. E.C. Europe | 15.00 | 10.00 | 6.50 | 1.25 | 1.30 |
| ☐28–29 | 40¢,80¢ U.N. Art-Sert | 14.00 | 11.00 | 7.00 | 1.35 | 1.60 |

**1973.**

| ☐30–31 | 60¢,1.10 fr. Disarm | 15.00 | 13.00 | 8.00 | 1.70 | 1.60 |
|---|---|---|---|---|---|---|
| ☐32 | 60¢ Drug Abuse | 8.00 | 7.00 | 3.50 | .70 | .60 |
| ☐33 | 80¢ U.N. Volunteers | 8.50 | 7.00 | 3.50 | .85 | .80 |
| ☐34 | 60¢ Namibia | 8.50 | 7.00 | 3.00 | .75 | .70 |

| Scott No. | Name Block 6 | Name Block 4 | Plain Block 4 | Unused Each | Used Each |
|---|---|---|---|---|---|
| ☐35–36 40¢, 80¢ Human Rights | 10.00 | 8.00 | 6.50 | 1.20 | .90 |

**1974.**

| | | | | | |
|---|---|---|---|---|---|
| ☐37–38 60¢, 80¢ ILO Hdqrs. | 11.00 | 8.50 | 6.50 | 1.35 | 1.20 |
| ☐39–40 30¢, 60¢ UPU Centenary | 8.00 | 7.50 | 4.00 | .90 | .85 |
| ☐41–42 60¢, 1 fr. Brazil Mural | 11.00 | 10.00 | 6.00 | 1.50 | 1.60 |
| ☐43–44 60¢, 80¢ Population | 11.00 | 9.00 | 7.50 | 1.40 | 1.10 |
| ☐45 1.30 fr. Law of Sea | 11.00 | 9.00 | 6.50 | 1.40 | 1.10 |

**1975.**

| | | | | | |
|---|---|---|---|---|---|
| ☐46–47 60¢, 80¢ Space Usage | 15.00 | 9.00 | 6.50 | 1.30 | 1.15 |
| ☐48–49 60¢, 90¢ Women's Year | 14.00 | 8.00 | 7.50 | 1.60 | 1.50 |
| ☐50–51 60¢, 90¢ U.N. Anniv. | 14.00 | 9.00 | 6.00 | 1.40 | 1.25 |
| ☐52 1.50 fr. Same, Souv. Sheet | — | — | — | 1.30 | 1.30 |
| ☐53–54 50¢, 1.30 fr. Namibia | 14.00 | 9.00 | 7.50 | 1.50 | 1.45 |
| ☐55–56 60¢, 70¢ Peacekeeping | 14.00 | 9.00 | 6.00 | 1.35 | 1.10 |

**1976.**

| | | | | | |
|---|---|---|---|---|---|
| ☐57 90¢ WFUNA | 9.50 | 6.50 | 6.00 | 1.10 | .90 |
| ☐58 .10 fr. UNCTAD | 9.00 | 6.50 | 5.50 | 1.15 | 1.10 |
| ☐59–60 40¢ 1.50 fr. HABITAT | 15.00 | 9.00 | 7.50 | 1.50 | 1.45 |
| ☐61–62 80¢, 1.10 fr. U.N. Postal Anniv. | | | | | |
| | 55.00 | 42.00 | 26.00 | 5.00 | 4.50 |
| ☐63 70¢ World Food Council | | | | | |
| | 8.00 | 5.50 | 4.00 | .85 | .70 |

**1977.**

| | | | | | |
|---|---|---|---|---|---|
| ☐64 80¢ WIPO | 7.50 | 6.00 | 4.50 | .80 | .75 |
| ☐65–66 80¢, 1.10 fr. Water Conf. | 12.00 | 10.00 | 8.00 | 1.60 | 1.40 |
| ☐67–68 80¢, 1.10 fr. Security Council | | | | | |
| | 12.00 | 10.00 | 8.00 | 1.60 | 1.40 |
| ☐69–70 40¢, 1.10 fr. Combat Racism | | | | | |
| | 12.00 | 10.00 | 7.50 | 1.50 | 1.25 |
| ☐71–72 80¢, 1.10 fr. Atomic Energy | | | | | |
| | 14.00 | 11.00 | 8.50 | 1.75 | 1.40 |
| ☐73 35¢ Doves | 8.00 | 4.00 | 2.50 | .50 | .40 |
| ☐74–75 80¢, 1.10 fr. Smallpox | 13.00 | 10.00 | 8.00 | 1.65 | 1.45 |
| ☐76 80¢ Namibia | 8.00 | 7.00 | 6.00 | 1.00 | .80 |
| ☐77–78 70¢, 80¢ ICAO-Air Safety | | | | | |
| | 11.00 | 8.50 | 7.50 | 1.40 | 1.15 |

| Scott No. | Name Block 6 | Name Block 4 | Plain Block 4 | Unused Each | Used Each |
|---|---|---|---|---|---|
| ☐79–80 70¢, 1.10 Fr. General Assembly | | | | | |
| | 11.00 | 8.50 | 10.00 | 1.65 | 1.30 |
| ☐81     80¢ Technical Cooperation | | | | | |
| | 8.50 | 6.00 | 4.00 | .85 | .70 |

## 1979.

| Scott No. | Name Block 6 | Name Block 4 | Plain Block 4 | Unused Each | Used Each |
|---|---|---|---|---|---|
| ☐82–83 80¢, 1.50 UNDRO | 16.00 | 13.00 | 10.00 | 2.10 | 1.90 |
| ☐84–85 80¢, 1.10 Intl. Year of the Child | | | | | |
| | 18.00 | 15.00 | 8.00 | 1.75 | 1.35 |
| ☐86   1.10 fr. Namibia | 11.00 | 8.50 | 5.00 | 1.00 | .90 |
| ☐87–88 80¢, 1.10 Court of Justice | | | | | |
| | 15.00 | 12.00 | 8.00 | 1.75 | 1.50 |

## 1980.

| Scott No. | Name Block 6 | Name Block 4 | Plain Block 4 | Unused Each | Used Each |
|---|---|---|---|---|---|
| ☐89     80¢ Economic Order | 9.00 | 7.50 | 4.00 | .85 | .70 |
| ☐90–91 40¢, 70¢ Women's Decade | | | | | |
| | 11.00 | 8.50 | 7.00 | 1.30 | 1.15 |
| ☐92   1.10 fr. Peacekeeping | 10.00 | 8.00 | 6.00 | 1.10 | 1.00 |
| ☐93–94 40¢, 70¢, 35th Anniversary | | | | | |
| | 10.00 | 8.00 | 6.00 | 1.30 | 1.70 |
| ☐95     40¢, 70¢ Sheet | — | — | — | 1.40 | 1.25 |
| 96–97   40¢, 70¢ Economic and Social Council | | | | | |
| | 10.00 | 8.00 | 6.00 | 1.10 | 1.00 |

## 1981.

| Scott No. | Name Block 6 | Name Block 4 | Plain Block 4 | Unused Each | Used Each |
|---|---|---|---|---|---|
| ☐98     80¢ Palestinian People | 7.50 | 6.00 | 5.00 | .85 | .70 |
| ☐99–100 40¢, 1.50 fr. Disabled Persons | | | | | |
| | 15.00 | 10.00 | 8.00 | 1.65 | 1.40 |
| ☐101     80¢ Bulgarian Mural | 8.00 | 6.00 | 5.00 | .90 | .70 |
| ☐102   1.10 fr. Energy Sources | 10.00 | 7.50 | 6.00 | 1.30 | 1.20 |
| ☐103–04 40¢, 70¢ Volunteers | 10.00 | 7.50 | 6.00 | 1.25 | 1.15 |

## 1982.

| Scott No. | Name Block 6 | Name Block 4 | Plain Block 4 | Unused Each | Used Each |
|---|---|---|---|---|---|
| ☐105–06 1 fr., Definitives | 11.00 | 8.50 | 9.00 | 1.40 | 1.25 |
| ☐107–08 40¢, 1.20 fr., Human Environment | | | | | |
| | 11.00 | 8.50 | 8.00 | 1.75 | 1.60 |

| Scott No. | | | Fine | Ave. |
|---|---|---|---|---|
| **UNUSED BOOKLET PANES** | | | | |
| ☐319g | 2¢ | Carmine | 125.00 | 74.00 |
| ☐331a | 1¢ | Green | 140.00 | 100.00 |
| ☐332a | 2¢ | Carmine | 110.00 | 80.00 |
| ☐374a | 1¢ | Green | 135.00 | 80.00 |
| ☐375a | 2¢ | Carmine | 100.00 | 75.00 |
| ☐405b | 1¢ | Green | 50.00 | 39.00 |
| ☐406a | 2¢ | Carmine | 70.00 | 38.00 |
| ☐424d | 1¢ | Green | 5.00 | 4.00 |
| ☐425e | 2¢ | Carmine | 12.00 | 9.00 |
| ☐462a | 1¢ | Green | 11.00 | 7.00 |
| ☐463a | 2¢ | Carmine | 66.00 | 46.00 |
| ☐498e | 1¢ | Green | 3.00 | 2.00 |
| ☐499e | 2¢ | Rose | 3.00 | 2.00 |
| ☐501b | 3¢ | Violet I | 52.00 | 36.00 |
| ☐502b | 3¢ | Violet II | 46.00 | 35.00 |
| ☐552b | 1¢ | Dark Green | 6.50 | 4.00 |
| ☐554c | 2¢ | Carmine | 8.00 | 5.00 |
| ☐583a | 2¢ | Carmine | 65.00 | 42.00 |
| ☐632a | 1¢ | Green | 5.00 | 3.75 |
| ☐634d | 2¢ | Carmine | 1.80 | 1.25 |
| ☐720b | 3¢ | Dark Violet | 30.00 | 20.00 |
| ☐804b | 1¢ | Green | 12.00 | 3.00 |
| ☐806b | 2¢ | Red Carmine | 15.00 | 6.00 |
| ☐807a | 3¢ | Dark Violet | 12.00 | 7.00 |
| ☐1035a | 3¢ | Dark Violet | 5.00 | 3.00 |
| ☐1036a | 4¢ | Red Violet | 4.00 | 3.00 |
| ☐1213a | 5¢ | "ZIP" | 3.00 | 2.50 |
| ☐1213x | 5¢ | Mailman | 6.00 | 4.00 |
| ☐1213y | 5¢ | Zone No | 8.50 | 5.00 |
| ☐1278a | 1¢ | Jeff. (8) | 3.00 | 1.50 |
| ☐1278ae | 1¢ | Gum (8) | 2.75 | 1.50 |
| ☐1278b | 1¢ | Green (4) | 12.00 | .50 |
| ☐1280a | 2¢ | Blue Gray (5) | 2.75 | .90 |
| ☐1280c | 2¢ | Blue Gray (6) | 11.00 | .65 |
| ☐1284b | 6¢ | F.D.R. (8) | 2.50 | 1.65 |
| ☐1284c | 6¢ | F.D.R. (5) | 2.00 | 1.50 |
| ☐1393a | 6¢ | Ike (8) | 2.10 | 1.50 |
| ☐1393ae | 6¢ | T. Gum | 3.00 | 1.70 |
| ☐1393b | 6¢ | Ike (5) | 4.00 | 1.00 |

| Scott No. | | | Fine | Ave. |
|---|---|---|---|---|
| ☐1395a | 8¢ | Ike (8) | 2.60 | 1.65 |
| ☐1395b | 8¢ | Ike (6) | 2.50 | 1.50 |
| ☐1395c | 8¢ | Ike (4) | 2.10 | 1.60 |
| ☐1395d | 8¢ | Ike (7) | 2.60 | 1.80 |
| ☐1510b | 10¢ | Mem'l (5) | 2.00 | 1.25 |
| ☐1510c | 10¢ | Mem'l (8) | 2.00 | 1.40 |
| ☐1510d | 10¢ | Mem'l (6) | 3.00 | 2.50 |
| ☐1595a | 13¢ | Bell (6) | 2.30 | 1.60 |
| ☐1595b | 13¢ | Bell (7) | 3.00 | 1.80 |
| ☐1595c | 13¢ | Bell (8) | 2.75 | 1.60 |
| ☐1595d | 13¢ | Bell (5) | 2.10 | 1.60 |
| ☐1623a | 13¢ | (7), 9¢ (1) | 3.50 | 2.50 |
| ☐1623c | | Same, Perf. 10 | 30.00 | 24.00 |
| ☐1736a | | "A" Eagle (no denomination) | 3.75 | 2.75 |
| ☐1737a | 15¢ | Multicolored | 4.10 | 3.00 |
| ☐1742a | 15¢ | Multicolored | 5.00 | 3.00 |
| ☐C10a | 10¢ | Lindbergh | 100.00 | 80.00 |
| ☐C25a | 6¢ | Carmine | 21.00 | 4.00 |
| ☐C39a | 6¢ | Small | 9.00 | 6.00 |
| ☐C51a | 7¢ | Blue | 10.00 | 7.00 |
| ☐C60a | 7¢ | Carmine | 12.00 | 8.00 |
| ☐C64c | 8¢ | Carmine "Zip" | 2.00 | 1.50 |
| ☐C64bx | 8¢ | Mailman | 10.00 | 6.00 |
| ☐C64by | 8¢ | Zone No | 50.00 | 28.00 |
| ☐C72b | 10¢ | Carmine (8) | 4.00 | 3.00 |
| ☐C72c | 10¢ | Carmine (5) | 6.00 | 3.50 |
| ☐C78a | 11¢ | Carmine (4) | 2.10 | 1.50 |
| ☐C79a | 13¢ | Letter (5) | 2.50 | 1.75 |

## SOUVENIR CARDS

| Scott No. | | Fine | Scott No. | | Fine |
|---|---|---|---|---|---|
| ☐1 | Truck w/gum | 70.00 | ☐ | Ana '69 | 70.00 |
| ☐ | Truck w/o gum | 11.00 | ☐ | FRESNO | 490.00 |
| ☐2 | Barcelona | 430.00 | ☐6 | ASDA '69 | 24.00 |
| ☐3 | SIPEX Scenes | 180.00 | ☐7 | INTERPEX '70 | 60.00 |
| ☐3a | SIPEX Miner | 11.00 | ☐8 | COMPEX '70 | 15.00 |
| ☐4 | EFIMEX | 3.50 | ☐ | ANA 1970 | 100.00 |
| ☐5 | SANDIPEX | 68.00 | ☐9 | PHILYMPIA | 2.50 |
| | | | ☐10 | HAPEX | 16.00 |

| Scott No. | | Fine | Scott No. | | Fine |
|---|---|---|---|---|---|
| ☐11 | INTERPEX '71 | 2.50 | ☐ | ANA 1975 | 12.00 |
| ☐12 | WESTPEX | 2.50 | ☐44 | ASDA '75 | 40.00 |
| ☐13 | NAPEX '71 | 3.00 | ☐45 | WERABA '76 | 4.10 |
| ☐ | ANA 1971 | 4.50 | ☐46 | INTERPHIL '76 | 8.00 |
| ☐14 | TEXANEX | 3.00 | ☐ | INTERPHIL Program | |
| ☐15 | EXFILIMA | 2.10 | | with BEP Card. | 9.00 |
| ☐16 | ASDA '71 | 2.50 | ☐47 | Science BEP | 8.50 |
| ☐17 | ANPHILEX | 1.80 | ☐48 | Science U.S.P.S. | 5.00 |
| ☐18 | INTERPEX '72 | 1.60 | ☐49 | Stamp Expo '76 | 8.50 |
| ☐19 | NOPEX | 1.60 | ☐50 | Colorado Statehood | |
| ☐20 | BELGICA | 1.60 | | | 3.50 |
| ☐ | ANA 1972 | 4.00 | ☐51 | HAFNIA '76 | 3.50 |
| ☐21 | Olympia Phil. Munchen | | ☐ | ANA 1976 | 8.00 |
| | | 1.85 | ☐52 | ITALIA '76 | 4.50 |
| ☐22 | EXFILBRA | 1.85 | ☐53 | NORDPOSTA '76 | 4.10 |
| ☐23 | Postal Forum | 1.90 | ☐54 | MILCOPEX '77 | 3.50 |
| ☐24 | SEPAD '72 | 1.90 | ☐55 | ROMPEX '77 | 3.00 |
| ☐25 | ASDA '72 | 1.60 | ☐56 | AMPHILEX '77 | 4.50 |
| ☐26 | Stamp Expo '75 | 2.10 | ☐ | ANA 1977 | 4.00 |
| ☐27 | INTERPEX '73 | 1.80 | ☐57 | SAN MARCO | 4.10 |
| ☐28 | IBRA | 2.40 | ☐58 | Puripex | 3.50 |
| ☐29 | COMPEX '73 | 2.10 | ☐59 | ASDA '77 | 3.75 |
| ☐30 | APEX | 2.40 | ☐60 | ROPEX '78 | 6.00 |
| ☐ | ANA 1973 | 7.50 | ☐ | Paper Money Show | |
| ☐31 | PLOSKA | 2.50 | | | 4.50 |
| ☐32 | NAPEX '73 | 2.30 | ☐61 | NAPOSTA '78 | 4.10 |
| ☐33 | ASDA '73 | 1.80 | ☐62 | CENTEX '78 | 3.50 |
| ☐34 | Stamps Expo '73 | 2.40 | ☐63 | BRASILIANA '79 | 7.00 |
| ☐35 | Hobby Show Chicago | | ☐64 | JAPEX '79 | 6.50 |
| | | 3.75 | ☐ | ANA '80 | 21.00 |
| ☐36 | MILCOPEX '72 | 3.00 | ☐65 | LONDON '80 | 6.50 |
| ☐37 | INTERNABA 1974 | 2.75 | ☐ | Money Show '80 | 12.00 |
| ☐ | ANA 1974 | 12.00 | ☐66 | NORWEX '80 | 5.50 |
| ☐38 | STOCKHOLMIA '74 | | ☐67 | NAPEX '80 | 14.00 |
| | | 3.50 | ☐ | Visitor Center | 9.00 |
| ☐39 | EXFILMEX '74 | 3.00 | ☐68 | ASDA STAMP | |
| ☐40 | ESPANA '75 | 2.50 | | FESTIVAL '80 | 17.00 |
| ☐41 | NAPEX '75 | 9.50 | ☐69 | ESSEN '80 | 6.00 |
| ☐42 | ARPHILA '75 | 3.00 | ☐70 | STAMP EXPO '81 | 20.00 |
| ☐43 | Women's Year | 26.00 | ☐ | Visitor Center | 9.00 |

| Scott No. | | Fine | Scott No. | | Fine |
|---|---|---|---|---|---|
| ☐71 | WIPA '81 | 6.00 | ☐73 | PHILATOKYO '81 | |
| ☐ | Paper Money | 18.00 | | | 6.00 |
| ☐ | ANA '81 | 16.00 | ☐74 | NORD POSKTA '81 | |
| ☐72 | STAMP COLLECTORS MONTH | 5.00 | | | 6.00 |

| Scott No. | Fine Unused Each | Ave. Unused Each | Fine Used Each | Ave. Used Each |
|---|---|---|---|---|

## POSTAGE DUE STAMPS
### 1879. PERFORATED 12 (N-H ADD 80%)

| Scott No. | | Fine Unused Each | Ave. Unused Each | Fine Used Each | Ave. Used Each |
|---|---|---|---|---|---|
| ☐J1 | 1¢ Brown | 34.00 | 21.00 | 7.00 | 4.00 |
| ☐J2 | 2¢ Brown | 190.00 | 110.00 | 5.00 | 2.40 |
| ☐J3 | 3¢ Brown | 24.00 | 15.00 | 3.00 | 1.70 |
| ☐J4 | 5¢ Brown | 290.00 | 180.00 | 32.00 | 16.00 |
| ☐J5 | 10¢ Brown | 315.00 | 210.00 | 16.00 | 9.50 |
| ☐J6 | 30¢ Brown | 170.00 | 100.00 | 33.00 | 18.00 |
| ☐J7 | 50¢ Brown | 200.00 | 125.00 | 38.00 | 20.00 |

### 1884–1889. SAME DESIGN—PERF. 12 (N-H ADD 80%)

| Scott No. | | Fine Unused Each | Ave. Unused Each | Fine Used Each | Ave. Used Each |
|---|---|---|---|---|---|
| ☐J15 | 1¢ Red Brown | 33.00 | 18.00 | 3.30 | 2.00 |
| ☐J16 | 2¢ Red Brown | 40.00 | 21.00 | 3.30 | 2.00 |
| ☐J17 | 3¢ Red Brown | 430.00 | 270.00 | 95.00 | 56.00 |
| ☐J18 | 5¢ Red Brown | 210.00 | 125.00 | 16.00 | 8.00 |
| ☐J19 | 10¢ Red Brown | 200.00 | 120.00 | 10.00 | 6.00 |
| ☐J20 | 30¢ Red Brown | 100.00 | 60.00 | 30.00 | 18.00 |
| ☐J21 | 50¢ Red Brown | 900.00 | 550.00 | 130.00 | 70.00 |

### 1891–1893. SAME DESIGN—PERF. 12 (N-H ADD 80%)

| Scott No. | | Fine Unused Each | Ave. Unused Each | Fine Used Each | Ave. Used Each |
|---|---|---|---|---|---|
| ☐J22 | 1¢ Bright Claret | 12.00 | 7.50 | .62 | .40 |
| ☐J23 | 2¢ Bright Claret | 12.00 | 8.00 | .60 | .34 |
| ☐J24 | 3¢ Bright Claret | 30.00 | 17.00 | 5.00 | 2.50 |
| ☐J25 | 5¢ Bright Claret | 32.00 | 19.00 | 4.50 | 2.50 |
| ☐J26 | 10¢ Bright Claret | 65.00 | 36.00 | 12.00 | 6.50 |
| ☐J27 | 30¢ Bright Claret | 210.00 | 125.00 | 90.00 | 48.00 |
| ☐J28 | 50¢ Bright Claret | 240.00 | 140.00 | 90.00 | 49.00 |

| Scott No. | | Fine Unused Each | Ave. Unused Each | Fine Used Each | Ave. Used Each |
|---|---|---|---|---|---|
| **1894. NEW SMALL DESIGN—NO WTMK.— PERF. 12 (N-H ADD 55%)** | | | | | |
| ☐J29 1¢ | Vermilion | 500.00 | 400.00 | 150.00 | 80.00 |
| ☐J30 2¢ | Vermilion | 300.00 | 215.00 | 70.00 | 36.00 |
| ☐J31 1¢ | Claret | 30.00 | 18.00 | 9.50 | 4.00 |
| ☐J32 2¢ | Claret | 24.00 | 12.00 | 9.00 | 3.00 |
| ☐J33 3¢ | Claret | 100.00 | 50.00 | 19.00 | 12.00 |
| ☐J34 5¢ | Claret | 100.00 | 45.00 | 25.00 | 18.00 |
| ☐J35 10¢ | Claret | 100.00 | 45.00 | 16.00 | 12.00 |
| ☐J36 30¢ | Claret (Shades) | 300.00 | 150.00 | 60.00 | 50.00 |
| ☐J37 50¢ | Claret (Shades) | 500.00 | 270.00 | 160.00 | 80.00 |
| **1895. SAME NEW SMALL DESIGN—D.L. WTMK.— PERF. 12 (N-H ADD 80%)** | | | | | |
| ☐J38 1¢ | Claret | 7.00 | 4.00 | .45 | .27 |
| ☐J39 2¢ | Claret | 7.00 | 3.00 | .30 | .20 |
| ☐J40 3¢ | Claret | 40.00 | 16.00 | 1.35 | .70 |
| ☐J41 5¢ | Claret | 50.00 | 16.00 | 1.20 | .70 |
| ☐J42 10¢ | Claret | 60.00 | 19.00 | 2.60 | 1.50 |
| ☐J43 30¢ | Claret | 400.00 | 150.00 | 31.00 | 14.00 |
| ☐J44 50¢ | Claret | 200.00 | 98.00 | 23.00 | 14.00 |
| **1910–1912. SMALL DESIGN—S.L. WTMK.— PERF. 12 (N-H ADD 80%)** | | | | | |
| ☐J45 1¢ | Claret | 18.00 | 10.50 | 2.30 | 1.30 |
| ☐J46 2¢ | Claret | 18.00 | 10.50 | .35 | .16 |
| ☐J47 3¢ | Claret | 300.00 | 175.00 | 19.00 | 12.00 |
| ☐J48 5¢ | Claret | 56.00 | 32.00 | 5.00 | 2.10 |
| ☐J49 10¢ | Claret | 72.00 | 45.00 | 9.00 | 4.75 |
| ☐J50 50¢ | Claret | 510.00 | 285.00 | 76.00 | 40.00 |
| **1914–1916. SAME SMALL DESIGN—S.L. WTMK. PERF. 10. (N-H ADD 80%)** | | | | | |
| ☐J52 1¢ | Carmine | 36.00 | 20.00 | 7.50 | 4.00 |
| ☐J53 2¢ | Carmine | 32.00 | 15.00 | .28 | .16 |
| ☐J54 3¢ | Carmine | 400.00 | 210.00 | 21.00 | 11.00 |
| ☐J55 5¢ | Carmine | 21.00 | 10.00 | 1.90 | 1.00 |

| Scott No. | Fine Unused Each | Ave. Unused Each | Fine Used Each | Ave. Used Each |
|---|---|---|---|---|
| ☐J56 10¢ Carmine | 35.00 | 20.00 | 1.10 | .60 |
| ☐J57 30¢ Carmine | 135.00 | 80.00 | 15.00 | 8.50 |
| ☐J58 50¢ Carmine | 5000.00 | 3000.00 | 400.00 | 220.00 |
| ☐J59 1¢ Rose (No Wtmk.) | | | | |
| | 1000.00 | 600.00 | 210.00 | 120.00 |
| ☐J60 2¢ Rose (No Wtmk.) | | | | |
| | 76.00 | 42.00 | 13.00 | 8.00 |

| Scott No. | Fine Unused Plate Blk | Ave. Unused Plate Blk | Fine Unused Each | Ave. Unused Each | Fine Used Each | Ave. Used Each |
|---|---|---|---|---|---|---|
| **1917–1926. SAME SMALL DESIGN—NO WTMK.— PERF. 11(N-H ADD 40%)** | | | | | | |
| ☐J61 1¢ Carmine Rose | | | | | | |
| | 39.00 | 26.00 | 1.60 | 1.00 | .20 | .15 |
| ☐J62 2¢ Carmine Rose | | | | | | |
| | 30.00 | 26.00 | 1.50 | 1.00 | .20 | .15 |
| ☐J63 3¢ Carmine Rose | | | | | | |
| | 96.00 | 72.00 | 8.00 | 5.00 | .20 | .15 |
| ☐J64 5¢ Carmine Rose | | | | | | |
| | 96.00 | 72.00 | 8.00 | 5.00 | .20 | .15 |
| ☐J65 10¢ Carmine Rose | | | | | | |
| | 130.00 | 95.00 | 12.00 | 6.50 | .20 | .15 |
| ☐J66 30¢ Carmine Rose | | | | | | |
| | 400.00 | 300.00 | 56.00 | 32.00 | .60 | .31 |
| ☐J67 50¢ Carmine Rose | | | | | | |
| | 600.00 | 480.00 | 72.00 | 40.00 | .21 | .15 |
| ☐J68 ½¢ Dull Red | | | | | | |
| | 12.00 | 9.00 | .68 | .41 | .21 | .15 |
| **1930–1931. NEW DESIGN FLAT PRESS— PERF. 11 x 11 (N-H ADD 30%)** | | | | | | |
| ☐J69 ½¢ Carmine | | | | | | |
| | 36.00 | 25.00 | 3.50 | 1.80 | .85 | .50 |
| ☐J70 1¢ Carmine | | | | | | |
| | 30.00 | 20.00 | 2.50 | 1.65 | .21 | .16 |
| ☐J71 2¢ Carmine | | | | | | |
| | 42.00 | 30.00 | 3.10 | 2.50 | .21 | .16 |

| Scott No. | Fine Unused Plate Blk | Ave. Unused Plate Blk | Fine Unused Each | Ave. Unused Each | Fine Used Each | Ave. Used Each |
|---|---|---|---|---|---|---|
| ☐J72 3¢ Carmine | | | | | | |
| | 250.00 | 185.00 | 21.00 | 15.00 | 1.15 | .75 |
| ☐J73 5¢ Carmine | | | | | | |
| | 240.00 | 190.00 | 18.00 | 12.00 | 1.70 | 1.10 |
| ☐J74 10¢ Carmine | | | | | | |
| | 475.00 | 320.00 | 36.00 | 25.00 | .85 | .40 |
| ☐J75 30¢ Carmine | | | | | | |
| | 1200.00 | 1000.00 | 90.00 | 72.00 | 1.35 | .80 |
| ☐J76 50¢ Carmine | | | | | | |
| | 1300.00 | 100.00 | 120.00 | 80.00 | .41 | .26 |
| ☐J77 $1 Carmine | | | | | | |
| | 260.00 | 200.00 | 21.00 | 18.00 | .20 | .16 |
| ☐J78 $5 Carmine | | | | | | |
| | 360.00 | 275.00 | 31.00 | 21.00 | .21 | .16 |

## 1931–1956. SAME DESIGN—ROTARY PRESS— PERF. 10 x 10½ (N-H ADD 20%)

| Scott No. | Fine Unused Plate Blk | Ave. Unused Plate Blk | Fine Unused Each | Ave. Unused Each | Fine Used Each | Ave. Used Each |
|---|---|---|---|---|---|---|
| ☐J79 ½¢ Carmine | | | | | | |
| | 32.00 | 13.00 | 1.10 | .60 | .18 | .13 |
| ☐J80 1¢ Carmine | | | | | | |
| | 2.10 | 1.50 | .22 | .16 | .18 | .13 |
| ☐J81 2¢ Carmine | | | | | | |
| | 2.10 | 1.50 | .22 | .16 | .18 | .13 |
| ☐J82 3¢ Carmine | | | | | | |
| | 3.10 | 1.60 | .26 | .22 | .18 | .13 |
| ☐J83 5¢ Carmine | | | | | | |
| | 4.60 | 2.10 | .42 | .26 | .18 | .13 |
| ☐J84 10¢ Carmine | | | | | | |
| | 9.00 | 5.00 | 1.25 | .72 | .18 | .13 |
| ☐J85 30¢ Carmine | | | | | | |
| | 52.00 | 25.00 | 8.50 | 5.00 | .18 | .13 |
| ☐J86 50¢ Carmine | | | | | | |
| | 62.00 | 32.00 | 10.00 | 5.00 | .18 | .13 |
| ☐J87 $1 Red (10½ x 11) | | | | | | |
| | 240.00 | 200.00 | 38.00 | 28.00 | .19 | .14 |

| Scott No. | Mint Sheet | Plate Block | Fine Unused Each | Fine Used Each |
|---|---|---|---|---|

## 1959. NEW SERIES—NEW DESIGN—ROTARY PRESS—PERF. 11 x 10½ (N-H ADD 20%)

| Scott No. | Mint Sheet | Plate Block | Fine Unused Each | Fine Used Each |
|---|---|---|---|---|
| ☐J88 ½¢ Red & Black | 400.00 | 200.00 | 1.50 | 1.10 |
| ☐J89 1¢ Red & Black | 3.50 | .40 | .18 | .14 |
| ☐J90 2¢ Red & Black | 6.00 | .46 | .18 | .14 |
| ☐J91 3¢ Red & Black | 7.00 | .50 | .18 | .14 |
| ☐J92 4¢ Red & Black | 9.00 | .86 | .18 | .14 |
| ☐J93 5¢ Red & Black | 11.00 | .75 | .19 | .14 |
| ☐J94 6¢ Red & Black | 16.00 | 1.00 | .18 | .14 |
| ☐J95 7¢ Red & Black | 24.00 | 2.10 | .18 | .14 |
| ☐J96 8¢ Red & Black | 24.00 | 1.60 | .18 | .14 |
| ☐J97 10¢ Red & Black | 24.00 | 1.65 | .18 | .14 |
| ☐J98 30¢ Red & Black | 60.00 | 4.60 | .60 | .14 |
| ☐J99 50¢ Red & Black | 100.00 | 6.00 | .95 | .20 |
| ☐J100 $1 Red & Black | 180.00 | 12.00 | 2.00 | .20 |
| ☐J101 $5 Red & Black | 810.00 | 48.00 | 10.00 | .21 |

## 1978. SAME DESIGN, NEW VALUES

| Scott No. | Mint Sheet | Plate Block | Fine Unused Each | Fine Used Each |
|---|---|---|---|---|
| ☐J102 11¢ Red & Black | 29.00 | 4.00 | .31 | .21 |
| ☐J103 13¢ Red & Black | 38.00 | 3.00 | .36 | .26 |

## 1985. SAME DESIGN, NEW VALUES

| Scott No. | Mint Sheet | Plate Block | Fine Unused Each | Fine Used Each |
|---|---|---|---|---|
| ☐J104 17¢ Red & Black | 68.00 | 36.00 | .42 | .36 |

| Scott No. | Fine | Scott No. | Fine |
|---|---|---|---|

## U.S. UNUSED ZIP CODE BLOCKS OF FOUR

| | | | |
|---|---|---|---|
| ☐1181 5¢ Battle-Wilderness | .95 | ☐1252 5¢ American Music | .70 |
| ☐1182 5¢ Appomattox | 2.00 | ☐1253 5¢ Homemakers | .70 |
| ☐1242 5¢ Sam Houston | .80 | ☐1254–57 5¢ Christmas, 1964 | 1.50 |
| ☐1243 5¢ Chas. M. Russell | .80 | ☐1258 5¢ Verr.-Narr. Bridge | .70 |
| ☐1244 5¢ N.Y. World's Fair. | 70 | ☐1259 5¢ Modern Art | .70 |
| ☐1247 5¢ N.J. Tercentenary. | 80 | ☐1260 5¢ Radio Amateurs | .70 |
| ☐1248 5¢ Nevada Statehood | .70 | ☐1261 5¢ Battle—N. Orleans | .70 |
| ☐1249 5¢ Register & Vote | .70 | | |
| ☐1250 5¢ Wm. Shakespeare | .70 | ☐1262 5¢ Physical Fitness | .70 |
| ☐1251 5¢ Mayo Brothers | .70 | ☐1263 5¢ Cancer Crusade | .70 |
| | | ☐1264 5¢ Churchill Mem'l | .70 |

| Scott No. | | Fine |
|---|---|---|
| ☐1265 | 5¢ Magna Carta | .70 |
| ☐1266 | 5¢ Intl. Co-op Year | .70 |
| ☐1267 | 5¢ Salvation Army | .70 |
| ☐1268 | 5¢ Dante Alighieri | .70 |
| ☐1269 | 5¢ Herbert Hoover | .70 |
| ☐1270 | 5¢ Robert Fulton | .70 |
| ☐1272 | 5¢ Traffic Safety | .70 |
| ☐1273 | 5¢ John S. Copley | .70 |
| ☐1274 | 11¢ Intl. Telecom. Un. | 8.00 |
| ☐1276 | 5¢ Christmas, 1965 | .70 |
| ☐1278 | 1¢ Thomas Jefferson | .60 |
| ☐1280 | 2¢ F. Lloyd Wright | .65 |
| ☐1281 | 3¢ Francis Parkman | .70 |
| ☐1284 | 6¢ F.D. Roosevelt | .80 |
| ☐1285 | 8¢ Albert Einstein | 1.20 |
| ☐1286 | 10¢ Andrew Jackson | 1.40 |
| ☐1286A | 12¢ Henry Ford | 1.50 |
| ☐1288 | 15¢ O.W. Holmes | 2.10 |
| ☐1289 | 20¢ Geo. C. Marshall | 2.60 |
| ☐1290 | 25¢ F. Douglass | 3.00 |
| ☐1291 | 30¢ John Dewey | 3.50 |
| ☐1292 | 40¢ Thomas Paine | 4.90 |
| ☐1293 | 50¢ Lucy Stone | 11.00 |
| ☐1294 | $1 Eugene O'Neill | 10.00 |
| ☐1306 | 5¢ Migr. Bird Treaty | .70 |
| ☐1307 | 5¢ Humane to Animals | .70 |
| ☐1308 | 5¢ Indiana Statehood | .70 |
| ☐1309 | 5¢ American Circus | .70 |
| ☐1310 | 5¢ 6th Intl. Phil. Exh. | .90 |
| ☐1312 | 5¢ Bill of Rights | .85 |
| ☐1313 | 5¢ Polish Millennium | .70 |
| ☐1314 | 5¢ Natl. Park Service | .70 |
| ☐1315 | 5¢ Marine Reserves | .70 |

| Scott No. | | Fine |
|---|---|---|
| ☐1316 | 5¢ Women's Clubs | .70 |
| ☐1317 | 5¢ Johnny Appleseed | .70 |
| ☐1318 | 5¢ Beautify America | .70 |
| ☐1319 | 5¢ Great River Road | .70 |
| ☐1320 | 5¢ Servicemen-Bonds | .70 |
| ☐1321 | 5¢ Christmas, 1966 | .70 |
| ☐1322 | 5¢ Mary Cassatt | .90 |
| ☐1323 | 5¢ National Grange | .80 |
| ☐1324 | 5¢ Canada Centennial | .70 |
| ☐1325 | 5¢ Erie Canal | .70 |
| ☐1326 | 5¢ Search for Peace | .80 |
| ☐1327 | 5¢ Henry D. Thoreau | .80 |
| ☐1328 | 5¢ Nebraska Statehood | .85 |
| ☐1329 | 5¢ Voice of America | .70 |
| ☐1330 | 5¢ Davy Crockett | .70 |
| ☐1331–32 | 5¢ Twin Space | 2.00 |
| ☐1333 | 5¢ Urban Planning | .80 |
| ☐1334 | 5¢ Finnish Independ. | .80 |
| ☐1336 | 5¢ Christmas, 1967 | .70 |
| ☐1337 | 5¢ Miss. Statehood | .90 |
| ☐1338 | 6¢ American Flag | .80 |
| ☐1339 | 6¢ Illinois Statehood | .80 |
| ☐1341 | $1 Airlift | 10.00 |
| ☐1342 | 6¢ Support Our Youth | .80 |
| ☐1343 | 6¢ Law & Order | 1.00 |
| ☐1344 | 6¢ Register & Vote | .80 |
| ☐1353–54 | 6¢ Historic Flags | 2.00 |
| ☐1355 | 6¢ Walt Disney | 2.40 |
| ☐1356 | 6¢ Fr. Marquette | 1.00 |
| ☐1357 | 6¢ Daniel Boone | .80 |
| ☐1358 | 6¢ Arkansas River | .80 |
| ☐1359 | 6¢ Leif Erikson | .80 |
| ☐1360 | 6¢ Cherokee Strip | .90 |
| ☐1361 | 6¢ Trumbull Painting | 1.10 |

| Scott No. | Fine |
|---|---|
| ☐ 1362 6¢ Wildlife Conserv. | 1.15 |
| ☐ 1364 6¢ American Indian | 1.15 |
| ☐ 1365–68 6¢ Beautify America | 4.00 |
| ☐ 1369 6¢ American Legion | .80 |
| ☐ 1370 6¢ Grandma Moses | .90 |
| ☐ 1371 6¢ Apollo 8 | 1.15 |
| ☐ 1372 6¢ W.C. Handy | 1.00 |
| ☐ 1373 6¢ California | .70 |
| ☐ 1374 6¢ J.W. Powell | .80 |
| ☐ 1375 6¢ Alabama | .80 |
| ☐ 1376–79 6¢ Botanical | 6.00 |
| ☐ 1380 6¢ Dartmouth Case | 1.00 |
| ☐ 1381 6¢ Baseball | 4.10 |
| ☐ 1382 6¢ Football | 1.50 |
| ☐ 1383 6¢ Eisenhower | .80 |
| ☐ 1385 6¢ Rehabilitation | .90 |
| ☐ 1386 6¢ Wm. M. Harnett | .90 |
| ☐ 1387–90 6¢ Natural History | 1.10 |
| ☐ 1391 6¢ Maine Statehood | .85 |
| ☐ 1392 6¢ Buffalo | .85 |
| ☐ 1393 6¢ Eisenhower-Reg. | .85 |
| ☐ 1393D 7¢ Franklin | 1.20 |
| ☐ 1394 8¢ Eisenhower | 1.00 |
| ☐ 1396 8¢ Postal Service | 4.00 |
| ☐ 1397 14¢ F. LaGuardia | 1.50 |
| ☐ 1398 16¢ Ernie Pyle | 1.80 |
| ☐ 1399 18¢ Dr. E. Blackwell | 2.10 |
| ☐ 1400 21¢ A.P. Giannini | 2.15 |
| ☐ 1405 6¢ E.L. Masters | .80 |
| ☐ 1406 6¢ Women's Suffrage | .80 |
| ☐ 1407 6¢ So. Carolina | .80 |
| ☐ 1408 6¢ Stone Mountain | .80 |
| ☐ 1409 6¢ Fort Snelling | .80 |
| ☐ 1410–13 6¢ Anti-Pollution | 1.90 |

| Scott No. | Fine |
|---|---|
| ☐ 1414 6¢ Nativity | 1.75 |
| ☐ 1414a 6¢ Precancelled | 1.60 |
| ☐ 1415–18 6¢ Christmas Toys | 3.00 |
| ☐ 1415–18a 6¢ Precancelled | 10.00 |
| ☐ 1419 6¢ United Nations | .80 |
| ☐ 1420 6¢ Pilgrim Landing | .80 |
| ☐ 1421–22 6¢ D.A.V & P.O.W. | 1.60 |
| ☐ 1423 6¢ Sheep | .80 |
| ☐ 1424 6¢ D. MacArthur | .80 |
| ☐ 1425 6¢ Blood Donors | .80 |
| ☐ 1426 8¢ Mo. Statehood | 3.00 |
| ☐ 1427–30 8¢ Wildlife Cons. | 1.15 |
| ☐ 1431 8¢ Antarctic Treaty | 1.10 |
| ☐ 1432 8¢ Amer. Revolution | 1.25 |
| ☐ 1433 8¢ John Sloan | 1.10 |
| ☐ 1434–35 8¢ Space Achievement | 1.25 |
| ☐ 1436 8¢ Emily Dickinson | 1.00 |
| ☐ 1437 8¢ San Juan | 1.00 |
| ☐ 1438 8¢ Drug Addiction | 1.50 |
| ☐ 1439 8¢ CARE | 2.00 |
| ☐ 1440–43 8¢ Historic Pres. | 2.00 |
| ☐ 1444 8¢ Nativity | 3.00 |
| ☐ 1445 8¢ Partridge | 3.00 |
| ☐ 1446 8¢ Sidney Lanier | 1.15 |
| ☐ 1447 8¢ Peace Corps | 1.50 |
| ☐ 1448–51 2¢ Cape Hatteras | .75 |
| ☐ 1452 6¢ Wolf Trap Farm | .80 |
| ☐ 1453 8¢ Yellowstone | 1.00 |
| ☐ 1454 15¢ Mt. McKinley | 2.00 |
| ☐ 1455 8¢ Family Planning | 1.10 |
| ☐ 1456–59 8¢ Colonial Crafts | 1.10 |

| Scott No. | Fine | Scott No. | Fine |
|---|---|---|---|
| ☐1460 6¢ Olympic Games | 2.00 | ☐1511 10¢ Zip Code | 2.10 |
| ☐1461 8¢ Olympic Games | 2.60 | ☐1525 10¢ V.F.W. | 1.25 |
| ☐1462 15¢ Olympic Games | 4.50 | ☐1526 10¢ Robert Frost | 1.25 |
| ☐1463 8¢ P.T.A. | 1.00 | ☐1527 10¢ EXPO"74—Envir. | 3.50 |
| ☐1464 8¢ Wildlife | 1.10 | | |
| ☐1468 8¢ Mail Order | 3.00 | ☐1528 10¢ Horse Racing | 3.40 |
| ☐1469 8¢ Osteopathic | 1.50 | ☐1529 10¢ Skylab Project | 1.25 |
| ☐1470 8¢ Tom Sawyer | 1.10 | ☐1538–41 10¢ Minerals | 1.20 |
| ☐1471 8¢ Xmas-Religious | 3.00 | ☐1542 10¢ Fort Harrod | 1.25 |
| ☐1472 8¢ Xmas-Santa Claus | 3.00 | ☐1543–46 10¢ Cont. Congress | 1.25 |
| ☐1473 8¢ Pharmacy | 1.30 | ☐1547 10¢ Energy Conserv. | 1.10 |
| ☐1474 8¢ Stamp Collectors | 1.10 | | |
| | | ☐1548 10¢ Sleepy Hollow | 1.10 |
| ☐1475 8¢ Love | 1.40 | ☐1549 10¢ Retarded Children | 1.10 |
| ☐1476 8¢ Pamphlet Printing | 1.10 | | |
| | | ☐1550 10¢ Xmas-Religious | 3.00 |
| ☐1477 8¢ Posting Broadside | 1.10 | ☐1551 10¢ Xmas-Sleigh | 3.20 |
| ☐1478 8¢ Post Rider | 1.10 | ☐1553 10¢ B. West | 3.10 |
| ☐1479 8¢ Drummer | 1.10 | ☐1554 10¢ P. Dunbar | 3.10 |
| ☐1480–83 8¢ Bost. Tea Party | 1.20 | ☐1555 10¢ D.W. Griffith | 1.30 |
| ☐1484 8¢ George Gershwin | 3.50 | ☐1556 10¢ Pioneer-Jupiter | 1.35 |
| | | ☐1557 10¢ Mariner 10 | 1.35 |
| ☐1485 8¢ Robinson Jeffers | 3.00 | ☐1558 10¢ Collective Barg | 2.50 |
| | | ☐1559 8¢ Sybil Ludington | 2.25 |
| ☐1486 8¢ Tanner | 3.00 | ☐1560 10¢ Salem Poor | 2.40 |
| ☐1487 8¢ Willa Cather | 3.00 | ☐1561 10¢ Haym Solomon | 2.40 |
| ☐1488 8¢ N. Copernicus | 3.00 | ☐1562 18¢ Peter Francisco | 6.00 |
| ☐1500 6¢ Electronics | .95 | ☐1563 10¢ Lex.-Concord | 3.25 |
| ☐1501 8¢ Electronics | 1.00 | ☐1564 10¢ Bunker Hill | 3.25 |
| ☐1502 15¢ Electronics | 1.65 | ☐1565–68 10¢ Uniforms | 1.35 |
| ☐1504 8¢ Angus Cattle | 1.00 | ☐1569–70 10¢ Apollo-Soyuz | 1.15 |
| ☐1505 10¢ Chautauqua | 1.15 | | |
| ☐1506 10¢ Winter Wheat | 1.20 | ☐1571 10¢ Women's Year | 1.75 |
| ☐1507 8¢ Xmas-Religious | 3.00 | ☐1572–75 10¢ Postal Service | 1.20 |
| ☐1508 8¢ Xmas-Tree | 3.00 | | |
| ☐1510 10¢ Jefferson Mem'l | 1.25 | ☐1576 10¢ World Peace | 1.50 |
| | | ☐1577–78 10¢ Banking & Com. | 1.15 |

| Scott No. | Fine |
|---|---|
| ☐1579 10¢ Xmas-Religious | 3.50 |
| ☐1580 10¢ Xmas-Post Card | 3.50 |
| ☐1581 1¢ Ability to Write | .70 |
| ☐1582 2¢ Freedom to Speak | .70 |
| ☐1585 4¢ Public that Reads | .65 |
| ☐1591 9¢ Freedom to Assemble | 1.00 |
| ☐1592 10¢ Justice | 1.40 |
| ☐1593 11¢ Freedom of Press | 1.20 |
| ☐1596 13¢ Eagle & Shield | 4.35 |
| ☐1603 24¢ Old North Church | 2.60 |
| ☐1629–31 13¢ Spirit of '76 | 3.00 |
| ☐1632 13¢ Interphil '76 | 1.60 |
| ☐1633–82 13¢ State Flags | 1.50 |
| ☐1683 13¢ Telephone | 1.65 |
| ☐1684 13¢ Aviation | 3.90 |
| ☐1685 13¢ Chemistry | 4.50 |
| ☐1690 13¢ Ben Franklin | 1.70 |
| ☐1691–94 13¢ Dec. of Indep. | 2.00 |
| ☐1695–98 13¢ Olympic Games | 1.75 |
| ☐1699 13¢ Clara Maass | 4.75 |
| ☐1700 13¢ Adolph Ochs | 1.60 |
| ☐1701 13¢ Nativity | 5.00 |
| ☐1702 13¢ Winter Pastime | 4.00 |
| ☐1704 13¢ Wash. at Princeton | 3.90 |
| ☐1705 13¢ Sound Recording | 1.50 |
| ☐1706–09 13¢ Pueblo Art (6) | 2.00 |
| ☐1710 13¢ Transatlantic Flight | 4.60 |

| Scott No. | Fine |
|---|---|
| ☐1711 13¢ Colorado | 4.60 |
| ☐1712 13¢ Butterflies | 1.50 |
| ☐1716 13¢ Lafayette | 1.60 |
| ☐1717–20 20¢,13¢ Skilled Hands | 1.85 |
| ☐1721 13¢ Peace Bridge | 1.60 |
| ☐1722 13¢ Herkimer | 3.75 |
| ☐1723–24 24¢ ,13¢ Energy | 1.60 |
| ☐1725 13¢ Alta | 1.50 |
| ☐1726 13¢ Confederation | 1.60 |
| ☐1727 13¢ Pictures | 1.60 |
| ☐1728 13¢ Saratoga | 4.15 |
| ☐1730 13¢ Mailbox | 4.00 |
| ☐1731 13¢ Sandburg | 1.50 |
| ☐1732 13¢ Capt. Cook | 1.55 |
| ☐1733 13¢ Capt. Cook R&S | 1.50 |
| ☐1734 13¢ Indian Cent | 1.80 |
| ☐1735 15¢ No Value "A" Eagle | 1.80 |
| ☐1744 13¢ Harriet Tubman | 7.00 |
| ☐1745–48 13¢ Quilts | 1.90 |
| ☐1749–52 13¢ Dance | 2.00 |
| ☐1753 13¢ French Alliance | 1.50 |
| ☐1754 13¢ Papanicolau | 1.80 |
| ☐1755 13¢ Jimmie Rodgers | 5.00 |
| ☐1756 15¢ George M. Cohan | 6.00 |
| ☐1757 13¢ Capex SS | 2.90 |
| ☐1758 15¢ Photography | 6.00 |
| ☐1759 15¢ Viking | 1.85 |
| ☐1760–63 15¢ Owls | 1.80 |
| ☐1764–67 15¢ Trees | 1.90 |
| ☐1768 15¢ Madonna | 6.00 |
| ☐1769 15¢ Xmas Hobby Horse | 6.00 |
| ☐1770 15¢ R.F. Kennedy | 1.90 |
| ☐1771 15¢ M.L. King | 5.00 |

| Scott No. | Fine | Scott No. | Fine |
|---|---|---|---|
| ☐1772 15¢ Intl. Year of Child | 1.85 | ☐1838–41 15¢ Architecture | 2.10 |
| ☐1773 15¢ Steinbeck | 1.85 | ☐1842 15¢ Christmas Madonna | 6.00 |
| ☐1774 15¢ Einstein | 1.85 | ☐1849 17¢ Rachel Carson | 4.00 |
| ☐1775–78 15¢ Toleware | 2.75 | ☐1850 18¢ Geo. Mason | 5.00 |
| ☐1779–82 15¢ Architecture | 2.00 | ☐1851 19¢ Sequoyah | 1.30 |
| ☐1783–86 15¢ Endangered Flora | 2.00 | ☐1859 35¢ Dr. Charles Drew | 3.00 |
| ☐1788 15¢ Special Olympics | 5.00 | ☐1874 15¢ Everett Dirksen | 1.90 |
| ☐1789 15¢ John Paul Jones | 5.00 | ☐1875 15¢ Whitney Young | 1.90 |
| ☐1790 10¢ Olympics | 5.00 | ☐1876–79 18¢ Flowers | 2.30 |
| ☐1791–94 15¢ Summer Olympics | 1.80 | ☐1910 18¢ Red Cross | 2.75 |
| ☐1795–98 15¢ Winter Olympics | 2.25 | ☐1911 18¢ Savings & Loan | 2.75 |
| ☐1799 15¢ Madonna | 6.00 | ☐1912–19 18¢ Space Achievement | 6.00 |
| ☐1800 15¢ Xmas Santa | 6.00 | ☐1920 18¢ Management | 2.50 |
| ☐1801 15¢ Will Rogers | 5.50 | ☐1921–24 18¢ Habitats | 2.15 |
| ☐1802 15¢ Vietnam Veterans | 6.00 | ☐1925 18¢ Disabled | 2.50 |
| ☐1803 15¢ Fields | 5.50 | ☐1926 18¢ Edna St. Vincent Millay | 2.50 |
| ☐1804 15¢ Banneker | 5.50 | ☐1928–31 18¢ Architecture | 2.50 |
| ☐1805–10 15¢ Letter Writing | 6.00 | ☐1932 18¢ Babe Zaharias | 3.00 |
| ☐1811 15¢ Perkins | .65 | ☐1933 18¢ Bobby Jones | 4.00 |
| ☐1822 15¢ Madison | 1.80 | ☐1934 18¢ Remington | 2.30 |
| ☐1823 15¢ Bissell | 1.80 | ☐1935 18¢ James Hoban | 2.30 |
| ☐1824 15¢ Keller/Sullivan | 1.80 | ☐1936 20¢ James Hoban | 2.60 |
| ☐1825 15¢ Vets. Admin. | 1.65 | ☐1937–38 18¢ Yorktown, Virginia | 2.40 |
| ☐1826 15¢ De Galvez | 1.65 | ☐1939 20¢ Christmas Madonna | 2.40 |
| ☐1827–30 15¢ Coral Reefs | 2.25 | ☐1940 20¢ Christmas Child Art | 2.40 |
| ☐1831 15¢ Org. Labor | 6.00 | ☐1941 20¢ John Hanson | 2.60 |
| ☐1832 15¢ Wharton | 4.00 | ☐1942–45 20¢ Desert Plants | 2.60 |
| ☐1833 15¢ Education | 7.00 | ☐C69 8¢ Robert H. Goddard | 2.30 |
| ☐1834–37 15¢ Indian Masks | 2.40 | | |

| Scott No. | Fine |
|---|---|
| ☐C70 8¢ Alaska Purchase | 1.90 |
| ☐C71 20¢ Columbia Jays | 5.00 |
| ☐C72 10¢ Stars | 1.40 |
| ☐C74 10¢ 50 Years Airmail | 3.50 |
| ☐C75 20¢ U.S.A. & Jet | 3.00 |
| ☐C76 10¢ Moon Landing | 2.00 |
| ☐C77 9¢ Delta Plane | 1.25 |
| ☐C78 11¢ Plane Silhouette | 1.40 |
| ☐C79 13¢ Letter | 1.70 |
| ☐C80 17¢ Liberty Head | 2.60 |
| ☐C81 21¢ "USA" | 2.60 |
| ☐C84 11¢ City of Refuge | 1.50 |
| ☐C85 11¢ Olympic Games | 4.00 |
| ☐C86 11¢ Electronics | 1.40 |
| ☐C87 18¢ Statue of Liberty | 2.50 |
| ☐C88 26¢ Mount Rushmore | 3.00 |
| ☐C89 5¢ Plane & Globes | 3.00 |
| ☐C90 31¢ Plane, Flag & Globes | 4.00 |
| ☐C91–92 31¢ Wright Bros. | 5.00 |
| ☐C93–94 21¢ Chanute | 6.00 |
| ☐C95–96 25¢ Wiley Post | 11.00 |
| ☐C97 31¢ Olympics | 13.00 |
| ☐C98 40¢ Mazzel | 12.50 |
| ☐C99 28¢ Scott | 9.00 |
| ☐C100 35¢ Curtiss | 11.00 |
| ☐E22 45¢ Special Delivery | 7.00 |
| ☐E23 60¢ Special Delivery | 7.00 |

## U.S. UNUSED MAIL EARLY INSCRIPTION BLOCKS

| Scott No. | Fine |
|---|---|
| ☐1278 1¢ T. Jefferson | .60 |
| ☐1280 2¢ F.L. Wright | .65 |
| ☐1281 3¢ Parkman | .70 |
| ☐1284 6¢ F.D. Roosevelt | .80 |
| ☐1285 8¢ A. Einstein | 1.20 |
| ☐1286 10¢ A. Jackson | 1.40 |

| Scott No. | Fine |
|---|---|
| ☐1286A 12¢ Henry Ford | 1.50 |
| ☐1288 15¢ O.W. Holmes | 2.10 |
| ☐1289 20¢ G.C. Marshall | 2.60 |
| ☐1290 25¢ F. Douglass | 3.00 |
| ☐1291 30¢ John Dewey | 3.50 |
| ☐1292 40¢ T. Paine | 4.90 |
| ☐1293 50¢ Lucy Stone | 5.00 |
| ☐1294 $1 E. O'Neill | 11.00 |
| ☐1338 6¢ American Flag | .80 |
| ☐1340 6¢ Hemis Fair '68 | .80 |
| ☐1341 $1 Airlift | 10.00 |
| ☐1342 6¢ Support Our Youth | .80 |
| ☐1343 6¢ Law & Order | 1.00 |
| ☐1344 6¢ Register & Vote | .80 |
| ☐1347–49 6¢ Historic Flags | .70 |
| ☐1355 6¢ Walt Disney | 2.40 |
| ☐1356 6¢ Fr. Marquette | 1.00 |
| ☐1357 6¢ Daniel Boone | .80 |
| ☐1358 6¢ Arkansas River | .80 |
| ☐1359 6¢ Leif Erikson | .80 |
| ☐1360 6¢ Cherokee Strip | .90 |
| ☐1361 6¢ Trumbull Painting | 1.10 |
| ☐1362 6¢ Wildlife Conserv. | 1.15 |
| ☐1364 6¢ American Indian | 1.15 |
| ☐1365–68 6¢ Beautify America | 5.00 |
| ☐1369 6¢ American Legion | .80 |
| ☐1370 6¢ Grandma Moses | .90 |
| ☐1371 6¢ Apollo 8 | 1.15 |
| ☐1372 6¢ W.C. Handy | 1.00 |
| ☐1373 6¢ California | .70 |
| ☐1374 6¢ J.W. Powell | .80 |
| ☐1375 6¢ Alabama | .80 |
| ☐1376–79 6¢ Botanical | 7.00 |
| ☐1380 6¢ Dartmouth Case | 1.00 |

| Scott No. | Fine |
|---|---|
| ☐1381 6¢ Baseball | 4.70 |
| ☐1382 6¢ Football | 1.50 |
| ☐1383 6¢ Eisenhower | .80 |
| ☐1385 6¢ Rehabilitation | .90 |
| ☐1386 6¢ W.M. Harnett | .90 |
| ☐1387–90 6¢ Nat. History | 1.25 |
| ☐1391 6¢ Maine | .85 |
| ☐1392 6¢ Buffalo | .85 |
| ☐1393 6¢ Eisenhower | .85 |
| ☐1393D 7¢ B. Franklin | 1.20 |
| ☐1394 8¢ Eisenhower | 1.00 |
| ☐1396 8¢ Postal Service (4) | 4.00 |
| ☐1397 14¢ F. LaGuardia | 1.50 |
| ☐1398 16¢ Ernie Pyle | 1.80 |
| ☐1399 18¢ Dr. E. Blackwell | 2.10 |
| ☐1400 21¢ A.P. Giannini | 2.15 |
| ☐1405 6¢ E.L. Masters | .80 |
| ☐1406 6¢ Women's Suffrage | .80 |
| ☐1407 6¢ South Carolina | .80 |
| ☐1408 6¢ Stone Mountain | .80 |
| ☐1409 6¢ Fort Snelling | .80 |
| ☐1410–13 6¢ Anti-Pollution | 2.60 |
| ☐1414 6¢ Nativity | 1.75 |
| ☐1414a 6¢ Precancelled | 1.50 |
| ☐1415–18 6¢ Christmas Toys | 5.00 |
| ☐1415a–18a 6¢ Precancelled | 16.00 |
| ☐1419 6¢ United Nations | .80 |
| ☐1420 6¢ Pilgrim Landing | .80 |
| ☐1421–22 6¢ D.A. & P.O.W. | 1.80 |
| ☐1423 6¢ Sheep | .80 |
| ☐1424 6¢ Gen. MacArthur | .80 |
| ☐1425 6¢ Blood Donors | .80 |
| ☐1426 8¢ Missouri (4) | 3.00 |

| Scott No. | Fine |
|---|---|
| ☐1427–30 8¢ Wildlife | 1.75 |
| ☐1431 8¢ Antarctic | 1.10 |
| ☐1432 8¢ Bicentennial | 1.25 |
| ☐1433 8¢ J. Sloan Painting | 1.10 |
| ☐1434–35 8¢ Space Accomp. | 1.60 |
| ☐1436 8¢ Emily Dickinson | 1.00 |
| ☐1437 8¢ San Juan | 1.00 |
| ☐1438 8¢ Drug Addiction | 1.50 |
| ☐1439 8¢ CARE | 2.00 |
| ☐1440–43 8¢ Historic Press | 1.25 |
| ☐1444 8¢ Nativity (4) | 4.00 |
| ☐1445 8¢ Partridge (4) | 4.00 |
| ☐1446 8¢ Sidney Lanier | 1.15 |
| ☐1447 8¢ Peace Corps | 1.50 |
| ☐1448–51 2¢ Hatteras (8) | 1.50 |
| ☐1452 6¢ Wolf Trap Farm | .80 |
| ☐1453 8¢ Yellowstone | 1.00 |
| ☐1454 15¢ Mt. McKinley | 2.00 |
| ☐1455 8¢ Family Planning | 1.10 |
| ☐1456–59 8¢ Craftman | 1.35 |
| ☐1460 6¢ Olympic Games | 2.00 |
| ☐1461 8¢ Olympic Games | 2.60 |
| ☐1462 15¢ Olympic Games | 2.75 |
| ☐1463 8¢ P.T.A. | 4.50 |
| ☐1464–67 8¢ Wildlife | 1.50 |
| ☐1468 8¢ Mail Order (4) | 3.00 |
| ☐1469 8¢ Osteopathic | 1.50 |
| ☐1470 8¢ Tom Sawyer | 1.10 |
| ☐1471 8¢ Religious | 3.00 |
| ☐1472 8¢ Santa Claus | 3.00 |
| ☐1473 8¢ Pharmacy | 1.30 |
| ☐1474 8¢ Stamp Collector | 1.10 |
| ☐1475 8¢ Love | 1.40 |
| ☐1476 8¢ Pamphlet Printing | 1.10 |
| ☐1477 8¢ Posting Broadside | 1.10 |

| Scott No. | Fine | Scott No. | Fine |
|---|---|---|---|
| ☐1478 8¢ Post Rider | 1.10 | ☐1559 8¢ Sybil Ludington | 2.25 |
| ☐1479 8¢ Drummer | 1.10 | ☐1560 10¢ Salem Poor | 2.40 |
| ☐1480–83 8¢ Bost. Tea | | ☐1561 10¢ Haym Salomon | 2.40 |
| Party | 1.70 | ☐1562 18¢ Peter Francisco | |
| ☐1488 8¢ Copernicus | 1.00 | | 6.00 |
| ☐1500 6¢ Electronics | .95 | ☐1565–68 10¢ Uniforms (4) | |
| ☐1501 8¢ Electronics | 1.00 | | 1.50 |
| ☐1502 15¢ Electronics | 1.65 | ☐1571 10¢ Women's Year | 1.75 |
| ☐1504 8¢ Angus Cattle | 1.00 | ☐1572–75 10¢ Postal Service | |
| ☐1505 10¢ Chautauqua | 1.20 | (4) | 1.20 |
| ☐1506 10¢ Winter Wheat | 1.20 | ☐1576 10¢ World Peace | 1.50 |
| ☐1507 8¢ Religious (4) | 3.00 | ☐1577–78 10¢ Banking & | |
| ☐1508 8¢ Xmas Tree (4) | 3.00 | Comm. | 1.65 |
| ☐1510 10¢ Jefferson Mem'l | | ☐1579 10¢ Xmas-Religious | |
| | 1.25 | | 3.50 |
| ☐1511 10¢ Zip Code | 2.10 | ☐1580 10¢ Xmas Post | |
| ☐1525 10¢ V.F.W. | 1.25 | Card (4) | 3.50 |
| ☐1526 10¢ Robert Frost | 1.25 | ☐1581 1¢ Ability Write | .70 |
| ☐1528 10¢ Horse Racing | | ☐1582 2¢ Freedom to Speak | |
| (4) | 3.40 | | .70 |
| ☐1529 10¢ Skylab Project | 1.25 | ☐1584 3¢ Cast A Ballot | .70 |
| ☐1538–41 10¢ Minerals | 1.65 | ☐1585 4¢ Public that Reads | .65 |
| ☐1542 10¢ Fort Harrod | 1.25 | ☐1591 9¢ Freedom to | |
| ☐1543–46 10¢ Cont. Cong. | | Assemble | 1.00 |
| | 1.65 | ☐1593 11¢ Freedom of | |
| ☐1547 10¢ Energy Cons. | 1.10 | Press | 1.15 |
| ☐1548 10¢ Sleepy Hollow | 1.10 | ☐1596 13¢ Eagle & Shield | 1.20 |
| ☐1549 10¢ Retarded Children | | ☐1603 24¢ Old North Church | |
| | 1.10 | | 2.60 |
| ☐1550 10¢ Xmas-Religious | | ☐1632 13¢ Interphil '76 | 1.60 |
| | 3.00 | ☐1633–82 13¢ State Flags | |
| ☐1551 10¢ Xmas-Sleigh (4) | | | 6.00 |
| | 3.20 | ☐1683 13¢ Telephone | 1.65 |
| ☐1553 10¢ Benjamin West | 3.10 | ☐1684 13¢ Aviation | 3.90 |
| ☐1554 10¢ Paul Dunbar | 3.10 | ☐1685 13¢ Chemistry | 4.50 |
| ☐1555 10¢ D.W. Griffith | 1.30 | ☐1690 13¢ Ben. Franklin | 1.70 |
| ☐1556 10¢ Pioneer-Jupiter | 1.35 | ☐1691–94 13¢ Independence | |
| ☐1557 10¢ Mariner 10 | 1.35 | | 3.50 |
| ☐1558 10¢ Coll. Bargaining | | ☐1695–98 13¢ Olympic | |
| | 2.50 | Games | 1.80 |

| Scott No. | | Fine |
|---|---|---|
| ☐1700 13¢ Adolph Ochs | | 1.60 |
| ☐1701 13¢ "Nativity" (4) | | 5.00 |
| ☐1702 13¢ "Winter Pastime" | | 4.00 |
| ☐1705 13¢ Sound Recording | | 7.00 |
| ☐1710 13¢ Transatlantic | | 4.60 |
| ☐1711 13¢ Colorado | | 4.60 |
| ☐1712–15 13¢ Butterflies | | 1.65 |
| ☐1716 13 ¢ Lafayette | | 1.60 |
| ☐1717–20 13¢ Skilled Hands (4) | | 1.80 |
| ☐1721 13¢ Peace Bridge | | 1.60 |
| ☐1725 13¢ California | | 1.50 |
| ☐1726 13¢ Articles of Conf. | | 1.60 |
| ☐1727 13¢ Talking Pictures | | 1.60 |
| ☐1730 13¢ Mailbox | | 4.00 |
| ☐1735 15¢ Eagle Issue "A" | | 1.80 |
| ☐1818 18¢ Eagle Issue "B" | | 2.30 |

| Scott No. | | Fine |
|---|---|---|
| ☐C72 10¢ Stars | | 1.40 |
| ☐C74 10¢ Airmail 50th Ann. | | 3.50 |
| ☐C75 20¢ U.S.A. Airmail | | 3.00 |
| ☐C76 10¢ Moon Landing | | 2.00 |
| ☐C77 9¢ Delta Plane | | 1.25 |
| ☐C78 1¢ Silhouette | | 1.40 |
| ☐C79 13¢ Letter | | 1.70 |
| ☐C80 17¢ Liberty Head | | 2.60 |
| ☐C81 21¢ U.S.A. Airmail | | 2.60 |
| ☐C84 11¢ City of Refuge | | 1.50 |
| ☐C85 11¢ Olympic Games | | 4.00 |
| ☐C86 11¢ Electronics | | 1.40 |
| ☐C87 18¢ Liberty | | 2.50 |
| ☐C88 26¢ Mt. Rushmore | | 3.00 |
| ☐C89 25¢ Plane & Globes | | 3.00 |
| ☐C90 31¢ Plane/Flag/Globes | | 4.00 |
| ☐E22 45¢ Arrows | | 7.00 |
| ☐E23 60¢ Arrows | | 7.00 |

| Scott No. | | | Fine Ctr Line Blk of 4 | Fine Arrow Blk of 4 |
|---|---|---|---|---|

## U.S. UNUSED CENTER LINE AND ARROW BLOCKS

| | Scott No. | | | Fine Ctr Line Blk of 4 | Fine Arrow Blk of 4 |
|---|---|---|---|---|---|
| ☐314 | 1¢ | Imperforate | | 190.00 | 150.00 |
| ☐320 | 2¢ | Imperforate | | 190.00 | 150.00 |
| ☐343 | 1¢ | Imperforate | | 70.00 | 42.00 |
| ☐344 | 2¢ | Imperforate | | 80.00 | 45.00 |
| ☐345 | 3¢ | Imperforate | | 140.00 | 85.00 |
| ☐346 | 4¢ | Imperforate | | 280.00 | 190.00 |
| ☐347 | 5¢ | Imperforate | | 400.00 | 250.00 |
| ☐368 | 2¢ | Lincoln, Imp. | | 190.00 | 115.00 |
| ☐371 | 2¢ | Alaska-Yukon, Imperf. | | 265.00 | 185.00 |
| ☐373 | 2¢ | Hudson-Fulton, Imperf. | | 300.00 | 200.00 |
| ☐383 | 1¢ | Imperforate | | 40.00 | 20.00 |
| ☐384 | 2¢ | Imperforate | | 70.00 | 30.00 |
| ☐408 | 1¢ | Imperforate | | 13.00 | 8.00 |

| Scott No. | | | Fine Ctr Line Blk of 4 | Fine Arrow Blk of 4 |
|---|---|---|---|---|
| ☐409 | 2¢ | Imperforate | 16.00 | 9.50 |
| ☐481 | 1¢ | Imperforate | 13.00 | 6.00 |
| ☐482 | 2¢ | Imperforate | 14.00 | 9.00 |
| ☐484 | 3¢ | Imperforate Type II | 125.00 | 75.00 |
| ☐524 | 5¢ | Green & Blk | 900.00 | 650.00 |
| ☐531 | 1¢ | Offset, Imperf. | 60.00 | 48.00 |
| ☐532 | 2¢ | Offset, Imperf. Type IV | 190.00 | 200.00 |
| ☐534 | 2¢ | Offset, Imperf. Type Va. | 95.00 | 70.00 |
| ☐534A | 2¢ | Offset, Imp. Type VI | 240.00 | 175.00 |
| ☐535 | 3¢ | Offset, Imperf. | 52.00 | 40.00 |
| ☐573 | $5 | Carm. & Blk | 900.00 | 750.00 |
| ☐575 | 1¢ | Imperforate | 60.00 | 45.00 |
| ☐576 | 1¹/₂¢ | Imperforate | 20.00 | 9.00 |
| ☐577 | 2¢ | Imperforate | 23.00 | 11.00 |
| ☐611 | 2¢ | Harding Imperf. | 80.00 | 36.00 |
| ☐620 | 2¢ | Norse-Amer'n | 38.00 | 27.00 |
| ☐621 | 5¢ | Norse-Amer'n | 92.00 | 62.00 |
| ☐631 | 1¹/₂¢ | Harding, Rotary Imperf. | 24.00 | 14.00 |
| ☐703 | 2¢ | Yorktown | 3.75 | 2.75 |
| ☐832 | $1 | Purple & Blk | 46.00 | 39.00 |
| ☐833 | $2 | Yel./Grn./Blk | 120.00 | 105.00 |
| ☐834 | $5 | Red & Blk | 530.00 | 440.00 |
| ☐C1 | 6¢ | Airmail | 360.00 | 280.00 |
| ☐C2 | 16¢ | Airmail | 485.00 | 440.00 |
| ☐C3 | 24¢ | Airmail | 500.00 | 420.00 |
| ☐C23 | 36¢ | Airmail | 3.00 | 2.50 |
| ☐CE2 | 16¢ | Spec. Del. Airmail | 3.10 | 2.75 |

| Scott No. | | Fine | Scott No. | | Fine |
|---|---|---|---|---|---|
| **1927–1940. MINT SHEETS** | | | ☐650 | 5¢ Aeronautics | 415.00 |
| ☐643 | 2¢ Vermont | 290.00 | ☐651 | 2¢ George R. Clark | |
| ☐644 | 2¢ Burgoyne | 300.00 | | | 44.00 |
| ☐645 | 2¢ Valley Forge | 180.00 | ☐654 | 2¢ Edison-Flat | 125.00 |
| ☐646 | 2¢ Molly Pitcher | 190.00 | ☐655 | 2¢ Edison-Rotary | 135.00 |
| ☐647 | 2¢ Hawaii | 650.00 | ☐657 | 2¢ Sullivan | 140.00 |
| ☐648 | 5¢ Hawaii | 1800.00 | ☐680 | 2¢ Fallen Timbers | |
| ☐649 | 2¢ Aeronautics | 92.00 | | | 150.00 |

| Scott No. | | Fine |
|---|---|---|
| ☐681 | 2¢ Ohio River Canal | 125.00 |
| ☐682 | 2¢ Mass. Bay | 100.00 |
| ☐683 | 2¢ Carolina-Charleston | 190.00 |
| ☐688 | 2¢ Braddock | 150.00 |
| ☐689 | 2¢ Von Steuben | 80.00 |
| ☐690 | 2¢ Pulaski | 50.00 |
| ☐702 | 2¢ Red Cross | 21.00 |
| ☐703 | 2¢ Yorktopwn | 27.00 |
| ☐704 | 1/2¢ Wash. Bicent'l | 18.00 |
| ☐705 | 1¢ Wash. Bicent'l | 20.00 |
| ☐706 | 1½¢ Wash. Bicent'l | 70.00 |
| ☐707 | 2¢ Wash. Bicent'l | 13.00 |
| ☐708 | 3¢ Wash. Bicent'l | 91.00 |
| ☐709 | 4¢ Wash. Bicent'l | 42.00 |
| ☐710 | 5¢ Wash. Bicent'l | 220.00 |
| ☐711 | 6¢ Wash. Bicent'l | 500.00 |
| ☐712 | 7¢ Wash. Bicent'l | 42.00 |
| ☐713 | 8¢ Wash. Bicent'l | 510.00 |
| ☐714 | 9¢ Wash. Bicent'l | 415.00 |
| ☐715 | 10¢ Wash. Bicent'l | 1700.00 |
| ☐716 | 2¢ Lake Placid | 70.00 |
| ☐717 | 2¢ Arbor Day | 28.00 |
| ☐718 | 2¢ Olympics | 190.00 |
| ☐719 | 5¢ Olympics | 300.00 |
| ☐724 | 3¢ Penn | 52.00 |
| ☐725 | 3¢ Webster | 80.00 |
| ☐726 | 3¢ Oglethorpe | 52.00 |
| ☐727 | 3¢ Newburgh | 24.00 |
| ☐728 | 1¢ Chicago | 16.00 |
| ☐729 | 3¢ Chicago | 23.00 |
| ☐732 | 3¢ N.R.A. | 15.00 |
| ☐733 | 3¢ Byrd | 45.00 |
| ☐734 | 5¢ Kosciuszko | 100.00 |

| Scott No. | | Fine |
|---|---|---|
| ☐736 | 3¢ Maryland | 32.00 |
| ☐737 | 3¢ Mother's Day (R) | 10.00 |
| ☐738 | 3¢ Mother's Day (F) | 14.00 |
| ☐739 | 3¢ Wisconsin | 16.00 |
| ☐740 | 1¢ Natl. Parks | 7.00 |
| ☐741 | 2¢ Natl. Parks | 10.00 |
| ☐742 | 3¢ Natl. Parks | 12.00 |
| ☐743 | 4¢ Natl. Parks | 32.00 |
| ☐744 | 5¢ Natl. Parks | 52.00 |
| ☐745 | 6¢ Natl. Parks | 82.00 |
| ☐746 | 7¢ Natl. Parks | 45.00 |
| ☐747 | 8¢ Natl. Parks | 110.00 |
| ☐748 | 9¢ Natl. Parks | 115.00 |
| ☐749 | 10¢ Natl. Parks | 210.00 |
| ☐772 | 3¢ Connecticut | 10.00 |
| ☐773 | 3¢ San Diego | 7.50 |
| ☐774 | 3¢ Boulder Dam | 9.00 |
| ☐775 | 3¢ Michigan | 7.00 |
| ☐776 | 3¢ Texas | 8.50 |
| ☐777 | 3¢ Rhode Island | 10.00 |
| ☐782 | 3¢ Arkansas | 8.50 |
| ☐783 | 3¢ Oregon | 8.50 |
| ☐784 | 3¢ Susan B. Anthony | 12.00 |
| ☐785 | 1¢ Army | 7.00 |
| ☐786 | 2¢ Army | 8.00 |
| ☐787 | 3¢ Army | 12.00 |
| ☐788 | 4¢ Army | 32.00 |
| ☐789 | 5¢ Army | 45.00 |
| ☐790 | 1¢ Navy | 5.00 |
| ☐791 | 2¢ Navy | 6.00 |
| ☐792 | 3¢ Navy | 8.50 |
| ☐793 | 4¢ Navy | 32.00 |
| ☐794 | 5¢ Navy | 46.00 |
| ☐795 | 3¢ N.W. Territory | 7.50 |
| ☐796 | 5¢ Virginia Dare | 14.00 |
| ☐798 | 3¢ Constitution | 9.00 |
| ☐799 | 3¢ Hawaii | 8.10 |

| Scott No. | | Fine | Scott No. | | Fine |
|---|---|---|---|---|---|
| ☐800 | 3¢ Alaska | 8.10 | ☐874 | 1¢ Audubon | 6.50 |
| ☐801 | 3¢ Puerto Rico | 8.10 | ☐875 | 2¢ Long | 7.00 |
| ☐802 | 3¢ Virgin Islands | 8.10 | ☐876 | 3¢ Burbank | 9.00 |
| ☐835 | 3¢ Ratification | 17.00 | ☐877 | 5¢ Reed | 22.00 |
| ☐836 | 3¢ Swede-Finn | 8.50 | ☐878 | 10¢ Addams | 115.00 |
| ☐837 | 3¢ N.W. Territory | 20.00 | ☐879 | 1¢ Fosters | 6.00 |
| ☐838 | 3¢ Iowa | 15.00 | ☐880 | 2¢ Sousa | 9.00 |
| ☐852 | 3¢ Golden Gate | 8.50 | ☐881 | 3¢ Herbert | 9.00 |
| ☐853 | 3¢ N.Y. Fair | 9.00 | ☐882 | 5¢ MacDowell | 36.00 |
| ☐854 | 3¢ Inauguration | 27.00 | ☐883 | 10¢ Nevin | 320.00 |
| ☐855 | 3¢ Baseball | 72.00 | ☐884 | 1¢ Sturat | 5.00 |
| ☐856 | 3¢ Canal Zone | 12.00 | ☐885 | 2¢ Whistler | 7.00 |
| ☐857 | 3¢ Printing | 7.50 | ☐886 | 3¢ St. Gaudens | 8.00 |
| ☐858 | 3¢ Four States | 7.50 | ☐887 | 5¢ French | 42.00 |
| ☐859 | 1¢ Irving | 6.50 | ☐888 | 10¢ Remington | 155.00 |
| ☐860 | 2¢ Cooper | 6.50 | ☐889 | 1¢ Whitney | 8.00 |
| ☐861 | 3¢ Emerson | 7.00 | ☐890 | 2¢ Morse | 8.00 |
| ☐862 | 5¢ Alcott | 30.00 | ☐891 | 3¢ McCormick | 24.00 |
| ☐863 | 10¢ Clemens | 140.00 | ☐892 | 5¢ Howe | 82.00 |
| ☐864 | 1¢ Longfellow | 7.50 | ☐893 | 10¢ Bell | 850.00 |
| ☐865 | 2¢ Whittier | 8.50 | ☐894 | 3¢ Pony Express | 17.00 |
| ☐866 | 3¢ Lowell | 10.00 | ☐895 | 3¢ Pan American | 17.00 |
| ☐867 | 5¢ Whitman | 38.00 | ☐896 | 3¢ Idaho | 11.00 |
| ☐868 | 10¢ Riley | 170.00 | ☐897 | 3¢ Wyoming | 10.00 |
| ☐869 | 1¢ Mann | 7.00 | ☐898 | 3¢ Coronado | 10.00 |
| ☐870 | 2¢ Hopkins | 7.75 | ☐899 | 1¢ Defense | 7.00 |
| ☐871 | 3¢ Elliot | 15.00 | ☐900 | 2¢ Defense | 9.00 |
| ☐872 | 5¢ Willard | 43.00 | ☐901 | 3¢ Defense | 11.00 |
| ☐873 | 10¢ B.T. Washington 170.00 | | ☐902 | 3¢ Emancipation | 14.00 |

| Scott No. | Fine Unused Each | Ave. Unused Each | Fine Used Each | Ave. Used Each |
|---|---|---|---|---|

## OFFICIAL STAMPS
## 1873. CONTINENTAL PRINTING (N-H ADD 70%)

| | | | | | |
|---|---|---|---|---|---|
| ☐01 | 1¢ Agricultural Department | | | | |
| | | 75.00 | 40.00 | 50.00 | 28.00 |
| ☐02 | 2¢ | 62.00 | 30.00 | 20.00 | 13.00 |

| Scott No. | | Fine Unused Each | Ave. Unused Each | Fine Used Each | Ave. Used Each |
|---|---|---|---|---|---|
| ☐ O3 | 3¢ | 55.00 | 32.00 | 4.10 | 2.70 |
| ☐ O4 | 4¢ | 68.00 | 36.00 | 14.00 | 8.00 |
| ☐ O5 | 10¢ | 120.00 | 65.00 | 55.00 | 36.00 |
| ☐ O6 | 12¢ | 180.00 | 100.00 | 80.00 | 50.00 |
| ☐ O7 | 15¢ | 115.00 | 60.00 | 48.00 | 28.00 |
| ☐ O8 | 24¢ | 136.00 | 70.00 | 60.00 | 35.00 |
| ☐ O9 | 30¢ | 190.00 | 90.00 | 90.00 | 52.00 |
| ☐ O10 | 1¢ Executive Department | | | | |
| | | 280.00 | 150.00 | 90.00 | 51.00 |
| ☐ O11 | 2¢ | 180.00 | 95.00 | 75.00 | 42.00 |
| ☐ O12 | 3¢ | 220.00 | 120.00 | 60.00 | 36.00 |
| ☐ O13 | 6¢ | 340.00 | 185.00 | 210.00 | 130.00 |
| ☐ O14 | 10¢ | 300.00 | 160.00 | 170.00 | 100.00 |
| ☐ O15 | 1¢ Interior Department | | | | |
| | | 18.00 | 10.00 | 4.50 | 2.10 |
| ☐ O16 | 2¢ | 18.00 | 10.00 | 2.40 | 1.30 |
| ☐ O17 | 3¢ | 24.00 | 14.00 | 3.00 | 1.25 |
| ☐ O18 | 6¢ | 18.50 | 10.00 | 3.00 | 1.30 |
| ☐ O19 | 10¢ | 20.00 | 10.00 | 7.00 | 3.40 |
| ☐ O20 | 12¢ | 30.00 | 17.00 | 5.00 | 2.50 |
| ☐ O21 | 15¢ | 45.00 | 24.00 | 11.00 | 6.00 |
| ☐ O22 | 24¢ | 36.00 | 19.00 | 8.00 | 4.50 |
| ☐ O23 | 30¢ | 45.00 | 24.00 | 9.00 | 6.00 |
| ☐ O24 | 90¢ | 86.00 | 50.00 | 17.00 | 10.00 |
| ☐ O25 | 1¢ Justice Department | | | | |
| | | 55.00 | 28.00 | 21.00 | 12.00 |
| ☐ O26 | 2¢ | 80.00 | 45.00 | 25.00 | 13.00 |
| ☐ O27 | 3¢ | 78.00 | 43.00 | 9.00 | 6.00 |
| ☐ O28 | 6¢ | 75.00 | 40.00 | 13.00 | 7.00 |
| ☐ O29 | 10¢ | 90.00 | 46.00 | 27.00 | 15.00 |
| ☐ O30 | 12¢ | 62.00 | 35.00 | 16.00 | 9.00 |
| ☐ O31 | 15¢ | 140.00 | 70.00 | 50.00 | 26.00 |
| ☐ O32 | 24¢ | 380.00 | 200.00 | 130.00 | 72.00 |
| ☐ O33 | 30¢ | 360.00 | 180.00 | 90.00 | 48.00 |
| ☐ O34 | 90¢ | 475.00 | 260.00 | 180.00 | 105.00 |
| ☐ O35 | 1¢ Navy Department | | | | |
| | | 38.00 | 20.00 | 11.00 | 7.00 |
| ☐ O36 | 2¢ | 32.00 | 18.00 | 10.00 | 6.00 |
| ☐ O37 | 3¢ | 32.00 | 17.00 | 4.50 | 2.50 |

| Scott No. | | Fine Unused Each | Ave. Unused Each | Fine Used Each | Ave. Used Each |
|---|---|---|---|---|---|
| ☐O38 | 6¢ | 32.00 | 18.00 | 7.00 | 4.00 |
| ☐O39 | 7¢ | 190.00 | 100.00 | 70.00 | 40.00 |
| ☐O40 | 10¢ | 42.00 | 24.00 | 14.00 | 8.00 |
| ☐O41 | 12¢ | 54.00 | 30.00 | 11.00 | 7.00 |
| ☐O42 | 15¢ | 85.00 | 45.00 | 29.00 | 16.00 |
| ☐O43 | 24¢ | 85.00 | 45.00 | 34.00 | 20.00 |
| ☐O44 | 30¢ | 76.00 | 40.00 | 16.00 | 10.00 |
| ☐O45 | 90¢ | 335.00 | 170.00 | 90.00 | 55.00 |
| ☐O47 | 1¢ Post Office Department | | | | |
| | | 8.00 | 4.50 | 4.00 | 1.90 |
| ☐O48 | 2¢ | 9.00 | 5.00 | 3.00 | 1.70 |
| ☐O49 | 3¢ | 2.50 | 1.15 | .95 | .60 |
| ☐O50 | 6¢ | 8.00 | 4.00 | 2.00 | 1.25 |
| ☐O51 | 10¢ | 36.00 | 20.00 | 19.00 | 11.00 |
| ☐O52 | 12¢ | 21.00 | 12.00 | 5.00 | 3.00 |
| ☐O53 | 15¢ | 32.00 | 13.00 | 11.00 | 5.00 |
| ☐O54 | 24¢ | 32.00 | 17.00 | 11.00 | 7.00 |
| ☐O55 | 30¢ | 32.00 | 18.00 | 10.00 | 6.00 |
| ☐O56 | 90¢ | 49.00 | 26.00 | 14.00 | 8.00 |
| ☐O57 | 1¢ State Department | | | | |
| | | 60.00 | 29.00 | 14.00 | 8.00 |
| ☐O58 | 2¢ | 105.00 | 60.00 | 30.00 | 18.00 |
| ☐O59 | 3¢ | 40.00 | 22.00 | 10.00 | 6.00 |
| ☐O60 | 6¢ | 38.00 | 21.00 | 10.00 | 6.00 |
| ☐O61 | 7¢ | 76.00 | 40.00 | 20.00 | 12.00 |
| ☐O62 | 10¢ | 70.00 | 36.00 | 18.00 | 10.00 |
| ☐O63 | 12¢ | 90.00 | 49.00 | 27.00 | 18.00 |
| ☐O64 | 15¢ | 90.00 | 48.00 | 20.00 | 13.00 |
| ☐O65 | 24¢ | 185.00 | 100.00 | 75.00 | 40.00 |
| ☐O66 | 30¢ | 190.00 | 90.00 | 50.00 | 32.00 |
| ☐O67 | 90¢ | 360.00 | 200.00 | 125.00 | 65.00 |
| ☐O68 | $2 | 525.00 | 290.00 | 240.00 | 150.00 |
| ☐O72 | 1¢ Treasury Department | | | | |
| | | 18.00 | 10.00 | 2.10 | 1.15 |
| ☐O73 | 2¢ | 21.00 | 12.00 | 2.10 | 1.15 |
| ☐O74 | 3¢ | 13.00 | 8.00 | 1.50 | .72 |
| ☐O75 | 6¢ | 19.00 | 11.00 | 1.50 | .72 |
| ☐O76 | 7¢ | 46.00 | 24.00 | 13.00 | 7.50 |
| ☐O77 | 10¢ | 52.00 | 26.00 | 5.00 | 3.40 |

| Scott No. | | Fine Unused Each | Ave. Unused Each | Fine Used Each | Ave. Used Each |
|---|---|---|---|---|---|
| ☐078 12¢ | | 53.00 | 27.00 | 4.00 | 2.00 |
| ☐079 15¢ | | 41.00 | 23.00 | 5.00 | 3.00 |
| ☐080 24¢ | | 210.00 | 105.00 | 48.00 | 26.00 |
| ☐081 30¢ | | 74.00 | 36.00 | 6.00 | 3.10 |
| ☐082 90¢ | | 78.00 | 40.00 | 6.00 | 3.10 |
| ☐083 1¢ | War Department | 70.00 | 36.00 | 4.80 | 2.80 |
| ☐084 2¢ | | 62.00 | 32.00 | 7.00 | 3.20 |
| ☐085 3¢ | | 56.00 | 30.00 | 2.00 | 1.00 |
| ☐086 6¢ | | 240.00 | 125.00 | 4.50 | 2.40 |
| ☐087 7¢ | | 58.00 | 30.00 | 32.00 | 20.00 |
| ☐088 10¢ | | 21.00 | 12.00 | 4.00 | 3.00 |
| ☐089 12¢ | | 62.00 | 34.00 | 5.00 | 2.60 |
| ☐090 15¢ | | 19.00 | 10.00 | 3.00 | 2.00 |
| ☐091 24¢ | | 19.00 | 10.00 | 4.00 | 2.00 |
| ☐092 30¢ | | 21.00 | 12.00 | 4.00 | 1.80 |
| ☐093 90¢ | | 45.00 | 24.00 | 13.00 | 8.00 |

## 1879. AMERICAN PRINTING—SOFT POROUS PAPER (N-H ADD 80%)

| Scott No. | | Fine Unused Each | Ave. Unused Each | Fine Used Each | Ave. Used Each |
|---|---|---|---|---|---|
| ☐094 1¢ | Agricultural Department | | | | |
| | | 1300.00 | 750.00 | — | — |
| ☐095 3¢ | | 185.00 | 100.00 | 35.00 | 21.00 |
| ☐096 1¢ | Interior Department | | | | |
| | | 132.00 | 70.00 | 65.00 | 36.00 |
| ☐097 2¢ | | 2.60 | 1.25 | 1.00 | .52 |
| ☐098 3¢ | | 2.00 | 1.00 | .90 | .45 |
| ☐099 6¢ | | 3.00 | 1.40 | 1.15 | .60 |
| ☐0100 10¢ | | 32.00 | 18.00 | 20.00 | 13.00 |
| ☐0101 12¢ | | 70.00 | 36.00 | 34.00 | 22.00 |
| ☐0102 15¢ | | 150.00 | 90.00 | 72.00 | 41.00 |
| ☐0103 24¢ | | 1200.00 | 700.00 | — | — |
| ☐0106 3¢ | Justice Department | | | | |
| | | 50.00 | 26.00 | 21.00 | 12.00 |
| ☐0107 6¢ | | 105.00 | 60.00 | 70.00 | 38.00 |
| ☐0108 3¢ | Post Office Department | | | | |
| | | 9.00 | 5.00 | 1.50 | 1.00 |
| ☐0109 3¢ | Treasury Department | | | | |
| | | 26.00 | 14.00 | 4.10 | 2.10 |
| ☐0110 6¢ | | 51.00 | 26.00 | 18.00 | 10.00 |

| Scott No. | Fine Unused Each | Ave. Unused Each | Fine Used Each | Ave. Used Each |
|---|---|---|---|---|
| ☐O111 10¢ | 65.00 | 34.00 | 15.00 | 9.00 |
| ☐O112 30¢ | 710.00 | 380.00 | 140.00 | 75.00 |
| ☐O113 90¢ | 735.00 | 400.00 | 140.00 | 76.00 |
| ☐O114  1¢ War Department | 2.40 | 1.15 | 1.00 | .60 |
| ☐O115  2¢ | 3.50 | 1.80 | 1.15 | .60 |
| ☐O116  3¢ | 3.00 | 1.50 | .80 | .50 |
| ☐O117  6¢ | 3.10 | 1.70 | .85 | .50 |
| ☐O118 10¢ | 21.00 | 11.00 | 10.00 | 6.00 |
| ☐O119 12¢ | 17.00 | 9.00 | 3.10 | 2.00 |
| ☐O120 30¢ | 48.00 | 24.00 | 26.00 | 16.00 |

## 1910–1911. POSTAL SAVINGS STAMPS (N-H ADD 70%)

| Scott No. | Fine Unused Each | Ave. Unused Each | Fine Used Each | Ave. Used Each |
|---|---|---|---|---|
| ☐O121 2¢  Black, D.L. Wmk | 10.00 | 5.00 | 1.30 | .86 |
| ☐O122 50¢ Dark Green, D.L. Wmk | 105.00 | 60.00 | 32.00 | 18.00 |
| ☐O123 $1 Ultramarine, D.L. Wmk | 100.00 | 55.00 | 10.00 | 6.00 |
| ☐O124 1¢  Dark Violet, S.L. Wmk | 4.00 | 3.00 | 1.40 | .80 |
| ☐O125 2¢  Black, S.L. Wmk | 30.00 | 16.00 | 4.00 | 2.60 |
| ☐O126 10¢ Carmine, S.L. Wmk | 9.00 | 5.00 | 1.25 | .75 |

| Scott No. | Fine Unused Block | Ave. Unused Block | Fine Unused Each | Ave. Unused Each | Fine Used Each | Ave. Used Each |
|---|---|---|---|---|---|---|

## 1912. PARCEL POST DUE STAMPS (N-H ADD 45%)

| Scott No. | Fine Unused Block | Ave. Unused Block | Fine Unused Each | Ave. Unused Each | Fine Used Each | Ave. Used Each |
|---|---|---|---|---|---|---|
| ☐JQ1 1¢  Dark Green | 275.00 | 200.00 | 7.50 | 6.00 | 4.00 | 2.50 |
| ☐JQ2 2¢  Dark Green | 400.00 | 275.00 | 60.00 | 45.00 | 14.00 | 9.00 |
| ☐JQ3 5¢  Dark Green | 100.00 | 60.00 | 9.00 | 7.00 | 4.00 | 3.00 |
| ☐JQ4 10¢ Dark Green | 1100.00 | 850.00 | 140.00 | 100.00 | 38.00 | 24.00 |
| ☐JQ5 25¢ Dark Green | 510.00 | 375.00 | 80.00 | 41.00 | 4.50 | 2.50 |

| Scott No. | Fine Unused Block | Ave. Unused Block | Fine Unused Each | Ave. Unused Each | Fine Used Each | Ave. Used Each |
|---|---|---|---|---|---|---|

## 1912–1913. PARCEL POST STAMPS (N-H ADD 45%)

| Scott No. | | Fine Unused Block | Ave. Unused Block | Fine Unused Each | Ave. Unused Each | Fine Used Each | Ave. Used Each |
|---|---|---|---|---|---|---|---|
| ☐Q1 | 1¢ P.O. Clerk | 50.00 | 40.00 | 3.50 | 2.40 | 1.30 | .80 |
| ☐Q2 | 2¢ City Carrier | 65.00 | 45.00 | 4.00 | 3.00 | 1.00 | .70 |
| ☐Q3 | 3¢ Railway Clerk | 100.00 | 80.00 | 7.00 | 5.00 | 4.50 | 3.40 |
| ☐Q4 | 4¢ Rural Carrier | 500.00 | 350.00 | 18.00 | 14.00 | 2.60 | 1.80 |
| ☐Q5 | 5¢ Mail Train | 500.00 | 360.00 | 18.00 | 13.00 | 1.90 | 1.25 |
| ☐Q6 | 10¢ Steamship | 300.00 | 170.00 | 30.00 | 21.00 | 2.30 | 1.60 |
| ☐Q7 | 15¢ Mail Truck | 360.00 | 225.00 | 42.00 | 28.00 | 9.00 | 6.00 |
| ☐Q8 | 20¢ Airplane | 410.00 | 360.00 | 91.00 | 60.00 | 18.00 | 12.00 |
| ☐Q9 | 25¢ Manufacturing | 390.00 | 300.00 | 45.00 | 30.00 | 6.50 | 4.50 |
| ☐Q10 | 50¢ Dairying | 1400.00 | 1100.00 | 180.00 | 140.00 | 32.00 | 25.00 |
| ☐Q11 | 75¢ Harvesting | 525.00 | 380.00 | 60.00 | 40.00 | 24.00 | 18.00 |
| ☐Q12 | $1 Fruit Growing | 1600.00 | 1100.00 | 290.00 | 180.00 | 20.00 | 14.00 |

## 1925–1929 SPECIAL HANDLING STAMPS (N-H ADD 35%)

| Scott No. | | Fine Unused Block | Ave. Unused Block | Fine Unused Each | Ave. Unused Each | Fine Used Each | Ave. Used Each |
|---|---|---|---|---|---|---|---|
| ☐QE1 | 10¢ Yellow Green | 25.00 | 16.00 | 1.75 | 1.00 | 1.00 | .70 |
| ☐QE2 | 15¢ Yellow Green | 30.00 | 24.00 | 1.50 | 1.00 | .90 | .70 |
| ☐QE3 | 20¢ Yellow Green | 42.00 | 24.00 | 1.95 | 2.00 | 2.00 | 1.10 |
| ☐QE4 | 25¢ Yellow Green | 250.00 | 160.00 | 17.00 | 13.00 | 8.50 | 4.50 |
| ☐QE4A | 25¢ Deep Green | 310.00 | 180.00 | 23.00 | 16.00 | 5.00 | 3.50 |

| Scott No. | Fine Unused Block | Ave. Unused Block | Fine Unused Each | Ave. Unused Each | Fine Used Each | Ave. Used Each |
|---|---|---|---|---|---|---|

## 1919–1922 U.S. OFFICES IN CHINA ISSUES (N-H ADD 60%) SHANGHAI 2¢ CHINA

| Scott No. | | Fine Unused Block | Ave. Unused Block | Fine Unused Each | Ave. Unused Each | Fine Used Each | Ave. Used Each |
|---|---|---|---|---|---|---|---|
| ☐K1 | 2¢ on 1¢ | 100.00 | 75.00 | 26.00 | 12.00 | 21.00 | 12.50 |
| ☐K2 | 4¢ on 2¢ | 100.00 | 75.00 | 26.00 | 12.00 | 21.00 | 12.50 |
| ☐K3 | 6¢ on 3¢ | 210.00 | 140.00 | 35.00 | 23.00 | 46.00 | 26.00 |
| ☐K4 | 8¢ on 4¢ | 225.00 | 170.00 | 40.00 | 24.00 | 46.00 | 27.00 |
| ☐K5 | 10¢ on 2¢ | 300.00 | 210.00 | 46.00 | 30.00 | 52.00 | 32.00 |
| ☐K6 | 12¢ on 6¢ | 275.00 | 200.00 | 56.00 | 36.00 | 68.00 | 42.00 |
| ☐K7 | 14¢ on 7¢ | 300.00 | 210.00 | 58.00 | 36.00 | 80.00 | 45.00 |
| ☐K8 | 16¢ on 8¢ Olive Bistre | 285.00 | 210.00 | 45.00 | 28.00 | 54.00 | 32.00 |
| ☐K8a | 16¢ on 8¢ Olive Green | 290.00 | 200.00 | 44.00 | 28.00 | 46.00 | 30.00 |
| ☐K9 | 18¢ on 9¢ | 290.00 | 190.00 | 45.00 | 30.00 | 58.00 | 36.00 |
| ☐K10 | 20¢ on 10¢ | 290.00 | 200.00 | 44.00 | 28.00 | 52.00 | 32.00 |
| ☐K11 | 24¢ on 12¢ Br. Car. | 290.00 | 190.00 | 48.00 | 32.00 | 60.00 | 36.00 |
| ☐K11a | 24¢ on 12¢ Cl. Br. | 310.00 | 250.00 | 70.00 | 44.00 | 76.00 | 50.00 |
| ☐K12 | 30¢ on 15¢ | 315.00 | 225.00 | 58.00 | 38.00 | 75.00 | 45.00 |
| ☐K13 | 40¢ on 20¢ | 400.00 | 300.00 | 85.00 | 55.00 | 110.00 | 70.00 |
| ☐K14 | 60¢ on 30¢ | 400.00 | 300.00 | 80.00 | 50.00 | 100.00 | 68.00 |
| ☐K15 | $1 on 50¢ | 2500.00 | 1500.00 | 400.00 | 280.00 | 425.00 | 280.00 |
| ☐K16 | $2 on $1 | 1900.00 | 1350.00 | 320.00 | 250.00 | 350.00 | 265.00 |

| Scott No. | Fine Unused Block | Ave. Unused Block | Fine Unused Each | Ave. Unused Each | Fine Used Each | Ave. Used Each |
|---|---|---|---|---|---|---|
| ☐K17 2¢ on 1¢ Loc. Sur | | | | | | |
| | 370.00 | 300.00 | 85.00 | 44.00 | 72.00 | 45.00 |
| ☐K18 4¢ on 2¢ Loc. Sur | | | | | | |
| | 350.00 | 250.00 | 70.00 | 46.00 | 65.00 | 47.00 |

| Scott No. | Imperforated (a) Fine | Ave. | Part Perforated (b) Fine | Ave. | Perforated (c) Fine | Ave. |
|---|---|---|---|---|---|---|
| **1862–1971. U.S. REVENUE STAMPS** | | | | | | |
| ☐R1 1¢ Express | | | | | | |
| | 51.00 | 28.00 | 34.00 | 18.50 | 1.00 | .58 |
| ☐R2 1¢ Play Cards | | | | | | |
| | 750.00 | 410.00 | 390.00 | 240.00 | 91.00 | 48.00 |
| ☐R3 1¢ Proprietary | | | | | | |
| | 500.00 | 265.00 | 95.00 | 52.00 | .38 | .26 |
| ☐R4 1¢ Telegraph | | | | | | |
| | 300.00 | 165.00 | — | — | 7.60 | 4.00 |
| ☐R5 2¢ Bank Ck., Blue | | | | | | |
| | .80 | .48 | 1.00 | .62 | .21 | .16 |
| ☐R6 2¢ Bank Ck., Orange | | | | | | |
| | — | — | 70.00 | 40.00 | .21 | .16 |
| ☐R7 2¢ Certif., Blue | | | | | | |
| | 10.50 | 6.00 | — | — | 28.00 | 12.00 |
| ☐R8 2¢ Certif., Orange | | | | | | |
| | — | — | — | — | 25.00 | 12.50 |
| ☐R9 2¢ Express, Blue | | | | | | |
| | 10.00 | 5.00 | 14.00 | 7.50 | .31 | .16 |
| ☐R10 2¢ Express, Orange | | | | | | |
| | — | — | — | — | 6.00 | 3.10 |
| ☐R11 2¢ Ply. Cds., Blue | | | | | | |
| | — | — | 100.00 | 60.00 | 2.65 | 1.50 |
| ☐R12 2¢ Ply. Cds., Orange | | | | | | |
| | — | — | — | — | 23.00 | 13.00 |
| ☐R13 2¢ Proprietary, Blue | | | | | | |
| | — | — | 90.00 | 50.00 | .32 | .21 |
| ☐R14 2¢ Proprietary, Orange | | | | | | |
| | — | — | — | — | 32.00 | 17.00 |

*No hinge pricing from 1941 to date is figured at (N-H ADD 15%)

| Scott No. | | Imperforated (a) Fine | Ave. | Part Perforated (b) Fine | Ave. | Perforated (c) Fine | Ave. |
|---|---|---|---|---|---|---|---|
| □R15 | 2¢ U.S.I.R. | — | — | — | — | .20 | .15 |
| □R16 | 3¢ Foreign Ex. | — | — | 140.00 | 81.00 | 2.25 | 1.00 |
| □R17 | 3¢ Playing Cds. | — | — | — | — | 96.00 | 50.00 |
| □R18 | 3¢ Proprietary | — | — | 170.00 | 100.00 | 1.80 | .90 |
| □R19 | 3¢ Telegraph | 40.00 | 21.00 | 13.00 | 7.50 | 2.80 | 1.25 |
| □R20 | 4¢ Inland Exch. | — | — | — | — | 1.60 | .90 |
| □R21 | 4¢ Playing Cards | — | — | — | — | 350.00 | 180.00 |
| □R22 | 4¢ Proprietary | — | — | 175.00 | 100.00 | 3.00 | 2.00 |
| □R23 | 5¢ Agreement | — | — | — | — | .31 | .16 |
| □R24 | 5¢ Certificate | 2.40 | 1.30 | 9.00 | 5.00 | .21 | .16 |
| □R25 | 5¢ Express | 3.70 | 2.10 | 4.50 | 3.00 | .34 | .20 |
| □R26 | 5¢ Foreign Ex. | — | — | — | — | .34 | .21 |
| □R27 | 5¢ Inland Exch. | 3.50 | 2.10 | 3.50 | 2.10 | .26 | .16 |
| □R28 | 5¢ Playing Cds. | — | — | — | — | 16.00 | 9.00 |
| □R29 | 5¢ Proprietary | — | — | — | — | 18.00 | 8.00 |
| □R30 | 6¢ Inland Exch. | — | — | — | — | 1.10 | .60 |
| □R32 | 10¢ Bill of Ldg. | 45.00 | 23.00 | 140.00 | 74.00 | .80 | .41 |
| □R33 | 10¢ Certificate | 80.00 | 42.00 | 110.00 | 61.00 | .31 | .18 |
| □R34 | 10¢ Contract Bill | — | — | 95.00 | 52.00 | .32 | .18 |
| □R35 | 10¢ For Ex. Bill | — | — | — | — | 5.00 | 3.00 |

*No hinge pricing from 1941 to date is figured at (N-H ADD 15%)

| Scott No. | Imperforated (a) Fine | Ave. | Part Perforated (b) Fine | Ave. | Perforated (c) Fine | Ave. |
|---|---|---|---|---|---|---|
| ☐R36 10¢ Inland Exch. | | | | | | |
| | 115.00 | 62.00 | 2.90 | 1.90 | .24 | .16 |
| ☐R37 10¢ Power of Aty. | | | | | | |
| | 300.00 | 160.00 | 18.00 | 10.00 | .38 | .22 |
| ☐R38 10¢ Proprietary | | | | | | |
| | — | — | — | — | 13.00 | 6.50 |
| ☐R39 15¢ Foreign Exch. | | | | | | |
| | — | — | — | — | 12.00 | 6.00 |
| ☐R40 15¢ Inland Exch. | | | | | | |
| | 24.00 | 13.00 | 10.00 | 6.10 | 1.00 | .60 |
| ☐R41 20¢ Foreign Exch. | | | | | | |
| | 41.00 | 23.00 | — | — | 30.00 | 14.50 |
| ☐R42 20¢ Inland Exch. | | | | | | |
| | 13.00 | 7.00 | 16.00 | 9.00 | .41 | .24 |
| ☐R43 25¢ Bond | | | | | | |
| | 94.00 | 50.00 | 6.00 | 3.40 | 1.70 | 1.00 |
| ☐R44 25¢ Certificate | | | | | | |
| | 6.00 | 3.10 | 6.00 | 3.00 | .20 | .16 |
| ☐R45 25¢ Entry of Gds. | | | | | | |
| | 16.00 | 9.00 | 32.00 | 19.00 | .60 | .28 |
| ☐R46 25¢ Insurance | | | | | | |
| | 9.00 | 5.50 | 10.00 | 6.00 | .28 | .16 |
| ☐R47 25¢ Life Insr. | | | | | | |
| | 30.00 | 18.00 | 95.00 | 54.00 | 5.50 | 3.50 |
| ☐R48 25¢ Power of Atty. | | | | | | |
| | 5.00 | 3.50 | 15.00 | 10.00 | .28 | .16 |
| ☐R49 25¢ Protest | | | | | | |
| | 21.00 | 11.00 | 140.00 | 72.00 | 6.00 | 3.00 |
| ☐R50 25¢ Warehouse Rct. | | | | | | |
| | 35.00 | 20.00 | 130.00 | 75.00 | 20.00 | 10.00 |
| ☐R51 30¢ Foreign Exch. | | | | | | |
| | 55.00 | 25.00 | 410.00 | 250.00 | 36.00 | 16.00 |
| ☐R52 30¢ Inland Exch. | | | | | | |
| | 38.00 | 20.00 | 40.00 | 21.00 | 2.50 | 1.30 |
| ☐R53 40¢ Inland Exch. | | | | | | |
| | 410.00 | 240.00 | 4.00 | 2.40 | 2.40 | 1.30 |
| ☐R54 50¢ Convey, Blue | | | | | | |
| | 10.00 | 6.00 | 1.10 | .75 | .21 | .16 |
| ☐R55 50¢ Entry of Gds. | | | | | | |
| | — | — | 10.00 | 5.80 | .31 | .16 |

*No hinge pricing from 1941 to date is figured at (N-H ADD 15%)

| Scott No. | Imperforated (a) | | Part Perforated (b) | | Perforated (c) | |
|---|---|---|---|---|---|---|
| | Fine | Ave. | Fine | Ave. | Fine | Ave. |
| ☐R56 50¢ Foreign Exch. | | | | | | |
| | 35.00 | 20.00 | 30.00 | 17.00 | 4.00 | 2.10 |
| ☐R57 50¢ Lease | | | | | | |
| | 21.00 | 12.00 | 50.00 | 30.00 | 5.00 | 2.65 |
| ☐R58 50¢ Life Insur. | | | | | | |
| | 26.00 | 15.00 | 51.00 | 28.00 | .80 | .45 |
| ☐R59 50¢ Mortgage | | | | | | |
| | 9.00 | 5.00 | 1.50 | 1.00 | .42 | .26 |
| ☐R60 50¢ Orig. Process | | | | | | |
| | 2.40 | 1.50 | — | — | .36 | .21 |
| ☐R61 50¢ Passage Tkt. | | | | | | |
| | 65.00 | 34.00 | 105.00 | 52.00 | .54 | .30 |
| ☐R62 50¢ Prob. of Will | | | | | | |
| | 30.00 | 17.00 | 41.00 | 24.00 | 16.00 | 8.75 |
| ☐R63 50¢ Sty. Bond, Bl. | | | | | | |
| | 105.00 | 59.00 | 2.75 | 1.40 | .31 | .16 |
| ☐R64 60¢ Inland Exch. | | | | | | |
| | 76.00 | 42.00 | 43.00 | 24.00 | 4.85 | 2.85 |
| ☐R65 70¢ Foreign Exch. | | | | | | |
| | 300.00 | 160.00 | 80.00 | 45.00 | 5.00 | 2.75 |
| ☐R66 $1 Conveyance | | | | | | |
| | 10.00 | 6.00 | 240.00 | 136.00 | 2.40 | 1.15 |
| ☐R67 $1 Entry of Gds. | | | | | | |
| | 24.00 | 13.00 | — | — | 1.50 | .85 |
| ☐R68 $1 Foreign Exch. | | | | | | |
| | 48.00 | 26.00 | — | — | .70 | .40 |
| ☐R69 $1 Inland Exch. | | | | | | |
| | 10.00 | 6.00 | 210.00 | 110.00 | .52 | .30 |
| ☐R70 $1 Lease | | | | | | |
| | 31.00 | 17.00 | — | — | 1.35 | .80 |
| ☐R71 $1 Life Insur. | | | | | | |
| | 135.00 | 76.00 | — | — | 4.60 | 2.40 |
| ☐R72 $1 Manifest | | | | | | |
| | 45.00 | 25.00 | — | — | 20.00 | 11.50 |
| ☐R73 $1 Mortgage | | | | | | |
| | 15.50 | 9.00 | — | — | 121.00 | 65.00 |
| ☐R74 $1 Passage Tkt. | | | | | | |
| | 148.00 | 87.00 | — | — | 135.00 | 66.00 |

*No hinge pricing from 1941 to date is figured at (N-H ADD 15%)

| Scott No. | Imperforated (a) Fine | Ave. | Part Perforated (b) Fine | Ave. | Perforated (c) Fine | Ave. |
|---|---|---|---|---|---|---|
| ☐R75 $1 Power of Atty. | 56.00 | 30.00 | — | — | 1.75 | .95 |
| ☐R76 $1 Prob. of Will | 53.00 | 29.00 | — | — | 32.00 | 17.50 |
| ☐R77 $1.30 Foreign Exch. | 1300.00 | 1000.00 | — | — | 43.00 | 24.00 |
| ☐R78 $1.50 Finland Exch. | 20.00 | 11.00 | — | — | 3.00 | 1.50 |
| ☐R79 $1.60 Foreign Exch. | 600.00 | 325.00 | — | — | 85.00 | 45.00 |
| ☐R80 $1.90 Foreign Exch. | 1800.00 | 1100.00 | — | — | 56.00 | 29.00 |
| ☐R81 $2 Conveyance | 85.00 | 50.00 | 700.00 | 400.00 | 2.00 | .95 |
| ☐R82 $2 Mortgage | 74.00 | 41.00 | — | — | 2.40 | 1.35 |
| ☐R83 $2 Prob. of Will | 1800.00 | 1300.00 | — | — | 40.00 | 21.00 |
| ☐R84 $2.50 Inland Exch. | 940.00 | 500.00 | — | — | 3.00 | 1.60 |
| ☐R85 $3 Chart. Pty. | 90.00 | 50.00 | — | — | 3.75 | 1.95 |
| ☐R86 $3 Manifest | 85.00 | 48.00 | — | — | 20.00 | 11.00 |
| ☐R87 $3.50 Inland Exch. | 1000.00 | 700.00 | — | — | 43.00 | 24.00 |
| ☐R88 $5 Chtr. Party | 200.00 | 115.00 | — | — | 4.50 | 2.65 |
| ☐R89 $5 Conveyance | 30.00 | 16.00 | — | — | 4.50 | 2.65 |
| ☐R90 $5 Manifest | 80.00 | 43.00 | — | — | 80.00 | 45.00 |
| ☐R91 $5 Mortgage | 78.00 | 45.00 | — | — | 16.00 | 9.00 |
| ☐R92 $5 Prob. of Will | 365.00 | 200.00 | — | — | 16.00 | 9.00 |
| ☐R93 $10 Chrt. Party | 400.00 | 215.00 | — | — | 20.00 | 10.00 |
| ☐R94 $10 Conveyance | 72.00 | 42.00 | — | — | 52.00 | 30.00 |

*No hinge pricing from 1941 to date is figured at (N-H ADD 15%)

| Scott No. | Imperforated (a) Fine | Ave. | Part Perforated (b) Fine | Ave. | Perforated (c) Fine | Ave. |
|---|---|---|---|---|---|---|
| ☐R95 $10 Mortgage | | | | | | |
| | 300.00 | 160.00 | — | — | 20.00 | 11.00 |
| ☐R96 $10 Prob. of Will | | | | | | |
| | 900.00 | 500.00 | — | — | 20.00 | 11.00 |
| ☐R97 $15 Mortgage | | | | | | |
| | 850.00 | 460.00 | — | — | 85.00 | 48.00 |
| ☐R98 $20 Conveyance | | | | | | |
| | 56.00 | 31.00 | — | — | 30.00 | 18.00 |
| ☐R99 $20 Prob. of Will | | | | | | |
| | 810.00 | 450.00 | — | — | 775.00 | 450.00 |
| ☐R100 $25 Mortgage | | | | | | |
| | 675.00 | 380.00 | — | — | 80.00 | 45.00 |
| ☐R101 $50 U.S.I.R | | | | | | |
| | 150.00 | 90.00 | — | — | 76.00 | 43.00 |
| ☐R102 $200 U.S.I.R. | | | | | | |
| | 950.00 | 510.00 | — | — | 500.00 | 300.00 |

| Scott No. | Fine Used Each | Ave. Used Each |
|---|---|---|

## 1871. SECOND ISSUE R103 THROUGH R131 HAVE BLUE FRAMES AND A BLACK CENTER

| Scott No. | | Fine Used Each | Ave. Used Each |
|---|---|---|---|
| ☐R103 | 1¢ | 24.00 | 13.00 |
| ☐R104 | 2¢ | 1.00 | .60 |
| ☐R105 | 3¢ | 12.00 | 6.50 |
| ☐R106 | 4¢ | 40.00 | 23.00 |
| ☐R107 | 5¢ | 1.00 | .62 |
| ☐R108 | 6¢ | 65.00 | 35.00 |
| ☐R109 | 10¢ | .86 | .48 |
| ☐R110 | 15¢ | 19.00 | 10.00 |
| ☐R111 | 20¢ | 4.50 | 2.40 |
| ☐R112 | 25¢ | .65 | .36 |
| ☐R113 | 30¢ | 48.00 | 26.00 |
| ☐R114 | 40¢ | 26.00 | 16.00 |
| ☐R115 | 50¢ | .62 | .38 |
| ☐R116 | 60¢ | 57.00 | 30.00 |
| ☐R117 | 70¢ | 24.00 | 12.00 |

*No hinge pricing from 1941 to date is figured at (N-H ADD 15%)

| Scott No. | | Fine Used Each | Ave. Used Each |
|---|---|---|---|
| ☐R118 | $1 | 3.00 | 1.60 |
| ☐R119 | $1.30 | 225.00 | 120.00 |
| ☐R120 | $1.50 | 10.00 | 6.00 |
| ☐R121 | $1.60 | 265.00 | 150.00 |
| ☐R122 | $1.90 | 125.00 | 65.00 |
| ☐R123 | $2 | 10.00 | 5.50 |
| ☐R124 | $2.50 | 19.00 | 10.00 |
| ☐R125 | $3 | 30.00 | 17.00 |
| ☐R126 | $3.50 | 110.00 | 54.00 |
| ☐R127 | $5 | 16.00 | 9.00 |
| ☐R128 | $10 | 80.00 | 48.00 |
| ☐R129 | $20 | 260.00 | 140.00 |
| ☐R130 | $25 | 260.00 | 140.00 |
| ☐R131 | $50 | 280.00 | 160.00 |

## 1871-1872. THIRD ISSUE SAME DESIGNS AS SECOND ISSUE

| | | | Fine Used Each | Ave. Used Each |
|---|---|---|---|---|
| ☐R134 | 1¢ | Claret & Blk. | 22.00 | 12.00 |
| ☐R135 | 2¢ | Org. & Blk. | .21 | .16 |
| ☐R136 | 4¢ | Bm. & Blk. | 26.00 | 14.00 |
| ☐R137 | 5¢ | Org. & Blk. | .31 | .16 |
| ☐R138 | 6¢ | Rog. & Blk. | 27.00 | 15.00 |
| ☐R139 | 15¢ | Bm. & Blk. | 10.00 | 5.00 |
| ☐R140 | 30¢ | Org. & Blk. | 10.00 | 6.00 |
| ☐R141 | 40¢ | Bm. & Blk. | 21.00 | 12.00 |
| ☐R142 | 60¢ | Org. & Blk. | 45.00 | 25.00 |
| ☐R143 | 70¢ | Gm. & Blk. | 30.00 | 16.00 |
| ☐R144 | $1 | Gm. & Blk. | 1.25 | .70 |
| ☐R145 | $2 | Verm'n & Blk. | 19.00 | 10.00 |
| ☐R146 | $2.50 | Claret & Blk. | 29.00 | 15.00 |
| ☐R147 | $3 | Gm. & Blk. | 30.00 | 17.00 |
| ☐R148 | $5 | Verm'n & Blk. | 17.00 | 8.00 |
| ☐R149 | $10 | Gm. & Blk. | 64.00 | 34.00 |
| ☐R150 | $20 | Org. & Blk. | 360.00 | 210.00 |

## 1874. FOURTH ISSUE

| | | | Fine Used Each | Ave. Used Each |
|---|---|---|---|---|
| ☐R151 | 2¢ | Org. & Blk, Gm. Paper | .21 | .16 |

| Scott No. | | | Fine Used Each | Ave. Used Each |
|---|---|---|---|---|

## 1875. ISSUE

| Scott No. | | | | Fine Used Each | Ave. Used Each |
|---|---|---|---|---|---|
| ☐R152a | 2¢ | Blue, Silk Paper | | .21 | .16 |
| ☐R152b | 2¢ | Blue, Watermarked | | .21 | .16 |
| ☐R152c | 2¢ | Blue, Rouletted | | 26.00 | 13.00 |

| Scott No. | | | Fine Uncancelled Each | Ave. Uncancelled Each | Fine Used Each | Ave. Used Each |
|---|---|---|---|---|---|---|

## 1898. POSTAGE AND NEWSPAPER STAMPS SURCHARGED I.R.

| | | Fine Uncancelled Each | Ave. Uncancelled Each | Fine Used Each | Ave. Used Each |
|---|---|---|---|---|---|
| ☐R153 | 1¢ Green, Small I.R. | 1.10 | .60 | .80 | .40 |
| ☐R154 | 1¢ Green, Large I.R. | .26 | .21 | .21 | .16 |
| ☐R154a | 1¢ Green Inverted Surch | 8.00 | 4.00 | 5.00 | 2.80 |
| ☐R155 | 2¢ Carmine, Large I.R. | .25 | .21 | .60 | .31 |
| ☐R155a | 2¢ Carmine, Inverted Surch | 1.20 | .75 | .90 | .72 |
| ☐R159 | $5 Blue, Surch. down | 185.00 | 100.00 | 124.00 | 70.00 |
| ☐R160 | $5 Blue, Surch. up | 85.00 | 48.00 | 56.00 | 32.00 |

## 1898. DOCUMENTARY "BATTLESHIP" DESIGN

| | | Fine Uncancelled Each | Ave. Uncancelled Each | Fine Used Each | Ave. Used Each |
|---|---|---|---|---|---|
| ☐R161 | ½¢ Orange | 2.50 | 2.00 | 6.00 | 3.60 |
| ☐R162 | ½¢ Dark Gray | .26 | .21 | .21 | .16 |
| ☐R163 | 1¢ Pale Blue | .26 | .21 | .21 | .16 |
| ☐R164 | 2¢ Carmine | .26 | .21 | .21 | .16 |
| ☐R165 | 3¢ Dark Blue | .86 | .48 | .21 | .16 |
| ☐R166 | 4¢ Pale Rose | .38 | .26 | — | .16 |
| ☐R167 | 5¢ Lilac | .26 | .21 | .20 | .16 |
| ☐R168 | 10¢ Dark Brown | .50 | .30 | .20 | .16 |
| ☐R169 | 25¢ Purple Brown | .50 | .30 | .20 | .16 |
| ☐R170 | 40¢ Blue Lilac (cut .25) | 55.00 | 30.00 | 1.15 | .90 |
| ☐R171 | 50¢ Slate Violet | 6.00 | 3.00 | .20 | .16 |
| ☐R172 | 80¢ Bistre (cut .15) | 24.00 | 14.00 | .41 | .26 |

## 1898–1899. DOCUMENTARY STAMPS

| | | Fine Uncancelled Each | Ave. Uncancelled Each | Fine Used Each | Ave. Used Each |
|---|---|---|---|---|---|
| ☐R173 | $1 Dark Green | 4.50 | 3.10 | .20 | .16 |
| ☐R174 | $3 Dark Brown (cut .18) | 9.00 | 6.00 | .46 | .31 |

| Scott No. | Fine Un-cancelled Each | Ave. Un-cancelled Each | Fine Used Each | Ave. Used Each |
|---|---|---|---|---|
| ☐R175 $5 Orange (cut .25) | — | — | 1.00 | .60 |
| ☐R176 $10 Black (cut .75) | — | — | 2.70 | 1.60 |
| ☐R177 $30 Red (cut 25.00) | — | — | 70.00 | 42.00 |
| ☐R178 $50 Gray Brown (cut 1.50) | — | — | 3.80 | 2.65 |
| ☐R179 $100 Brown & Black (cut 12.00) | — | — | 26.00 | 14.00 |
| ☐R180 $500 Lake & Black (cut 180.00) | — | — | 420.00 | 260.00 |
| ☐R181 $100 Green & Black (cut 100.00) | — | — | 310.00 | 260.00 |

## 1900. DOCUMENTARY STAMPS

| Scott No. | Fine Un-cancelled Each | Ave. Un-cancelled Each | Fine Used Each | Ave. Used Each |
|---|---|---|---|---|
| ☐R182 $1 Carmine (cut .15) | 7.50 | 4.50 | .52 | .36 |
| ☐R183 $3 Lake (cut 8.00) | 62.00 | 40.00 | 40.00 | 23.00 |

## 1900–1902. SURCHARGED LARGE BLACK NUMERALS

| Scott No. | Fine Un-cancelled Each | Ave. Un-cancelled Each | Fine Used Each | Ave. Used Each |
|---|---|---|---|---|
| ☐R184 $1 Gray (cut .09) | 4.00 | 2.10 | .21 | .16 |
| ☐R185 $2 Gray (cut .09) | 4.00 | 2.00 | .21 | .16 |
| ☐R186 $3 Gray (cut 1.15) | 32.00 | 18.00 | 10.00 | 6.10 |
| ☐R187 $5 Gray (cut .40) | 20.00 | 12.00 | 5.00 | 3.10 |
| ☐R188 $10 Gray (cut 3.25) | 40.00 | 25.00 | 11.00 | 5.50 |
| ☐R189 $50 Gray (cut 80.00) | 540.00 | 290.00 | 310.00 | 190.00 |
| ☐R190 $1 Green (cut .35) | 8.00 | 4.00 | 2.50 | 1.60 |
| ☐R191 $2 Green (cut .30) | 7.50 | 4.00 | 1.00 | .65 |
| ☐R192 $5 Green (cut 1.60) | 46.00 | 30.00 | 17.00 | 11.00 |
| ☐R193 $10 Green (cut 27.50) | 225.00 | 130.00 | 140.00 | 75.00 |
| ☐R194 $50 Green (cut 220.00) | 940.00 | 510.00 | 600.00 | 375.00 |

## 1914. DOCUMENTARY SINGLE LINE WATERMARK

| Scott No. | Fine Un-cancelled Each | Ave. Un-cancelled Each | Fine Used Each | Ave. Used Each |
|---|---|---|---|---|
| ☐R195 ½¢ Rose | 4.60 | 2.65 | 2.40 | 1.60 |

| Scott No. | Fine Un-cancelled Each | Ave. Un-cancelled Each | Fine Used Each | Ave. Used Each |
|---|---|---|---|---|
| ☐R196 1¢ Rose | 1.15 | .62 | .21 | .16 |
| ☐R197 2¢ Rose | 1.15 | .62 | .21 | .16 |
| ☐R198 3¢ Rose | 27.00 | 15.00 | 21.00 | 11.00 |
| ☐R199 4¢ Rose | 7.00 | 4.00 | 1.00 | .50 |
| ☐R200 5¢ Rose | 2.60 | 1.25 | .21 | .16 |
| ☐R201 10¢ Rose | 2.10 | 1.15 | .21 | .16 |
| ☐R202 25¢ Rose | 14.00 | 8.00 | .50 | .31 |
| ☐R203 40¢ Rose | 9.00 | 5.00 | .60 | .36 |
| ☐R204 50¢ Rose | 3.50 | 2.00 | .21 | .16 |
| ☐R205 80¢ Rose | 40.00 | 22.00 | 6.50 | 4.00 |

## 1914. DOCUMENTARY DOUBLE LINE WATERMARK

| Scott No. | Fine Un-cancelled Each | Ave. Un-cancelled Each | Fine Used Each | Ave. Used Each |
|---|---|---|---|---|
| ☐R206 ½¢ Rose | 1.20 | .50 | .52 | .35 |
| ☐R207 1¢ Rose | .23 | .21 | .21 | .16 |
| ☐R208 2¢ Rose | .23 | .21 | .21 | .16 |
| ☐R209 3¢ Rose | 1.15 | .55 | .26 | .20 |
| ☐R210 4¢ Rose | 2.00 | 1.10 | .34 | .21 |
| ☐R211 5¢ Rose | 1.15 | .51 | .21 | .16 |
| ☐R212 10¢ Rose | .42 | .24 | .21 | .16 |
| ☐R213 25¢ Rose | 3.30 | 2.00 | .82 | .48 |
| ☐R214 40¢ Rose (cut .60) | 36.00 | 21.00 | 7.50 | 4.00 |
| ☐R215 50¢ Rose | 7.50 | 4.50 | .21 | .16 |
| ☐R216 80¢ Rose (cut 1.10) | 42.00 | 22.00 | 9.00 | 5.00 |
| ☐R217 $1 Green (cut .06) | 13.00 | 7.50 | .21 | .16 |
| ☐R218 $2 Carmine (cut .10) | 24.00 | 15.00 | .21 | .16 |
| ☐R219 $2 Carmine (cut .25) | 38.00 | 21.00 | 1.00 | .60 |
| ☐R220 $5 Blue (cut .65) | 31.00 | 17.00 | 2.00 | 1.00 |
| ☐R221 $10 Orange (cut 1.10) | | | | |
| | 70.00 | 40.00 | 4.50 | 3.00 |
| ☐R222 $30 Vermilion (cut 2.35) | | | | |
| | 130.00 | 80.00 | 9.00 | 6.00 |
| ☐R223 $50 Violet (cut 200.00) | | | | |
| | 850.00 | 450.00 | 610.00 | 335.00 |
| ☐R224 $60 Brown (cut 47.50) | | | | |
| | — | — | 105.00 | 64.00 |
| ☐R225 $100 Green (cut 14.50) | | | | |
| | — | — | 40.00 | 21.00 |

| Scott No. | Fine Un-cancelled Each | Ave. Un-cancelled Each | Fine Used Each | Ave. Used Each |
|---|---|---|---|---|
| **1917–1933. TENTH ISSUE DOCUMENTARY STAMPS—PERF. 11** | | | | |
| ☐R228 1¢ Rose | .24 | .22 | .21 | .16 |
| ☐R229 2¢ Rose | .24 | .22 | .21 | .16 |
| ☐R230 3¢ Rose | .40 | .30 | .26 | .16 |
| ☐R231 4¢ Rose | .35 | .22 | .21 | .16 |
| ☐R232 5¢ Rose | .30 | .22 | .21 | .16 |
| ☐R233 8¢ Rose | 1.25 | .70 | .21 | .16 |
| ☐R234 10¢ Rose | .26 | .21 | .21 | .16 |
| ☐R235 20¢ Rose | .90 | .50 | .21 | .16 |
| ☐R236 25¢ Rose | .90 | .50 | .21 | .16 |
| ☐R237 40¢ Rose | .90 | .50 | .21 | .16 |
| ☐R238 50¢ Rose | 1.10 | .65 | .21 | .16 |
| ☐R239 80¢ Rose | 3.00 | 1.70 | .21 | .16 |
| ☐R240 $1 Green | 4.00 | 2.50 | .22 | .16 |
| ☐R241 $2 Rose | 7.50 | 5.00 | .22 | .16 |
| ☐R242 $3 Violet (cut .15) | 22.00 | 14.00 | .55 | .30 |
| ☐R243 $4 Brown (cut .20) | 14.00 | 8.50 | 1.00 | .64 |
| ☐R244 $5 Blue (cut .13) | 9.00 | 5.00 | .26 | .16 |
| ☐R245 $10 Orange (cut .20) | 19.00 | 12.00 | .64 | .40 |
| **1917. DOCUMENTARY STAMPS—PERF. 12** | | | | |
| ☐R246 $30 Vermilion (cut .80) | 27.00 | 16.00 | 2.10 | 1.40 |
| ☐R247 $60 Brown (cut 1.00) | 38.00 | 24.00 | 7.50 | 4.00 |
| ☐R248 $100 Green (cut .45) | 23.00 | 14.00 | 1.00 | .52 |
| ☐R249 $500 Blue (cut 9.50) | — | — | 32.00 | 18.00 |
| ☐R250 $1000 Orange (cut 3.50) | 90.00 | 55.00 | 30.00 | 20.00 |
| **1928–1929. DOCUMENTARY STAMPS—PERF. 10** | | | | |
| ☐R251 1¢ Carmine Rose | 1.90 | 1.10 | .90 | .65 |
| ☐R252 2¢ Carmine Rose | .52 | .36 | .21 | .16 |
| ☐R253 4¢ Carmine Rose | 5.50 | 3.00 | 3.10 | 1.90 |
| ☐R254 5¢ Carmine Rose | 1.15 | .50 | .32 | .21 |
| ☐R255 10¢ Carmine Rose | 1.70 | .95 | .90 | .58 |
| ☐R256 20¢ Carmine Rose | 5.00 | 3.00 | 4.15 | 2.65 |
| ☐R257 $1 Green (cut 1.90) | 58.00 | 36.00 | 28.00 | 17.00 |
| ☐R258 $2 Rose | 17.00 | 8.50 | 1.60 | .95 |
| ☐R259 $10 Orange (cut 8.00) | 80.00 | 55.00 | 28.00 | 18.00 |

| Scott No. | Fine Un-cancelled Each | Ave. Un-cancelled Each | Fine Used Each | Ave. Used Each |
|---|---|---|---|---|
| **1929–1930. DOCUMENTARY STAMPS— PERF. 11 x 10** | | | | |
| ☐ R260 2¢ Carmine Rose | 2.40 | 1.50 | 2.00 | 1.00 |
| ☐ R261 5¢ Carmine Rose | 1.90 | 1.25 | 1.00 | .70 |
| ☐ R262 10¢ Carmine Rose | 7.00 | 4.00 | 6.00 | 3.75 |
| ☐ R263 20¢ Carmine Rose | 14.00 | 8.00 | 7.00 | 5.00 |

| Scott No. | Fine Used Each | Ave. Used Each | Fine Used Each | Ave. Used Each |
|---|---|---|---|---|
| | Violet Paper (a) | | Green Paper (b) | |
| **1871–1874. PROPRIETARY STAMPS—ALL USED** | | | | |
| ☐ RB1 1¢ Green & Black | 3.50 | 2.00 | 6.00 | 3.00 |
| ☐ RB2 2¢ Green & Black | 4.00 | 2.40 | 11.00 | 7.00 |
| ☐ RB3 3¢ Green & Black | 10.00 | 6.00 | 35.00 | 19.00 |
| ☐ RB4 4¢ Green & Black | 7.00 | 4.00 | 12.00 | 6.75 |
| ☐ RB5 4¢ Green & Black | 100.00 | 56.00 | 100.00 | 65.00 |
| ☐ RB6 6¢ Green & Black | 26.00 | 15.00 | 80.00 | 44.00 |
| ☐ RB7 10¢ Green & Black | 140.00 | 80.00 | 33.00 | 18.00 |
| ☐ RB8 50¢ Green & Black | 600.00 | 350.00 | 850.00 | 485.00 |

| Scott No. | Silk Paper (a) Fine | Ave. | Watermarked (b) Fine | Ave. | Rouletted (c) Fine | Ave. |
|---|---|---|---|---|---|---|
| **1875–1881. PROPRIETARY STAMPS—ALL USED** | | | | | | |
| ☐ RB11 1¢ Green | | | | | | |
| | 2.00 | 1.00 | .38 | .21 | 40.00 | 21.00 |
| ☐ RB12 2¢ Brown | | | | | | |
| | 2.10 | 1.10 | 1.10 | .75 | 50.00 | 28.00 |
| ☐ RB13 3¢ Orange | | | | | | |
| | 8.00 | 4.00 | 2.00 | 1.30 | 54.00 | 29.00 |
| ☐ RB14 4¢ Red Brown | | | | | | |
| | 4.10 | 2.25 | 3.60 | 2.10 | — | — |
| ☐ RB15 4¢ Red | | | | | | |
| | — | — | 3.60 | 2.10 | 62.00 | 40.00 |
| ☐ RB16 5¢ Black | | | | | | |
| | 92.00 | 51.00 | 70.00 | 36.00 | 480.00 | 390.00 |

| Scott | Silk Paper (a) | | Watermarked (b) | | Rouletted (c) | |
|-------|------|------|------|------|------|------|
| No. | Fine | Ave. | Fine | Ave. | Fine | Ave. |
| ☐RB17 6¢ Violet Blue | | | | | | |
| | 19.00 | 12.00 | 12.00 | 7.00 | 142.00 | 85.00 |
| ☐RB18 6¢ Violet | | | | | | |
| | — | — | 18.00 | 11.00 | 180.00 | 95.00 |
| ☐RB19 10¢ Blue | | | | | | |
| | — | — | 190.00 | 115.00 | — | — |

| Scott No. | Fine Un-cancelled Each | Ave. Un-cancelled Each | Fine Used Each | Ave. Used Each |
|-----------|------|------|------|------|

## 1898. PROPRIETARY STAMPS—BATTLESHIP

| | Fine Un-cancelled Each | Ave. Un-cancelled Each | Fine Used Each | Ave. Used Each |
|---|------|------|------|------|
| ☐RB20 1/8¢ Yellow Green | .25 | .22 | .20 | .16 |
| ☐RB21 1/4¢ Pale Green | .25 | .22 | .20 | .16 |
| ☐RB22 3/8¢ Deep Orange | .26 | .22 | .20 | .16 |
| ☐RB23 5/8¢ Deep Ultramarine | .26 | .22 | .20 | .16 |
| ☐RB24 1¢ Dark Green | .41 | .26 | .24 | .16 |
| ☐RB25 1 1/4¢ Violet | .26 | .21 | .21 | .16 |
| ☐RB26 1 7/8¢ Dull Blue | 2.50 | 1.50 | .90 | .48 |
| ☐RB27 2¢ Violet Brown | .41 | .28 | .26 | .16 |
| ☐RB28 2 1/2¢ Lake | 1.00 | .60 | .21 | .16 |
| ☐RB29 3 3/4¢ Olive Gray | 10.00 | 6.00 | 3.00 | 2.00 |
| ☐RB30 4¢ Purple | 3.25 | 2.00 | .90 | .60 |
| ☐RB31 5¢ Brown Orange | 3.75 | 2.00 | .95 | .60 |

## 1914. BLACK PROPRIETARY STAMPS—S.L. WTMK

| | Fine Un-cancelled Each | Ave. Un-cancelled Each | Fine Used Each | Ave. Used Each |
|---|------|------|------|------|
| ☐RB32 1/8¢ Black | .26 | .21 | .21 | .16 |
| ☐RB33 1/4¢ Black | 1.20 | .70 | .90 | .50 |
| ☐RB34 3/8¢ Black | .26 | .21 | .21 | .16 |
| ☐RB35 5/8¢ Black | 2.40 | 1.60 | 1.45 | .90 |
| ☐RB36 1 1/4¢ Black | 1.50 | 1.10 | .75 | .42 |
| ☐RB37 1 7/8¢ Black | 24.00 | 14.00 | 15.00 | 9.00 |
| ☐RB38 2 1/4¢ Black | 4.00 | 2.50 | 2.75 | 1.75 |
| ☐RB39 3 1/8¢ Black | 60.00 | 38.00 | 42.00 | 26.00 |
| ☐RB40 3 3/4¢ Black | 24.00 | 16.00 | 18.00 | 10.00 |
| ☐RB41 4¢ Black | 42.00 | 23.00 | 26.00 | 15.00 |
| ☐RB42 4 3/8¢ Black | 750.00 | 450.00 | — | — |
| ☐RB43 5¢ Black | 84.00 | 50.00 | 54.00 | 32.00 |

| Scott No. | Fine Un-cancelled Each | Ave. Un-cancelled Each | Fine Used Each | Ave. Used Each |
|---|---|---|---|---|
| **1914. BLACK PROPRIETARY STAMPS— D.L. WTMK.** | | | | |
| ☐ RB44 ⅛¢ Black | .26 | .21 | .20 | .16 |
| ☐ RB45 ¼¢ Black | .26 | .21 | .20 | .16 |
| ☐ RB46 ⅜¢ Black | .58 | .36 | .32 | .21 |
| ☐ RB47 ½¢ Black | 2.50 | 1.40 | 2.00 | 1.15 |
| ☐ RB48 ⅝¢ Black | .26 | .22 | .21 | .16 |
| ☐ RB49 1¢ Black | 3.15 | 1.90 | 2.40 | 1.35 |
| ☐ RB50 1¼¢ Black | .32 | .22 | .21 | .16 |
| ☐ RB51 1½¢ Black | 3.00 | 1.80 | 2.10 | 1.15 |
| ☐ RB52 1⅞¢ Black | .80 | .50 | .55 | .36 |
| ☐ RB53 2¢ Black | 4.80 | 2.90 | 3.80 | 2.00 |
| ☐ RB54 2½¢ Black | 1.20 | .75 | .95 | .60 |
| ☐ RB55 3¢ Black | 3.20 | 1.90 | 2.30 | 1.40 |
| ☐ RB56 3⅛¢ Black | 4.00 | 2.10 | 2.80 | 1.60 |
| ☐ RB57 3¾¢ Black | 9.00 | 5.00 | 6.50 | 4.00 |
| ☐ RB58 4¢ Black | .34 | .22 | .20 | .16 |
| ☐ RB59 4⅜¢ Black | 10.00 | 6.00 | 7.00 | 4.00 |
| ☐ RB60 5¢ Black | 2.40 | 1.15 | 2.00 | 1.10 |
| ☐ RB61 6¢ Black | 45.00 | 25.00 | 36.00 | 22.00 |
| ☐ RB62 8¢ Black | 12.00 | 7.00 | 10.00 | 6.00 |
| ☐ RB63 10¢ Black | 8.50 | 5.50 | 7.00 | 4.00 |
| ☐ RB64 20¢ Black | 17.00 | 10.00 | 14.00 | 8.50 |
| **1919. PROPRIETARY STAMPS** | | | | |
| ☐ RB65 1¢ Dark Blue | .26 | .21 | .16 | .14 |
| ☐ RB66 2¢ Dark Blue | .26 | .21 | .16 | .14 |
| ☐ RB67 3¢ Dark Blue | 1.00 | .60 | .50 | .35 |
| ☐ RB68 4¢ Dark Blue | 1.00 | .60 | .52 | .26 |
| ☐ RB69 5¢ Dark Blue | 1.10 | .62 | .55 | .36 |
| ☐ RB70 8¢ Dark Blue | 10.00 | 6.00 | 7.10 | 4.60 |
| ☐ RB71 10¢ Dark Blue | 2.80 | 1.75 | 1.85 | 1.15 |
| ☐ RB72 20¢ Dark Blue | 4.50 | 3.00 | 2.60 | 1.50 |
| ☐ RB73 40¢ Dark Blue | 22.00 | 14.00 | 10.00 | 5.50 |
| **1918–1934. FUTURE DELIVERY STAMPS** | | | | |
| ☐ RC1 2¢ Carmine Rose | 1.35 | .90 | .21 | .16 |
| ☐ RC2 3¢ Carmine Rose (cut 7.50) | | | | |
| | 27.00 | 16.00 | 19.00 | 12.00 |

| Scott No. | Fine Un-cancelled Each | Ave. Un-cancelled Each | Fine Used Each | Ave. Used Each |
|---|---|---|---|---|
| ☐RC3  4¢ Carmine Rose | 2.00 | 1.25 | .21 | .16 |
| ☐RC3A 5¢ Carmine Rose | — | — | 3.10 | 2.25 |
| ☐RC4 10¢ Carmine Rose | 4.75 | 2.90 | .21 | .16 |
| ☐RC5 20¢ Carmine Rose | 4.75 | 2.90 | .22 | .16 |
| ☐RC6 25¢ Carmine Rose (cut .10) | | | | |
| | 11.00 | 7.50 | .60 | .46 |
| ☐RC7 40¢ Carmine Rose (cut .10) | | | | |
| | 11.00 | 5.00 | .60 | .40 |
| ☐RC8 50¢ Carmine Rose | 3.80 | 2.40 | .38 | .16 |
| ☐RC9 80¢ Carmine Rose (cut .75) | | | | |
| | 18.00 | 12.00 | 6.00 | 4.00 |
| ☐RC10 $1 Green (cut .10) | — | — | .26 | .16 |
| ☐RC11 $2 Rose (cut .08) | — | — | .26 | .16 |
| ☐RC12 $3 Violet (cut .12) | — | — | 1.15 | .75 |
| ☐RC13 $5 Dark Blue (cut .09) | — | — | .45 | .26 |
| ☐RC14 $10 Orange (cut .20) | — | — | .60 | .40 |
| ☐RC15 $20 Olive Bistre (cut .50) | — | — | 3.70 | 2.00 |
| ☐RC16 $30 Vermilion (cut .95) | — | — | 3.40 | 1.85 |
| ☐RC17 $50 Olive Green (cut .30) | — | — | 1.00 | .60 |
| ☐RC18 $60 Brown (cut .55) | — | — | 1.85 | 1.10 |
| ☐RC19 $100 Yellow Green (cut 5.00) | | | | |
| | — | — | 25.00 | 15.00 |
| ☐RC20 $500 Blue (cut 3.00) | — | — | 9.00 | 6.00 |
| ☐RC21 $1000 Orange (cut 1.60) | — | 1.00 | 4.00 | 3.00 |
| ☐RC22  1¢ Carmine Rose Narrow Overprint | | | | |
| | .60 | .32 | .19 | .16 |
| ☐RC23 80¢ Narrow Overprint (cut .20) | | | | |
| | — | — | 1.55 | 1.10 |
| ☐RC25 $1 Serif Overprint (cut .08) | | | | |
| | 7.00 | 4.50 | .65 | .40 |
| ☐RC26 $10 Serif Overprint (cut 4.50) | | | | |
| | — | — | 12.00 | 8.00 |

## 1918–1929. STOCK TRANSFER STAMPS— PERF. 11 OR 12

| | | | | |
|---|---|---|---|---|
| ☐RD1  1¢ Carmine Rose, Perf. 11 | | | | |
| | .40 | .36 | .21 | .16 |
| ☐RD2  1¢ Carmine Rose, Perf. 11 | | | | |
| | .25 | .21 | .21 | .16 |

| Scott No. | Fine Un-cancelled Each | Ave. Un-cancelled Each | Fine Used Each | Ave. Used Each |
|---|---|---|---|---|
| ☐RD3 4¢ Carmine Rose, Perf. 11 | | | | |
| | .25 | .21 | .21 | .16 |
| ☐RD4 5¢ Carmine Rose, Perf. 11 | | | | |
| | .25 | .21 | .21 | .16 |
| ☐RD5 10¢ Carmine Rose, Perf. 11 | | | | |
| | .25 | .21 | .21 | .16 |
| ☐RD6 20¢ Carmine Rose, Perf. 11 | | | | |
| | .36 | .26 | .21 | .16 |
| ☐RD7 25¢ Carmine Rose, Perf. 12 (cut .07) | | | | |
| | .72 | .42 | .21 | .16 |
| ☐RD8 40¢ Carmine Rose, Perf. 11 | | | | |
| | .65 | .41 | .21 | .16 |
| ☐RD9 50¢ Carmine Rose, Perf. 11 | | | | |
| | .45 | .26 | .21 | .16 |
| ☐RD10 80¢ Carmine Rose, Perf. 11 (cut .07) | | | | |
| | 1.40 | .95 | .26 | .18 |
| ☐RD11 $1 Green, perf. 11, Red Ovpt. (cut .40) | | | | |
| | 32.00 | 20.00 | 8.00 | 4.65 |
| ☐RD12 $1 Green, Perf. 11, Black Ovpt | | | | |
| | 1.40 | .80 | .21 | .16 |
| ☐RD13 $2 Rose, Perf. 11 | 1.40 | .80 | .21 | .16 |
| ☐RD14 $3 Violet, Perf. 11 (cut .17) | | | | |
| | 6.00 | 4.25 | 1.85 | .75 |
| ☐RD15 $4 Y. Brown, Perf. 11 (cut .07) | | | | |
| | 4.00 | 2.25 | .21 | .16 |
| ☐RD16 $5 Blue, Perf. 11 (cut .07) | | | | |
| | 2.60 | 1.40 | .21 | .16 |
| ☐RD17 $10 Orange, Perf. 11 (cut .07) | | | | |
| | 4.00 | 2.75 | .21 | .16 |
| ☐RD18 $20 Bistre, Perf. 11 (cut 4.25) | | | | |
| | 36.00 | 24.00 | 18.00 | 11.00 |
| ☐RD19 $30 Vermilion (cut 1.05) | | | | |
| | 14.00 | 9.00 | 4.00 | 2.65 |
| ☐RD20 $50 Olive Green (cut 9.75) | | | | |
| | 80.00 | 46.00 | 40.00 | 32.00 |
| ☐RD21 $60 Brown (cut 4.60) | | | | |
| | 56.00 | 33.00 | 17.00 | 12.00 |
| ☐RD22 $100 Green (cut 1.10) | | | | |
| | 16.00 | 11.00 | 4.50 | 3.00 |

| Scott No. | Fine Un-cancelled Each | Ave. Un-cancelled Each | Fine Used Each | Ave. Used Each |
|---|---|---|---|---|
| □RD23 $500 Blue (cut 38.00) | — | — | 108.00 | 72.00 |
| □RD24 $1000 Strange (cut 10.00) | — | — | 75.00 | 48.00 |
| □RD25 2¢ Carmine Rose, Perf. 10 | .50 | .30 | .21 | .14 |
| □RD26 4¢ Carmine Rose, Perf. 10 | .50 | .30 | .21 | .14 |
| □RD27 10¢ Carmine Rose, Perf. 10 | .40 | .26 | .21 | .14 |
| □RD28 20¢ Carmine Rose, Perf. 10 | .40 | .26 | .21 | .14 |
| □RD29 50¢ Carmine Rose, Perf. 10 | 1.00 | .60 | .21 | .14 |
| □RD30 $1 Green, Perf. 10 | 2.00 | 1.25 | .21 | .14 |
| □RD31 $2 Carmine Rose, Perf. 10 | 2.00 | 1.25 | .21 | .14 |
| □RD32 $10 Orange, Perf. 10 (cut .07) | 8.50 | 5.00 | .21 | .14 |

## 1919–1928.
## STOCK TRANSFER STAMPS, SERIF OVERPRINT

| Scott No. | Fine Un-cancelled Each | Ave. Un-cancelled Each | Fine Used Each | Ave. Used Each |
|---|---|---|---|---|
| □RD33 2¢ Carmine Rose, Perf. 11 | 3.00 | 1.60 | .55 | .36 |
| □RD34 10¢ Carmine Rose, Perf. 11 | .60 | .24 | .21 | .15 |
| □RD35 20¢ Carmine Rose, Perf. 11 | .65 | .31 | .22 | .15 |
| □RD36 50¢ Carmine Rose, Perf. 11 | 1.25 | .70 | .30 | .15 |
| □RD37 $1 Green, Perf. 11 (cut .11) | 12.50 | 8.00 | 6.00 | 4.00 |
| □RD38 $2 Rose, Perf, 11 (cut .12) | 9.00 | 6.00 | 5.50 | 3.50 |
| □RD39 2¢ Rose, Perf. 11 (cut .12) | 3.00 | 1.80 | .36 | .21 |
| □RD40 10¢ Carmine Rose, Perf. 10 | .80 | .40 | .21 | .15 |
| □RD41 20¢ Carmine Rose, Perf. 10 | 1.15 | .70 | .21 | .15 |

| Scott No. | | | Fine Unused Block | Ave. Unused Block | Fine Unused Each | Ave. Unused Each | Fine Used Each | Ave. Used Each |
|---|---|---|---|---|---|---|---|---|

## CONFEDERATE STATES OF AMERICA STAMPS (N-H ADD 80%)

| Scott No. | | | Fine Unused Block | Ave. Unused Block | Fine Unused Each | Ave. Unused Each | Fine Used Each | Ave. Used Each |
|---|---|---|---|---|---|---|---|---|
| ☐1 | 5¢ | J. Davis, Green | — | 1250.00 | 140.00 | 100.00 | 100.00 | 62.00 |
| ☐2 | 10¢ | Jefferson, Blue | — | 1500.00 | 200.00 | 115.00 | 140.00 | 96.00 |
| ☐3 | 2¢ | Jackson, Green | — | — | 400.00 | 250.00 | 460.00 | 340.00 |
| ☐4 | 5¢ | J. Davis, Blue | 650.00 | 540.00 | 110.00 | 60.00 | 82.00 | 52.00 |
| ☐5 | 10¢ | Jefferson, Rose | — | — | 730.00 | 460.00 | 400.00 | 260.00 |
| ☐6 | 5¢ | Davis, Lon. Print | 95.00 | 82.00 | 8.00 | 6.00 | 17.00 | 11.00 |
| ☐7 | 5¢ | Davis, Local Print | 130.00 | 95.00 | 12.00 | 7.00 | 10.00 | 7.00 |

### 1863.

| Scott No. | | | Fine Unused Block | Ave. Unused Block | Fine Unused Each | Ave. Unused Each | Fine Used Each | Ave. Used Each |
|---|---|---|---|---|---|---|---|---|
| ☐8 | 2¢ | Jackson, Br. Red | 400.00 | 315.00 | 45.00 | 24.00 | 260.00 | 165.00 |
| ☐9 | 10¢ | Davis (len) | — | — | 650.00 | 440.00 | 415.00 | 280.00 |
| ☐10 | 10¢ | Davis (w fr. lin.) | — | — | 2400.00 | 1600.00 | 1100.00 | 725.00 |
| ☐11 | 10¢ | Davis (no fr.) | 78.00 | 63.00 | 9.00 | 7.00 | 13.00 | 7.50 |
| ☐12 | 10¢ | Davis (fill. com) | 90.00 | 84.00 | 9.50 | 7.00 | 13.00 | 7.50 |
| ☐13 | 20¢ | Washington | 380.00 | 310.00 | 36.00 | 24.00 | 360.00 | 240.00 |

### 1862.

| Scott No. | | | Fine Unused Block | Ave. Unused Block | Fine Unused Each | Ave. Unused Each | Fine Used Each | Ave. Used Each |
|---|---|---|---|---|---|---|---|---|
| ☐14 | 1¢ | J.C. Calhoun | 750.00 | 580.00 | 78.00 | 50.00 | — | — |

| | | | Fine Plate Block | Block | Fine Unused Each | Fine Used Each |
|---|---|---|---|---|---|---|

## 1935. "FARLEY SPECIAL PRINTINGS"

| | | | Fine Plate Block | Block | Fine Unused Each | Fine Used Each |
|---|---|---|---|---|---|---|
| ☐752 | 3¢ | Newburgh | 16.00 | 6.00 | .21 | .16 |

| | | | Fine Plate Block | Block | Fine Unused Each | Fine Used Each |
|---|---|---|---|---|---|---|
| ☐753 | 3¢ | Byrd, Perf. | 20.00 | 3.75 | .62 | .60 |
| ☐754 | 3¢ | Mother's Day | 20.00 | 3.75 | .65 | .58 |
| ☐755 | 3¢ | Wisconsin | 20.00 | 4.00 | .65 | .60 |
| ☐756 | 1¢ | Park | 6.00 | 1.60 | .21 | .16 |
| ☐757 | 2¢ | Park | 7.00 | 1.60 | .28 | .18 |
| ☐758 | 3¢ | Park | 18.00 | 6.00 | .65 | .60 |
| ☐759 | 4¢ | Park | 24.00 | 9.00 | 1.15 | 1.00 |
| ☐760 | 5¢ | Park | 30.00 | 15.00 | 2.30 | 1.80 |
| ☐761 | 6¢ | Park | 50.00 | 19.00 | 2.80 | 2.30 |
| ☐762 | 7¢ | Park | 40.00 | 17.00 | 2.00 | 1.90 |
| ☐763 | 8¢ | Park | 50.00 | 18.00 | 2.30 | 1.90 |
| ☐764 | 9¢ | Park | 58.00 | 21.00 | 2.25 | 2.00 |
| ☐765 | 10¢ | Park | 60.00 | 34.00 | 4.25 | 3.50 |
| ☐766a | 1¢ | Chicago | — | 16.00 | .80 | .50 |
| ☐767a | 3¢ | Chicago | — | 16.00 | .80 | .50 |
| ☐768a | 3¢ | Byrd | — | 20.00 | 3.00 | 2.80 |
| ☐769a | 1¢ | Park | — | 12.00 | 1.90 | 1.45 |
| ☐770a | 3¢ | Park | — | 27.00 | 3.50 | 2.90 |
| ☐771 | 16¢ | Air Spec. Del | 87.00 | — | 3.00 | 2.70 |

| Scott No. | Center Line Block | Fine Arrow Block | Block W/Vert. Line | Pair W/Vert. Line | Block W/Horiz. Line | Pair W/Horiz. Line |
|---|---|---|---|---|---|---|

## 1935. FARLEY POSITION ON BLOCKS AND PAIRS

| | | | | | | |
|---|---|---|---|---|---|---|
| ☐752 | 3¢ Newburgh | | | | | |
| | 49.00 | 26.00 | 18.00 | 8.00 | 8.00 | 4.25 |
| ☐753 | 3¢ Byrd | | | | | |
| | 92.00 | 114.00 | 80.00 | 40.00 | — | 1.60 |
| ☐754 | 3¢ Mother's Day | | | | | |
| | 10.00 | 16.00 | 4.00 | 1.60 | 4.00 | 1.70 |
| ☐755 | 3¢ Wisconsin | | | | | |
| | 10.00 | 16.00 | 4.00 | 1.60 | 4.00 | 1.70 |
| ☐756 | 1¢ Park | | | | | |
| | 4.00 | 9.00 | 1.70 | .70 | 1.25 | 55 |
| ☐757 | 2¢ Park | | | | | |
| | 6.00 | 9.00 | 1.60 | .75 | 2.00 | .80 |
| ☐758 | 3¢ Park | | | | | |
| | 7.00 | 14.00 | 3.75 | 1.60 | 3.75 | 1.60 |

| Scott No. | Center Line Block | Fine Arrow Block | Block W/Vert. Line | Pair W/Vert. Line | Block W/Horiz. Line | Pair W/Horiz. Line |
|---|---|---|---|---|---|---|
| ☐759 4¢ Park | | | | | | |
| | 10.00 | 38.00 | 6.00 | 2.60 | 6.00 | 3.00 |
| ☐760 5¢ Park | | | | | | |
| | 17.00 | 46.00 | 11.00 | 5.00 | 11.00 | 4.10 |
| ☐761 6¢ Park | | | | | | |
| | 21.00 | 70.00 | 16.00 | 7.00 | 10.00 | 7.00 |
| ☐762 7¢ Park | | | | | | |
| | 19.00 | 50.00 | 12.00 | 5.10 | 11.00 | 5.00 |
| ☐763 8¢ Park | | | | | | |
| | 19.00 | 50.00 | 16.00 | 6.50 | 13.00 | 5.00 |
| ☐764 9¢ Park | | | | | | |
| | 21.00 | 54.00 | 15.00 | 6.00 | 7.00 | 6.00 |
| ☐765 10¢ Park | | | | | | |
| | 32.00 | 150.00 | 27.00 | 12.00 | 23.00 | 10.00 |
| ☐766a 1¢ Chicago | | | | | | |
| | 17.00 | — | 15.00 | 9.50 | 12.00 | 6.75 |
| ☐767a 3¢ Chicago | | | | | | |
| | 17.00 | — | 15.00 | 9.50 | 10.00 | 6.75 |
| ☐768a 3¢ Byrd | | | | | | |
| | 20.00 | — | 16.00 | 8.00 | 14.00 | 6.75 |
| ☐769a 1¢ Park | | | | | | |
| | 11.00 | — | 14.00 | 6.00 | 10.00 | 5.00 |
| ☐770a 3¢ Park | | | | | | |
| | 26.00 | — | 20.00 | 11.00 | 18.00 | 12.00 |
| ☐771 16¢ Air Spec. Del | | | | | | |
| | 80.00 | 90.00 | 28.00 | 7.00 | 19.00 | 7.00 |

| Scott No. | Fine Plate Block | Ave. Plate Block | Fine Unused Each | Ave. Unused Each | Fine Used Each | Ave. Used Each |
|---|---|---|---|---|---|---|

## HUNTING PERMIT STAMPS

| | | | | | | |
|---|---|---|---|---|---|---|
| ☐RW1 (1934) $1 Blue | | | | | | |
| | 6000.00 | 4500.00 | 350.00 | 230.00 | 100.00 | 80.00 |
| ☐RW2 (1935) $1 Rose Lake | | | | | | |
| | 7000.00 | 5500.00 | 325.00 | 220.00 | 130.00 | 90.00 |
| ☐RW3 (1936) $1 Brown Blk | | | | | | |
| | 2800.00 | 2000.00 | 170.00 | 115.00 | 70.00 | 48.00 |

| Scott No. | Fine Plate Block | Ave. Plate Block | Fine Unused Each | Ave. Unused Each | Fine Used Each | Ave. Used Each |
|---|---|---|---|---|---|---|
| □RW4 (1937)$1 Lt. Green | | | | | | |
| | 1800.00 | 1400.00 | 125.00 | 90.00 | 42.00 | 28.00 |
| □RW5 (1938)$1 Lt. Violet | | | | | | |
| | 1900.00 | 1500.00 | 141.00 | 100.00 | 48.00 | 30.00 |
| □RW6 (1939)$1 Chocolate | | | | | | |
| | 1200.00 | 1000.00 | 95.00 | 67.00 | 26.00 | 16.00 |
| □RW7 (1940)$1 Sepia | | | | | | |
| | 1250.00 | 900.00 | 95.00 | 67.00 | 26.00 | 16.00 |
| □RW8 (1941)$1 Brn. Carmine | | | | | | |
| | 1250.00 | 800.00 | 95.00 | 65.00 | 26.00 | 16.00 |
| □RW9 (1942)$1 Violet Brn. | | | | | | |
| | 1250.00 | 800.00 | 95.00 | 65.00 | 21.00 | 15.00 |
| □RW10 (1943)$1 Deep Rose | | | | | | |
| | 410.00 | 300.00 | 40.00 | 27.00 | 21.00 | 15.00 |
| □RW11 (1944)$1 Red Org. | | | | | | |
| | 400.00 | 290.00 | 40.00 | 27.00 | 21.00 | 15.00 |
| □RW12 (1945)$1 Black | | | | | | |
| | 250.00 | 180.00 | 28.00 | 19.00 | 17.00 | 13.00 |
| □RW13 (1946)$1 Red Brn | | | | | | |
| | 250.00 | 180.00 | 28.00 | 19.00 | 15.00 | 10.00 |
| □RW14 (1947)$1 Black | | | | | | |
| | 250.00 | 180.00 | 28.00 | 19.00 | 14.00 | 10.00 |
| □RW15 (1948)$1 Brt. Blue | | | | | | |
| | 250.00 | 180.00 | 30.00 | 21.00 | 14.50 | 10.00 |
| □RW16 (1949)$2 Brt. Green | | | | | | |
| | 250.00 | 180.00 | 31.00 | 22.00 | 10.00 | 8.00 |
| □RW17 (1950)$1 Violet | | | | | | |
| | 350.00 | 250.00 | 36.00 | 24.00 | 10.00 | 8.00 |
| □RW18 (1951)$2 Gray Blk | | | | | | |
| | 350.00 | 250.00 | 36.00 | 24.00 | 8.50 | 6.00 |
| □RW19 (1952)$2 Ultramarine | | | | | | |
| | 350.00 | 250.00 | 36.00 | 24.00 | 8.50 | 6.00 |
| □RW20 (1953)$2 Dk. Rose Brn | | | | | | |
| | 350.00 | 250.00 | 36.00 | 24.00 | 8.50 | 6.00 |
| □RW21 (1954)$2 Black | | | | | | |
| | 350.00 | 250.00 | 36.00 | 24.00 | 8.50 | 6.00 |
| □RW22 (1955)$2 Dk. Blue | | | | | | |
| | 350.00 | 250.00 | 36.00 | 24.00 | 8.50 | 6.00 |

| Scott No. | Fine Plate Block | Ave. Plate Block | Fine Unused Each | Ave. Unused Each | Fine Used Each | Ave. Used Each |
|---|---|---|---|---|---|---|
| ☐RW23 (1956)$2 Black | | | | | | |
| | 350.00 | 250.00 | 36.00 | 24.00 | 8.50 | 6.00 |
| ☐RW24 (1957)$2 Emerald | | | | | | |
| | 350.00 | 250.00 | 36.00 | 24.00 | 8.50 | 6.00 |
| ☐RW25 (1958)$2 Black | | | | | | |
| | 350.00 | 250.00 | 36.00 | 24.00 | 8.50 | 6.00 |
| ☐RW26 (1959)$3 Bl./Ochre/Blk | | | | | | |
| | 340.00 | 220.00 | 50.00 | 36.00 | 8.50 | 6.00 |
| ☐RW27 (1960)$3 Red Brn./Bl./Bist | | | | | | |
| | 340.00 | 220.00 | 50.00 | 36.00 | 8.50 | 8.00 |
| ☐RW28 (1961)$3 Bl./Bist./Brn | | | | | | |
| | 380.00 | 220.00 | 50.00 | 36.00 | 8.50 | 8.00 |
| ☐RW29 (1962)$3 Bl./Brn./Blk | | | | | | |
| | 420.00 | 240.00 | 60.00 | 40.00 | 11.00 | 9.00 |
| ☐RW30 (1963)$3 Blk./Bl. Yel./Grn | | | | | | |
| | 420.00 | 240.00 | 60.00 | 40.00 | 11.00 | 9.00 |
| ☐RW31 (1964)$3 Bl./Bl./Bist | | | | | | |
| | 2000.00 | 1600.00 | 60.00 | 40.00 | 11.00 | 9.00 |
| ☐RW32 (1965)$3 Grn./Blk./Brn | | | | | | |
| | 400.00 | 260.00 | 60.00 | 40.00 | 11.00 | 9.00 |
| ☐RW33 (1966)$3 Bl./Grn./Blk | | | | | | |
| | 400.00 | 260.00 | 60.00 | 40.00 | 11.00 | 9.00 |
| ☐RW34 (1967)$3 Multicolored | | | | | | |
| | 400.00 | 260.00 | 60.00 | 40.00 | 11.00 | 9.00 |
| ☐RW35 (1968)$3 Grn./Blk./Brn | | | | | | |
| | 250.00 | 170.00 | 40.00 | 30.00 | 8.00 | 9.00 |
| ☐RW36 (1969)$3 Multicolored | | | | | | |
| | 250.00 | 130.00 | 40.00 | 33 .00 | 8.00 | 7.00 |
| ☐RW37 (1970)$3 Multicolored | | | | | | |
| | 250.00 | 130.00 | 36.00 | 30.00 | 8.00 | 7.00 |
| ☐RW38 (1971)$3 Multicolored | | | | | | |
| | 165.00 | 130.00 | 32.00 | 24.00 | 8.00 | 7.00 |
| ☐RW39 (1972)$5 Multicolored | | | | | | |
| | 120.00 | 80.00 | 22.00 | 19.00 | 7.00 | 6.00 |
| ☐RW40 (1973)$5 Multicolored | | | | | | |
| | 100.00 | 80.00 | 21.00 | 18.00 | 7.00 | 6.00 |
| ☐RW41 (1974)$5 Multicolored | | | | | | |
| | 85.00 | 46.00 | 16.50 | 12.00 | 7.00 | 6.00 |

| Scott No. | Fine Plate Block | Ave. Plate Block | Fine Unused Each | Ave. Unused Each | Fine Used Each | Ave. Used Each |
|---|---|---|---|---|---|---|
| ☐RW42 (1975)$5 Multicolored | | | | | | |
| | 65.00 | 46.00 | 14.00 | 11.00 | 7.00 | 6.00 |
| ☐RW43 (1976)$5 Emerald & Blk | | | | | | |
| | 65.00 | 46.00 | 14.00 | 11.00 | 7.00 | 5.00 |
| ☐RW44 (1977)$5 Multicolored | | | | | | |
| | 65.00 | 46.00 | 16.00 | 13.00 | 7.00 | 5.00 |
| ☐RW45 (1978)$5 Multicolored | | | | | | |
| | 65.00 | 46.00 | 14.00 | 12.00 | 7.00 | 5.00 |
| ☐RW46 (1979)$7.50 Multicolored | | | | | | |
| | 70.00 | 44.00 | 17.00 | 15.00 | 6.00 | 5.00 |
| ☐RW47 (1980)$7.50 Multicolored | | | | | | |
| | 70.00 | 44.00 | 17.00 | 15.00 | 6.00 | 5.00 |
| ☐RW48 (1981)$7.50 Multicolored | | | | | | |
| | 70.00 | 44.00 | 17.00 | 15.00 | 6.00 | 5.00 |
| ☐RW49 (1982)$7.50 Multicolored | | | | | | |
| | 70.00 | 44.00 | 17.00 | 14.00 | 6.00 | 5.00 |
| ☐RW50 (1983)$7.50 Multicolored | | | | | | |
| | 70.00 | 44.00 | 17.00 | 14.00 | 6.00 | 5.00 |
| ☐RW51 (1984)$7.50 Multicolored | | | | | | |
| | 70.00 | 44.00 | 17.00 | 14.00 | 6.00 | 5.00 |
| ☐RW52 (1985)$7.50 Multicolored | | | | | | |
| | 70.00 | 44.00 | 17.00 | 14.00 | 6.00 | 5.00 |
| ☐RW53 (1986)$7.50 Multicolored | | | | | | |
| | 70.00 | 44.00 | 17.00 | 14.00 | 6.00 | 5.00 |
| ☐RW54 (1987)$10.00 Multicolored | | | | | | |
| | 75.00 | 54.00 | 20.00 | 16.00 | 10.00 | 8.00 |
| ☐RW55 (1988)$10.00 Multicolored | | | | | | |
| | 75.00 | 54.00 | 20.00 | 16.00 | 10.00 | 8.00 |
| ☐RW56 (1989)$12.50 Multicolored | | | | | | |
| | 95.00 | 60.00 | 21.00 | 17.00 | 11.00 | 9.00 |
| ☐RW57 (1990)$12.50 Multicolored | | | | | | |
| | 95.00 | 60.00 | 21.00 | 17.00 | 11.00 | 9.00 |
| ☐RW58 (1991)$15.00 Multicolored | | | | | | |
| | 145.00 | 90.00 | 31.00 | 21.00 | 14.00 | 12.00 |
| ☐RW59 (1992)$15.00 Multicolored | | | | | | |
| | 145.00 | 90.00 | 31.00 | 21.00 | 14.00 | 12.00 |

| Scott No. | | Fine Unused Each | Ave. Unused Each | Fine Used Each | Ave. Used Each |
|---|---|---|---|---|---|

## HAWAIIAN ISSUES
## 1851–1952. "MISSIONARIES"

| | | | | | |
|---|---|---|---|---|---|
| ☐1 | 2¢ Blue | — | 450,000.00 | — | 190,000.00 |
| ☐ | On Cover | | | | 425,000.00 |
| ☐2 | 5¢ Blue | — | 40,000.00 | — | 24.000.00 |
| ☐ | On Cover | | | | 50,000.00 |
| ☐3 | 13¢ Blue | — | 20,000.00 | — | 11,000.00 |
| ☐ | On Cover | | | | 35,000.00 |
| ☐4 | 13¢ Blue | — | 42,000.00 | — | 25,000.00 |
| ☐ | On Cover | | | | 40,000.00 |

NOTE: Prices on the above classic stamps of Hawaii vary greatly depending on the individual specimen and circumstances of sale.

NOTE: Beware of fake cancels on Hawaiian stamps, when the value is higher used than unused.

## 1853. KING KAMEHAMEHA III

| | | | | | |
|---|---|---|---|---|---|
| ☐5 | 5¢ Blue | — | 800.00 | — | 600.00 |
| ☐6 | 13¢ Dark Red | — | 460.00 | — | 390.00 |
| ☐7 | 5¢ on 13¢ Dark Red | — | 6000.0¢ | — | 5000.00 |

## 1857.

| | | | | | |
|---|---|---|---|---|---|
| ☐8 | 5¢ Blue | — | 350.00 | — | 310.00 |

## 1861.

| | | | | | |
|---|---|---|---|---|---|
| ☐9 | 5¢ Blue | — | 100.00 | — | 80.00 |

## 1868. RE-ISSUE

| | | | | | |
|---|---|---|---|---|---|
| ☐10 | 5¢ Blue | — | 16.00 | — | — |
| ☐11 | 13¢ Rose | — | 150.00 | — | — |

## 1869–1862.

| | | | | | |
|---|---|---|---|---|---|
| ☐12 | 1¢ Light Blue | — | 3000.00 | — | 2600.00 |
| ☐13 | 2¢ Light Blue | — | 3000.00 | — | 2400.00 |
| ☐14 | 2¢ Black | — | 3000.00 | — | 1800.00 |

## 1863.

| | | | | | |
|---|---|---|---|---|---|
| ☐15 | 1¢ Black | — | 275.00 | — | 300.00 |
| ☐16 | 2¢ Black | — | 375.00 | — | 340.00 |

| Scott No. | | | Fine Unused Each | Ave. Unused Each | Fine Used Each | Ave. Used Each |
|---|---|---|---|---|---|---|
| ☐17 | 2¢ | Dark Blue | — | 4000.00 | — | 2400.00 |
| ☐18 | 2¢ | Black | — | 750.00 | — | 900.00 |

### 1864–1865.
| | | | | | | |
|---|---|---|---|---|---|---|
| ☐19 | 1¢ | Black | — | 330.00 | — | 500.00 |
| ☐20 | 2¢ | Black | — | 380.00 | — | 400.00 |
| ☐21 | 5¢ | Blue | — | 400.00 | — | 400.00 |
| ☐22 | 5¢ | Blue | — | 275.00 | — | 300.00 |

### 1864. LAID PAPER
| | | | | | | |
|---|---|---|---|---|---|---|
| ☐23 | 1¢ | Black | 160.00 | 100.00 | 650.00 | 600.00 |
| ☐24 | 2¢ | Black | 160.00 | 100.00 | 650.00 | 500.00 |

### 1865. WOVE PAPER
| | | | | | | |
|---|---|---|---|---|---|---|
| ☐25 | 1¢ | Blue | 190.00 | 100.00 | 145.00 | 125.00 |
| ☐26 | 2¢ | Blue | 180.00 | 100.00 | 140.00 | 125.00 |
| ☐27 | 2¢ | Rose | 170.00 | 120.00 | 140.00 | 110.00 |
| ☐28 | 2¢ | Rose Vert | 170.00 | 120.00 | 140.00 | 110.00 |

### 1869. ENGRAVED
| | | | | | | |
|---|---|---|---|---|---|---|
| ☐29 | 2¢ | Red | 60.00 | 34.00 | — | — |

### 1864–1871.
| | | | | | | |
|---|---|---|---|---|---|---|
| ☐30 | 1¢ | Purple | 9.00 | 5.00 | 6.00 | 4.00 |
| ☐31 | 2¢ | Vermilion | 11.00 | 6.00 | 7.00 | 4.00 |
| ☐32 | 5¢ | Blue | 75.00 | 40.00 | 16.00 | 10.00 |
| ☐33 | 6¢ | Green | 20.00 | 10.00 | 6.00 | 4.00 |
| ☐34 | 18¢ | Rose | 100.00 | 60.00 | 16.00 | 8.50 |

### 1875.
| | | | | | | |
|---|---|---|---|---|---|---|
| ☐35 | 2¢ | Brown | 6.00 | 3.00 | 2.50 | 1.60 |
| ☐36 | 12¢ | Black | 36.00 | 24.00 | 19.00 | 11.00 |
| ☐37 | 1¢ | Blue | 4.00 | 3.00 | 5.50 | 4.00 |
| ☐38 | 2¢ | Lilac Rose | 73.00 | 48.00 | 27.00 | 17.00 |
| ☐39 | 5¢ | Ultramarine | 11.00 | 8.00 | 2.00 | 1.10 |
| ☐40 | 10¢ | Black | 21.00 | 14.00 | 16.00 | 9.00 |
| ☐41 | 15¢ | Red Brown | 38.00 | 22.00 | 20.00 | 12.00 |

### 1883–1886.
| | | | | | | |
|---|---|---|---|---|---|---|
| ☐42 | 1¢ | Green | 2.15 | 1.45 | 1.45 | .80 |

| Scott No. | | | Fine Unused Each | Ave. Unused Each | Fine Used Each | Ave. Used Each |
|---|---|---|---|---|---|---|
| ☐43 | 2¢ | Rose | 3.50 | 2.00 | .90 | .50 |
| ☐44 | 10¢ | Red Brown | 17.00 | 10.00 | 7.00 | 4.00 |
| ☐45 | 10¢ | Vermilion | 21.00 | 12.00 | 11.00 | 8.00 |
| ☐46 | 12¢ | Red Lilac | 52.00 | 33.00 | 29.00 | 17.00 |
| ☐47 | 25¢ | Dark Violet | 78.00 | 48.00 | 38.00 | 22.00 |
| ☐48 | 50¢ | Red | 120.00 | 90.00 | 68.00 | 44.00 |
| ☐49 | $1 | Rose Red | 190.00 | 120.00 | 82.00 | 48.00 |
| ☐50 | 2¢ | Orange | 115.00 | 92.00 | — | — |
| ☐51 | 2¢ | Carmine | 20.00 | 15.00 | — | — |

**1890–1891.**

| ☐52 | 2¢ | Dull Violet | 6.00 | 2.50 | 1.25 | .80 |
|---|---|---|---|---|---|---|
| ☐52c | 5¢ | Dark Blue | 90.00 | 58.00 | 76.00 | 45.00 |

**1893. PROVISIONAL GOVT. RED OVERPRINT**

| ☐53 | 1¢ | Purple | 4.00 | 2.60 | 4.00 | 2.15 |
|---|---|---|---|---|---|---|
| ☐54 | 1¢ | Blue | 4.00 | 2.50 | 6.00 | 3.00 |
| ☐55 | 1¢ | Green | 1.60 | .90 | 2.50 | 1.60 |
| ☐56 | 2¢ | Brown | 4.50 | 2.60 | 9.50 | 6.00 |
| ☐57 | 2¢ | Dull Violet | 1.40 | .90 | 1.25 | 1.00 |
| ☐58 | 5¢ | Dark Blue | 9.00 | 5.00 | 15.00 | 11.00 |
| ☐59 | 5¢ | Ultramarine | 5.00 | 2.75 | 3.10 | 2.00 |
| ☐60 | 6¢ | Green | 9.00 | 5.00 | 18.00 | 10.00 |
| ☐61 | 10¢ | Black | 7.00 | 4.00 | 8.50 | 4.50 |
| ☐62 | 12¢ | Black | 7.50 | 4.10 | 11.00 | 7.00 |
| ☐63 | 12¢ | Red Lilac | 115.00 | 62.00 | 145.00 | 85.00 |
| ☐64 | 25¢ | Dark Violet | 20.00 | 11.00 | 24.00 | 16.00 |

**BLACK OVERPRINT**

| ☐65 | 2¢ | Vermilion | 44.00 | 28.00 | 43.00 | 29.00 |
|---|---|---|---|---|---|---|
| ☐66 | 2¢ | Rose | 1.25 | .80 | 2.50 | 1.40 |
| ☐67 | 10¢ | Vermilion | 9.50 | 6.00 | 19.00 | 11.00 |
| ☐68 | 10¢ | Red Brown | 6.50 | 4.00 | 9.00 | 5.00 |
| ☐69 | 12¢ | Red Lilac | 200.00 | 115.00 | 280.00 | 160.00 |
| ☐70 | 15¢ | Red Brown | 17.00 | 10.00 | 29.00 | 16.00 |
| ☐71 | 18¢ | Dull Rose | 20.00 | 11.00 | 32.00 | 18.00 |
| ☐72 | 50¢ | Red | 50.00 | 28.00 | 80.00 | 46.00 |
| ☐73 | $1 | Rose Red | 95.00 | 58.00 | 135.00 | 75.00 |
| ☐74 | 1¢ | Yellow | 2.00 | 1.60 | 1.30 | .80 |

| Scott No. | | | Fine Unused Each | Ave. Unused Each | Fine Used Each | Ave. Used Each |
|---|---|---|---|---|---|---|
| □75 | 2¢ | Brown | 2.00 | 2.00 | .75 | .46 |
| □76 | 5¢ | Rose Lake | 3.90 | 3.00 | 1.75 | 1.10 |
| □77 | 10¢ | Yellow Green | 5.00 | 4.00 | 5.10 | 3.00 |
| □78 | 12¢ | Blue | 9.50 | 6.00 | 11.00 | 7.00 |
| □79 | 25¢ | Deep Blue | 9.50 | 6.00 | 11.00 | 7.00 |

**1899.**

| | | | | | | |
|---|---|---|---|---|---|---|
| □80 | 1¢ | Dark Green | 1.60 | 1.15 | 1.25 | .80 |
| □81 | 2¢ | Rose | 1.60 | 1.15 | 1.25 | .80 |
| □82 | 5¢ | Blue | 4.50 | 3.50 | 3.40 | 2.00 |

**1896. OFFICIAL STAMPS**

| | | | | | | |
|---|---|---|---|---|---|---|
| □O1 | 2¢ | Green | 30.00 | 17.00 | 17.00 | 11.00 |
| □O2 | 5¢ | Dark Brown | 30.00 | 17.00 | 17.00 | 11.00 |
| □O3 | 6¢ | Deep Ultramarine | 38.00 | 19.00 | 17.00 | 11.00 |
| □O4 | 10¢ | Rose | 29.00 | 16.00 | 17.00 | 11.00 |
| □O5 | 12¢ | Orange | 58.00 | 32.00 | 17.00 | 11.00 |
| □O6 | 25¢ | Gray Violet | 75.00 | 42.00 | 17.00 | 12.00 |

| Scott No. | | | Single | Block Of 4 |
|---|---|---|---|---|

**FIRST DAY COVER ISSUES UNCACHETED**

| | | | Single | Block Of 4 |
|---|---|---|---|---|
| □551 | ½¢ | Hale | 14.00 | 18.00 |
| □552 | 1¢ | Franklin | 24.00 | 36.00 |
| □553 | 1½¢ | Harding | 26.00 | 40.00 |
| □554 | 2¢ | Washington | 36.00 | 52.00 |
| □555 | 3¢ | Lincoln | 31.00 | 46.00 |
| □556 | 4¢ | Martha Washington | 54.00 | 76.00 |
| □557 | 5¢ | Roosevelt | 115.00 | 160.00 |
| □558 | 6¢ | Garfield | 140.00 | 180.00 |
| □559 | 7¢ | McKinley | 130.00 | 180.00 |
| □560 | 8¢ | Grant | 130.00 | 180.00 |
| □561 | 9¢ | Jefferson | 130.00 | 180.00 |
| □562 | 10¢ | Monroe | 150.00 | 180.00 |
| □563 | 11¢ | Hayes | 610.00 | 850.00 |
| □564 | 12¢ | Cleveland | 160.00 | 220.00 |
| □565 | 14¢ | Indian | 310.00 | 415.00 |

| Scott No. | | | Single | Block Of 4 |
|---|---|---|---|---|
| ☐566 | 15¢ | Statue of Liberty | 380.00 | — |
| ☐568 | 25¢ | Niagara Falls | 550.00 | 710.00 |
| ☐569 | 30¢ | Bison | 615.00 | 850.00 |
| ☐570 | 50¢ | Arlington | 850.00 | — |
| ☐571 | $1 | Lincoln Memorial | 4500.00 | — |
| ☐572 | $2 | U.S. Capitol | 10,000.00 | — |
| ☐573 | $5 | America | 14,000.00 | — |
| ☐576 | 1½¢ | Harding | 42.00 | 58.00 |
| ☐581 | 1¢ | Franklin | 1800.00 | — |
| ☐582 | 1½¢ | Harding | 36.00 | 50.00 |
| ☐583a | 2¢ | Washington | 60.00 | — |
| ☐584 | 3¢ | Lincoln | 46.00 | 65.00 |
| ☐585 | 4¢ | Martha Washington | 46.00 | — |
| ☐586 | 5¢ | Roosevelt | 47.00 | — |
| ☐587 | 6¢ | Garfield | 56.00 | 70.00 |
| ☐588 | 7¢ | McKinley | 72.00 | 92.00 |
| ☐589 | 8¢ | Grant | 60.00 | — |
| ☐590 | 9¢ | Jefferson | 65.00 | 92.00 |
| ☐591 | 10¢ | Monroe | 80.00 | — |
| ☐597 | 1¢ | Franklin | 550.00 | — |
| ☐598 | 1½¢ | Harding | 40.00 | 60.00 |
| ☐599 | 2¢ | Washington | 700.00 | — |
| ☐600 | 3¢ | Lincoln | 65.00 | 115.00 |
| ☐602 | 5¢ | Roosevelt | 70.00 | 95.00 |
| ☐603 | 10¢ | Monroe | 85.00 | 115.00 |
| ☐604 | 1¢ | Franklin | 76.00 | 100.00 |
| ☐605 | 1½¢ | Harding | 48.00 | 80.00 |
| ☐606 | 2¢ | Washington | 26.00 | 40.00 |
| ☐610 | 2¢ | Harding | 24.00 | 36.00 |
| ☐611 | 2¢ | Harding | 73.00 | 100.00 |
| ☐612 | 2¢ | Harding | 85.00 | 125.00 |
| ☐614 | 1¢ | Huguenot-Walloon | 28.00 | 40.00 |
| ☐615 | 2¢ | Huguenot-Walloon | 28.00 | 40.00 |
| ☐616 | 5¢ | Huguenot-Walloon | 58.00 | — |
| ☐617 | 1¢ | Lexington-Concord | 24.00 | — |
| ☐618 | 2¢ | Lexington Concord | 30.00 | — |
| ☐619 | 5¢ | Lexington-Concord | 72.00 | — |
| ☐620 | 2¢ | Norse-American | 21.00 | — |
| ☐621 | 5¢ | Norse-American | 24.00 | — |
| ☐622 | 13¢ | Harrison | 16.00 | — |

| Scott No. | | | Single | Block Of 4 |
|---|---|---|---|---|
| ☐623 | 17¢ | Wilson | 17.00 | — |
| ☐627 | 2¢ | Sesquicentennial | 9.00 | 16.00 |
| ☐628 | 5¢ | Erikson | 14.00 | 17.00 |
| ☐629 | 2¢ | White Plains | 7.00 | 10.00 |
| ☐630 | 2¢ | White Plains Sheet | 11.00 | — |
| ☐631 | 1¹/₂¢ | Harding | 32.00 | 80.00 |
| ☐632 | 1¢ | Franklin | 43.00 | 58.00 |
| ☐633 | 1¹/₂¢ | Harding | 43.00 | 58.00 |
| ☐634 | 2¢ | Washington | 45.00 | 62.00 |
| ☐635 | 3¢ | Lincoln | 40.00 | 55.00 |
| ☐635a | 3¢ | Bright Violet | 17.00 | 21.00 |
| ☐636 | 4¢ | Martha Washington | 43.00 | — |
| ☐637 | 5¢ | Roosevelt | 44.00 | 62.00 |
| ☐638 | 6¢ | Garfield | 52.00 | 70.00 |
| ☐639 | 7¢ | McKinley | 50.00 | 75.00 |
| ☐640 | 8¢ | Grant | 55.00 | 76.00 |
| ☐641 | 9¢ | Jefferson | 72.00 | 90.00 |
| ☐642 | 10¢ | Monroe | 70.00 | 98.00 |
| ☐643 | 2¢ | Vermont | 5.00 | 6.50 |
| ☐644 | 2¢ | Burgoyne | 8.00 | 10.00 |
| ☐645 | 2¢ | Valley Forge | 4.00 | 6.00 |
| ☐646 | 2¢ | Molly Pitcher | 10.00 | 14.00 |
| ☐647 | 2¢ | Hawaii | 13.00 | 18.00 |
| ☐648 | 5¢ | Hawaii | 18.00 | 22.00 |
| ☐649 | 2¢ | Aero Conf. | 6.00 | 8.00 |
| ☐650 | 5¢ | Aero Conf. | 8.00 | 11.00 |
| ☐651 | 2¢ | Clark | 5.00 | 8.00 |
| ☐653 | ¹/₂¢ | Hale | 29.00 | 36.00 |
| ☐654 | 2¢ | Electric Light | 7.00 | 10.00 |
| ☐655 | 2¢ | Electric Light | 70.00 | 90.00 |
| ☐656 | 2¢ | Electric Light | 90.00 | — |
| ☐657 | 2¢ | Sullivan | 4.00 | 6.00 |
| ☐658 | 1¢ | Kansas | 29.00 | 41.00 |
| ☐659 | 1¹/₂¢ | Kansas | 30.00 | 60.00 |
| ☐660 | 2¢ | Kansas | 31.00 | 58.00 |
| ☐661 | 3¢ | Kansas | 38.00 | 54.00 |
| ☐662 | 4¢ | Kansas | 42.00 | 60.00 |
| ☐663 | 5¢ | Kansas | 42.00 | 60.00 |
| ☐664 | 6¢ | Kansas | 56.00 | 65.00 |
| ☐665 | 7¢ | Kansas | 60.00 | 90.00 |

| Scott No. | | | Single | Block Of 4 |
|---|---|---|---|---|
| ☐666 | 8¢ | Kansas | 73.00 | 110.00 |
| ☐667 | 9¢ | Kansas | 85.00 | 115.00 |
| ☐668 | 10¢ | Kansas | 110.00 | 140.00 |
| ☐669 | 1¢ | Nebraska | 30.00 | 40.00 |
| ☐670 | 1¹/₂¢ | Nebraska | 33.00 | — |
| ☐671 | 2¢ | Nebraska | 33.00 | 45.00 |
| ☐672 | 3¢ | Nebraska | 38.00 | 52.00 |
| ☐673 | 4¢ | Nebraska | 44.00 | 60.00 |
| ☐674 | 5¢ | Nebraska | 43.00 | 61.00 |
| ☐675 | 6¢ | Nebraska | 62.00 | 85.00 |
| ☐676 | 7¢ | Nebraska | 64.00 | 90.00 |
| ☐677 | 8¢ | Nebraska | 72.00 | 100.00 |
| ☐678 | 9¢ | Nebraska | 92.00 | 110.00 |
| ☐679 | 10¢ | Nebraska | 100.00 | 140.00 |
| ☐680 | 2¢ | Fallen Timbers | 3.10 | 5.00 |
| ☐681 | 2¢ | Ohio River | 3.10 | 5.00 |
| ☐682 | 2¢ | Massachusetts Bay Colony | 3.10 | 5.00 |
| ☐683 | 2¢ | Carolina-Charleston | 3.10 | 5.00 |
| ☐684 | 1¹/₂¢ | Harding | 4.00 | 5.50 |
| ☐685 | 4¢ | Taft | 5.50 | 7.50 |
| ☐686 | 1¹/₂¢ | Harding | 4.00 | 6.00 |
| ☐687 | 4¢ | Taft | 24.00 | — |
| ☐688 | 2¢ | Braddock | 3.75 | 6.00 |
| ☐689 | 2¢ | Von Steuben | 4.00 | 6.00 |
| ☐690 | 2¢ | Pulaski | 3.50 | 5.00 |
| ☐692 | 11¢ | Hayes | 90.00 | 115.00 |
| ☐693 | 12¢ | Cleveland | 90.00 | 115.00 |
| ☐694 | 13¢ | Harrison | 90.00 | 115.00 |
| ☐695 | 14¢ | Indian | 90.00 | 125.00 |
| ☐696 | 15¢ | Liberty | 110.00 | 150.00 |
| ☐697 | 17¢ | Wilson | 290.00 | — |
| ☐698 | 20¢ | Golden Gate | 260.00 | — |
| ☐699 | 25¢ | Niagara Falls | 310.00 | — |
| ☐700 | 30¢ | Bison | 220.00 | — |
| ☐701 | 50¢ | Arlington | 350.00 | — |
| ☐702 | 2¢ | Red Cross | 3.00 | 4.00 |
| ☐703 | 2¢ | Yorktown | 3.00 | 5.00 |
| ☐704 | ¹/₂¢ | Olive Brown | 14.50 | 18.50 |
| ☐705 | 1¢ | Green | 14.50 | 18.50 |
| ☐706 | 1¹/₂¢ | Brown | 14.50 | 18.50 |

| Scott No. | | | Single | Block Of 4 |
|---|---|---|---|---|
| ☐707 | 2¢ | Carmine Rose | 14.50 | 18.50 |
| ☐708 | 3¢ | Deep Violet | 14.50 | 18.50 |
| ☐709 | 4¢ | Light Brown | 14.50 | 18.50 |
| ☐710 | 5¢ | Blue | 14.50 | 18.50 |
| ☐711 | 6¢ | Red Orange | 14.50 | 18.50 |
| ☐712 | 7¢ | Black | 16.50 | 20.00 |
| ☐713 | 8¢ | Olive Bistre | 16.50 | 20.00 |
| ☐714 | 9¢ | Pale Red | 16.50 | 20.00 |
| ☐715 | 10¢ | Orange Yellow | 16.50 | 20.00 |
| ☐716 | 2¢ | Olympic Winter Games | 21.00 | 23.00 |
| ☐717 | 2¢ | Arbor Day | 16.00 | 21.00 |
| ☐718 | 3¢ | Olympic Summer Games | 22.00 | 26.00 |
| ☐719 | 5¢ | Olympic Summer Games | 23.00 | 35.00 |
| ☐720 | 3¢ | Washington | 33.00 | 42.00 |
| ☐721 | 3¢ | Washington (coil) | 34.00 | — |
| ☐722 | 3¢ | Washington (coil) | 34.00 | — |
| ☐723 | 6¢ | garfield (coil) | 34.00 | — |
| ☐724 | 3¢ | William Penn | 11.00 | 15.00 |
| ☐725 | 3¢ | Daniel Webster | 11.00 | 15.00 |
| ☐726 | 3¢ | Gen. Oglethorpe | 11.00 | 15.00 |
| ☐727 | 3¢ | Peace Proclamation | 14.00 | 16.00 |
| ☐728 | 1¢ | Century of Progress | 14.00 | 16.00 |
| ☐729 | 3¢ | Century of Progress | 14.00 | 16.00 |
| ☐730 | 1¢ | American Philatelic Society, full sheet on cover | 170.00 | — |
| ☐730a | 1¢ | American Philatelic Society | 14.00 | 16.00 |
| ☐731 | 3¢ | American Philatelic Society | 165.00 | — |
| ☐731a | 3¢ | American Philatelic Society | 14.00 | 16.00 |
| ☐732 | 3¢ | National Recovery Administration | 16.00 | 21.00 |
| ☐733 | 3¢ | Byrd Antarctic | 24.00 | 30.00 |
| ☐734 | 5¢ | Kosciuszko | 18.00 | 25.00 |
| ☐735 | 3¢ | National Exhibition | 48.00 | — |
| ☐735a | 3¢ | National Exhibition | 16.00 | — |
| ☐736 | 3¢ | Maryland Tercentenary | 11.00 | 16.00 |
| ☐737 | 3¢ | Mothers of America | 11.00 | 16.00 |
| ☐738 | 3¢ | Mothers of America | 11.00 | 16.00 |
| ☐739 | 3¢ | Wisconsin | 11.00 | 16.00 |
| ☐740 | 1¢ | Parks, Yosemite | 11.00 | 16.00 |
| ☐741 | 2¢ | Parks, Grand Canyon | 11.00 | 16.00 |
| ☐742 | 3¢ | Parks, Mt. Rainier | 11.00 | 16.00 |

| Scott No. | | | Single | Block Of 4 |
|---|---|---|---|---|
| ☐743 | 4¢ | Parks, Mesa Verde | 11.00 | 16.00 |
| ☐744 | 5¢ | Parks, Yellowstone | 11.00 | 16.00 |
| ☐745 | 6¢ | Parks, Crater Lake | 11.00 | 16.00 |
| ☐746 | 7¢ | Parks, Acadia | 11.00 | 16.00 |
| ☐747 | 8¢ | Parks, Zion | 11.00 | 16.00 |
| ☐748 | 9¢ | Parks, Glacier Park | 11.00 | 16.00 |
| ☐749 | 10¢ | Parks, Smoky Mountains | 11.00 | 16.00 |
| ☐750 | 3¢ | American Philatelic Society, full sheet on cover | 48.00 | — |
| ☐750a | 3¢ | American Philatelic Society | 11.00 | 16.00 |
| ☐751 | 1¢ | Trans-Mississippi Philatelic Expo, full sheet on cover | 50.00 | — |
| ☐751a | 1¢ | Trans-Mississippi Philatelic Expo. | 11.00 | 16.00 |
| ☐752 | 3¢ | Peace Commemoration | 36.00 | 50.00 |
| ☐753 | 34¢ | Byrd | 36.00 | 50.00 |
| ☐754 | 3¢ | Mothers of America | 36.00 | 50.00 |
| ☐755 | 3¢ | Wisconsin | 36.00 | 50.00 |
| ☐756 | 1¢ | Parks, Yosemite | 21.00 | 26.00 |
| ☐757 | 2¢ | Parks, Grand Canyon | 21.00 | 25.00 |
| ☐758 | 3¢ | Parks, Mount Ranier | 21.00 | 25.00 |
| ☐759 | 4¢ | Parks, Mesa Verde | 21.00 | 25.00 |
| ☐760 | 5¢ | Parks, Yellowstone | 21.00 | 25.00 |
| ☐761 | 6¢ | Parks, Crater Lake | 22.00 | 31.00 |
| ☐762 | 7¢ | Parks, Acadia | 22.00 | 31.00 |
| ☐763 | 8¢ | Parks, Zion | 22.00 | 31.00 |
| ☐764 | 9¢ | Parks, Glacier Park | 22.00 | 31.00 |
| ☐765 | 10¢ | Parks, Smoky Mountains | 22.00 | 31.00 |
| ☐766a | 1¢ | Century of Progress | 38.00 | 54.00 |
| ☐767a | 3¢ | Century of Progress | 38.00 | 54.00 |
| ☐768a | 3¢ | Byrd | 38.00 | 54.00 |
| ☐769a | 1¢ | Parks, Yosemite | 38.00 | 54.00 |
| ☐770a | 3¢ | Parks, Mount Ranier | 38.00 | 54.00 |
| ☐771 | 16¢ | Airmail, special delivery | 38.00 | 54.00 |

## FIRST DAY COVER ISSUES CACHETED

| | | | | |
|---|---|---|---|---|
| ☐610 | 2¢ | Harding | 650.00 | — |
| ☐617 | 1¢ | Lexington-Concord | 130.00 | — |
| ☐618 | 2¢ | Lexington-Concord | 130.00 | — |
| ☐619 | 5¢ | Lexington-Concord | 172.00 | — |

| Scott No. | | | Single | Block Of 4 |
|---|---|---|---|---|
| ☐623 | 17¢ | Wilson | 280.00 | — |
| ☐627 | 2¢ | Sesquicentennial | 60.00 | — |
| ☐628 | 5¢ | Erikson | 425.00 | — |
| ☐629 | 2¢ | White Plains | 48.00 | — |
| ☐630 | 2¢ | White Plains Sheet | 1200.00 | — |
| ☐635a | 3¢ | Bright Violet | 42.00 | — |
| ☐643 | 2¢ | Vermont | 48.00 | 70.00 |
| ☐644 | 2¢ | Burgoyne | 52.00 | 80.00 |
| ☐645 | 2¢ | Valley Forge | 42.00 | 60.00 |
| ☐646 | 2¢ | Molly Pitcher | 82.00 | — |
| ☐647 | 2¢ | Hawaii | 52.00 | 70.00 |
| ☐648 | 5¢ | Hawaii | 60.00 | 85.00 |
| ☐649 | 2¢ | Aero Conf. | 32.00 | 45.00 |
| ☐650 | 5¢ | Aero Conf. | 32.00 | 42.00 |
| ☐651 | 2¢ | Clark | 29.00 | 42.00 |
| ☐654 | 2¢ | Electric Light | 29.00 | 42.00 |
| ☐655 | 2¢ | Electric Light | 165.00 | — |
| ☐656 | 2¢ | Electric Light | 250.00 | — |
| ☐657 | 2¢ | Sullivan, Auburn N.Y. | 28.00 | 43.00 |
| ☐680 | 2¢ | Fallen Timbers | 28.00 | 43.00 |
| ☐681 | 2¢ | Ohio River | 28.00 | 42.00 |
| ☐682 | 2¢ | Massachusetts Bay Colony | 32.00 | 46.00 |
| ☐683 | 2¢ | California-Charleston | 32.00 | 46.00 |
| ☐684 | 1¹/₂¢ | Harding | 32.00 | 46.00 |
| ☐685 | 4¢ | Taft | 42.00 | 58.00 |
| ☐686 | 1¹/₂¢ | Harding | 36.00 | 50.00 |
| ☐687 | 4¢ | Taft | 76.00 | 90.00 |
| ☐688 | 2¢ | Braddock | 29.00 | 42.00 |
| ☐689 | 2¢ | Von Steuben | 29.00 | 42.00 |
| ☐690 | 2¢ | Pulaski | 29.00 | 42.00 |
| ☐702 | 2¢ | Red Cross | 24.00 | 32.00 |
| ☐703 | 2¢ | Yorktown | 35.00 | 50.00 |
| ☐704 | 1¹/₂¢ | Olive Brown | 14.00 | 18.00 |
| ☐705 | 1¢ | Green | 14.00 | 18.00 |
| ☐706 | 1¹/₂¢ | Brown | 14.00 | 18.00 |
| ☐707 | 2¢ | Carmine Rose | 14.00 | 18.00 |
| ☐708 | 3¢ | Deep Violet | 14.00 | 18.00 |
| ☐709 | 4¢ | Light Brown | 14.00 | 18.00 |
| ☐710 | 5¢ | Blue | 14.00 | 18.00 |
| ☐711 | 6¢ | Red Orange | 14.00 | 18.00 |

| Scott No. | | | Single | Block Of 4 |
|---|---|---|---|---|
| ☐712 | 7¢ | Black | 14.00 | 18.00 |
| ☐713 | 8¢ | Olive Bistre | 18.00 | 25.00 |
| ☐714 | 9¢ | Pale Red | 18.00 | 25.00 |
| ☐715 | 10¢ | Orange Yellow | 18.00 | 25.00 |
| ☐716 | 2¢ | Olympic Winter Games | 21.00 | 30.00 |
| ☐717 | 2¢ | Arbor Day | 17.00 | 24.00 |
| ☐718 | 3¢ | Olympic Summer Games | 21.00 | 30.00 |
| ☐719 | 5¢ | Olympic Summer Games | 21.00 | 30.00 |
| ☐720 | 3¢ | Washington | 33.00 | 42.00 |
| ☐720b | 3¢ | Booklet pane | 140.00 | — |
| ☐721 | 3¢ | Washington (coil) | 36.00 | — |
| ☐722 | 3¢ | Washington (coil) | 35.00 | — |
| ☐723 | 6¢ | Garfield (coil) | 35.00 | — |
| ☐724 | 3¢ | William Penn | 16.00 | 22.00 |
| ☐725 | 3¢ | Daniel Webster | 16.00 | 22.00 |
| ☐726 | 3¢ | Gen. Oglethorpe | 16.00 | 22.00 |
| ☐727 | 3¢ | Peace Proclamation | 16.00 | 22.00 |
| ☐728 | 1¢ | Century of Progress | 16.00 | 22.00 |
| ☐729 | 3¢ | Century of Progress | 16.00 | 22.00 |
| ☐730 | 1¢ | American Philatelic Society, full sheet on cover. | 165.00 | — |
| ☐730a | 1¢ | American Philatelic Society | 15.00 | 21.00 |
| ☐731 | 3¢ | American Philatelic Society | 165.00 | — |
| ☐731a | 3¢ | American Philatelic Society | 15.00 | 21.00 |
| ☐732 | 3¢ | National Recovery Administration | 16.00 | 22.00 |
| ☐733 | 3¢ | Byrd Antarctic | 26.00 | 36.00 |
| ☐734 | 5¢ | Kosciuszko | 21.00 | 29.00 |
| ☐735 | 3¢ | National Exhibition | 52.00 | — |
| ☐735a | 3¢ | National Exhibition | 16.00 | — |
| ☐736 | 3¢ | Maryland Tercentenary | 11.00 | 16.00 |
| ☐737 | 3¢ | Mothers of America | 11.00 | 16.00 |
| ☐738 | 3¢ | Mothers of America | 11.00 | 16.00 |
| ☐739 | 2¢ | Wisconsin | 11.00 | 16.00 |
| ☐740 | 1¢ | Parks, Yosemite | 11.00 | 16.00 |
| ☐741 | 2¢ | Parks, Grand Canyon | 11.00 | 16.00 |
| ☐742 | 35¢ | Parks, Mt. Ranier | 11.00 | 16.00 |
| ☐743 | 4¢ | Parks, Mesa Verde | 11.00 | 16.00 |
| ☐744 | 5¢ | Parks, Yellowstone | 11.00 | 16.00 |
| ☐745 | 6¢ | Parks, Crater Lake | 11.00 | 16.00 |
| ☐746 | 7¢ | Parks, Acadia | 11.00 | 16.00 |

| Scott No. | | | Single | Block Of 4 |
|---|---|---|---|---|
| ☐747 | 8¢ | Parks, Zion | 11.00 | 16.00 |
| ☐748 | 9¢ | Parks, Glacier Park | 11.00 | 16.00 |
| ☐749 | 10¢ | Parks, Smoky Mountains | 11.00 | 16.00 |
| ☐750 | 3¢ | American Philatelic Society, full sheet on cover | 48.00 | — |
| ☐750a | 3¢ | American Philatelic Society | 12.00 | 17.00 |
| ☐751 | 1¢ | Trans-Mississippi Philatelic Expo., full sheet on cover | 48.00 | — |
| ☐751a | 1¢ | Trans-Mississippi Philatelic Expo. | 12.00 | 17.00 |
| ☐752 | 3¢ | Peace Commemoration | 35.00 | 42.00 |
| ☐753 | 3¢ | Byrd | 35.00 | 42.00 |
| ☐754 | 3¢ | Mothers of America | 36.00 | 42.00 |
| ☐755 | 3¢ | Wisconsin Tercentenary | 34.00 | 40.00 |
| ☐756 | 1¢ | Parks, Yosemite | 21.00 | 28.00 |
| ☐757 | 2¢ | Parks, Grand Canyon | 21.00 | 28.00 |
| ☐758 | 3¢ | Parks, Mount Rainier | 21.00 | 28.00 |
| ☐759 | 4¢ | Parks, Mesa Verde | 21.00 | 28.00 |
| ☐760 | 5¢ | Parks, Yellowstone | 21.00 | 28.00 |
| ☐761 | 6¢ | Parks, Crater Lake | 21.00 | 28.00 |
| ☐762 | 7¢ | Parks, Acadia | 21.00 | 28.00 |
| ☐763 | 8¢ | Parks, Zion | 21.00 | 28.00 |
| ☐764 | 9¢ | Parks, Glacier Park | 21.00 | 28.00 |
| ☐765 | 10¢ | Parks, Smoky Mountains | 21.00 | 28.00 |
| ☐766a | 1¢ | Century of Progress | 42.00 | 60.00 |
| ☐767a | 3¢ | Century of Progress | 42.00 | 60.00 |
| ☐768a | 3¢ | Byrd | 42.00 | 60.00 |
| ☐769a | 1¢ | Parks, Yosemite | 42.00 | 60.00 |
| ☐770a | 3¢ | Parks, Mount Rainier | 42.00 | 60.00 |
| ☐771 | 16¢ | Airmail, special delivery | 42.00 | 60.00 |

| Scott No. | | | Single | Block | Plate Block |
|---|---|---|---|---|---|
| ☐772 | 3¢ | Connecticut Tercentenary | 7.00 | 8.50 | 15.00 |
| ☐773 | 3¢ | California Exposition | 8.50 | 8.50 | 16.00 |
| ☐774 | 3¢ | Boulder Dam | 9.00 | 10.00 | 17.00 |
| ☐775 | 3¢ | Michigan Centenary | 7.50 | 8.50 | 15.00 |
| ☐776 | 3¢ | Texas Centennial | 10.00 | 14.00 | 20.00 |
| ☐777 | 3¢ | Rhode Island Tercentenary | 7.00 | 8.50 | 16.00 |
| ☐778 | 3¢ | TIPEX | 14.00 | 19.00 | — |

| Scott No. | | Single | Block | Plate Block |
|---|---|---|---|---|
| ☐782 | 3¢ Arkansas Centennial | 7.00 | 8.50 | 15.00 |
| ☐783 | 3¢ Oregon Territory | 6.50 | 8.50 | 15.00 |
| ☐784 | 3¢ Susan B. Anthony | 6.50 | 8.50 | 15.00 |
| ☐785 | 1¢ Army | 5.00 | 7.00 | 12.00 |
| ☐786 | 2¢ Army | 5.00 | 7.00 | 12.00 |
| ☐787 | 3¢ Army | 5.00 | 7.00 | 12.00 |
| ☐788 | 5¢ Army | 5.00 | 7.00 | 12.00 |
| ☐790 | 1¢ Navy | 5.00 | 7.00 | 12.00 |
| ☐791 | 2¢ Navy | 5.00 | 7.00 | 12.00 |
| ☐792 | 3¢ Navy | 5.00 | 7.00 | 12.00 |
| ☐793 | 4¢ Navy | 5.00 | 7.00 | 12.00 |
| ☐794 | 5¢ Navy | 5.00 | 7.00 | 12.00 |
| ☐795 | 3¢ Ordinance of 1787 | 6.50 | 7.00 | 14.00 |
| ☐796 | 5¢ Virginia Dare | 6.50 | 7.00 | 14.00 |
| ☐797 | 10¢ Souvenir Sheet | 6.50 | — | — |
| ☐798 | 3¢ Constitution | 6.00 | 8.50 | 14.00 |
| ☐799 | 3¢ Hawaii | 6.00 | 8.50 | 14.00 |
| ☐800 | 3¢ Alaska | 6.00 | 8.50 | 14.00 |
| ☐801 | 3¢ Puerto Rico | 6.00 | 8.50 | 14.00 |
| ☐802 | 3¢ Virgin Islands | 6.00 | 8.50 | 14.00 |
| ☐803 | ½¢ Franklin | 2.50 | 4.50 | 8.50 |
| ☐804 | 1¢ Washington | 2.50 | 4.50 | 8.50 |
| ☐805 | 1½¢ Martha Washington | 2.35 | 4.50 | 8.50 |
| ☐806 | 2¢ Adams | 2.35 | 4.50 | 8.50 |
| ☐807 | 3¢ Jefferson | 2.35 | 4.50 | 8.50 |
| ☐808 | 4¢ Madison | 2.35 | 4.50 | 8.50 |
| ☐809 | 4½¢ White House | 2.35 | 4.50 | 8.50 |
| ☐810 | 5¢ Monroe | 2.35 | 4.50 | 8.50 |
| ☐811 | 6¢ Adams | 2.35 | 4.50 | 8.50 |
| ☐812 | 7¢ Jackson | 2.35 | 4.50 | 8.50 |
| ☐813 | 8¢ VanBuren | 2.35 | 4.50 | 8.50 |
| ☐814 | 9¢ Harrison | 2.35 | 4.50 | 8.50 |
| ☐815 | 10¢ Tyler | 2.35 | 4.50 | 8.75 |
| ☐816 | 11¢ Polk | 2.50 | 4.25 | 8.75 |
| ☐817 | 12¢ Taylor | 2.50 | 4.25 | 8.75 |
| ☐818 | 13¢ Fillmore | 2.50 | 4.25 | 8.75 |
| ☐819 | 14¢ Pierce | 2.50 | 4.25 | 8.75 |
| ☐820 | 15¢ Buchanan | 2.50 | 4.25 | 8.75 |
| ☐821 | 16¢ Lincoln | 3.50 | 5.50 | 7.50 |
| ☐822 | 17¢ Johnson | 3.50 | 5.50 | 7.50 |

| Scott No. | | | Single | Block | Plate Block |
|---|---|---|---|---|---|
| ☐823 | 18¢ | Grant | 3.50 | 5.50 | 7.50 |
| ☐824 | 19¢ | Hayes | 3.50 | 5.50 | 7.50 |
| ☐825 | 20¢ | Garfield | 4.00 | 6.00 | 7.50 |
| ☐826 | 21¢ | Arthur | 4.00 | 6.00 | 11.50 |
| ☐827 | 22¢ | Cleveland | 4.00 | 6.00 | 11.50 |
| ☐828 | 24¢ | Harrison | 4.00 | 6.00 | 11.50 |
| ☐829 | 25¢ | McKinley | 4.00 | 6.00 | 12.00 |
| ☐830 | 30¢ | Roosevelt | 6.00 | 8.50 | 13.00 |
| ☐831 | 50¢ | Taft | 13.00 | 18.00 | 25.00 |
| ☐832 | $1 | Wilson | 50.00 | 75.00 | 126.00 |
| ☐832c | $1 | Wilson | 32.00 | 48.00 | 72.00 |
| ☐833 | $2 | Harding | 120.00 | 185.00 | 250.00 |
| ☐834 | $5 | Coolidge | 180.00 | 270.00 | 360.00 |
| ☐835 | 3¢ | Constitution | 5.50 | 8.50 | 11.50 |
| ☐836 | 3¢ | Swedes and Finns | 5.50 | 8.50 | 11.50 |
| ☐837 | 3¢ | Northwest Sesquicentennial | 5.50 | 8.50 | 11.50 |
| ☐838 | 3¢ | Iowa | 5.50 | 8.50 | 11.50 |
| ☐852 | 3¢ | Golden Gate Expo | 5.50 | 8.50 | 11.50 |
| ☐853 | 3¢ | N.Y. World's Fair | 5.50 | 8.50 | 11.50 |
| ☐854 | 3¢ | Washington Inauguration | 5.50 | 8.50 | 11.50 |
| ☐855 | 3¢ | Baseball Centennial | 24.00 | 35.00 | 43.00 |
| ☐856 | 3¢ | Panama Canal | 5.50 | 8.50 | 11.00 |
| ☐857 | 3¢ | Printing Tercentenary | 5.50 | 8.50 | 11.00 |
| ☐858 | 3¢ | 50th Statehood Anniversary | 5.50 | 7.50 | 12.00 |
| ☐859 | 1¢ | Washington Irving | 2.50 | 4.00 | 5.00 |
| ☐860 | 2¢ | James Fenimore Cooper | 2.50 | 4.00 | 5.00 |
| ☐861 | 3¢ | Ralph Waldo Emerson | 2.50 | 4.00 | 5.00 |
| ☐862 | 5¢ | Louisa May Alcott | 3.50 | 7.00 | 8.00 |
| ☐863 | 10¢ | Samuel L. Clemens | 5.00 | 8.00 | 11.00 |
| ☐864 | 1¢ | Henry W. Longfellow | 2.50 | 4.00 | 7.00 |
| ☐865 | 2¢ | John Greenleaf Whittier | 2.50 | 4.00 | 7.00 |
| ☐866 | 3¢ | James Russell Lowell | 2.50 | 4.00 | 7.00 |
| ☐867 | 5¢ | Walt Whitman | 3.50 | 8.00 | 9.00 |
| ☐868 | 10¢ | James Whitcomb Riley | 5.00 | 7.50 | 12.00 |
| ☐869 | 1¢ | Horace Mann | 2.50 | 4.00 | 5.50 |
| ☐870 | 2¢ | Mark Hopkins | 2.50 | 4.00 | 5.50 |
| ☐871 | 3¢ | Charles W. Eliot | 2.50 | 4.00 | 5.50 |
| ☐872 | 5¢ | Frances E. Willard | 3.50 | 6.50 | 6.00 |
| ☐873 | 10¢ | Booker T. Washington | 7.50 | 13.00 | 16.00 |
| ☐874 | 1¢ | John James Audubon | 2.50 | 4.00 | 5.50 |

| Scott No. | | | Single | Block | Plate Block |
|---|---|---|---|---|---|
| ☐875 | 2¢ | Dr. Crawford W. Long | 2.50 | 4.00 | 5.50 |
| ☐876 | 3¢ | Luther Burbank | 2.50 | 4.00 | 5.50 |
| ☐877 | 5¢ | Dr. Walter Reed | 3.50 | 4.50 | 8.50 |
| ☐878 | 10¢ | Jane Addams | 5.50 | 8.50 | 12.00 |
| ☐879 | 1¢ | Stephen Collins Foster | 2.50 | 4.00 | 5.00 |
| ☐880 | 2¢ | John Philip Sousa | 2.50 | 4.00 | 5.00 |
| ☐881 | 3¢ | Victor Herbert | 2.50 | 4.00 | 5.00 |
| ☐882 | 5¢ | Edward A. MacDowell | 3.50 | 5.00 | 8.00 |
| ☐883 | 10¢ | Ethelbert Nevin | 4.50 | 8.00 | 12.00 |
| ☐884 | 1¢ | Gilbert Charles Stuart | 2.50 | 4.00 | 5.00 |
| ☐885 | 2¢ | James A. McNeill Whistler | 2.50 | 4.00 | 5.00 |
| ☐886 | 3¢ | Augustus Saint-Gaudens | 2.50 | 4.00 | 5.00 |
| ☐887 | 5¢ | Daniel Chester French | 3.50 | 7.50 | 11.00 |
| ☐888 | 10¢ | Frederic Remington | 4.00 | 7.50 | 11.00 |
| ☐889 | 1¢ | Eli Whitney | 2.50 | 4.00 | 7.00 |
| ☐890 | 2¢ | Samuel F.B. Morse | 2.50 | 4.00 | 7.00 |
| ☐891 | 3¢ | Cyrus Hall McCormick | 2.50 | 4.00 | 7.00 |
| ☐892 | 5¢ | Elias Howe | 3.50 | 8.00 | 11.00 |
| ☐893 | 10¢ | Alexander Graham Bell | 6.00 | 8.50 | 15.00 |
| ☐894 | 3¢ | Pony Express | 4.00 | 7.00 | 10.00 |
| ☐895 | 3¢ | Pan American Union | 4.00 | 7.00 | 10.00 |
| ☐896 | 3¢ | Idaho Statehood | 4.00 | 7.00 | 10.00 |
| ☐897 | 3¢ | Wyoming Statehood | 4.00 | 7.00 | 10.00 |
| ☐898 | 3¢ | Coronado Expedition | 4.00 | 7.00 | 10.00 |
| ☐899 | 1¢ | Defense | 3.50 | 7.50 | 11.00 |
| ☐900 | 2¢ | Defense | 3.50 | 7.50 | 11.00 |
| ☐901 | 3¢ | Defense | 3.50 | 7.50 | 11.00 |
| ☐902 | 3¢ | Thirteenth Amendment | 4.50 | 7.50 | 11.00 |
| ☐903 | 3¢ | Vermont Statehood | 4.50 | 7.50 | 9.00 |
| ☐904 | 3¢ | Kentucky Statehood | 3.00 | 4.50 | 7.50 |
| ☐905 | 3¢ | "Win the War" | 2.50 | 7.00 | 10.00 |
| ☐906 | 5¢ | Chinese Commemorative | 7.50 | 10.00 | 15.00 |
| ☐907 | 2¢ | United Nations | 3.25 | 6.00 | 7.00 |
| ☐908 | 1¢ | Four Freedoms | 4.25 | 7.50 | 10.00 |
| ☐909 | 5¢ | Poland | 4.25 | 7.50 | 11.00 |
| ☐910 | 5¢ | Czechoslovakia | 3.25 | 5.25 | 8.50 |
| ☐911 | 5¢ | Norway | 3.25 | 5.25 | 8.50 |
| ☐912 | 5¢ | Luxembourg | 3.25 | 5.25 | 8.50 |
| ☐913 | 5¢ | Netherlands | 3.25 | 5.25 | 8.50 |
| ☐914 | 5¢ | Belgium | 3.25 | 5.25 | 8.50 |

| Scott No. | | | Single | Block | Plate Block |
|---|---|---|---|---|---|
| ☐915 | 5¢ | France | 3.25 | 5.25 | 8.50 |
| ☐916 | 5¢ | Greece | 3.25 | 5.25 | 8.50 |
| ☐917 | 5¢ | Yugoslavia | 3.25 | 5.25 | 8.50 |
| ☐918 | 5¢ | Albany | 3.25 | 5.25 | 8.50 |
| ☐919 | 5¢ | Austria | 3.25 | 5.25 | 8.50 |
| ☐920 | 5¢ | Denmark | 3.25 | 5.25 | 8.50 |
| ☐921 | 5¢ | Korea | 3.25 | 5.25 | 8.50 |
| ☐922 | 3¢ | Railroad | 3.50 | 7.50 | 9.00 |
| ☐923 | 3¢ | Steamship | 3.00 | 4.75 | 7.50 |
| ☐924 | 3¢ | Telegraph | 3.00 | 4.75 | 7.50 |
| ☐925 | 3¢ | Philippines | 3.00 | 4.75 | 7.50 |
| ☐926 | 3¢ | Motion Picture | 3.00 | 4.75 | 7.50 |
| ☐927 | 3¢ | Florida | 3.00 | 4.75 | 7.50 |
| ☐928 | 5¢ | United Nations Conference | 3.00 | 4.75 | 7.50 |
| ☐929 | 3¢ | Iwo Jima | 4.00 | 7.50 | 9.50 |
| ☐930 | 1¢ | Roosevelt | 2.90 | 4.30 | 6.50 |
| ☐931 | 2¢ | Roosevelt | 2.90 | 4.30 | 6.50 |
| ☐932 | 3¢ | Roosevelt | 2.90 | 4.30 | 6.50 |
| ☐933 | 3¢ | Roosevelt | 2.90 | 4.30 | 6.50 |
| ☐934 | 3¢ | Army | 2.90 | 4.30 | 6.50 |
| ☐935 | 3¢ | Navy | 2.90 | 4.30 | 6.50 |
| ☐936 | 3¢ | Coast Guard | 3.50 | 4.30 | 7.00 |
| ☐937 | 3¢ | Alfred E. Smith | 3.50 | 4.30 | 7.00 |
| ☐938 | 3¢ | Texas | 3.50 | 4.30 | 7.00 |
| ☐939 | 3¢ | Merchant Marine | 2.90 | 4.30 | 7.00 |
| ☐940 | 3¢ | Honorable Discharge | 2.90 | 4.30 | 7.00 |
| ☐941 | 3¢ | Tennessee | 2.90 | 4.30 | 7.00 |
| ☐942 | 3¢ | Iowa | 2.90 | 4.30 | 7.00 |
| ☐943 | 3¢ | Smithsonian | 2.90 | 4.30 | 7.00 |
| ☐944 | 3¢ | Santa Fe | 2.90 | 4.30 | 7.00 |
| ☐945 | 3¢ | Thomas A. Edison | 2.90 | 4.30 | 7.00 |
| ☐946 | 3¢ | Joseph Pulitzer | 2.90 | 4.30 | 7.00 |
| ☐947 | 3¢ | Stamp Centenary | 2.90 | 4.30 | 7.00 |
| ☐948 | 5¢ and 10¢ Centenary Exhibition Sheet | | 3.50 | — | — |
| ☐949 | 3¢ | Doctors | 3.50 | 4.30 | 7.00 |
| ☐950 | 3¢ | Utah | 2.90 | 4.30 | 7.00 |
| ☐951 | 3¢ | "Constitution" | 3.50 | 4.30 | 7.00 |
| ☐952 | 3¢ | Everglades Park | 2.90 | 4.30 | 7.00 |
| ☐953 | 3¢ | Carver | 2.90 | 4.30 | 7.00 |

| Scott No. | | | Single | Block | Plate Block |
|---|---|---|---|---|---|
| ☐954 | 3¢ | California Gold | 2.25 | 4.00 | 4.50 |
| ☐955 | 3¢ | Mississippi Territory | 2.25 | 4.00 | 4.50 |
| ☐956 | 3¢ | Four Chaplains | 2.25 | 4.00 | 4.50 |
| ☐957 | 3¢ | Wisconsin Centennial | 2.25 | 4.00 | 4.50 |
| ☐958 | 5¢ | Swedish Pioneers | 2.25 | 4.00 | 4.50 |
| ☐959 | 3¢ | Women's Progress | 2.25 | 4.00 | 4.50 |
| ☐960 | 3¢ | William Allen White | 2.25 | 4.00 | 4.50 |
| ☐961 | 3¢ | U.S.-Canada Friendship | 2.25 | 4.00 | 4.50 |
| ☐962 | 3¢ | Francis Scott Key | 2.50 | 4.00 | 5.00 |
| ☐963 | 3¢ | Salute to Youth | 2.25 | 4.00 | 4.50 |
| ☐964 | 3¢ | Oregon Territory | 2.25 | 4.00 | 4.50 |
| ☐965 | 3¢ | Harlan Fiske Stone | 2.25 | 4.00 | 4.50 |
| ☐966 | 3¢ | Palomar Observatory | 2.50 | 4.00 | 4.50 |
| ☐967 | 3¢ | Clara Barton | 2.50 | 4.00 | 5.50 |
| ☐968 | 3¢ | Poultry Industry | 2.25 | 4.50 | 4.50 |
| ☐969 | 3¢ | Gold Star Mothers | 2.25 | 4.50 | 4.50 |
| ☐970 | 3¢ | Volunteer Fireman | 2.25 | 4.50 | 4.50 |
| ☐972 | 3¢ | Indian Centennial | 2.25 | 4.50 | 4.50 |
| ☐973 | 3¢ | Rough Riders | 2.25 | 4.50 | 4.50 |
| ☐974 | 3¢ | Juliette Low | 3.50 | 4.50 | 7.50 |
| ☐975 | 3¢ | Will Rogers | 2.25 | 4.50 | 4.50 |
| ☐976 | 3¢ | Fort Bliss | 3.00 | 4.75 | 6.00 |
| ☐977 | 3¢ | Moina Michael | 2.25 | 4.00 | 6.00 |
| ☐978 | 3¢ | Gettysburg Address | 3.00 | 7.00 | 7.50 |
| ☐979 | 3¢ | American Turners Society | 2.25 | 4.50 | 6.00 |
| ☐980 | 3¢ | Joel Chandler Harris | 2.25 | 4.50 | 6.00 |
| ☐981 | 3¢ | Minnesota Territory | 1.95 | 4.50 | 6.00 |
| ☐982 | 3¢ | Washington and Lee University | 1.95 | 4.50 | 6.00 |
| ☐983 | 3¢ | Puerto Rico Election | 1.95 | 4.50 | 6.00 |
| ☐984 | 3¢ | Annapolis, Md. | 1.95 | 4.50 | 6.00 |
| ☐985 | 3¢ | G.A.R. | 1.95 | 4.50 | 6.00 |
| ☐986 | 3¢ | Edgar Allan Poe | 2.25 | 4.50 | 4.50 |
| ☐987 | 3¢ | American Bankers Association | 1.95 | 4.25 | 5.00 |
| ☐988 | 3¢ | Samuel Gompers | 1.95 | 4.25 | 5.00 |
| ☐990 | 3¢ | Nat. Capital Sesqui. (Executive) | 1.95 | 4.25 | 5.00 |
| ☐991 | 3¢ | Nat. Capital Sesqui. (Judicial) | 1.95 | 4.25 | 5.00 |
| ☐992 | 3¢ | Nat. Capital Sesqui. (Legislative) | 1.95 | 4.25 | 5.00 |
| ☐993 | 3¢ | Railroad Engineers | 1.95 | 4.25 | 5.00 |
| ☐994 | 3¢ | Kansas City Centenary | 1.95 | 4.25 | 5.00 |
| ☐995 | 3¢ | Boy Scout | 3.00 | 7.00 | 8.00 |

| Scott No. | | | Single | Block | Plate Block |
|---|---|---|---|---|---|
| ☐996 | 3¢ | Indiana Ter. Sesquicentennial | 1.80 | 4.00 | 4.00 |
| ☐997 | 3¢ | California Statehood | 1.80 | 4.00 | 4.00 |
| ☐998 | 3¢ | United Confederate Veterans | 1.80 | 4.00 | 4.00 |
| ☐999 | 3¢ | Nevada Centennial | 1.80 | 4.00 | 4.00 |
| ☐1000 | 3¢ | Landing of Cadillac | 1.80 | 4.00 | 4.00 |
| ☐1001 | 3¢ | Colorado Statehood | 1.80 | 4.00 | 4.00 |
| ☐1002 | 3¢ | American Chemical Society | 1.80 | 4.00 | 4.00 |
| ☐1003 | 3¢ | Battle of Brooklyn | 1.80 | 4.00 | 4.00 |
| ☐1004 | 3¢ | Betsy Ross | 2.40 | 5.00 | 7.50 |
| ☐1005 | 3¢ | 4-H Clubs | 1.80 | 4.00 | 5.00 |
| ☐1006 | 3¢ | B & O Railroad | 1.80 | 4.00 | 5.00 |
| ☐1007 | 3¢ | American Automobile Assoc. | 1.80 | 4.00 | 5.00 |
| ☐1008 | 3¢ | NATO | 1.80 | 4.00 | 5.00 |
| ☐1009 | 3¢ | Grand Coulee Dam | 1.80 | 4.00 | 5.00 |
| ☐1010 | 3¢ | Lafayette | 1.80 | 4.00 | 5.00 |
| ☐1011 | 3¢ | Mt. Rushmore Memorial | 1.80 | 4.00 | 5.00 |
| ☐1012 | 3¢ | Civil Engineers | 1.80 | 4.00 | 5.00 |
| ☐1013 | 3¢ | Service Women | 1.80 | 4.00 | 5.00 |
| ☐1014 | 3¢ | Gutenberg Bible | 1.80 | 4.00 | 5.00 |
| ☐1015 | 3¢ | Newspaper boys | 1.80 | 4.00 | 5.00 |
| ☐1016 | 3¢ | Red Cross | 1.80 | 4.00 | 5.00 |
| ☐1017 | 3¢ | National Guard | 1.80 | 4.00 | 5.00 |
| ☐1018 | 3¢ | Ohio Sesquicentennial | 1.80 | 4.00 | 5.00 |
| ☐1019 | 3¢ | Washington Territory | 1.80 | 4.00 | 5.00 |
| ☐1020 | 3¢ | Louisiana Purchase | 1.80 | 4.00 | 5.00 |
| ☐1021 | 5¢ | Opening of Japan | 1.80 | 4.00 | 5.00 |
| ☐1022 | 3¢ | American Bar Association | 1.80 | 4.00 | 5.00 |
| ☐1023 | 3¢ | Sagamore Hill | 1.80 | 4.00 | 5.00 |
| ☐1024 | 3¢ | Future Farmers | 1.80 | 4.00 | 5.00 |
| ☐1025 | 3¢ | Trucking Industry | 1.80 | 4.00 | 5.00 |
| ☐1026 | 3¢ | Gen. G.S. Patton, Jr. | 1.80 | 4.00 | 5.00 |
| ☐1027 | 3¢ | New York City | 1.80 | 4.00 | 5.00 |
| ☐1028 | 3¢ | Gadsden Purchase | 1.80 | 4.00 | 5.00 |
| ☐1029 | 3¢ | Columbia University | 1.80 | 4.00 | 5.00 |
| ☐1030 | ½¢ | Franklin | 1.80 | 4.00 | 5.00 |
| ☐1031 | 1¢ | Washington | 1.80 | 4.00 | 5.00 |
| ☐1031a | 1¼¢ | Palace | 1.80 | 4.00 | 5.00 |
| ☐1032 | 1½¢ | Mount Vernon | 1.80 | 4.00 | 5.00 |
| ☐1033 | 2¢ | Jefferson | 1.80 | 4.00 | 5.00 |
| ☐1034 | 2½¢ | Bunker Hill | 1.80 | 4.00 | 5.00 |

| Scott No. | Single | Block | Plate Block |
|---|---|---|---|
| ☐1035 3¢ Statue of Liberty | 1.80 | 4.00 | 5.00 |
| ☐1036 4¢ Lincoln | 1.80 | 4.00 | 5.00 |
| ☐1037 4½¢ Hermitage | 1.80 | 4.00 | 5.00 |
| ☐1038 5¢ Monroe | 1.80 | 4.00 | 5.00 |
| ☐1039 6¢ Roosevelt | 1.80 | 4.00 | 5.00 |
| ☐1040 7¢ Wilson | 1.80 | 4.00 | 5.00 |
| ☐1041 8¢ Statue of Liberty | 1.80 | 4.00 | 5.00 |
| ☐1042 8¢ Statue of Liberty | 1.80 | 4.00 | 5.00 |
| ☐1042a 8¢ Pershing | 2.75 | 6.00 | 7.50 |
| ☐1043 9¢ The Alamo | 1.80 | 4.00 | 7.00 |
| ☐1044 10¢ Independence Hall | 1.80 | 4.00 | 7.00 |
| ☐1045 12¢ Harrison | 1.80 | 4.00 | 7.00 |
| ☐1046 15¢ John Jay | 1.80 | 4.00 | 5.50 |
| ☐1046a 15¢ John Jay | 1.80 | 4.00 | 5.00 |
| ☐1047 20¢ Monticello | 1.80 | 4.00 | 5.50 |
| ☐1048 25¢ Paul Revere | 1.80 | 4.00 | 5.50 |
| ☐1049 30¢ Robert E. Lee | 2.50 | 5.50 | 7.50 |
| ☐1050 40¢ John Marshall | 3.25 | 7.00 | 8.50 |
| ☐1051 50¢ Susan Anthony | 4.25 | 8.00 | 12.00 |
| ☐1052 $1 Patrick Henry | 7.00 | 14.00 | 20.00 |
| ☐1053 $5 Alexander Hamilton | 48.00 | 75.00 | 100.00 |
| ☐1054 1¢ Washington | 1.80 | — | — |
| ☐1055 2¢ Jefferson | 1.80 | — | — |
| ☐1056 2½¢ Bunker Hill | 1.80 | — | — |
| ☐1057 3¢ Statue of Liberty | 1.80 | — | — |
| ☐1058 4¢ Lincoln | 1.80 | — | — |
| ☐1059 4½¢ The Hermitage | 1.80 | — | — |
| ☐1059a 25¢ Paul Revere | 2.25 | — | — |
| ☐1059b 25¢ Tagged | 24.00 | — | — |
| ☐1060 3¢ Nebraska Territory | 1.80 | 3.75 | 7.00 |
| ☐1061 3¢ Kansas Territory | 1.80 | 3.75 | 7.00 |
| ☐1062 3¢ George Eastman | 1.80 | 3.75 | 7.00 |
| ☐1063 3¢ Lewis & Clark | 1.80 | 3.75 | 7.00 |
| ☐1064 3¢ Pennsylvania Academy of the Fine Arts | | | |
| | 1.80 | 3.75 | 7.00 |
| ☐1065 3¢ Land Grant Colleges | 2.25 | 4.50 | 6.50 |
| ☐1066 8¢ Rotary International | 2.25 | 4.50 | 6.50 |
| ☐1067 3¢ Armed Forces Reserve | 2.10 | 4.50 | 6.50 |
| ☐1068 3¢ New Hampshire | 1.80 | 4.00 | 5.00 |
| ☐1069 3¢ Soo Locks | 1.80 | 4.00 | 5.00 |

| Scott No. | | Single | Block | Plate Block |
|---|---|---|---|---|
| ☐1070 | 3¢ Atoms for Peace | 1.80 | 4.00 | 5.00 |
| ☐1071 | 3¢ Fort Ticonderoga | 1.80 | 4.00 | 5.00 |
| ☐1072 | 3¢ Andrew W. Mellon | 1.80 | 4.00 | 5.00 |
| ☐1073 | 3¢ Benjamin Franklin | 1.80 | 4.00 | 5.00 |
| ☐1074 | 3¢ Booker T. Washington | 1.80 | 4.00 | 5.00 |
| ☐1075 | 3¢, 8¢ FIPEX Souvenir Sheet | 4.00 | 8.00 | 11.00 |
| ☐1076 | 3¢ FIPEX | 1.80 | 3.50 | 5.00 |
| ☐1077 | 3¢ Wildlife (Turkey) | 1.80 | 3.50 | 5.00 |
| ☐1078 | 3¢ Wildlife (Antelope) | 1.80 | 3.50 | 5.00 |
| ☐1079 | 3¢ Wildlife (Salmon) | 1.80 | 3.50 | 5.00 |
| ☐1080 | 3¢ Pure Food and Drug Laws | 1.80 | 3.50 | 5.00 |
| ☐1081 | 3¢ Wheatland | 1.80 | 3.50 | 5.00 |
| ☐1082 | 3¢ Labor Day | 1.80 | 3.50 | 5.00 |
| ☐1083 | 3¢ Nassau Hall | 1.80 | 3.50 | 5.00 |
| ☐1084 | 3¢ Devils Tower | 1.80 | 3.50 | 5.00 |
| ☐1085 | 3¢ Children | 1.80 | 3.50 | 5.00 |
| ☐1086 | 3¢ Alexander Hamilton | 1.80 | 3.50 | 5.00 |
| ☐1087 | 3¢ Polio | 1.80 | 3.50 | 5.00 |
| ☐1088 | 3¢ Coast & Geodetic Survey | 1.80 | 3.50 | 5.00 |
| ☐1089 | 3¢ Architects | 1.80 | 3.50 | 5.00 |
| ☐1090 | 3¢ Steel Industry | 1.80 | 3.50 | 5.00 |
| ☐1091 | 3¢ Naval Review | 1.80 | 3.50 | 5.00 |
| ☐1092 | 3¢ Oklahoma Statehood | 1.80 | 3.50 | 5.00 |
| ☐1093 | 3¢ School Teachers | 1.80 | 3.50 | 5.00 |
| ☐1094 | 4¢ Flag | 1.80 | 3.50 | 5.00 |
| ☐1095 | 3¢ Shipbuilding | 1.75 | 2.80 | 4.25 |
| ☐1096 | 8¢ Ramon Magsaysay | 1.75 | 2.80 | 4.25 |
| ☐1097 | 3¢ Lafayette Bicentenary | 1.75 | 2.80 | 4.25 |
| ☐1098 | 3¢ Wildlife (Whooping Crane) | 1.75 | 2.80 | 4.25 |
| ☐1099 | 3¢ Religious Freedom | 1.75 | 2.80 | 4.25 |
| ☐1100 | 3¢ Gardening Horticulture | 1.75 | 2.80 | 4.25 |
| ☐1104 | 3¢ Brussels Exhibition | 1.75 | 2.80 | 4.25 |
| ☐1105 | 3¢ James Monroe | 1.75 | 2.80 | 4.25 |
| ☐1106 | 3¢ Minnesota Statehood | 1.75 | 2.80 | 4.25 |
| ☐1107 | 3¢ International Geophysical Year | 1.75 | 2.80 | 4.25 |
| ☐1108 | 3¢ Gunston Hall | 1.75 | 2.80 | 4.25 |
| ☐1109 | 3¢ Mackinac Bridge | 1.75 | 2.80 | 4.25 |
| ☐1110 | 4¢ Simon Bolivar | 1.75 | 2.80 | 4.25 |
| ☐1111 | 8¢ Simon Bolivar | 1.75 | 2.80 | 4.25 |
| ☐1112 | 4¢ Atlantic Cable | 1.75 | 2.80 | 4.25 |

| Scott No. | | Single | Block | Plate Block |
|---|---|---|---|---|
| ☐1113 1¢ | Lincoln Sesquicentennial | 1.75 | 2.80 | 4.25 |
| ☐1114 3¢ | Lincoln Sesquicentennial | 1.75 | 2.80 | 4.25 |
| ☐1115 4¢ | Lincoln-Douglas Debates | 1.75 | 2.80 | 4.25 |
| ☐1116 4¢ | Lincoln Sesquicentennial | 1.75 | 2.80 | 4.25 |
| ☐1117 4¢ | Lajos Kossuth | 1.75 | 2.80 | 4.25 |
| ☐1118 8¢ | Lajos Kossuth | 1.75 | 2.80 | 4.25 |
| ☐1119 4¢ | Freedom of Press | 1.75 | 2.80 | 4.25 |
| ☐1120 4¢ | Overland Mail | 1.75 | 2.80 | 4.25 |
| ☐1121 4¢ | Noah Webster | 1.75 | 2.80 | 4.25 |
| ☐1122 4¢ | Forest Conservation | 1.75 | 2.80 | 4.25 |
| ☐1123 4¢ | Fort Duquesne | 1.75 | 2.80 | 4.25 |
| ☐1124 4¢ | Oregon Statehood | 1.75 | 2.80 | 4.25 |
| ☐1125 4¢ | San Martin | 1.75 | 2.80 | 4.25 |
| ☐1126 8¢ | San Martin | 1.75 | 2.80 | 4.25 |
| ☐1127 4¢ | NATO | 1.75 | 2.80 | 4.25 |
| ☐1128 4¢ | Arctic Explorations | 1.75 | 2.80 | 4.25 |
| ☐1129 8¢ | World Trade | 1.75 | 2.80 | 4.25 |
| ☐1130 4¢ | Silver Centennial | 1.75 | 2.80 | 4.25 |
| ☐1131 4¢ | St. Lawrence Seaway | 1.75 | 2.80 | 4.25 |
| ☐1132 4¢ | Flag | 1.75 | 2.75 | 4.25 |
| ☐1133 4¢ | Soil Conservation | 1.75 | 2.75 | 4.25 |
| ☐1134 4¢ | Petroleum Industry | 1.75 | 2.75 | 4.25 |
| ☐1135 4¢ | Dental Health | 1.75 | 2.75 | 4.25 |
| ☐1136 4¢ | Reuter | 1.75 | 2.75 | 4.25 |
| ☐1137 8¢ | Reuter | 1.75 | 2.75 | 4.25 |
| ☐1138 4¢ | Dr. Ephraim McDowell | 1.75 | 2.75 | 4.25 |
| ☐1139 4¢ | Washington "Credo" | 1.75 | 2.75 | 4.25 |
| ☐1140 4¢ | Franklin "Credo" | 1.75 | 2.75 | 4.25 |
| ☐1141 4¢ | Jefferson "Credo" | 1.75 | 2.75 | 4.25 |
| ☐1142 4¢ | Frances Scott Key "Credo" | 1.75 | 2.75 | 4.25 |
| ☐1143 4¢ | Lincoln "Credo" | 1.75 | 2.75 | 4.25 |
| ☐1144 4¢ | Patrick Henry "Credo" | 1.75 | 2.75 | 4.25 |
| ☐1145 4¢ | Boy Scouts | 1.75 | 2.75 | 4.25 |
| ☐1146 4¢ | Olympic Winter Games | 1.65 | 2.80 | 4.50 |
| ☐1147 4¢ | Masaryk | 1.65 | 2.80 | 4.50 |
| ☐1148 8¢ | Masaryk | 1.65 | 2.80 | 4.50 |
| ☐1149 4¢ | World Refugee Year | 1.65 | 2.80 | 4.50 |
| ☐1150 4¢ | Water Conservation | 1.65 | 2.80 | 4.50 |
| ☐1151 4¢ | SEATO | 1.65 | 2.80 | 4.50 |
| ☐1152 4¢ | American Woman | 1.65 | 2.80 | 4.50 |

| Scott No. | | Single | Block | Plate Block |
|---|---|---|---|---|
| ☐1153 | 4¢ 50-Star Flag | 1.65 | 2.80 | 4.50 |
| ☐1154 | 4¢ Pony Express Centennial | 2.10 | 3.00 | 5.00 |
| ☐1155 | 4¢ Employ the Handicapped | 1.65 | 2.80 | 4.50 |
| ☐1156 | 4¢ World Forestry Congress | 1.65 | 2.80 | 4.50 |
| ☐1157 | 4¢ Mexican Independence | 1.80 | 2.80 | 4.50 |
| ☐1158 | 4¢ U.S. Japan Treaty | 1.65 | 2.80 | 4.50 |
| ☐1159 | 4¢ Paderewski | 1.65 | 2.80 | 4.50 |
| ☐1160 | 8¢ Paderewski | 1.65 | 2.80 | 4.50 |
| ☐1161 | 4¢ Robert A. Taft | 1.65 | 2.80 | 4.50 |
| ☐1162 | 4¢ Wheels of Freedom | 1.65 | 2.80 | 4.50 |
| ☐1163 | 4¢ Boys' Clubs | 1.65 | 2.80 | 4.50 |
| ☐1164 | 4¢ Automated P.O. | 1.65 | 2.80 | 4.50 |
| ☐1165 | 4¢ Mannerheim | 1.65 | 2.80 | 4.50 |
| ☐1166 | 8¢ Mannerheim | 1.65 | 2.80 | 4.50 |
| ☐1167 | 4¢ Camp Fire Girls | 1.65 | 2.80 | 4.50 |
| ☐1168 | 4¢ Garibaldi | 1.65 | 2.80 | 4.50 |
| ☐1169 | 8¢ Garibaldi | 1.65 | 2.80 | 4.50 |
| ☐1170 | 4¢ Senator George | 1.65 | 2.80 | 4.50 |
| ☐1171 | 4¢ Andrew Carnegie | 1.65 | 2.80 | 4.50 |
| ☐1172 | 4¢ John Foster Dulles | 1.65 | 2.80 | 4.50 |
| ☐1173 | 4¢ Echo I | 1.65 | 2.80 | 4.50 |
| ☐1174 | 4¢ Gandhi | 1.65 | 2.80 | 4.50 |
| ☐1175 | 8¢ Gandhi | 1.65 | 2.80 | 4.50 |
| ☐1176 | 4¢ Range Conservation | 1.65 | 2.80 | 4.50 |
| ☐1177 | 4¢ Horace Greeley | 1.65 | 2.80 | 4.50 |
| ☐1178 | 4¢ Fort Sumter | 2.40 | 3.75 | 5.00 |
| ☐1179 | 4¢ Battle of Shiloh | 2.40 | 3.75 | 5.00 |
| ☐1180 | 5¢ Battle of Gettysburg | 2.40 | 3.75 | 5.00 |
| ☐1181 | 5¢ Battle of Wilderness | 2.40 | 3.75 | 5.00 |
| ☐1182 | 5¢ Appomattox | 2.40 | 3.75 | 5.00 |
| ☐1183 | 4¢ Kansas Statehood | 2.40 | 3.75 | 5.00 |
| ☐1184 | 4¢ Senator Norris | 1.65 | 3.50 | 5.00 |
| ☐1185 | 4¢ Naval Aviation | 1.65 | 2.75 | 4.50 |
| ☐1186 | 4¢ Workmen's Compensation | 1.65 | 2.75 | 4.50 |
| ☐1187 | 4¢ Frederic Remington | 2.00 | 2.90 | 5.00 |
| ☐1188 | 4¢ China Republic | 3.00 | 4.00 | 6.00 |
| ☐1189 | 4¢ Naismith | 4.00 | 6.00 | 6.00 |
| ☐1190 | 4¢ Nursing | 7.00 | 10.00 | 18.00 |
| ☐1191 | 4¢ New Mexico Statehood | 2.50 | 4.00 | 7.50 |
| ☐1192 | 4¢ Arizona Statehood | 2.50 | 4.00 | 7.50 |

| Scott No. | | Single | Block | Plate Block |
|---|---|---|---|---|
| ☐1193 4¢ | Project Mercury | 3.00 | 5.00 | 7.00 |
| ☐1194 4¢ | Malaria Eradication | 1.55 | 2.40 | 4.00 |
| ☐1195 4¢ | Charles Evans Hughes | 1.55 | 2.40 | 4.00 |
| ☐1196 4¢ | Seattle World's Fair | 1.55 | 2.40 | 4.00 |
| ☐1197 4¢ | Louisiana Statehood | 1.55 | 2.40 | 4.00 |
| ☐1198 4¢ | Homestead Act | 1.55 | 2.40 | 4.00 |
| ☐1199 4¢ | Girl Scouts | 2.10 | 3.50 | 5.00 |
| ☐1200 4¢ | Brien McMahon | 1.55 | 2.40 | 5.00 |
| ☐1201 4¢ | Apprenticeship | 1.55 | 2.40 | 5.00 |
| ☐1202 4¢ | Sam Rayburn | 1.55 | 2.40 | 5.00 |
| ☐1203 4¢ | Dag Hammarskjold | 1.55 | 2.40 | 5.00 |
| ☐1204 4¢ | Hammarskjold "Error" | 4.50 | 7.50 | 11.00 |
| ☐1205 4¢ | Christmas | 1.65 | 2.70 | 4.50 |
| ☐1206 4¢ | Higher Education | 2.00 | 2.90 | 4.00 |
| ☐1207 4¢ | Winslow Homer | 2.00 | 2.90 | 4.00 |
| ☐1208 4¢ | Flag | 1.80 | 2.80 | 4.00 |
| ☐1209 4¢ | Jackson | 1.65 | 2.75 | 4.00 |
| ☐1213 5¢ | Washington | 1.65 | 2.75 | 4.00 |
| ☐1225 1¢ | Jackson (coil) | 1.65 | 2.75 | 4.00 |
| ☐1229 5¢ | Washington (coil) | 1.65 | 2.75 | 4.00 |
| ☐1230 5¢ | Carolina Charter | 1.65 | 2.75 | 4.00 |
| ☐1231 5¢ | Food for Peace | 1.65 | 2.75 | 4.00 |
| ☐1232 5¢ | West Virginia Statehood | 1.65 | 2.75 | 4.00 |
| ☐1233 5¢ | Emancipation Proclamation | 1.65 | 2.75 - | 4.00 |
| ☐1234 5¢ | Alliance for Progress | 1.65 | 2.75 | 4.00 |
| ☐1235 5¢ | Cordell Hull | 1.65 | 2.75 | 4.00 |
| ☐1236 5¢ | Eleanor Roosevelt | 1.65 | 2.75 | 4.00 |
| ☐1237 5¢ | Science | 1.65 | 2.75 | 4.00 |
| ☐1238 5¢ | City Mail Delivery | 1.65 | 2.75 | 4.00 |
| ☐1239 5¢ | Red Cross | 1.65 | 2.75 | 4.00 |
| ☐1240 5¢ | Christmas | 1.65 | 2.75 | 4.00 |
| ☐1241 5¢ | Audubon | 1.65 | 2.75 | 4.00 |
| ☐1242 5¢ | Sam Houston | 1.65 | 2.75 | 4.00 |
| ☐1243 5¢ | Charles Russell | 2.50 | 4.50 | 7.00 |
| ☐1244 5¢ | N.Y. World's Fair | 1.65 | 2.75 | 4.00 |
| ☐1245 5¢ | John Muir | 1.65 | 2.75 | 4.00 |
| ☐1246 5¢ | John F. Kennedy | 2.10 | 3.50 | 4.00 |
| ☐1247 5¢ | New Jersey Tercentenary | 1.65 | 2.75 | 4.00 |
| ☐1248 5¢ | Nevada Statehood | 1.65 | 2.75 | 4.00 |
| ☐1249 5¢ | Register & Vote | 1.65 | 2.75 | 4.00 |

| Scott No. | Single | Block | Plate Block |
|---|---|---|---|
| ☐1250 5¢ Shakespeare | 2.10 | 3.00 | 4.25 |
| ☐1251 5¢ Drs. Mayo | 2.75 | 4.50 | 6.00 |
| ☐1252 5¢ American Music | 1.65 | 2.75 | 4.00 |
| ☐1253 5¢ Homemakers | 1.65 | 2.75 | 4.00 |
| ☐1254–57 5¢ Christmas | 5.00 | 7.00 | 10.00 |
| ☐1258 5¢ Verrazano-Narrows Bridge | 1.65 | 2.70 | 4.00 |
| ☐1259 5¢ Fine Arts | 1.65 | 2.70 | 4.00 |
| ☐1260 5¢ Amateur Radio | 2.10 | 3.00 | 4.00 |
| ☐1261 5¢ Battle of New Orleans | 1.65 | 2.70 | 4.00 |
| ☐1262 5¢ Physical Fitness | 1.80 | 3.00 | 5.50 |
| ☐1263 5¢ Cancer Crusade | 2.10 | 3.50 | 7.00 |
| ☐1264 5¢ Churchill | 1.70 | 2.60 | 5.00 |
| ☐1265 5¢ Magna Carta | 1.70 | 2.60 | 5.00 |
| ☐1266 5¢ Intl. Cooperation Year | 1.70 | 2.60 | 5.00 |
| ☐1267 5¢ Salvation Army | 1.70 | 2.60 | 5.00 |
| ☐1268 5¢ Dante | 1.70 | 2.60 | 5.00 |
| ☐1269 5¢ Herbert Hoover | 1.70 | 2.60 | 5.00 |
| ☐1270 5¢ Robert Fulton | 1.70 | 2.60 | 5.00 |
| ☐1271 5¢ Florida Settlement | 1.70 | 2.60 | 5.00 |
| ☐1272 5¢ Traffic Safety | 1.70 | 2.60 | 5.00 |
| ☐1273 5¢ Copley | 1.70 | 2.60 | 5.00 |
| ☐1274 11¢ Intl. Telecommunication Union | 1.70 | 2.60 | 5.00 |
| ☐1275 5¢ Adlai Stevenson | 1.70 | 2.60 | 5.00 |
| ☐1276 5¢ Christmas | 1.70 | 2.60 | 5.00 |
| ☐1278 1¢ Jefferson | 1.70 | 2.60 | 5.00 |
| ☐1279 1¼¢ Gallatin | 1.70 | 2.60 | 5.00 |
| ☐1280 2¢ Wright | 1.70 | 2.60 | 5.00 |
| ☐1281 3¢ Parkman | 1.70 | 2.60 | 5.00 |
| ☐1282 4¢ Lincoln | 1.70 | 2.60 | 5.00 |
| ☐1283 5¢ Washington | 1.70 | 2.60 | 5.00 |
| ☐1283B 5¢ Washington | 1.70 | 2.60 | 5.00 |
| ☐1284 6¢ Roosevelt | 1.70 | 2.60 | 5.00 |
| ☐1285 8¢ Einstein | 2.10 | 3.00 | 4.00 |
| ☐1286 10¢ Jackson | 1.70 | 3.50 | 4.50 |
| ☐1286a 12¢ Ford | 1.70 | 3.50 | 4.50 |
| ☐1287 13¢ Kennedy | 2.50 | 5.00 | 7.00 |
| ☐1288 15¢ Holmes | 1.85 | 3.50 | 4.50 |
| ☐1289 20¢ Marshall | 2.10 | 4.00 | 7.00 |
| ☐1290 25¢ Douglas | 2.10 | 4.00 | 7.00 |
| ☐1291 30¢ Dewey | 2.50 | 5.00 | 7.00 |

| Scott No. | Single | Block | Plate Block |
|---|---|---|---|
| ☐1292 40¢ Paine | 2.75 | 5.00 | 7.50 |
| ☐1293 50¢ Stone | 3.50 | 7.00 | 9.00 |
| ☐1294 $1 O'Neill | 4.50 | 7.50 | 12.00 |
| ☐1295 $5 Moore | 45.00 | 85.00 | 110.00 |
| ☐1304 5¢ Washington (coil) | — | pr. 1.50 | lp. 3.00 |
| ☐1305 6¢ Roosevelt (coil) | — | pr. 1.50 | lp. 3.00 |
| ☐1305c $1 O'Neill (coil) | — | pr. 1.50 | lp. 3.00 |
| ☐1306 5¢ Migratory Bird Treaty | 1.65 | 2.50 | 4.00 |
| ☐1307 5¢ Humane Treatment of Animals | 1.65 | 2.50 | 4.00 |
| ☐1308 5¢ Indiana Statehood | 1.65 | 2.50 | 4.00 |
| ☐1309 5¢ Circus | 1.65 | 2.50 | 4.00 |
| ☐1310 5¢ SIPEX | 1.65 | 2.50 | 4.00 |
| ☐1311 5¢ SIPEX | 1.65 | 2.50 | 4.00 |
| ☐1312 5¢ Bill of Rights | 1.65 | 2.50 | 4.00 |
| ☐1313 5¢ Polish Millennium | 1.65 | 2.50 | 4.00 |
| ☐1314 5¢ National Park Service | 1.65 | 2.50 | 4.00 |
| ☐1315 5¢ Marine Corps Reserve | 1.65 | 2.50 | 4.00 |
| ☐1316 5¢ Genl. Fed. of Women's Clubs | 1.90 | 3.00 | 4.50 |
| ☐1317 5¢ Johnny Appleseed | 1.70 | 2.60 | 4.00 |
| ☐1318 5¢ Beautification of America | 1.70 | 2.60 | 4.00 |
| ☐1319 5¢ Great River Road | 1.70 | 2.60 | 4.00 |
| ☐1320 5¢ Savings Bonds | 1.90 | 3.00 | 6.00 |
| ☐1321 5¢ Christmas | 1.90 | 3.00 | 6.00 |
| ☐1322 5¢ Mary Cassatt | 1.60 | 2.60 | 5.00 |
| ☐1323 5¢ National Grange | 1.60 | 2.60 | 5.00 |
| ☐1324 5¢ Canada Centenary | 1.60 | 2.60 | 5.00 |
| ☐1325 5¢ Erie Canal | 1.60 | 2.60 | 5.00 |
| ☐1326 5¢ Search for Peace | 1.60 | 2.60 | 5.00 |
| ☐1327 5¢ Thoreau | 1.60 | 2.60 | 5.00 |
| ☐1328 5¢ Nebraska Statehood | 1.60 | 2.60 | 5.00 |
| ☐1329 5¢ Voice of America | 1.60 | 2.60 | 5.00 |
| ☐1330 5¢ Davy Crockett | 1.75 | 3.00 | 5.50 |
| ☐1331–1332 5¢ Space Accomplishments | 12.00 | pr. 20.00 | 24.00 |
| ☐1333 5¢ Urban Planning | 1.60 | 2.60 | 5.00 |
| ☐1334 5¢ Finland Independence | 1.60 | 2.60 | 5.00 |
| ☐1335 5¢ Thomas Eakins | 1.60 | 2.60 | 5.00 |
| ☐1336 5¢ Christmas | 1.90 | 3.00 | 5.00 |
| ☐1337 5¢ Mississippi Statehood | 1.60 | 2.60 | 5.00 |

| Scott No. | | Single | Block | Plate Block |
|---|---|---|---|---|
| ☐1338 6¢ | Flag | 1.60 | 2.60 | 5.00 |
| ☐1339 6¢ | Illinois Statehood | 1.60 | 2.60 | 5.00 |
| ☐1340 6¢ | Hemis Fair '68 | 1.60 | 2.60 | 5.00 |
| ☐1341 $1 | Airlift | 8.00 | 12.00 | 17.00 |
| ☐1342 6¢ | Youth-Elks | 1.60 | 2.60 | 5.00 |
| ☐1343 6¢ | Law and Order | 3.00 | 4.50 | 7.50 |
| ☐1344 6¢ | Register and Vote | 1.60 | 2.60 | 3.60 |
| ☐1345–1354 6¢ | Historic Flag series of 10, all on one cover | | | |
| | | 11.00 | — | — |
| ☐1355 6¢ | Disney | 8.50 | 12.00 | 25.00 |
| ☐1356 6¢ | Marquette | 1.60 | 2.60 | 4.50 |
| ☐1357 6¢ | Daniel Boone | 1.60 | 2.60 | 4.50 |
| ☐1358 6¢ | Arkansas River | 1.60 | 2.60 | 4.50 |
| ☐1359 6¢ | Leif Erikson | 1.60 | 2.60 | 4.50 |
| ☐1360 6¢ | Cherokee Strip | 1.60 | 2.60 | 4.50 |
| ☐1361 6¢ | John Trumbull | 2.10 | 3.50 | 5.50 |
| ☐1362 6¢ | Waterfowl Conservation | 2.10 | 3.50 | 5.50 |
| ☐1363 6¢ | Christmas | 2.10 | 3.50 | 5.50 |
| ☐1364 6¢ | American Indian | 1.60 | 2.60 | 4.50 |
| ☐1365–1368 6¢ | Beautification of America | | | |
| | | 4.00 | 7.00 | 11.00 |
| ☐1369 6¢ | American Legion | 1.60 | 2.70 | 4.50 |
| ☐1370 6¢ | Grandma Moses | 1.60 | 2.70 | 4.50 |
| ☐1371 6¢ | Apollo 8 | 3.10 | 6.00 | 8.50 |

NOTE: From number 1372 to date, most First Day Covers have a value of $1.50 to $2.00 for single stamps, $2.75 to $4.00 for blocks of four and $3.50 to $5.00 for plate blocks of four.

# MEMBERSHIP IN THE ANA COULD BE YOUR BEST INVESTMENT THIS YEAR.

*As a rare coin collector or hobbyist, you continually deal with a variety of questions. How can you know that the coin you're about to purchase is not counterfeit? How can you find the detailed, current information you need to build your collection? There is no authority to help you solve all these problems. Unless you belong to the American Numismatic Association.*

**Coin Certification and Grading.** ANA experts examine rare coins for authenticity to help safeguard against counterfeiting and misrepresentation. ANA now offers the ANACS Grading Service—third party expert opinions as to the condition of U.S. coins submitted for examination, and will issue certificates of authenticity.

**Library Service.** The largest circulating numismatic library in the world is maintained by the ANA. Its sole purpose is to provide you with free access to invaluable information that can't be found anywhere else.

**The Numismatist.** The Association's fully illustrated magazine, considered *the* outstanding publication devoted exclusively to all phases of numismatics, is mailed free to all members.

And there are more benefits available through the ANA. Like coin insurance, special seminars, free booklets and photographic services. You can't find benefits like these anywhere else. Don't you owe it to yourself to join.

# I want some recognition!
# Make me an ANA Member.

Check One:
- ☐ Regular $26 plus $6 first-year processing fee
- ☐ Junior $11 (age 17 or younger)
- ☐ Senior $22 plus $6 first-year processing fee (age 65 or older)

- ☐ 5-year $120
- ☐ Life $750
- ☐ Foreign $28 plus $6 first-year processing fee

☐ Mr.  ☐ Mrs.  ☐ Ms.

Name _____

*Please Print*

Street _____

City _____ State _____ Zip _____

Birthdate _____ / _____ / _____

I agree to abide by the American Numismatic Association's bylaws and Code of Ethics which require the publiation of each applicant's name and state.

_____        _____
Signature of Applicant                        Signature of Parent or Guardian
                                                        (required for Junior applicant)

- ☐ Check here if you DO NOT want your name and address forwarded to an ANA Club Representative in your area.

- ☐ Check here if you want your name provided to numismatic-related companies.

- ☐ Check
- ☐ MasterCard
- ☐ AmExpress

- ☐ Money Order
- ☐ VISA

_____        Expiration Date _____
Credit Card Account No.

_____
Signature of Cardholder (required)

SPONSOR_____         ANA No._____
(optional)

Foreign applications must be accompanied by U.S. Funds drawn on a U.S. bank.
OR JOIN BY PHONE: Use your VISA, MasterCard or American Express Card.
Call 719-632-2646

**Return application with payment to:**
**American Numismatic Association**
**818 N. Cascade Ave.**
**Colorado Springs, CO 80903-3279**

# THE BLACKBOOKS!